A HISTORY OF
THE MARCONI COMPANY
1874–1965

A replica of Marconi's first transmitter which he used
in his earliest experiments in Italy in 1895.

A History of
THE MARCONI
COMPANY

W. J. Baker

First published 1970
by Methuen & Co Ltd
Reprinted 1979, 1984 and 1990

Reprinted 1996, 1999
by Routledge
11 New Fetter Lane, London EC4P 4EE

Printed in Great Britain by
George Over Limited, London and Rugby

British Library Cataloguing in Publication Data
A catalogue record for this book is available from the British Library

ISBN 0-415-14624-0

Contents

CONTENTS

List of Plates

ACKNOWLEDGEMENTS

My warm thanks go to The Marconi Company Limited for so kindly allowing me to reproduce a large number of plates from the Company archives, to The Marconi International Marine Co, Ltd for permission to reproduce plates 7 and 16 and to The Imperial War Museum for permission to reproduce plates 9, 10, and 11. The cartoon on the back of the jacket has been reproduced by kind permission of *Punch*.

List of Figures

Preface

The idea for this book was born when a senior executive of Methuen's chanced to read a short account of The Marconi Company's history in a jubilee issue of a local paper, *The Essex Chronicle*. This outline convinced him that here was a story which should be told in full and accordingly wheels were set in motion to achieve that end.

I think this circumstance is worth recording if only to establish to the reader that the book is not a product of Company sponsorship. The archives were made available to me and and everyone concerned has been extremely helpful but no commercial censorship was exercised and the history was written as an extra-mural task. In short, the 'downs' are recorded as well as the 'ups'.

Although some circuit diagrams of early equipments are given for the interest of electronics engineers, the non-technical reader will not find himself out of his depth. I hope that students of industrial history will find something of value in the account, for this was a main objective in the writing.

I could fill several pages with names of those who have given generously of their time and experience to set the record straight. I have not done so because almost inevitably someone would get left out in error, to their hurt and mine. So, will the executives, engineers, physicists, veterans, secretaries and other Marconi people – including four Company historians, past and present – please take this as an acknowledgement of my indebtedness?

As for the Marconi Company itself, it is still fashioning its history. Since 1965, the date at which this account ends, it has won the Queen's Award to Industry in four consecutive years – the only electronics firm to do so. But I must not encroach on the preserves of a later historian.

Great Baddow
4 December 1969.

W. J. BAKER

PART ONE

I

The Stage is Set

The employment of electromagnetic waves for purposes of communication is no modern invention; on the contrary, its origins are lost in time. A boy winks; a girl smiles. Communication via the optical electromagnetic frequencies has taken place, although the participants are unlikely to be thinking of the process in those terms. The discovery of means of making fire, the greatest single forward step in human history, put the power of the artificial generation of electromagnetic waves into the hands of primitive man, giving him means to warm himself and cook his food by the use of infra-red frequencies and the facility of communication at night (camp-fires and beacons).

We are not, however, primarily concerned here with the optical and near-optical frequencies – although modern researches have extended the domain of electronics into those regions – but rather with the bands of radiation which lie roughly between the frequencies of 10 kHz and 300 GHz* and for which the human body has no direct means of detection.

The history of scientific progress is closely analogous to the history of an individual. We celebrate the birth of a baby, not the miracle of conception, and tend to take the incredibly complex chemistry of the gestation period rather for granted. Similarly, in science; it is the birth of an invention which is remembered, not its conception or the patient development which made the device practicable.

The discovery of a practical means of wireless communication is a typical instance of this. Every schoolboy – in the Western hemisphere at least – associates the name of Marconi with it, whereas the names of those concerned with the gestation period are much less known outside of scientific circles, although without them there could have been no birth.

In tracing the evolution of any given discovery, the problem is to

---

* One Hertz (1 Hz) is an oscillation of 1 cycle per second; one kiloHertz=10^3 cycles/second; one MegaHertz=10^6 cycles/second; one GigaHertz=10^9 cycles/second.

know where to start, and the history of wireless communication provides no exception. Pursuing the human analogy, we can conveniently attribute its conception to Clerk Maxwell, the first quickening to Hertz and the actual birth to Marconi. This is all very well as far as it goes, but it takes no account of the fact that all these owed a great deal to the efforts of others; Maxwell, for instance, took over from Faraday, and Faraday, in turn, inherited much from his predecessors, who likewise had built upon the findings of even earlier workers – and so on (or rather, back) until we find ourselves with the ancient Greeks and Chinese. As with biological evolution, there is a spark of life which has been present from the very beginning, having been transmitted from generation to generation.

This is an oblique way of reminding ourselves that electronics is not a science in its own right, but an off-shoot of electrical engineering. In order, therefore, to put the advent of wireless telegraphy into perspective it is necessary to consider, in the briefest outline, the history of electricity and magnetism. For purposes of a summary it is reasonable to start at the first Elizabethan period, for although both phenomena were known to the ancients, no sensible growth of information about them had occurred until the sixteenth century. By comparison, optics had made much more headway.

It was Dr Gilbert (or Gilberd), physician to Queen Elizabeth I, who gave the initial impetus to scientific interest in electricity and magnetism by publishing his findings. Over the subsequent three centuries the original trickle of experimental work grew into something approaching a stream, with many important discoveries emerging. Devices for generating electric charges were invented and this circumstance originated a need for a means of storing such charges, thereby bringing the Leyden jar into being. The discovery of chemical means whereby electricity could be made available in a steady flow was another great step forward.

The physics of light was also being investigated, with such giants as Newton and, later, Huygens, dominating scientific thought. Physics in general made great strides between the sixteenth and nineteenth centuries and by the beginning of the nineteenth century a great deal had been found out about electricity and to a lesser extent, magnetism, although the interchangeable nature of these had not been discovered. In 1822 Georg Simon Ohm tore another veil from the mystery of electricity by establishing the mathematical relationship between voltage, current and resistance.

Another genius now arose in the person of Michael Faraday, who, building upon previous work, notably by Ampere and Oersted, announced his discovery of the principle of electromagnetic induction. This great step forward, which was made in 1831, opened the door to a host of possibilities, including those of the large-scale generation of alternating and direct currents.

At that time the nature of the force which Faraday had discovered was not understood, and although it was patent that when a loop of wire was rotated between the poles of a magnet a transfer of energy took place across the gap, opinion was divided as to how this was effected. The majority school of thought held that this 'action at a distance' could only be accounted for by the presence of some medium of contiguous matter. Faraday himself had other ideas, suggesting that the 'lines of force' he had discovered spread themselves out in all directions from a point of electric charge or magnetic pole and that any alteration in the state of these must have its consequences throughout the space they permeated.

But Faraday was no mathematician, and unfortunately his concept needed the backing of mathematical proof before it could be accepted. In 1855, James Clerk Maxwell, already at twenty-three a mathematician of some note, read his first paper on *Faraday's Lines of Force*, but while this succeeded in expressing Faraday's findings mathematically it did not carry matters to the point where the 'action at a distance' hypothesis could be positively rejected.

Maxwell was by now deeply engrossed in the problem. He devised a mechanical model to illustrate Faraday's Law of electromagnetic induction, whereby changes in a magnetic field were stated to produce an electric force; this it did successfully and Maxwell discovered on using it that it suggested that the process was reversible – that is, that changes in the electric force would produce a magnetic field. The realization of this concept of interchangeability led directly to the thought that all changes in electric and magnetic fields cause electromagnetic waves in space.

This model was used in conjunction with Maxwell's paper of 1862 *Physical Lines of Force*, in which the forerunners of the Maxwell Equations appear. These were fully developed in his classic treatise of 1865 *A Dynamical Theory of the Electromagnetic Field* in which the electromagnetic wave theory was mathematically expounded. Experiments conducted by Maxwell gave a rate of propagation of these waves which tallied closely with that of light as determined by Fizeau (it is a curious fact that although Fizeau's and Maxwell's calculations agreed to within thirty miles per second the figure they arrived at was subsequently found to be more than 6,000 miles per second in error). But the almost perfect agreement had led Maxwell to state:

> ... we have strong reason to believe that light itself – including radiant heat and other radiations if any – is an electromagnetic disturbance in the form of waves propagated through their electromagnetic field according to electromagnetic laws.

The seed of Maxwell's theory fell on rather stony ground because it upset too many preconceived ideas all at once, and because his mathematical presentation was obscure. It took many years to establish a significant following for the Maxwellian theory and in the interim the invisible waves which the master had postulated were discovered by accident. This circumstance took place in 1875 when Professor Elihu Thomson was demonstrating an induction coil at a lecture at the Central High School, Philadelphia, and had connected one terminal of the apparatus to a water-pipe and the other to a piece of metal insulated from earth. Thomson made the fortuitous discovery that tiny sparks were produced when the point of a pencil was brought near to a metal door knob in the lecture hall; it is stated that he pursued this phenomenon to various floors in the building and found the effect present in a room a hundred feet away from the induction coil.

The discovery was not widely publicized and Professor Thomson seems not to have carried out further investigation; neither did he connect it with Maxwell's work. The field of practical discovery thereafter lay dormant until 1883 when Fitzgerald, a new convert to the Maxwell school of thought, suggested that it might be possible to generate invisible waves by employing the discharge of a Leyden jar, which was already known to be oscillatory in character.

What would today be known as the breakthrough came in 1888 when Heinrich Hertz announced in Weidemann's *Annalen der Physik* that he had succeeded in producing what he described as an 'outspreading of electric force' (it was Lord Kelvin, in a translation of Hertz' work, who coined the expression 'æther waves'). It is significant that Hertz had been a pupil of Von Helmholtz who was one of the first in Europe to accept Maxwell's theory; without doubt Von Helmholtz' influence was responsible for Hertz' pursuance of the matter.

The Hertzian apparatus used was beautifully simple. The transmitter consisted of a pair of flat metal plates, each of which was joined to a short metal rod terminating at the far end in a metal ball. These two units were supported end-on, with the metal knobs innermost and

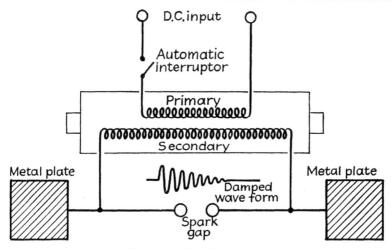

Figure 1.1 Hertz Transmitter

nearly touching each other; each unit was connected to one output terminal of an induction coil which formed a high voltage supply. This assembly formed, in essence, a capacitor or Leyden jar around which a strong electric displacement was created as the induction coil charged it.

At a critical potential the capacitor broke down, discharging itself in the form of a spark across the air dielectric between the two metal balls; this resulted in a sudden disruption of the electric field, which in turn created a magnetic flux in space. The persistence of this flux produced an electric displacement in the reverse direction and so an oscillatory process was initiated. Assuming that this oscillation was started sufficiently suddenly, some of the energy was radiated by the Hertzian dipole in the form of a damped wave. With the induction coil permanently switched on, a series or train of damped waves was radiated.

The receiver, or resonator, consisted of a metal circlet broken at one point, with the two ends terminating in small metal balls just out of contact with one another. The radiation was detected visually by the presence of tiny sparks jumping the gap.

At this point the question may be raised as to why Hertz and not Thomson is regarded as the discoverer of aether waves. The answer to this must surely be that, whereas Professor Thomson's discovery was accidental, and incidental to his immediate purpose, the work of Professor Hertz was a deliberate series of experiments designed to test Maxwell's theory. Just how completely Hertz achieved this is shown by

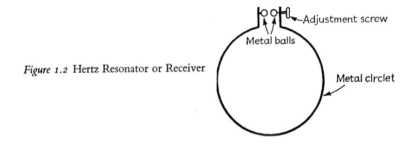

Figure 1.2 Hertz Resonator or Receiver

the fact that he not only succeeded in generating the waves, but also showed that they obeyed the optical laws governing reflection, refraction and interference, and furthermore that they travelled at the same velocity as light.

In view of the intense interest which the discovery aroused in scientific circles it is curious that no mention of the possibility of using these waves as conveyors of intelligence seems to have been made until 1892, when Sir William Crookes suggested that they might conceivably be employed for this purpose; at the same time he foreshadowed the use of some form of tuning in order to avoid interference between two transmissions.

The years which intervened between Hertz' discovery and the practical utilization of his waves were nevertheless not wasted, for valuable – indeed essential – pieces of apparatus were evolved during this time. Before discussing these, however, it might be appropriate first to mention various other means of communicating through space which were already in existence, and which from time to time (usually in the daily Press) still give rise to a statement that this inventor or that was the 'Father of Wireless'.

The methods which were being investigated fall into one or other of the following categories:

1. The conduction of electric currents through water or moist earth. Many names are associated with this approach, notably Morse, Lindsay, Trowbridge, Preece, Rathenau, Stecker, Wilkins and Melhuish.
2. Electromagnetic induction between parallel conductors, either in the form of complete circuits or by using the earth return method. Trowbridge, Preece and Lodge were among the investigators. Preece, by combining methods (1) and (2), evolved a practical system for the British Post Office, although this was limited in its range and scope.

3. Electrostatic induction between separated conductors. This method was pioneered with some success by Edison, Gilliland, Phelps, W. Smith and others, chiefly as a means of communicating with railway trains in motion.

In the assessment of claims made on behalf of individual workers in these fields we have to consider carefully the meaning of words. If the word 'wireless' is taken to mean 'signalling through space' then it must be conceded that those experimenters in fields (2) and (3) above undoubtedly achieved communication between two points and therefore would have prior claims. But the term 'wireless' means more than this. It relates to a method of signalling through space by a particular means – that of causing electromagnetic waves to radiate from an antenna system: broadly speaking, one of the fundamental differences between the conduction and induction methods and 'wireless' lies in the frequencies employed, the former using speech frequencies of only a few kHz and the latter much higher frequencies, with about 16 kHz as the minimum.

From the practical point of view the conduction or induction methods are limited in usefulness by their very short range. The G.P.O. system mentioned above, which was easily the most successful within the 'induction' category, needed the installation of two parallel conductors roughly equal in length to the distance to be bridged; as a consequence, on an overland circuit it would be cheaper to string one conductor between the two points to be bridged, using an earth return. The only place where the induction system might be used with advantage would be for communication with an off-shore island; indeed, the G.P.O. used it in this capacity.

Not all the alleged inventions of signalling without wires which were devised in the nineteenth century will bear critical scrutiny. Marconi himself, in an unpublished document in the Company's archives, mentions, in passing, two of these. One was a belief of the Rosicrucians, that if little pieces of flesh were transplanted from one person to another, each piece being tattooed with a letter of the alphabet, it was only necessary to prick the graft corresponding to a particular letter and its original owner would feel the pain in the very spot from which the skin had been taken.

Even more bizarre, about 1850 a Monsieur Benoit of Paris was alleged to have talked to a compatriot, M. Bial Cretien, in America, by means of snails. It seems that two snails, once placed in contact, are ever after in sympathetic communion; the basis of the invention was similar metal bowls in Paris and New York, in which snails were placed in contact with letters of the alphabet. When a snail was touched in Paris its sympathetic counterpart in New York would put out its horns and in this way messages could be exchanged. The medium of transmission was stated to be 'escargotic fluid' which was described as 'galvano-terrestrial-magnetic-animal and adamic force'.

Far more feasible was the claim made in 1872 by Mahlon Loomis, an American dentist, who took out a patent for 'establishing an electrical current for telegraphic or other purposes without the aid of wires, batteries or cables'. Loomis elevated two kites, using wires in place of string, on two adjacent mountain tops and is stated to have signalled from one to the other by discharging the static electricity collected by the 'transmitter' cable. Although this scheme is clearly impractical from the commercial point of view, it would, at least, seem to make use of a sudden discharge to create electromagnetic waves and to indicate that Loomis was the first to use elevated antennas for signalling purposes.

Another candidate with a claim to have generated electromagnetic waves and received them at a distance was Professor D. E. Hughes, who in 1879 gave a private demonstration of his apparatus to prominent members of the Royal Society, including Sir William Crookes. Two years later he repeated his demonstration to other members.

Although scientific opinion at the time held that the signals were propagated by induction, the description of the apparatus used indicates that electromagnetic waves were radiated from the transmitting end by rapidly interrupting an inductive circuit (the well-known radiating properties of an electric bell when connected to an antenna, or those of the spark plugs of a petrol engine are examples of this approach). Hughes is stated to have received the radiations up to 500 yards from his transmitter, using a 'microphone' of his own devising as a detector, but as no account of his work was published until 1889, the work of Hertz, which was issued in the previous year, takes precedence.

Hughes was a remarkable man. Although a professor of music, not of science, he had, in 1859, invented a typewriting telegraph which was used by the G.P.O. for a great number of years. He is also generally credited with the invention of the microphone, which, in the form in which he used it for his wireless experiments, was a forerunner of the coherers used at the turn of the century.

In the matter of his wireless apparatus however, he stumbled upon his method of generating the waves by accident, and had even then no idea of what he had done. He seems to have had no knowledge of Maxwell's work, and attributed the reception of signals to conduction effects. Again, although he is stated to have used a radiating element (it was in fact a kitchen fender!) and an earth connection, he patently had no idea of their functions. In short, Hughes was a trial-and-error experimenter who, had he possessed a scientific training, might well have developed his apparatus to the point of commercial utility.

In turning now to a state-of-the-art survey of the years which elapsed between the publication of Hertz' paper and the evolution of a practical system of wireless telegraphy, it may be wondered why seven years went by with little apparent progress. The key word here is 'apparent'. In fact, some very valuable work was done in the interim period, although this was done for scientific ends and not with any objective of creating a commercial system for message-carrying.

The simple apparatus used by Hertz was plainly capable of improvement. In particular, a more efficient means of detecting the wave-trains was badly needed. In 1890, Professor E. Branly of Paris published an account of the very extensive research he had carried out into the curious behaviour of certain metallic powders which had the property of changing their conductivity whenever an electric spark was discharged in their vicinity. This was not an original discovery of Branly's. It had been described as far back as 1835 by Munk of Rosenchoeld and this scientific curio was subsequently resurrected at intervals, notably by Guitard (1850) and S. A. Varley (1866). Varley, in fact, made use of the effect in a patent lightning protective device for use with telegraph instruments.

In 1879 Professor Hughes, as mentioned earlier, employed a glass tube filled with zinc and silver filings as a detector for his apparatus, but nothing of this was published for another twenty years. In Italy Professor T. Calzecchi-Onesti made a scientific record of the change in resistance of various metallic powders. His findings were published in 1884 and 1886 but attracted no particular interest.

Branly's work also constituted a very careful investigation into the phenomenon, but again little general notice was taken of it at the time. It was not until two years after publication that the significance of the change in resistance began to dawn. This was at a meeting of the British Association in which the speaker, Dr Dawson Turner, described Branly's experiments and those of his own. On this occasion the subsequent discussion prompted Professor G. Forbes to inquire whether Hertzian waves might not act in the same way as a spark from a Leyden jar.

Shortly afterwards Professor G. H. Minchin asserted that the change in conductivity of the powder was brought about by invisible electro-magnetic waves and not (as was generally believed) by action of the light emitted by the spark.

By 1893 a few scientists had come to the same conclusion as Minchin. Among these was Professor (later Sir Oliver) Lodge, who in 1894, in the course of a lecture to the Royal Institution on 'The Work of Hertz', demonstrated the Branly tube of filings, as improved by himself, in a new and very important role, namely, that of a detector of Hertzian waves. Lodge christened the device a coherer, because the filings cohered whenever a Hertzian wavetrain was encountered.

This lecture is particularly noteworthy for two reasons. It publicized the fact to all scientific workers in the field that the Branly coherer was an important piece of apparatus for the detection of electromagnetic waves, but it is not less remarkable that despite Sir William Crookes' prophecy of wireless telegraphy two years earlier – of which Lodge must have known – absolutely no reference was made to any such possibility in the lecture.

This circumstance is at first sight all the more astonishing when it is recalled that nearly all the ingredients for a practical system of wireless telegraphy were to hand. The spark gap transmitter for wavetrain generation, the elevated antenna which had often been used as a collector of static electricity, and the sensitive coherer for detecting their presence – all were there. With hindsight, the next step, the assembling of these components into a signalling system, seems obvious enough.

In reality it was by no means as obvious as all that. By far the greater number of investigators in the Hertzian field at that time were totally unconcerned with anything but the pure physics of the subject. There was, moreover, one link missing. This was the elevated antenna in its role as radiator; for although aerial wires had been used in experi-ments in connection with static electricity since Benjamin Franklin's day, they had never been thought of in terms of radiators or collecting devices for use with man-made electromagnetic waves. The absence of this vital piece of information relegated the range of the apparatus, even with the Branly coherer, to a matter of a few hundred yards at best, and this with no apparent prospect of radical improvement. The appara-tus therefore remained a laboratory device; tremendously exciting within the preserves of the scientist, but offering no practical facilities whatever for the commercial transmission of messages. This, then, was the situa-tion as it existed in 1894-5.

2

The Young Signor Marconi

Although this book is not a biography of Guglielmo Marconi, nevertheless the history of the Company he founded is inextricably interwoven with the life of this remarkable Italian, and for that reason it is pertinent to recall briefly a little of his background.

Guglielmo Marconi was born on 25 April 1874 at No. 7 Via delle Asse in Bologna (the street was subsequently renamed Via IV Novembre in honour of an Italian victory in World War I). He was the second son of Giuseppe Marconi, a well-to-do landowner who was married to Annie Jameson, a member of the well-known 'whiskey' family of Ireland.

For the most part the boy was brought up at the family's country residence, the Villa Griffone, near Bologna. At the age of five however he was taken to England and received his first elementary education at a private school in Bedford, where he remained for two years. He then returned to Italy and attended school at Florence. He completed his formal education at Livorno, where he studied physics under Professor Rosa.

Marconi, from an early age, displayed an original and inventive mind and when in his 'teens he came into contact with the renowned Professor Righi and studied his papers on electromagnetic radiation, his attention, which up to that point had been veering between various branches of physics, became steadfast upon the subject of Hertzian waves.

The critical moment of his life came when, on holiday in the Italian Alps, he chanced to read yet another scientific paper on the experiments of Hertz. Out of this, the idea to use the waves as a means of communication was born, and fired his enthusiasm to the point where he curtailed his holiday and returned to his top-floor 'laboratory' – a spare room – at the Villa Griffone.

His apparatus was such as was being used by all other researchers of the day; a spark induction coil and the Branly type of coherer, coupled to a Hertzian radiator. He was soon achieving the typical ranges obtained by contemporary workers – a matter of yards and no more – which he increased marginally by improvements of detail in the apparatus. For a short time he side-tracked into conducting experiments in the detection of electric storms using an elevated antenna (Professor Popov of Russia was carrying out similar work at the time) but soon abandoned these to continue his Hertzian wave work.

Just when it seemed that the practical limits of range had been reached at a hundred yards or so, Marconi had the inspiration of combining the elevated antenna of the thunderstorm experiments with the Hertzian apparatus. Disconnecting the Hertzian dipoles at both transmitter and receiver, he attached one output terminal of his induction coil via a wire to a metal cylinder erected at the top of a pole. The other output terminal was connected to a metal plate in contact with the ground. At the receiving end, one side of the coherer was connected to a similar elevated cylinder and the other side to earth.

The improvement in range was magical and Marconi, by systematic experiments, found that the distance over which the waves could travel was directly related to the dimensions of the cylinders and their height above ground. Whereas, for example, cubes of tin of about 25 cm. side measurements placed at a height of 2 m. gave him an effective range of only 30 m., cubes with side measurements of 100 cm. placed 8 m. above ground level meant that signals could be received at a distance of 2,400 m. (one and a half miles).

Marconi had also added some components to the original apparatus; these were mainly to enable Morse telegraphic signals to be sent, as distinct from the mere transmission of Hertzian waves. Fig. 2.1 shows the transmitting and receiving apparatus he used. From Fig. 2.3 note that at the receiver he had inserted an r.f. choke in both the 'antenna' and 'earth' side of the relay circuit which is parallel with the coherer in order that the latter should receive the full amount of energy from the Hertzian oscillations. He also fitted shunt resistors across the tapper (decoherer) contacts, and also to the relay contacts, so as to minimize sparking which would otherwise be initiating spurious local oscillations in the vicinity of the coherer.

The relay was a small sensitive type, energized by a single voltaic cell whenever a wave-train caused the coherer to drop in resistance value and so complete the relay circuit, which in turn switched in a battery to operate the tapper and a Morse inker. The receiving equipment was mounted on a baseboard, with the coherer, tapper and relay

26

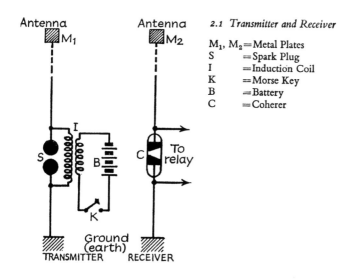

2.1 *Transmitter and Receiver*

M_1, M_2 = Metal Plates
S = Spark Plug
I = Induction Coil
K = Morse Key
B = Battery
C = Coherer

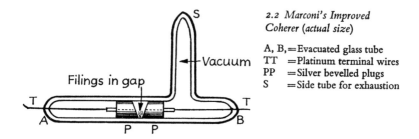

2.2 *Marconi's Improved Coherer (actual size)*

A, B, = Evacuated glass tube
TT = Platinum terminal wires
PP = Silver bevelled plugs
S = Side tube for exhaustion

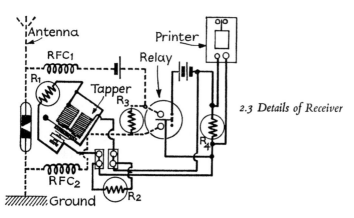

2.3 *Details of Receiver*

Figures 2.1, 2.2, 2.3 Marconi's Apparatus for
Wireless Telegraphy, 1894–5–6

enclosed in a metal box to shield them from the effects of extraneous interference.

At the transmitter, he originally used a Righi spark gap which consisted of four metal spheres immersed in insulating oil, the central ones being larger than the two outers connected to the secondary coil of the exciter. The presence of the oil demanded a greater electric strain to break it down and the spark was, as a consequence, more vigorous.

Marconi's first effort at a commercial exploitation of his apparatus was to offer the Italian Government a demonstration; it was a bitter blow, when, after the inevitable delay, the Government declared itself not interested.

After a family conference it was decided to act upon the advice of the Irish Jamesons and send the young man – he was twenty-one years old at that time – to England. This was a logical choice of country, for there were influential relatives living in London, notably Marconi's cousin Jameson Davis, who had promised all possible aid; furthermore, Britain was the hub of a great Empire and the workshop of the world, possessing the world's biggest mercantile fleet and the mightiest Navy – and it was in shipping that Marconi saw his best chance.

This, with good reason. Today it is difficult to visualize the utter isolation which enshrouded a ship of the 1890s once it had lost sight of land. Disaster could strike – and not infrequently did – with no one on shore or in nearby vessels being any the wiser. Some form of communication between ship and shore was sorely needed.

Marconi's entry into England was hardly auspicious. An overzealous Customs officer investigated his mysterious apparatus with such thoroughness that it arrived in London broken and useless. Hastily repairs were effected and the equipment demonstrated to cousin Jameson Davis, who, vastly impressed, set about establishing influential contacts.

On 2 June 1896, Guglielmo Marconi applied for the world's first patent for wireless telegraphy (Brit. Pat. No. 12,039), which was duly granted. The complete specification was filed on 2 March 1897.

By this time contact had been made with A. A. Campbell Swinton, an eminent electrical engineer of the day, who in turn provided Marconi with a letter of introduction to William H. Preece (later Sir William), the then Chief Engineer of the British Post Office. Marconi had also established touch with the War Office, offering a demonstration. Both Preece and the War Office showed interest, and the first official tests took place in June 1896. These were followed by further demonstrations in July and August, conducted between the Post Office building at St Martins-le-Grand and a station erected on the roof of the Savings Bank Department in Queen Victoria Street.

These brought a request for another demonstration, primarily for the Postal Telegraphy Dept, but also for Navy and Army observers. This took place on 2 September 1896, from a building on Three Mile Hill, Salisbury Plain, with the objective of establishing the feasibility of directional control by means of metallic reflectors. A range of one and three-quarter miles was recorded.

It is perhaps of interest to note that on this occasion the Naval observer was Captain H. Jackson, later to become Sir Henry Jackson and First Sea Lord. Captain Jackson had been carrying out communication experiments between ships since the previous year and had, in August 1896, succeeded in sending wireless signals between two naval vessels. Acting upon Admiralty instructions, he met Marconi at the War Office the day before the Salisbury Plain experiments took place. The two compared notes and found that both had been working along similar lines.

The Salisbury Plain demonstration evidently impressed the Army observer, Major Carr, for there was a quick reaction from the War Office. It was proposed that Marconi should attempt to develop apparatus which would activate either of two receivers enclosed in a common steel box immersed in the sea a mile off shore. This proposal, which was patently an idea for the detonating of underwater mines by remote control, was wholly beyond the capabilities of the Marconi apparatus at that time, and was not followed up.

William Preece gave an account of Marconi's experiments to the British Association later in September, and followed this with a lecture on wireless telegraphy at Toynbee Hall on 12 December, at which Marconi assisted the lecturer by giving practical demonstrations. For this, the first appearance of his apparatus in public, the young Italian astutely added a decorous degree of showmanship by enclosing his apparatus in two black boxes; the one containing the receiver was carried among the audience, so that whenever Preece depressed the transmitting key a bell rang in the box in Marconi's hands.

The lecture, which was attended by the Press, was something of a sensation and the next day Marconi awoke to find himself headline news. The Press, with a deadline to meet, had no time to sort out the niceties of the situation, and Marconi was widely advertised as the inventor of wireless. This, not unnaturally, was too much for the scientists, many of whom had made valuable contributions to the study of Hertzian waves and its associated apparatus, and they were, as a consequence, outraged. Dr (later Sir Oliver) Lodge was among the many who had some scathing remarks to make in print about the 'secret box', its owner, and the Chief Engineer of the G.P.O.

Preece was indeed furthering Marconi's interests in no small way and this was particularly commendable because in so doing he was closing the lid of the coffin on his own technical contribution to the problem of communication through space – the induction method – into which he had put a great deal of personal effort and which was already in limited usage by the G.P.O.

His championing of the cause was by no means disinterested however. Preece had a perfectly sound reason for keeping a close eye upon this new means of communication, in that he was Chief Engineer of an organization which had only just acquired a monopoly in telephonic and telegraphic communication in Britain, by the acquisition (in 1896) of the old National Telephone Company. If wireless telegraphy proved to be a success it could, if left to develop as a discrete and unsupervised entity, grow up to be a thorn in the G.P.O. flesh. Preece, as a faithful servant of his organization, was taking no chance on this happening.

So in his close liaison with Marconi, Preece was able to give every opportunity for the new system of communication to show its paces and at the same time to maintain the closest awareness of every new technical development, on the age-old principle that to be forewarned is to be forearmed. It says much for Preece's engineering integrity that he allowed his own inductive system to be sacrificed in the process.

One of the G.P.O. Chief Engineer's many practical contributions was to detail one of his own laboratory assistants, G. S. Kemp, to help Marconi in his work. This ex-Naval Chief Instructor in electrical and torpedo work was destined to become the young Italian's right-hand man, serving him and the Company, which was to be formed in the following year, with an almost fanatical loyalty for the rest of his life.

Marconi's apparatus was further improved and other tests carried out on behalf of the Post Office. In January 1897, Dr F. H. Bowman, consulting engineer to the G.P.O. reported:

> I have carefully examined the electrical receiver invented and patented by Mr Marconi and am of the opinion that the instrument embodies an entirely novel and practical means of intercepting electrical radiations and thus constitutes the really first successful application of wireless telegraphy.

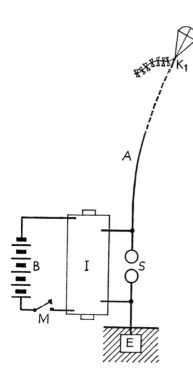

Figure 2.4 Marconi's Apparatus for Wireless Telegraphy, 1897; The Transmitting System

B = Battery
I = Induction Coil
M = Morse Key
S = Spark Gap
A = Antenna
K_1 = Kite Support
E = Ground (Earth) Plate

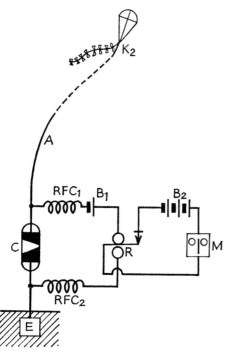

Figure 2.5 Marconi's Apparatus for Wireless Telegraphy, 1897; The Receiving System

B_1, B_2 = Batteries
C = Coherer
RFC_1
RFC_2 = R.F. Chokes
K_2 = Kite Support for Antenna
R = Relay
M = Morse Printer
A = Antenna
E = Ground (Earth) Plate

The word 'invented' will be noted as one which might have been expected of a lay member of the public, but not of an engineer. Dr Bowman would certainly have been in no doubt about the origin of the basic apparatus and we may fairly assume that this was a slip of the pen.

More experiments followed in rapid succession. In March 1897, in a demonstration on Salisbury Plain, ranges of up to four and a half miles were recorded. In these tests Marconi discarded the reflectors he had been using in favour of wires kept aloft by kites or balloons. (See Figs. 2.4, 2.5.)

At the demonstrations Marconi found himself playing host to a not too welcome guest. This was Professor A. Slaby of the Technical High School at Charlottenburg, Berlin, who witnessed the trials as the result of a request made through diplomatic channels by the German Emperor. Marconi's apprehension was not without cause, for Slaby was of international repute and was known to be experimenting with wireless telegraphy.

In the event, Professor Slaby proved to be a generous rival. In an article in *The Century Magazine* for April 1898, he gave full credit to Marconi for his discovery and admitted that he himself had never achieved a range of more than a hundred metres.

A little while after the 1897 demonstration Slaby suggested a commercial arrangement between Marconi and the Algemeine Elektrizitäts Gesellschaft (the General Electric Company of Berlin) whereby his powerful organization should be permitted to manufacture and sell the Marconi apparatus, but a failure to agree upon terms brought this proposal to nothing.

This was perhaps unfortunate, for the inspection of the Marconi apparatus had not only shown Slaby the answer to the problem which had been baffling him, but had also triggered some ideas of his own. He saw, for instance, that the original Marconi arrangement whereby the coherer was connected between the base of the antenna and the earth was inefficient, and that the ideal place would be between the upper end of the antenna (where the antinode of the stationary wave would be) and the earth. This arrangement, he also realized, was not possible, so he devised an alternative in the form of an antenna with both vertical and horizontal members, the horizontal section being of approximately equal length to the vertical and joined to it at a height of about three metres above ground level. This horizontal wire also had an antinode of potential at the far end which was quite accessible, and to this end

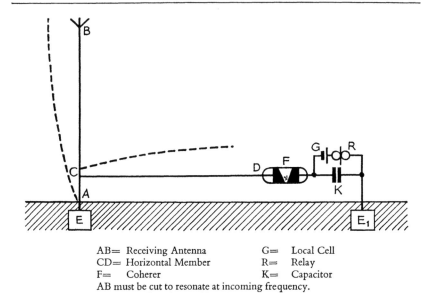

AB= Receiving Antenna   G= Local Cell
CD= Horizontal Member   R= Relay
F= Coherer   K= Capacitor
AB must be cut to resonate at incoming frequency.
CD to be of nearly equal length to AB.

Figure 2.6 Slaby-Arco Receiving Antenna
(Patented October 1900)

the coherer was fitted with its other terminal connected to earth via a capacitor.

This arrangement was successful and Slaby, in association with Count von Arco, followed it with other variants. Later (in 1903) their work on behalf of the German General Electric Company was to amalgamate with that of another brilliant German, Professor F. Braun, who was associated with the firm of Siemens and Halske. This alliance gave birth to a new company, Gesellschaft für Drahtlose Telegraphie, marketing the Telefunken system, a formidable rival to the Marconi Company to this day.

These circumstances have been related at some length to illustrate how rival systems were quickly (and quite legitimately) making their appearance. In short, time was not on the side of Guglielmo Marconi; it was essential that his new method of communication should be established on a sound business footing without delay if he were to maintain his head start.

This was indeed an especially worrying time. On the one hand frequent demonstrations were essential to convince the sceptical, whilst on the other Marconi needed every available minute to devote himself

c

to quiet experimentation to improve the apparatus still further. Over and above these problems was the financial one. Up to this time most of the money which had so far been spent had come from the Irish side of the family; and as the well was not bottomless it was essential to off-set expenditure to some degree with at least a token income.

Again, the publicity which had been given him by the Press had made enemies for him as well as friends. Many of the scientists were outraged at the misrepresentation of facts, and although Marconi himself had never overstated his case, their hostility was directed against this young interloper. Rumours were rife that the Marconi demonstrations were being heavily financed at the expense of the British tax-payer and to the detriment of British scientists, whereas in fact all that had happened was that the War Office had paid out-of-pocket expenses for their demonstrations and the Post Office had provided certain equipment and facilities, but no cash.

Despite these pressures, Marconi shrewdly resisted tempting offers by City financiers who wished to acquire his patents; instead, he entrusted the formation of a company to Jameson Davis, and such was his trust in his cousin that when registration took place, on 20 July 1897, Marconi himself was in Italy carrying out a demonstration for the Ministry of Marine.

3

The Infant Company

It is on 20 July 1897 that this history really begins, for on that day 'The Wireless Telegraph and Signal Company Limited'* came into being, with the objective of developing the Marconi apparatus commercially. It had a capital of £100,000. Marconi was awarded £15,000 for his patents, out of which he paid the formation expenses. In addition he received 60,000 of the 100,000 one pound shares. The remaining 40,000 shares were put on the market for public subscription, out of the proceeds of which Marconi was paid, and £25,000 was provided as working capital.

Jameson Davis was the Company's first Managing Director and Henry W. Allen became the first Secretary, operating from offices at 28, Mark Lane in the City of London, where demonstrations were given to interested parties by the transmission of signals from one part of the building to another.

The omens at first were good. Marconi, away in Italy, had succeeded in establishing wireless communication between the San Bartolemeo shipyard, Spezia, and the cruiser *San Martino*, a distance of 18 km. In the following month (August) he gave another successful demonstration watched by the King and Queen of Italy, as a result of which it was later announced that the Italian Navy was to adopt Marconi apparatus.

In England the strategy of trying to interest key people in the new means of communication was pursued with vigour and much publicity accrued, both in the lay and technical Press, but no sales. Returning to this country Marconi continued his experiments for the Post Office. In October, communication was established between Salisbury and Bath, a distance of thirty-four miles.

But now a disturbing phase set in. The Post Office themselves set up a station near Dover, using Marconi apparatus adapted by their own engineers, and began a series of experiments on their own account under

* The first title to be proposed was 'Marconi's Patent Telegraphs Ltd'. This was rejected by Marconi.

conditions of great secrecy. These were not very successful – ranges of not much more than four miles were achieved – but they were straws in the wind. Preece was now clearly looking upon The Wireless Telegraph and Signal Co. as a potential competitor which might in the not too distant future challenge the Post Office monopoly in the matter of a public telegraph service.

Furthermore, Preece had become possessed of an ambition which to many at that time must have seemed impossible to achieve. It was nothing less than the dream of establishing a wireless telegraphic service between England and France. But Preece was far too sound an engineer to entertain dreams which were impracticable, and he had realism on his side in the Salisbury-Bath demonstration over thirty-four miles – a considerably greater distance than that between Dover and Boulogne.

Marconi's mind was working in another direction, although before long the two paths were to meet. He was still on his original track of communication with (and eventually between) ships at sea. At this time (November 1897) his objectives were modest; a cautious exploration of possibilities within the sphere of interest of the shipping organizations.

His first move was to establish a coastal station; this was done at the Needles Hotel, Alum Bay, in the Isle of Wight, where a 120 foot mast was erected on the lawn to support a wire netting antenna. At the same time he negotiated an arrangement with the old London and South Western Railway Co., whereby he was permitted to experiment with receivers placed aboard their steamers *Solent* and *May Flower* which operated daily between Alum Bay and Bournemouth and Swanage piers. It was not long before the Alum Bay station was maintaining telegraphic contact (at four words per minute) with the steamers to the full extent of their excursions (Swanage Pier, eighteen and a half miles distant). A demonstration of this was given to the Post Office on December 23.

An incident which occurred a little later shows Marconi in another role, namely that of a publicist for his infant Company.

In January 1898 he had set up a station at Madeira House, Bournemouth, fourteen and a half miles from the Alum Bay station in the Isle of Wight. That winter a heavy snowstorm hit the south coast of England and for a time Bournemouth was isolated telegraphically from London because of broken lines, a circumstance which caused much concern to the many newspaper men who had gathered at Bournemouth on the arrival there of the dying William Ewart Gladstone.

Marconi heard of the reporters' predicament in being unable to get their messages through to Fleet Street and offered to contact his Isle of Wight station to find out whether the telegraph circuits between the island and the Capital were still intact. Luck was on his side, for they were. The reporters' messages were thereupon sent by wireless from Bournemouth to Alum Bay and then by the normal lines to London.

The incident was widely reported, not only giving Marconi some excellent publicity but making some good friends for him in the newspaper world. It was a continuation of the pattern of his relations with the Press, which, begun on his arrival in England, was to persist throughout his life. Marconi was fully aware of the value of good publicity and never hesitated to enlist its aid when occasion truly warranted it, but always with that reservation. The journalistic world, for its part, soon grew to realize that this young Italian never made a claim unless it could be substantiated, and respected him accordingly.

The common regard was exemplified in April 1898 when the Company invited the Press to Bournemouth for a demonstration. Messages were sent by various Press representatives in a private code which was unknown to the operators, whereupon the party was taken from the mainland to the Isle of Wight and given the coded tape as it had arrived on the printer. It was checked and found correct – proof positive that a perfect transmission had taken place, as the possibility that an operator had made an intelligent guess at indecipherable words was ruled out by the use of the private code.

May 1898 was a month of great promise for the new Company. In this month the Italian Ministry of Marine reaffirmed that the Italian Navy was to adopt the Marconi system. At home a successful demonstration was given, by invitation, in the House of Commons (with the receiving station at St Thomas's Hospital on the opposite side of the Thames). In May also, the first test of wireless telegraphy was made on behalf of Lloyd's Committee.

This last was a particularly significant event. Lloyd's had – as, indeed, they still have – a vital interest in furthering maritime communications. At that time the only means of reporting a ship's position was when it was sighted by coastal watchers and its presence notified to Headquarters by overland telegraph. The immediate question was – could the new wireless telegraphy augment this service in any way – for instance when fog blanketed the coast? Lloyd's Committee determined to explore the possibilities.

The venue for the experiment was Rathlin Island,* off Ballycastle on the Irish coast. This lies athwart the Western Approaches in an area which is often fogbound. Kemp (who had now joined the Company), took charge of the operation, which was entirely successful. In August 1898 Rathlin Island reported the passing of ten ships which were unseen by the coastal observers on the mainland, which was shrouded in fog.

While this demonstration was in progress another, just as momentous in its way, was being undertaken at the Alum Bay station. In June 1898, it was visited by Lord Kelvin, perhaps the most influential scientist of that time, and also by Lord Tennyson (son of the poet).

To Kelvin the visit was much more than a social occasion. He was intensely involved in the mystery of the medium of transmission of electromagnetic waves; in particular the Hertzian wavelengths needed much investigation, for little was known of their range limitations and of the modifications to their behaviour brought about by air and earth.

To carry out the experiments which Kelvin very rightly deemed to be necessary, he needed money and a lot of it. He also knew that university sources could not afford the sum required, and that even supposing the help of the Post Office could be enlisted, the Treasury would see to it that public expenditure on such a nebulous enterprise was limited.

To Kelvin, the work being carried out by Marconi and his Company was a ray of hope. Here was a public organization which was committed to the exploration of the medium of transmission for the compelling reason of commercial survival, and already Marconi and his researchers were piling up an exhaustive amount of data; they were, in fact, the only ones to be doing so on any significant scale. It was, to Kelvin, only commonsense to investigate, and should he be convinced, to back Marconi wholeheartedly.

Kelvin was in fact much impressed by the workmanlike atmosphere at Alum Bay and despatched telegrams for transmission to the mainland, thence to Cambridge and to Glasgow. He signified his approval in a rather curious way, namely by insisting on paying for the telegrams. There was, however, great significance attached to this apparent triviality, for he knew that both he and Marconi were breaking the law in making the matter a subject of a financial transaction. It was a deliberate throwing down of the gauntlet to the Post Office and their Parliament-granted monopoly. Furthermore, by implying an obligation on

* This was also the scene of an earlier experiment carried out by William Preece of the Post Office, who instigated tests of his inductive system of telegraphy there. The superficial similarity of these two series of tests has since proved a source of confusion.

the part of the new Company to complete a contract it underlined the fact that Kelvin was giving his approval to a practical new service, not a mere scientific laboratory toy.

Kelvin was to prove a very valuable friend to Marconi. As an instance, he pulled strings with the Italian Government which resulted in Marconi's temporary appointment as an assistant Marine Attaché to the Italian Embassy in London for the period when he, as an Italian subject, became liable for military training in his homeland. Thus, at a critical point in his career, Marconi was left free to pursue his experiments, for his official duties at the Embassy were nominal only.

Encouraged now by the active backing of the two men who, in all the country, could be the most influential to his cause – Preece, the Post Office Chief Engineer and Lord Kelvin, who was recognized as the chief authority of that era in the field of telegraphy – Marconi pressed on with renewed enthusiasm.

One of his new Company's first paid-for commissions was the successful reporting of the Kingstown Regatta of 1898, an assignment which was sponsored by the Dublin *Daily Express*. Seven hundred messages passed in all, over ranges of ten to twenty-five miles, to give the newspaper information on the progress and the result of each race well ahead of all its rivals. In addition to paying for the service, the journal gave generous publicity to the Company which had made the scoop possible, and news of the innovation appeared in the world's newspapers.

Another demonstration which fortuitously kept the Company in the public eye at this time was brought about by an injury sustained by the Prince of Wales (later King Edward VII). In the summer of 1898 Edward was convalescing aboard the yacht *Osborne* which was lying off Cowes, about two miles from Osborne House where Queen Victoria was in residence. The Queen wished to be kept informed of her son's progress, but intervening hills made visual signalling impossible; she consequently agreed to the suggestion that the new system of wireless telegraphy be given a trial and accordingly a 10-inch spark gap set was rigged aboard the yacht and another at Osborne House.

On 4 August 1898, the first medical bulletin ever transmitted by wireless was sent from the royal yacht to the Queen; during the next sixteen days, one hundred and fifty messages were exchanged, and naturally, the newspapers made the most of the circumstance. It was all grist to the Marconi mill, for at that time one of the prime requirements was to project what in modern jargon would be called the Company image – a picture, not of an organization dealing in fragile laboratory apparatus, but one which was in business to sell a new, robust and reliable means of communication.

Marconi's commercial acumen ran in many channels, one of which, as has been mentioned, was his shrewd appraisal of the power of the Press. Another lay in his ability to think ahead. He knew that at the moment he was technically ahead of such competition as existed, but he was also well aware that he could no longer carry out experimental investigations and mount demonstrations on a one-man basis. He needed technical assistance and characteristically he chose the best. It has already been recorded that he had acquired the valuable services of George Kemp for the practical work on hand; now he needed a physicist for the experimental aspect. In November 1898 Dr J. Erskine Murray resigned his Assistant Professorship of Physics at Heriott-Watt College, Edinburgh, and became Marconi's principal experimental assistant. Marconi was an adept at casting his bread upon the waters; at a time when the Company's financial resources were slender indeed, with no prospect of the situation improving for many years to come, he might well have been excused for adopting a cheeseparing attitude in his selection of new staff. But this, as will be seen later, was never his way.

He set Erskine-Murray to work at the Haven hotel at Poole, and demonstration after demonstration was given to organizations or individuals who could, in one way or another, further the cause.

One potentially useful market, the equipping of lighthouses and lightships, now lay in the sights. The Corporation of Trinity House had long wanted a reliable means of communication with their off-shore establishments and at least two systems had already been tried and found wanting. Cable connections to the lightships were short-lived because of fractures brought about by the combined efforts of rocks and tide-rips, whilst the Post Office inductive system had proved to be insufficiently satisfactory.

The way thus lay open and the Company made an offer to carry out a ship-to-shore demonstration for the Elder Brethren. This was accepted, the chosen line of communication being between the East Goodwin lightship and the South Foreland station some twelve miles distant.

Kemp carried out the lightship installation in foul weather. He was an indefatigable diarist and it is largely thanks to his efforts in this direction that a clear picture of the Company's early activities still exists. The following extract from one of his diaries is quoted at some length to throw light upon the life of an early installation engineer. After describing the technical problems attending the East Goodwin installation and how they were solved, Kemp goes on:

Dec. 20th. N.W. wind blowing sending seas over lightship. Fitted another earth wire to improve the spark ...

Dec. 23rd. Wind increased. Lightship began to toss about. At 7 p.m. and 8 p.m. it was almost unbearable.

Dec. 24th. Mr Marconi called me up [i.e. by wireless. Marconi was operating the South Foreland installation] by ringing V's in code on my bell and we went on working at good speed until 9 p.m., sending Compliments of the Season to all the editors of the *Daily Express*, all friends and relations of the lightship's crew and the Wireless Telegraph staff etc. I sent 'three cheers' for Mr Marconi and Compliments of the Season to the Supt. at Ramsgate. Then I went on deck and looked after the lighting and clockwork machine while the men below enjoyed themselves until the early hours of the morning.

Dec. 25th. Christmas Day. We managed to get over our Christmas dinner and then arose a S.W. gale and the ship began to plunge considerably. V. miserable on board esp. at high water slacks when the ship was kept broadside on to the tide by the gale. Seas which were v. heavy then came over her.

Dec. 26th. Weather still v. bad. I was called up [from South Foreland] at 2.15 p.m. and worked until 6.15 p.m. under v. great difficulties, the seas going right over the ship.

Dec. 27th. Weather worse. Waves washing over ship went down hatchways. The S. Foreland called me up at 11 a.m. and I worked until 11.30 a.m. Everything between decks as wet as on deck but I still gave S. Foreland a 1 cm. spark.

Dec. 28th. Weather still bad. Told S. Foreland I was feeling ill but I managed to send the 3 cm. spark ... Cold, wet, miserable; had v. little sleep.

Dec. 29th. Weather same as 28th. Could not go on deck. Could get no sleep all night. Pains spreading from back of my neck to shoulders and spine.

Dec. 30th. Weather again the same. Transmitted with 3 cm. spark and worked from 11 a.m. to noon, 3 p.m. to 4 p.m. with splendid results the signals received being the best so far. Told Mr Marconi I was not well enough to remain on board any longer and he must send for me when the wind dropped. He asked me to stop until the mast was up at S. Foreland [a temporary aerial was in use at the shore station] which he hoped would be on the following night. I told him we wanted fresh meat, vegetables, bread and bacon, but this was taken, it appeared, as a joke. The fact that I had come on board on December 19th with provisions for one week had evidently been forgotten, also that I had been on board for 12 days, living for the latter part on quarter rations – consequently I had to beg, borrow or steal from the lightshipmen. Fortunately during my stay on board I had taught the lightshipmen the Morse code, how to manage the aerial and the leading-in wire and how to manipulate the transmitter and receiver . . .

Kemp, in spite of his illness, did not leave the lightship until January 9, having spent twenty-two days on board. It should perhaps be noted that his indisposition was not solely one of mal-de-mer. Kemp was no landlubber but an ex-Petty Officer of the Royal Navy and a seasoned seaman.

In leaving Kemp aboard under such circumstances, Marconi was not being intentionally callous. The inclement weather left him no option as it was impossible to board the lightship until the gales abated. Nevertheless it is a fact that Marconi drove his men hard in those days, his saving grace being that he never pushed them further than he pushed himself.

Numerous two-way demonstrations between ship and shore took place and officials of Trinity House were shown that the lightship men themselves could operate the equipment efficiently. In early January when a savage sea tore away the best part of the lightship's bulwarks, she was able to report the damage by wireless to South Foreland and thence to Trinity House. When on 17 March 1899, the *Elbe* went ashore on the Goodwins in dense fog, the Ramsgate lifeboat was called out to her assistance by the same means. In April the lightship herself was rammed by the *R. F. Matthews* and the wireless installation saved the lives of her crew by calling out the Ramsgate lifeboat.

Alas! All to little purpose as far as orders were concerned. Trinity House at that time elected not to adopt the system, although Sir George Vivian, the executive chief of Trinity House, publicly confirmed the success of the experiment. And as his organization had from the outset refused to bear any of the cost, the Wireless Telegraph and Signal Co. emerged over £500 the poorer when the apparatus was dismantled in February 1900.

A vast amount of experimental and demonstration work was carried out during this period by the handful of men who constituted the staff. The experimental work was carried out at the Haven station at Poole, Dorset, where the 'small band of brothers' atmosphere was well in evidence.

One of the ground-floor rooms at the Haven served as the main laboratory, while other experimental work was carried out in huts in the hotel grounds. A visitor to the station in 1899 records that in the main laboratory he found two of the earliest employees, the brothers Cave, at one table making coherers; at another, P. W. Paget was winding receiver chokes and at a third Marconi himself was busy fitting V-gap plugs into an experimental coherer. Outside, along the foreshore, Dr Erskine Murray was conducting parabolic mirror reflector tests, using centimetric wavelengths.

At meal times, Marconi, his mother, his brother Alfonso (when present), Dr and Mrs Erskine Murray, the rest of the staff and any visitors all shared a common table. Often for relaxation in the evenings Murray would play his cello, Alfonso his violin, and Marconi would accompany them on the piano.

4

Successes and Setbacks

Influenced, possibly by confidence that an order for wireless equipment would come from Trinity House, it was decided that expansion was necessary, and accordingly, premises in Hall Street, Chelmsford, Essex, were acquired with the objective of turning it into a manufactory of Marconi equipment.

Much speculation has been made as to why Chelmsford was chosen; the probability is that it was brought about by a combination of circumstances. Essex is a flattish county and this was a favourable condition for the early wireless experiments. Chelmsford itself was sufficiently far out from London (about thirty-five miles) for land and property to be relatively cheap, but was conveniently near to the Port of London, with its vast amount of shipping – a promising potential source of revenue – and to Whitehall and the Post Office Headquarters. For the rest, it seems likely that Chelmsford itself was selected for the good and sufficient reason that the Hall Street premises came on to the market at just the right time.

The Hall Street building had been a silk factory and then a furniture warehouse. Now, in December 1898, it became the first wireless factory in the world.

Meanwhile, back on the South coast, while the East Goodwin tests were still going on, an even more ambitious role was being planned for the South Foreland station. In September 1898 the Company asked the French Government for permission to erect a wireless station on their side of the channel, but not until 2 March 1899 was the request officially approved.

At once the Boulogne area was surveyed and a site chosen at Wimereux, three miles north of Boulogne. By 26 March the station had been built and was ready to go on the air in an attempt to communicate with the South Foreland station, thirty-two miles away.

On the following day Marconi arrived at Wimereux to meet a Commission appointed by the French Government, representatives of the French Army, Navy and the Telegraph Service. A special correspondent of *The Times* was also present. With Marconi at the transmitting key the first wireless message ever to cross the English Channel was successfully picked up by the South Foreland station. Other test messages, set by the watching authorities, were sent to various prominent people in England; these likewise were received and forwarded to their respective destinations via overland telegraph. The French Government was impressed.

With the establishment of contact over ranges of thirty miles or more, the commercial potential of wireless telegraphy would seem to be established. There was, however, a big 'but'. When two stations were in communication everything was satisfactory; but when another station within range started to transmit, chaos was apt to ensue because the radiations spread over a very considerable band of frequencies and one transmission jammed the other.

There were two possible approaches to this problem. One was to ration the transmission time of every station, so that each could have exclusive use of the medium for a given period and then close down to give the others their turns. The second was to carry out research to reduce very considerably the spread of the radiation. In practice, with wireless stations multiplying to the extent visualized by the Company, only the second approach was realistic, so the Haven experimental station devoted a considerable amount of thought to the problem, making use of the three stations at East Goodwin, South Foreland and Wimereux to carry out practical tests. By April 11th, progress was such that South Foreland could communicate with East Goodwin without Wimereux receiving a single dot.

As a result of this step forward another series of demonstrations was given to the French Government which placed at the Company's disposal, first the gunboat *Ibis* and later the store ship *Vienne*. On 17 June 1899 the *Vienne*, with Marconi and a French Commission on board, steamed into the English Channel and a series of test communications was made with the South Foreland station which proved to all on board that the improvement in selectivity was no idle claim.

It is somehow out of period with wireless telegraphy to have to record that on that same evening when returning from Boulogne to Wimereux, Marconi, Kemp and another man were involved in a fairly serious accident in the horse-drawn cabriolet in which they were riding. The horse ran away on the brow of a hill and the three men – the third was the driver – were just able to jump clear before the vehicle smashed against a wall. Marconi injured his knee and was out of action for ten days; the others were unhurt.

The Admiralty had been following the French demonstrations with interest and in July 1899, the Wireless Telegraph and Signal Company was invited to install and operate their equipment on two warships for the duration of the forthcoming naval manœuvres.

The offer was accepted; one set was installed aboard the cruiser *Juno* which lay at Devonport Dockyard, and the second set was packed aboard for installation on the battleship *Alexandra* when the two vessels made rendezvous in Torbay. Marconi sailed with the *Juno*.

On July 14 he reported that he was picking up signals from the Needles station from a distance of eighty-seven miles. By the 16th the installation aboard the *Alexandra* was completed in Torbay. Subsequently, at the Admiralty's request, a third ship, the cruiser *Europa*, was equipped with wireless apparatus.

The manœuvres, which continued into August, showed clearly that wireless telegraphy was destined to be indispensable to any modern fleet. Communication between the *Europa* and the *Juno* was reliably maintained up to sixty nautical miles, and up to forty-five nautical miles between *Juno* and *Alexandra*. Messages were actually received at a distance of seventy-four nautical miles. These figures, although short ranges by modern standards, must be considered in relation to the fact that in all previous manœuvres, inter-ship communication was limited to the distances at which semaphore, flag or lamp signals could be read. If, for instance, a cruiser located the enemy main force at a point some seventy miles distant from the main battle fleet, she would, in the previous year, have had to steam back at full speed with the information and by the time the battleships had arrived in the area, the enemy might well have disappeared. With wireless telegraphy aboard the cruiser, the passing of the information was virtually instantaneous.

Important as these manœuvres were in assessing the value of wireless to the world's navies, there was another, more fundamental, matter of extreme value which emerged. This was the fact that, contrary to current scientific opinion of the day, the waves were somehow reaching far beyond the horizon. It was inexplicable; it appeared to confound all the work of Maxwell, Hertz and the others. Only a few months earlier the influential and usually well-informed journal *The Electrician* had stated:

... it is an absurdity to suggest that ether waves inherently followed the curvature of the earth.

The Electrician was, of course, right, the key word being 'inherently'. Some unknown factor was causing the waves to behave in a manner which was foreign to them. The more foresighted scientists began to seek for a rational explanation, but these, it is to be feared, were in a minority. The greater number, still incensed at the thought of an upstart young amateur stealing their thunder, took refuge behind a hill of doubts and continued their sniping from there.

In September 1899, another demonstration was undertaken. This one started out in a modest way and enlarged itself to very significant proportions.

The occasion was the annual meeting of the British Association, which, in that year, was to be held at Dover. The address was to be delivered to this body by Dr J. A. Fleming, Professor of Electrical Technology, University College, London, his subject being *A Centenary of the Electrical Current*. Dr Fleming suggested that a demonstration of wireless telegraphy would make an apt complement to his lecture, and accordingly apparatus had been installed in Dover Town Hall.

As originally visualized, nothing more ambitious than routine communication with the South Foreland station only four miles away was contemplated. Nevertheless, this four miles was significant, for the intervening area was occupied by the 400 ft. cliff upon which Dover Castle stands, and the demonstration had a serious purpose, namely to show the members of the Learned Society that the wireless waves would get to their destination regardless of this intervening obstacle.

It so happened that at times during the preparatory tests, the Wimereux station's signals were being received at Dover. By coincidence, the Association Scientifique Française was meeting at Boulogne during the same week as the British Association convened at Dover, while in Italy an Electrical Congress was being held at Como, birthplace of Volta. Enterprising as always, Guglielmo Marconi hit upon the idea of attempting a fraternal exchange of messages between the three scientific organizations; with all speed the Dover antenna system was heightened and this put the temporary Town Hall station in direct communication with Wimereux.

On September 18 the British Association began its meeting during which congratulatory messages were passed via Wimereux to the French and Italian scientific organizations, the messages for the latter being retransmitted from Boulogne over land wire to Como.

This bold, impromptu exercise impressed not only the scientists of the three countries concerned, but the world, for the Press seized upon it and made much of it. It was all valuable publicity for the infant Company.

The Wimereux station had by now served its useful purpose and plans were laid for dismantling it. It did not, however, die without enjoying a little further glory, for on September 23 its signals were received at Chelmsford, eighty-five miles away, of which fifty-eight were over land. The next day the mast was lowered and the equipment removed.

By this time Marconi was in New York supervising arrangements for the reporting of the America Cup yacht race on behalf of the *New York Herald* and *Evening Telegram*. Again, world publicity was the main motive, for this would be assured by the global interest occasioned by the event.

Marconi and his engineers made sure that no effort was spared to ensure as far as humanly possible that the apparatus, which was installed on a sea-going ship of 3,000 tons (rather improbably named the *Ponce*) and a cable ship, the *Mackay Bennett*, should work faultlessly. The *Ponce* was to follow the race and transmit the details to the *Mackay Bennett* which was moored in the river by Bowden, for onward transmission by line telegraph to the newspaper offices.

The operation was, indeed, a conspicuous success and the essentially practical nature of the equipment was underlined by the circumstance (unforeseen at the start and brought about by the extension of the races over seventeen days because of bad weather) that the seagoing equipment had to be transferred to another vessel, the *Grande Duchesse*, part-way through the period. Not only were the newspaper offices in possession of the race positions within seventy-five seconds, but the wireless telegraph also succeeded in scotching a rumour that two hundred lives had been lost in the sinking of one of the following ships crowded with sightseers. In fact, no accident had befallen this vessel, but the prompt reassurance to the shore clearly emphasized that the new form of communication could be of inestimable value to shipping.

Just for the record, the American yacht *Columbia* won the seventh race and retained the cup from her British rival *Shamrock*.

The Marconi apparatus was dismantled and, at the request of the U.S. Naval Department, reinstalled in the cruiser *New York* and the battleship *Massachusetts*, between which successful tests were carried out over ranges of up to thirty-five miles. On November 2 the *Massachusetts* equipment was transferred to the torpedo boat *Porter* which subsequently maintained contact with the *New York* while travelling at her maximum speed of twenty-four knots.

The ability of the equipment to serve the battle fleet and to withstand the vibration of small high-power boats was not lost on the Naval authorities, and the Secretary to the U.S. Navy duly sent the Company a letter of congratulation, but made no specific offer to purchase equipment. Unfortunately, the plaudits of onlookers (and they were many, for the Company was now very much in the public eye) do not pay shareholders' dividends and the order book was deplorably empty. The British military authorities had not so far backed their interest with tangible contracts; neither had Trinity House nor any of the commercial shipping interests. The Post Office, being already adequately served on its inland routes, had no real occasion to buy wireless apparatus. Abroad, the picture was dismally similar; great interest had been shown by France and America but not to the point of contracts.

One bright spot emerged from the gloom when Wall Street showed its confidence by forming, on 22 November 1899, an American Company which was to pay the Wireless Telegraph and Signal Company 7,000,000 dollars for patent rights. In the event this transaction never materialized; instead the original American Company was later merged into the parent Company with the title of Marconi Wireless Telegraph Company of America. Many years after, it was to become the Radio Corporation of America.

In our own era of thrust and bustle it is perhaps salutary to reflect that the Victorians could, when occasion demanded, do their share also.

As an instance of this, whilst Marconi was in the U.S.A., Kemp (who was at Hall Street, Chelmsford) received orders to dismantle both the Needles and the Haven stations. This was on November 2. Two days later, the Needles apparatus was *en route* to Chelmsford and the mast lowered. By the 8th, the Haven station had been similarly dealt with and Kemp was on his way to London to visit Head Office in Mark Lane.

Here he met with news that must have raised his blood-pressure considerably, for a cable had arrived saying that Mr Marconi wanted the Needles and Haven stations put into service again.

On that same day (the 8th) Marconi and his assistants sailed for England aboard the American Line ship *St Paul*, having first sent the cable to the London Office. The first few days were spent in rigging the wireless apparatus aboard, while in England, Kemp and his assistants worked to such good effect that both the Needles and the Haven stations were in operation again by the 13th.

On November 15 when the ship was sixty-six nautical miles from the English coast, the Needles station established contact with the *St Paul*, this being the first occasion that a transatlantic ship had reported her arrival by wireless. Marconi, ever an opportunist, borrowed the ship's small printing press and began to run off the news which the Needles station, by pre-arrangement, was transmitting. He christened his little newspaper *The Transatlantic Times* and sold it for a dollar a copy, the proceeds going to the Seamen's Fund.

In this casual fashion the first ship's newspaper containing up-to-the-minute intelligence was inaugurated. The passengers were vastly impressed, particularly as the *St Paul* was travelling through thick fog, which made the reception of the news all the more spectacular. The eighty-five subscribers were regaled with the latest available news about the Boer War: 'Ladysmith, Kimberley and Mafeking holding out well. No big battle. 15,000 men recently landed.'

The Boer War, which began on 11 October 1899, was the first in which wireless telegraphy was used in the field. One would like to be able to record that its use revolutionized the whole concept of the conduct of the war, but accuracy compels the admission that it did nothing of the kind.

The Company had initially suggested to the military authorities that wireless telegraphy should be used for ship-to-shore operation at Cape Town, Durban and other ports of disembarkation, where troop transports were arriving daily in the roadsteads and traffic congestion was causing problems. This suggestion was followed to the point where equipment for five such stations was sent to South Africa, together with engineers to install and operate it. But when the engineers arrived at Cape Town, they found that the military had changed the plan and they were invited to volunteer for service in the field. This they did and in a short space of time each found himself in charge of a unit consisting of a horse-drawn wagon in which the apparatus was mounted, and personnel drawn from the Telegraph Section of the Royal Engineers.

The power supplies consisted of large-capacity dry cells and jelly accumulators. Under the original agreement the War Office was to supply the antenna masts, and these, in the event, proved to be 50 ft. jointed bamboo rods, each unit being additionally issued with two six foot linen Baden-Powell box kites.

In service in the Kimberley area, static discharges proved to be extremely troublesome in that they made the coherers insensitive or even completely unserviceable at times. Cyclonic dust storms wrecked the bamboo masts; the kites proved to be difficult to synchronize in the air at the different stations and 14 ft. balloons, which were tried as alternatives, were torn adrift in the high winds. In short, the stations were unserviceable for half of the six-week period in which they had been tested.

Marconi was swift to spring to the defence of his engineers and the equipment. On 2 February 1900, in a paper he read to the Royal Institution in London, he criticized the War Office for supplying unsuitable masts. Ten days later the Director of Army Telegraphs in person gave orders for the Kimberley Line stations to be dismantled.

At this point the Admiralty stepped in and asked for the use of three of the five installations. These were installed on the *Forte*, *Thetis* and *Magicienne* of the Delagoa Bay squadron which were carrying out blockade duties. C. S. Franklin, one of the installation team, and later to become a very eminent engineer, once remarked dryly to the writer that the ship-board installations proved extremely useful to the officers for making their private arrangements when returning for shore leave. This, however, was a comment which should not be taken too seriously: in fact, the wireless apparatus did a useful job, for there were several occasions when a fast blockade runner had been captured by the slower naval vessels converging on her from different points, being able to act in unison by reason of their wireless equipment.

Subsequently the remaining two sets of gear were brought into service, and Warrant Officers and signal ratings were taught how to operate the equipment. The Marconi Company also gained valuable experience; as an instance, an experimental twin-wire horizontal aerial was rigged on the *Thetis* which proved so successful that it eventually became a standard feature of ship-board installations.

There can be no doubt that the British Admiralty were as impressed by their captains' reports as they had been by the performance of the wireless apparatus used during the 1899 manœuvres. In proof of this a contract was placed with the Company for the supply and installation of apparatus aboard twenty-six naval vessels and at six Admiralty coast stations. In addition, the Boer War apparatus was taken over as it stood.

This, the first big Admiralty contract for wireless apparatus, was placed on 4 July 1900; all the sea-going installations were tested and accepted by October of that year. The conditions of acceptance were stringent; satisfactory communication had to be maintained by naval signalmen between two ships, one anchored at Portsmouth and the other at Portland, a distance of sixty-two miles, of which eighteen miles was overland with intervening hills. The first ship to use the new apparatus was the *Diadem*.

5

Tuning: a Great Step Forward

The dawn of the twentieth century saw a change of name for the Company, for on 23 February 1900 the Wireless Telegraph and Signal Co. was reconstituted to become Marconi's Wireless Telegraph Co. Ltd. It is perhaps of interest to note that the choice of name was a Board decision with at least one dissentient voice – that of Guglielmo Marconi himself, who did not like it. History subsequently justified his opinion to some extent, for the newspapers in particular have never seemed to be able to get it right and it was, after all, something of a mouthful. However it did duty for over sixty years until it changed in 1963 to the more manageable title of 'The Marconi Company Ltd.'

Much history was to be made in the intervening years but before going on to this, 23 February 1900 seems a convenient date upon which to pause and consider the state of the art at the time, together with the technical problems which confronted the Company.

The apparatus used was still basically the same as that which had been evolved four years earlier – simple, battery-driven equipment which had been taken from the laboratory and made robust enough to withstand day-to-day usage. But with the aid of this the small band of engineers had accumulated a very considerable amount of valuable data, as a result of which a decision as to whether a given proposal was feasible or not could often be made in the light of past experience, and evaluation was becoming less dependent upon empiric trials.

Nevertheless it was a worrying time, for orders were distressingly few. The shipping interests, with the exception of the Royal Navy, were still not buying. The maritime world seemed quite content to carry on with the same primitive means of communication which had been in use from time immemorial.

This was not sheer conservatism and none knew this better than Marconi. He had long since realized that there were three main arguments against the use of wireless telegraphy, namely the limited range, the lack of privacy in the transmitting/receiving process and the dismal fact that because the spark transmission shock-excited a very broad band of frequencies into being, a receiving station which happened to lie within range of two or more transmitters could only receive a garbled mixture of all signals which happened to be reaching it, because no means existed of selecting the wanted from the unwanted message.

Life was made no easier by the knowledge that rival systems had made their appearance, notably, Popov-Ducretet, Slaby-Arco and the Siemens-Halske-Braun combine, but also others. Already the French naval authorities had veered towards the Popov-Ducretet system and the German Navy had adopted that of Slaby-Arco. All, however, suffered from the same defects; all were seeking the master-invention which would give a decisive lead over competitors.

At the onset Marconi had sought to improve his apparatus in detail, mostly by empiric research to find the most efficient form of antenna and by experimenting with various types of coherer. But he and his engineers soon realized that improvements along these lines would never be more than marginal, and the real problem lay in the inefficient dissipation of the radiation over such an extremely wide band of frequencies.

It will be recalled that Professor Slaby in witnessing the Salisbury Plain demonstration of 1897 had realized that Marconi was not using the coherer to best advantage by placing it as a direct connection between the lower end of the antenna and earth. Whether Slaby incautiously dropped a hint of this, or whether Marconi realized it simultaneously we shall

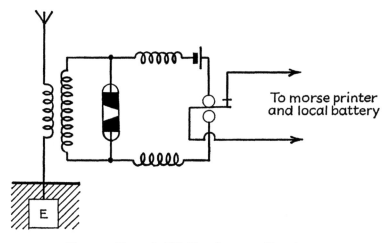

Figure 5.1 Marconi's H.F. Transformer or 'Jigger', 1897

never know; it can only be recorded that from the Salisbury Plain demonstration onward Marconi began to experiment with other ways of connecting the coherer, with the principal aim of applying the incoming signal to it as a voltage rather than as a current. In order to do this he introduced an r.f. transformer into the circuit, with the primary connected between antenna and earth and the tightly-coupled secondary winding connected to the coherer.*

The first results were disappointing. Far from improving the sensitivity of the receiver it diminished it considerably. Other transformers were wound, using different ratios of turns, different wire diameters and different couplings; some improved the receiver sensitivity; others did not. Between March and December of 1897, several hundred transformers of different design were wound and tested, and Marconi took out patents on three of the most promising ones.

The extent of his overall success at this time can be gauged by the gradual increase in the ranges recorded. In later years Marconi in recalling those days was able to say:

> The new methods of connection which I adopted in 1898, i.e. connecting the receiver aerial directly to earth instead of to the coherer, and by the introduction of a proper form of oscillation transformer in conjunction with a condenser so as to form a resonator tuned to respond best to waves given out by a given length of aerial wire, were important steps in the right direction.

His patent for this, No. 12,326, was applied for on 1 June 1898.

The principle of tuned circuits was not, of course, an original discovery of Marconi's. In 1889, Dr (later Sir Oliver) Lodge had demonstrated syntony (as he called it) in a closed circuit application and much later (10 May 1897) applied for a patent (No. 11,575) entitled 'Improvements in syntonized telegraphy without wires'. This employed identical antennas, inductances and capacitors at both the transmitting and receiving station, each antenna consisting of a pair of large sheet metal cones placed one above the other in a vertical line. These were referred to as 'capacity areas'.

It is tempting to jump to the conclusion that Marconi borrowed Lodge's idea and modified it to suit his own requirements. This, however, is not the case; Lodge's 'syntonic jars' experiment of 1889 did not permit the radiation of electromagnetic waves for any significant distance; furthermore, Marconi's experiments with oscillation transformers began well before Lodge's patent of 1897, the constructional

---

* Such a transformer was christened a 'jigger'.

details of which, in any event, were not published at the time of the application.

In his patent of June 1, Marconi makes his aims very clear:

It is desirable that the induction coil should be in tune or syntony with the electrical oscillations transmitted, the most appropriate number of turns and most appropriate thickness of wire varying with the length of wave transmitted.

In a further patent specification (No. 25,186) of 19 December 1899 he adds that:

. . . the best results are obtained when the length of wire of the secondary of the induction coil is equal to the length of the vertical wire used at the transmitting station. (Fig. 5.3.)

The problem was not as yet fully solved however, for whilst a degree of selectivity was now present, a receiver placed equidistant from two transmitting stations was still unable to separate the two sets of messages. Marconi now turned to a further patent taken out by Lodge in 1898 (N. 29069) but was unable to get any satisfactory results, probably because the antenna capacitance was too small in proportion to the

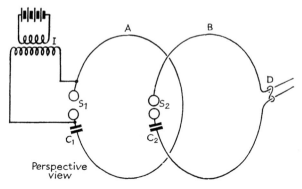

Figure 5.2 Lodge's 'Syntony' Experiment, 1889

In 1889 Sir Oliver Lodge demonstrated the phenomenon of resonance or 'syntony' as it was then termed. 'A' is a circlet of wire with a Leyden jar in series (capacitor C_1 in diagram) and with metal balls at the ends to form a spark gap. An induction coil I is connected across the gap.

'B' is a second circlet, similar to A except that the spark gap is smaller and that means of varying the length of wire is provided.

When the induction coil is switched on, capacitor C_1 charges and discharges across the gap S_1. With circlet B close to, and parallel with, A, minute sparks are observed across the gap S_2 when the slider D is adjusted to bring B into resonance with A.

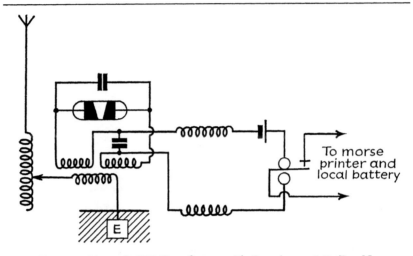

Figure 5.3 Marconi's H.F. Transformer with Capacitors, 1898. (Pat. No. 25,186, 19 December.) (The capacitor across the coherer and that across the split in the secondary winding constitutes a form of pre-set tuning.)

inductance. He tried large metal plates as antennas at transmitter and receiver but abandoned these because of the physical impracticability of their use on board ship in high winds. A step forward was made when a vertical wire, earthed at its base, was placed near the vertical radiator; the improvement effected by this gave encouragement to carry out further experimental work.

The next patent (N. 5387) was taken out on 21 March 1900. In this the transmitting antenna consisted of two concentric cylinders, the outside one forming the radiator and the inside one being earthed; the receiving antenna was similar. This provided a fair degree of syntony, but experimental work still proceeded.

At this point, Marconi and his assistants returned to Lodge's original syntonic jars experiment of 1889. This, as it stood, was essentially a closed circuit system; that is, its properties of radiation were virtually nil. Marconi found, however, that such a circuit could be made to radiate by coupling an aerial to it via an h.f. transformer (the idea of using such a coupling was not in itself new, having been incorporated in Lodge's patent of 1897 and Braun's of 1899). What was new was that the antenna inductance was tapped so as to be able to adjust the periodicity of the oscillation and also the Leyden jar or fixed capacitor was replaced by one which could be varied in capacity. The receiving circuit used similar arrangements.

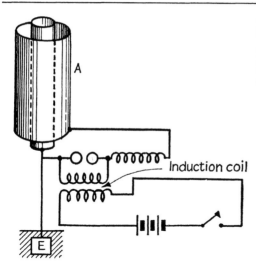

Figure 5.4 Marconi's Concentric Cylinder Antenna (1900).

Diagram shows transmitter, but the principle was also applied at the receiver.

This was it. The problem of syntony had been solved, and two major worries eliminated at one stroke, for the radiated power was no longer dissipating over a very broad band and consequently ranges improved considerably. Perhaps even more important, adjacent stations could now conduct their business without interfering one with the other. As soon as was humanly possible Marconi took out a master patent, No. 7777 (the famous 'Four Sevens') and this was granted on 26 April 1900.

Experiments with the syntonic transmitters and receivers were even more successful than had been hoped for. In a series of demonstrations to influential people, including an Admiralty Commission, it was shown that two differently tuned transmitters could be connected to a common antenna. A number of messages could also be received simultaneously on an antenna connected to differently tuned receivers. Diplex working had arrived, and other technical improvements which had been made enabled a keying speed of about twenty words per minute to be attained. This speed, although slow by later standards, was a considerable advance on what had been possible at the start of the Company's activities and made wireless telegraphy competitive with the ordinary inland telegraph service of the period.

While the technicalities of patenting the syntonic system were being implemented, some commercial encouragement had come the way of the Company in the form of an order for a wireless installation aboard a transatlantic liner. Not, as might have reasonably been expected, from one of the British shipping firms but from a German line, Norddeutscher

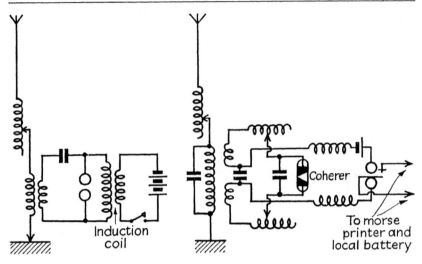

Figure 5.5 Marconi Transmitter, 1900.   *Figure 5.6* Marconi Receiver, 1900.

Lloyd of Bremen – a relatively unexpected source, seeing that extensive experimental work on wireless telegraphy was currently being carried out in Germany. However, there was the contract in black and white; an installation aboard the *Kaiser Wilhelm der Grosse* and permission from the German Government to fit wireless apparatus on the Borkum Riff lightship and at the Borkum Island lighthouse twenty miles or so distant.

The latter two installations were particularly challenging because previous attempts to connect the two by submarine cable had failed. In addition, both were so far off the main shipping line that visual signalling to passing vessels was only possible when visibility was very good.

On February 10 the apparatus was taken aboard the liner and, a few days later, in foul weather, other equipment was installed in the lightship and lighthouse.

On 28 February 1900 the *Kaiser Wilhelm* left Bremen with Kemp putting the final touches to the wireless equipment. Contact was established with both the lightship and the lighthouse, the latter being in touch for fifty miles. As the liner passed down Channel, the ship's telegraphist took over from Kemp and exchanged messages with the Marconi stations at the Needles and the Haven. The equipment was not of course the syntonic type, but nevertheless performed very successfully.

This installation not only made maritime history but also set the seal on a new project which in its turn underlined the emergence of two complementary attitudes within the Company. One was the engineering research outlook personified by Marconi and his small band of technicians; the other was headed by Major Flood Page, the new managing director (Jameson Davis had resigned a few months previously), representing the commercial aspect.

Flood Page, while appreciating that the Marconi team must continue the research and demonstration work unabated, was equally sensible of the fact that the Company must be made to pay its way. As the most striking successes of the Marconi system had been in ship-to-shore work, and because this was the obvious target for immediate returns, it was decided to form a subsidiary Company – the Marconi International Marine Communication Co. Ltd., and this was incorporated on 25 April 1900, with offices in London and Brussels and agencies in Paris and Rome. Its object was to carry out the maritime working of the Marconi system in all its applications, and this it has done ever since, except for naval installations which are the responsibility of the parent Company.

The main purpose behind the formation of the new Company was to challenge the Telegraph Acts of 1868 and 1869 and to clarify the nebulous situation which existed regarding a private Company's rights in handling messages sent by wireless telegraphy. In this connection it should be mentioned that the Post Office had ignored the challenge of Lord Kelvin's paid telegram, no doubt recognizing it for what it was – a deliberate exercise in kite-flying.

To summarize the situation, the salient features were as follows:

1. It was clear that clauses in the Acts would permit a private Company to send messages for its own use, but not for gain as a public telegraph service.
2. A private Company could own and maintain a private service on behalf of some other organization so long as no charge was made for the sending of telegrams.
3. A Company could therefore install its apparatus and operators aboard a vessel for the purpose of communication with shore stations provided no direct charge was made for messages handled.
4. The Company would be perfectly free to use its apparatus for gainful message traffic on the high seas.

It was against this background that the Marconi Marine Company was formed. In order to avoid the restrictive clauses in the Acts, the necessary apparatus was not offered for outright sale to the shipping Companies as this would have meant that each of them would have had to own and maintain shore stations. Instead, a hire service was offered, whereby the apparatus, the operators and use of Marconi shore stations were provided as an all-in system. (This hire service has, in fact, continued to the present day, although the shore stations are now under G.P.O. control.)

One major issue still remained in doubt. Although gainful message traffic was permitted on the high seas, it was not clear what would happen if a ship outside the three-mile limit passed a message to a shore station, or vice versa.

It so happened that this situation was soon to be resolved.

As the result of a successful Marconi demonstration given before the Belgian Royal Family and Belgian Ministers of State, a licence was granted by that Government for the erection of a coastal station at Ostend for the purpose of communicating with Belgian mail packets on the Ostend–Dover route. This service was inaugurated on 3 November 1900, when the first of the ships to be fitted, the *Princess Clementine*, maintained communication with the Ostend shore station all the way to Dover harbour.

This circumstance stung the British Post Office into prompt action. The ship was officially forbidden to transmit messages within the U.K. three-mile limit in view of the private gain which thereby accrued to the Marconi Company, but no objection was raised to communication outside territorial waters.

As a result, the hiring of complete systems as distinct from the outright sale of apparatus was extended to vessels of all nationalities. At the same time the construction of several coastal stations at strategic points along the British coastline was begun with all speed. The end of the year 1900 saw the Company feverishly planning and building stations at North Foreland, Holyhead, Caister, Withernsea, Rosslare, Crookhaven and Port Stewart. All of these were operational within a few months, although Port Stewart in Londonderry was later superseded by the Malin Head station in Donegal.

6

The Transatlantic Gamble

In a Company developments can and do materialize simultaneously, and the bigger the Company the more likely this is to happen. Very often these developments are in completely different directions and the recorder of events has to choose between providing a chronological string of disconnected facts or a series of discrete stories at the conclusion of each of which a return to an earlier date is necessary in order to begin the next.

Such a choice has to be made regarding the turn of the century, a momentous time for the Marconi Company on both the scientific and commercial fronts; to preserve some degree of coherence the events will be taken as separate narratives instead of in their actual interwoven form.

With the problem of multi-station operation without jamming solved by syntonic tuning (Marconi, in addition to his 'Four Sevens' patent, had also acquired the Lodge patent of 10 May 1897) the time had come to tackle the question of how to increase the working range.

Here was an enigma. Hertz in his early experiments had shown that the invisible wireless waves obeyed exactly the same laws of reflection and refraction as did light waves; that in fact the only fundamental difference between the two was one of frequency. These conclusions had been verified time and again. Yet, equally beyond dispute was the fact that the data amassed from the Marconi Company demonstrations showed a steady progress in the ranges achieved. At first these were so little beyond the calculated figures as to cause no great comment, but when they rose to about double the predicted figure – and sixty miles was now guaranteed – then it became a matter which could no longer be ignored.

Scientific opinion of the day – with a few notable exceptions, of which Lord Kelvin's was one – seems to have preserved a curious head-in-sand attitude to such ranges; because they could not be explained by any known circumstance the general scientific outlook was to regard them as of doubtful authenticity.

Marconi at this time had two ambitions in his researches. One was to quash the rumours regarding the accuracy of the ranges claimed; the second was to set his system into direct competition with the long-distance undersea cable interests, seeing that the Post Office monopoly – and similar restrictions in other countries – made it impossible to provide a revenue-earning inland wireless telegraph service. To achieve these aims he conceived a bold plan which, if successful, would realize both at one stroke.

To the lay mind, and to most of the scientists, his proposal was not so much bold as hare-brained. It was to attempt to send wireless signals across the Atlantic in one hop. Small wonder then, that he had difficulty in convincing his Board that it must be done, and in fairness to that body it would have been irresponsible of them if they had agreed out of hand, for the Company, far from making a profit, was eating steadily into its capital. Up until this point, the equipment which was being employed for ship-shore communication was small and relatively simple; now, for his transatlantic bid, Marconi was proposing to build super-power transmitting stations of a size, complexity and cost which was absolutely without precedent.

Quite apart from the cost, one objection which the Board very properly raised was that powerful transmissions such as those which were visualized, would swamp all the existing shipping sets. To this Marconi replied with a practical demonstration to the Board between the Haven* and Niton (an experimental station at St Catherine's Point, Isle of Wight, which had superseded the Needles Hotel station, also in the Isle of Wight). Using equipment embodying syntonic tuning he convinced them that their fears had no real substance. Under his powers of persuasion the Board uneasily acquiesced to his scheme.

Yet another of Marconi's attributes was a realistic assessment of his own practical limitations. If ever a problem lay outside the range of his own experience he would consider it no loss of face to call in outside help. Just such a situation had now materialized by reason of the super-power transmitting stations (one in the U.K., one in America) which were postulated, for it must be remembered that battery-driven, laboratory-type equipments were the only ones in use at this time;

* The Haven Hotel at Sandbanks, near Poole, Dorset; Marconi set up an experimental establishment in a room in the hotel on 30 September 1898 and extended his activities by building huts in the grounds.

nothing more powerful had ever been built. It was rather like proposing to build a cathedral in a world which had never seen anything more grandiose than a log hut.

Characteristically, Marconi enlisted the services of a man whose past experience had run closest to that needed for the job in hand – Dr J. A. Fleming. Fleming, a most distinguished scholar and University lecturer, had been extremely interested in electromagnetic waves ever since the publication of the Maxwell equations, and had duplicated Hertz' experiments and carried out many of his own. When the youthful Marconi arrived in England, Fleming had followed his progress with the keenest interest and on more than one occasion championed his cause.

But over and above all this, Fleming had carried out some very valuable work in connection with high-voltage alternating currents and had solved many of the problems which had manifested themselves when a high voltage cable was installed between Deptford and London in about 1890. In July 1900 he agreed to become the Marconi Company's Scientific Adviser while still retaining his position as Professor of Electrical Technology, University College, London.

First, a suitable site for the British station had to be found, preferably one which, while being on the English mainland, was physically as near as possible to America. In due course a lease was acquired of some land on the headland overlooking Poldhu cove in south-western Cornwall, and preliminary work on the site began in October 1900.

In order that early checks could be made upon the radiations of the Poldhu station, another site, this time at the Lizard, six miles from Poldhu, was also chosen. This station was to fulfil a three-fold purpose:

1. A local station for checking the Poldhu test transmissions.
2. An experimental station for testing the efficacy of syntonic circuits in the vicinity of a powerful transmitter.
3. An additional station for ship-to-shore traffic.

By 23 January 1901 the Lizard station was in commission and a record distance for syntonic transmission was achieved by the reception of the Niton, I.O.W. station 186 miles away.

At Poldhu, work was proceeding apace; the station building had been constructed and the power plant designed by Fleming was installed. By January 1901 preliminary tests of the power, control and high frequency circuits were in progress. The size of the Poldhu station in relation to its predecessors was tremendous. In place of the conventional battery power supply, a 32 hp Hornsby-Ackroyd oil engine drove a

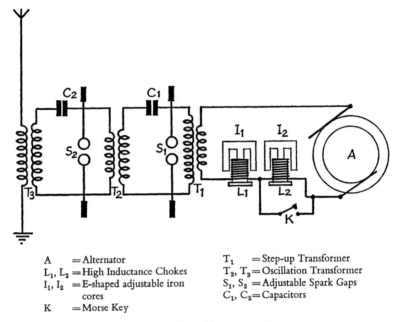

A   = Alternator
L₁, L₂ = High Inductance Chokes
I₁, I₂ = E-shaped adjustable iron
          cores
K   = Morse Key

T_1 = Step-up Transformer
T_2, T_3 = Oscillation Transformer
S_1, S_2 = Adjustable Spark Gaps
C_1, C_2 = Capacitors

Figure 6.1 The Poldhu Transmitter

25 kW Mather and Platt alternator, delivering a 2,000 volts, 50 cycles/sec supply. This was stepped up to 20,000 volts and fed to a closed oscillatory circuit in which a capacitor discharged across a spark gap via the primary of an r.f. transformer. The secondary of the transformer was connected to a second spark gap and capacitor and the primary of a second r.f. transformer. The secondary of this transformer was in series with the antenna. Keying was effected by short-circuiting chokes in the output of the alternator.

The capacitors referred to were made up of twenty glass plates, each sixteen inches square, coated on one side with one square foot of tinfoil. These plates were immersed in stoneware boxes filled with linseed oil, and each box had a capacitance of 0·05 microfarads.

The antenna system consisted of about four hundred wires suspended in an inverted cone from a 200 ft. circle of masts, there being twenty masts in all, each 200 ft. high. The wavelength was estimated as 366 m.

With the work all but completed by the beginning of March, Marconi accompanied by Vyvyan, one of his senior engineers who had been in charge of the constructional work at Poldhu, took ship to the U.S.A. where the site for the second super-power station was chosen among the sand-dunes of South Wellfleet, Cape Cod, Massachusetts. Leaving Vyvyan to be responsible for its construction, Marconi returned to England.

By June, experimental transmissions from Poldhu were being well received at Niton, 186 miles away, and, a little later, at the newly opened station at Crookhaven, County Cork, 225 miles distant. This was, of course, highly satisfactory, particularly as teething troubles with the transmitting equipment precluded the use of anything like full power. It also proved beyond all doubt that the radiation was not leaving the earth's surface tangentially as theoretically it should, but was following the curvature of the globe.

There were, however, troubles with the antenna system, only a part of which was in service because bad weather had delayed construction. Furthermore it had already been realized that although the theoretical design of the antenna system was good, its practical construction left something to be desired. In order to reduce to a minimum the absorption of r.f. energy in the stay wires, these were broken into sections by dead-eye and lanyard inserts (a recently-learned trick at that time), but only the radial stays were taken by anchor blocks, the circumferential staying being obtained by means of horizontal triatics between one mast and the next. The employment of these triatics had the obvious disadvantage that should one fail, the safety of all twenty masts could be jeopardized; technically, however, the system had the advantage that the horizontal wires absorbed little energy from the antenna wires within the circle of masts, being virtually at right angles to them. The danger was discussed, but as the advantage in technical performance was not to be set aside lightly in view of the great issues it might resolve, it was decided to take the calculated risk.

With hindsight, it was an ill-advised course of action, but no one could foresee that on 17 September 1901 the worst gale within living memory was to strike full force at the station. In one particularly vicious squall a lug was torn from a topgallant mast cap, breaking the retaining circle of the triatic. Inevitably the worst happened; all twenty masts collapsed in a shambles of shattered timber and tangled wire, although by a near-miracle the personnel and plant were spared.

Disaster, indeed; but worse was to follow. On November 26 the completed ring of masts erected by Vyvyan (to the same design) at the Cape Cod station suffered precisely the same humiliation.

The Marconi Board of Directors, having from the first committed the Company with reluctance to what seemed a wild-cat venture, were appalled. Fifty thousand pounds had been sunk in the scheme and nothing to show for it but chaos. But Marconi was not going to give up the struggle. Scarcely had the Poldhu masts reached the ground before he had organized a team under the indefatigable Kemp to clear the wreckage and re-erect a temporary antenna system. As a striking instance of the speed at which work was carried out in that so-called leisurely era, the catastrophe occurred on September 17; by the 24th an experimental antenna system had been erected and tests were resumed on the 26th!

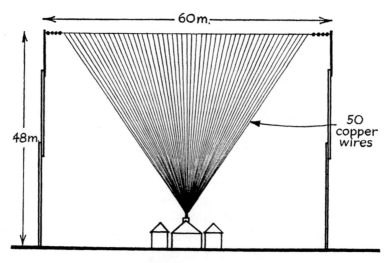

Figure 6.2 The Temporary Antenna used at Poldhu
for the Transatlantic Tests

By October 22, plans for a new permanent antenna system had been put forward by a Marconi engineer, and approved. Work on this began on November 1st, but in view of the promising signal strengths being received at Crookhaven using the improvised experimental antenna, Marconi elected not to wait for the new permanent array. He also decided (because of the diminished efficiency of the temporary Poldhu antenna) not to essay transatlantic reception at the Cape Cod station but to make the attempt with temporary equipment at the point of nearest landfall, which was Newfoundland. Under conditions of great secrecy – he was ostensibly following up an inquiry for a ship-to-shore installation – he set sail for Newfoundland on November 27 in company with Kemp and another assistant, Paget, and a miscellany of receiving apparatus, kites, balloons, antenna wire and gas accessories.

One can imagine the states of mind of the trio when, just before their ship sailed, they received the news of the disaster at Cape Cod. All hopes now of two-way transatlantic communication were gone for the time being; the immediate horizon was limited to single-way communication and for this the prospect was as bleak as the Atlantic weather. For in place of the mammoth antenna arrays on either side of the ocean, all that was available was a lashed-up structure at Poldhu, the product of eight days' feverish activity with no time for matching the load to the antenna, and, at Newfoundland, not even a solitary mast; only a small stock of kites and balloons to keep the wire aloft in as capable a manner as ingenuity and the elements would allow.

The party landed at St John's on December 6 and paid formal calls on the Governor, Sir Cavendish Boyle and on the Premier, Sir Robert Bond, both of whom received them kindly and promised them every assistance. A quick reconnoitre of the area showed that Signal Hill, a promontory rising some 600 ft. above the harbour, was the most suitable site for their proposed venture, and the authorities helpfully provided accommodation in an empty military hospital there. By coincidence it lay near the memorial tower which commemorates John Cabot's discovery of Newfoundland, whilst not far away is Heart's Content, where the first transatlantic cable was landed in 1858. Marine communication; communication by submarine cable; and now – perhaps – communication by wireless telegraphy?

On December 9 the apparatus was laid out on a table in a ground floor room of the hospital. The earth plates were buried and a balloon made ready for inflation. A cable was sent to Poldhu requesting that the Morse letter 'S' (a group of three dots) should be transmitted continuously from 3 p.m. to 7 p.m. G.M.T., the transmissions to begin on December 11. The letter 'S' was chosen, partly because the use of a single simple letter made it possible to send it automatically, but also because the keying system at Poldhu left something to be desired and the transmission of dashes would have imposed a greater strain on the apparatus, if carried out continuously. The three dots would also be more easily identifiable through heavy static.

On December 10, the weather being fair, an antenna was sent aloft by means of a kite. Meanwhile, at Poldhu, another transmitting antenna consisting of fifty stranded bare copper wires suspended from a triatic strained between two 160 ft. masts 200 ft. apart, had been rigged, these wires being brought together in a fan shape to form a common connection to the transmitter. Although Fleming was not wholly satisfied with the overall performance of the station, there was nothing he could do in the short time available before zero hour.

On the crucial day, the transmission started according to plan, the power employed being, according to Fleming, of the order of 10–12 kW. Because no means of measuring the length of the waves existed at that time, the actual wavelength has always been a matter for controversy. H. M. Dowsett, an eminent engineer of the Marconi Company, who joined the organization in 1899, but who was not directly concerned with the transatlantic enterprise, gives the wavelength as an estimated 366 m. at the time of the initial tests in June 1901. Other equally authoritative sources have opted for a wavelength lying between 2,000–3,000 m. – quite a difference.

At Signal Hill the wind had freshened, and Kemp was having great trouble with the balloon which was carrying the antenna aloft. Marconi was using one of his new syntonic receivers in conjunction with what was at the time described as a self-restoring coherer consisting of a glass tube in which a globule of mercury was retained between two iron or carbon rods.* This device, which had been developed by P. Castelli, a signalman in the Italian Navy, was, when on its best behaviour, a very sensitive detector although erratic in performance. Marconi employed it for its sensitivity, using it in conjunction with a telephone earpiece rather than trust to the coherer, relay and Morse inker combination which although supplying a positive printed record was not nearly so receptive to weak signals as the human ear.

Nothing which could be positively identified as the letter 'S' was heard and Marconi came to the conclusion that the rise and fall of the antenna in the strong wind was causing the antenna capacity to fluctuate so much that it was impossible to keep the syntonic circuit in tune. He therefore abandoned the new receiver for an older, untuned version, but before long the full gale which had developed tore the balloon free and put an end to all experiments until such time as another could be rigged.

On the 12th the gale was still vicious. A kite which was launched carrying two 510 ft. antenna wires was carried away within an hour. Another kite was flown, this time with 500 ft. of wire attached. Frantically it reared and plunged, threatening every instant to break loose like its predecessor.

At the receiver Marconi sat listening intently as the precious minutes

---

* Although termed a coherer, its action was more that of a semi-conductor rectifier, an oxide film on the mercury providing the semi-conductor element. This device, slightly modified by Lieutenant Luigi Solari of the Italian Navy, was subsequently known as the Solari or Italian Navy detector.

of the scheduled transmission slipped by. Suddenly, at 12.30 p.m. Newfoundland time, he handed the earpiece to George Kemp with a quiet 'Can you hear anything, Mr Kemp?'

Kemp took the headphone. Through the crash of static he could hear, faintly, the unmistakable rhythm of three clicks followed by a pause; then three more and a pause, and so on in constant repetition until, all too soon, the signals were lost once more in static . . .

One would like, at this point, to tell something of the jubilation which must have possessed both men (Paget, Marconi's other assistant, was unwell that day and was not present) but the archives are blank on this aspect. Kemp, who throughout his working life meticulously kept a detailed daily journal, records the victory as if it were scarcely of more account than the putting on of his boots. Marconi was no diarist but occasionally scribbled laconic entries in a pocket book. His entry for that fateful December 12 reads simply:

Sigs. at 12.30, 1.10 and 2.20.

And with these we have to be content.

On the following day the weather worsened. Three kites were elevated but not one of them would stay aloft. Snow, rain and hail fell at intervals. During the brief period when a kite was flying, faint signals were again heard.

On Saturday 14th the weather continued foul; Kemp, in charge of some local labour, rigged an antenna from Signal Hill to an iceberg in the harbour in a desperate attempt to pick up the Poldhu signals in defiance of the wind which had made kite-flying impossible. By this time it had become very obvious that a mast-supported antenna was the only solution. Where should it be? Signal Hill? Cape Race, where a mast for a proposed service to ships operating off the Grand Banks was all but ready for erection? One thing was certain; there could be no further tests until the weather improved to the point where a kite could be flown steadily, or alternatively, a mast erected. The adoption of either step meant a cessation of the tests for the time being.

Marconi was in a quandary. All human instincts urged that the world should know of the feat, but all reason told him that the world would want more conclusive proof than he could offer, for it must be remembered that no visible proof in the form of Morse inker tape existed as only a headphone had been used; moreover the only two witnesses, he and Kemp, were not exactly unbiased. Should he make a public statement or not?

In the event, Marconi cabled his London office with the news on December 14 and then, on the 16th, he gave his story to the Press.

The triumph was more bitter than sweet. The first reaction came that same evening from the solicitors of the Anglo-American Telegraph Company, whose lines had carried the cable to the London office two days earlier. It was in the form of a letter which was sharp and to the point. It called Marconi's attention to the fact that the Cable Company had a monopoly in the matter of communication throughout New-foundland and it forbade any further infringement of their rights under pain of legal action.

Although it could be argued that the work was a scientific experiment and not a message-carrying service, Marconi decided not to contest the matter, but to dismantle his apparatus and go elsewhere. It was, on the whole, a wise decision, for he had built no intricate and costly station at St John's, and Canada or the United States would serve his purpose almost as well geographically. Furthermore, no such monopolistic restrictions existed in either of these countries. To have got himself involved in a legal wrangle could easily have dissipated his energies and money for many precious months.

The embargo, as it turned out, indirectly operated to Marconi's advantage. The citizens of Newfoundland, on learning the news, were furious at the Anglo-American Telegraph Company's action, and when the news reached the New York papers, Dr Alexander Graham Bell, the inventor of the telephone, immediately offered Marconi the use of land at Cape Breton, Nova Scotia. The Canadian and United States Governments both reacted strongly in favour of the under-dog – circumstances which were later to be of considerable advantage to Marconi and his Company.

The world's Press for the most part received the news of the Anglo-American Telegraph Company incident with indignation. Nevertheless Marconi's claim to have bridged the Atlantic with wireless signals, whilst receiving world-wide attention, was treated with scepticism, not only by the lay Press, but in the technical journals also.

This attitude was very understandable. It must be remembered that Marconi had not an iota of practical proof with which to substantiate his claim, for only he and Kemp had heard the signals, and the threat of legal action had precluded the possibility of any form of public demon-stration.

It must be borne in mind also that in making his claim, Marconi was apparently challenging the validity of those fundamental laws of physics

which govern the behaviour of electromagnetic waves, and in particular those relating to diffraction, which had long since been proved,
both theoretically and empirically, to be unassailable. Wireless waves
would be expected to travel a little beyond the optical horizon, but
would then travel tangentially outward into space. For them to follow
the earth's curvature – a hump of ocean over a hundred miles high –
over a distance of nearly 2,000 miles, seemed scientifically impossible.
To believe it, one had to accept the unproven word of two men against
the proven might of Newton, Maxwell, Hertz and innumerable
others. Or so it seemed. It was not until later, when the reception of
signals across the Atlantic was demonstrated beyond all shadow of
doubt, that science was impelled to try to reconcile the practical achievement with the basic physical laws. As the state of knowledge stood in
1901 it was only reasonable to incline to the opinion that either Marconi
and Kemp had made a false claim, or that they were genuinely mistaken.
It says much for Marconi's reputation for integrity that most of the
sceptics opted for the latter explanation.

It must also, in fairness, be remembered that even today a few responsible people still contend that no signals were in fact heard, instancing
various factors in support of their belief. The receiving equipment for
example consisted of an inefficient antenna coupled to an untuned
receiver which possessed no form of amplification whatever, and a
rectifier which was less sensitive even than the crystal detector which
evolved a few years later. The onus of providing sufficient signal
strength to operate the headphones was therefore entirely upon the
Poldhu transmitter, which itself was an experimental rig. Again, if we
accept Dowsett's statement that the wavelength was 366 m.,* it later
transpired that the transmission took place at the worst possible times
of all for this wavelength, because the entire signal path was in daylight.
Had the experiment been conducted during hours when the Atlantic
was in darkness the available signal strength at the receiver would have
been many times greater because of the action of the Heaviside and
Appleton layers. Today, we know that radio signals can travel across
the Atlantic and far beyond. In 1901, anyone who believed that they
had, did so as an act of faith based on the integrity of one man.

Immediately the Anglo-American Telegraph Company's brusque
embargo became known, both the Government of the Province of
Nova Scotia and the Canadian Government demonstrated their sympathy

---

* In a lecture at the Royal Institution on 13 March 1908, Marconi quotes the wavelength as
1,200 ft. which is roughly 366 m.

in a practical manner by inviting Marconi to visit them and state his requirements. This he did, leaving St John's in company with Kemp on December 24, after seeing Paget and the dismantled equipment safely aboard the *Sardinian, en route* for England the previous day. Christmas Day was spent at North Sydney, Nova Scotia, where they were entertained by the Premier of Nova Scotia and members of his Government; the next few days were occupied in looking for possible sites, of which Glace Bay was provisionally selected.

A very cordial welcome awaited them at Ottawa, where they arrived on December 30 to be assured by the Governor-General of Canada, the Premier and various high government officials, that every practicable form of assistance would be given in order to further their work. As an earnest of this, the Government of Canada not only offered a free site, but financial help to the extent of £16,000 for development expenditure. A contract between the Canadian Government and the Marconi Company was ratified a little later.

When on January 12 Marconi arrived in New York he found that a similarly warm welcome had been prepared; on the following evening a dinner in his honour was given by the Institute of American Electrical Engineers at which he was gratified to meet such eminent personalities as Professors Steinmetz, Elihu Thomson, Alexander Graham Bell, Dr M. I. Pupin and many others.

Whilst in the U.S.A. Marconi inspected the transatlantic station at South Wellfleet, Cape Cod, the masts of which, it will be remembered, had collapsed shortly after the Poldhu catastrophe. Now four 210 ft. wooden towers had been erected and awaited only a decision as to the type of antenna to be used.

On January 22 Marconi sailed for Southampton and on arrival in England lost no time in giving his Directors and shareholders a first-hand account of the transatlantic experiment. This and further experiments with syntonic apparatus fully occupied his time until February 22, when he returned to the New World with the Canadian contract duly drawn up.

In the intervening period between the Newfoundland tests and the sailing date, much useful work had been done at Poldhu; the transmitting equipment had been improved and the keying system was now such that messages of reasonable length could be sent. The wavelength of 366 m. (?) remained unaltered.

This voyage was destined to be significant indeed. The ship was the one which had brought him home, the *Philadelphia* of the American

Line, whose owners agreed to a mast extension which would support a 4-wire cage inverted 'L' antenna at a height of 150 m. above deck.

Marconi's intention was to make a bold attempt to provide the world with proof that wireless signals could span the Atlantic and this time he made sure that reliable witnesses were to hand. Using syntonic receiving apparatus and a conventional coherer, he arranged for any messages to be recorded on Morse inker tape and attested by the ship's captain.

Further and further west steamed the *Philadelphia*. The Niton station lapsed into silence, but Poldhu still stuttered on. At a distance of 700 miles signals were being received in broad daylight but became too faint beyond this range to operate the tape machine.

It was at this point that a curious and then quite inexplicable phenomenon was noticed, in that after dark the Poldhu signals were again receivable, and in fact under these conditions messages were recorded at a distance of 1,550 miles from Poldhu, and 'S's up to 2,100 miles. Here was complete vindication of Marconi's claims. No one now could deny that transatlantic communication was possible in view of the proof afforded by the tape messages signed as completely authentic by the ship's master, Captain Miles. And at the same time there had been another important step forward in knowledge with the discovery of the 'night effect'.

(In parentheses it is perhaps of interest to record that the Marconi wireless operator on this voyage was C. S. Franklin, later to win renown as a prolific inventor and the architect of the beam system of radio communication.)

Proceeding from New York to Ottawa, Marconi completed the agreement with the Canadian Government and then set about making a final selection of the site for his new station. Table Head, Glace Bay was the ultimate choice. This done he returned to New York where, on 1 April 1902, the Marconi Wireless Telegraph Company of America was incorporated as a public Company (it had been registered on 22 November 1899), and the American rights in Marconi inventions were transferred from the parent Company for the sum of £50,000.

The cable companies now had reason for alarm and the stock exchange values of shares in these organizations slumped heavily round about this time. The spring of 1902 saw the beginning of a long and bitter struggle between the rival media for electric communication.

7

'A Transatlantic Service, but —'

Spurred on by his success and fully aware that he had now not merely to contend with foreign competitors in the field of wireless telegraphy, but also with the powerful cable companies, Marconi worked on at a prodigious speed.

Returning from the U.S.A. towards the end of April 1902, he put in an intensive burst of experimentation at Niton to such good effect that by June 12 he was able to describe to the Royal Society a new type of detector which was destined to become standard Marconi equipment aboard ship for many years – some even surviving to the period beyond the 1914–18 War. This apparatus was officially named the magnetic detector, but to sea-going wireless operators the world over it became the 'Maggie'.

Like most inventions, the 'Maggie' was derivative, its origins going back to 1842 when Joseph Henry demonstrated that magnetized steel needles could be demagnetized by discharging Leyden jars in their vicinity. Rutherford followed this up in 1895 by realizing that the demagnetizing agent was the oscillatory waves set up by the spark discharge and that the phenomenon might be turned to account by using it to detect Hertzian waves. He built apparatus to test his theory, using a resonator, to the rods of which were connected a bobbin of fine wire with a magnetized steel needle in its centre. On switching on his induction coil transmitter he found that the needle became demagnetized whenever an oscillation was received; by such means he was able to detect signals over a distance of about three-quarters of a mile.

This discovery was scientifically interesting but commercially impracticable because after each train of oscillations had passed the needle had to be remagnetized. Two years later Professor E. Wilson made a positive step towards removing this objection. Like Rutherford he used a magnetometer to register the change in magnetization but he so arranged matters that the magnetometer needle by its movement closed a battery circuit to remagnetize the needle.

This device worked, but was delicate. In 1900 Rutherford suggested that a detector might be constructed which used a moving steel band, upon which the incoming signals would be recorded. (An early form of tape recorder employing this principle was in fact exhibited in Paris later that year.)

Marconi in 1902 patented two forms of the Rutherford type of magnetic detector. The first used a stationary pair of wire coils and a rotating magnet; the second, which was the version which came into general use, uses an endless band of soft iron wires stranded together but insulated from each other, moving slowly past the poles of a pair of stationary permanent magnets. Just at the point where the wire passes the pole-pieces it runs through a short length of glass tube upon which is wound an r.f. transformer, one end of the primary of which is connected to the antenna and the other to earth, while the secondary winding is connected to headphones.

The band of soft iron wire is moved around by means of a clockwork mechanism at a rate of 7 cm. or 8 cm. per second. In the absence of a signal the wire is magnetized by the permanent magnets but the lines of force are being pulled out of position by the moving iron band which, because of the motion, is being taken away from the poles before it has time to become fully magnetized.

When an oscillation occurs in the primary winding, the hysteresis of the iron is annulled, the iron becomes fully magnetized and the lines of

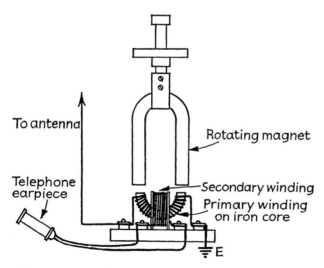

Figure 7.1 Marconi's First Magnetic Detector, or Cymoscope

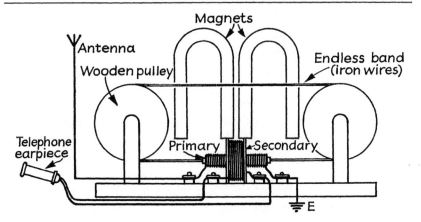

Figure 7.2 Marconi's Second Magnetic Detector, 1902 (The 'Maggie')

force slip back to a point exactly opposite to the pole-pieces. As a consequence of this movement a current is induced in the secondary winding and this creates a sound in the headphones.

This device constituted an important advance, in that it was more sensitive than a coherer and, because of the clear-cut signals it produced, a considerably higher speed of transmission and reception became possible; this brought wireless apparatus much more into line with the telegraphic speeds which were possible over cable circuits.

In May 1902 significant improvements were effected at the Poldhu transmitting station. The wavelength was increased to 1,100 m. using a fan-shaped antenna assembly, and the original two closed and coupled oscillating circuits designed by Fleming were replaced by a single closed circuit.

Shortly after this a first-class cruiser of the Italian Navy, the *Carlo Alberto,* arrived in British waters with King Victor Emmanuel III aboard to represent Italy at the forthcoming coronation of King Edward VII which was to take place on June 26. It was then learned that because of Edward's sudden illness the coronation would have to be postponed and the *Carlo Alberto* was making preparations to sail.

Marconi's stock was understandably high in Italy. He was, of course, an Italian subject whose name was already famous throughout the world. The Italian Navy were impressed by the excellent service which the four equipments purchased from the Marconi Company were giving, and national interest had been aroused to a peak by the trans-atlantic experiments, particularly as it was known that the so-called Italian Navy coherer had been used.

These were the factors which caused Marconi to be invited to take advantage of the unexpected change in plans occasioned by King Edward VII's illness by sailing to Italy in the *Carlo Alberto* and demonstrating long-distance reception.

This was an opportunity too good to miss. A four-wire cage antenna was hurriedly fitted to the ship and the latest syntonic receiving equipment together with a magnetic detector, installed. The cruiser sailed on July 7 bound for Kronstadt, where a ceremonial visit by King Victor to the Czar Alexander III had been arranged. The wireless apparatus performed splendidly, receiving signals from Poldhu after nightfall when the cruiser lay at anchor off Kronstadt, some 1,600 miles away. The meeting between the two potentates attracted world-wide interest, and the news of the long-distance wireless reception shared the headlines.

The ship returned to Portland to enable King Victor to attend the coronation, then, on August 23, sailed for the Mediterranean with Marconi still aboard. Reception of the Poldhu transmissions was maintained up to a distance of 500 miles during daylight, and for the whole of the way to Italy after nightfall. Greetings were sent from the Marconi Company to His Majesty King Victor on this, the occasion of the first wireless telegraph message direct from England to Italy.

The pride of the Italian nation in its distinguished son was soon expressed in a gesture of practical help when the Italian Government placed the *Carlo Alberto* with the full ship's complement of six hundred ratings at Marconi's disposal for purposes of long-range testing over the transatlantic route. The offer was gratefully accepted and, after sailing to Plymouth where a Poldhu fan-shaped antenna was fitted, the Italian cruiser crossed the Atlantic with Marconi and Lt. Solari* aboard. Valuable data were gathered on the voyage and when the *Carlo Alberto* dropped anchor in Sydney harbour, Novia Scotia, it was found that after dark the 1,100 m. transmission from Poldhu could be received.

Having now proved beyond all shadow of doubt, and on more than one occasion, that wireless telegraphy could span the Atlantic, Marconi was faced with an even more difficult task, namely to establish his triumph on to a solid commercial footing. To receive signals from Poldhu during transient experimental periods was one thing; to establish a reliable two-way commercial service was quite another.

For this, Marconi's hopes were pinned on his new station at Glace Bay, now completed with an antenna consisting of four hundred copper

---

* Solari was a notable pioneer of wireless telegraphy in the Italian Navy and a lifelong friend of Marconi.

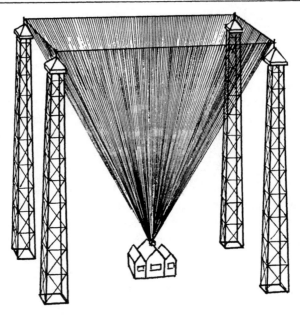

Figure 7.3 The Glace Bay Antenna, 1902

wires suspended in sections from triatics between four 200 ft. wooden towers, with the down leads brought together in an inverted cone at the point of entry to the station building, and so constructed that either the whole antenna system or sections of it could be used as desired.

The first transmission tests from Glace Bay began on 19 November 1902 and were frankly disappointing; not until the 28th did Poldhu report the reception of weak, unreliable signals, and this only after considerable modification to various circuits and to the antenna had been made.

Modifications continued and on December 5 Poldhu experienced the first readable recorded signals ever received from west to east across the Atlantic. But jubilation was premature; on the following night under identical transmitting and receiving conditions (the wavelength employed was 1,650 m.) no signals at all were received.

The reason was inexplicable at that time; not until later when the vagaries in the behaviour of the reflecting ionized layers were better understood did enlightenment come. But at that time the very existence of these layers was unknown, and as a consequence, many baffling experiences were recorded. Modifications which should (and in fact did) bring about substantial improvements apparently failed simply because on the occasion when testing took place, the ionosphere happened not to be reflecting the signals earthward to the same degree as it had the previous night. It was all very confusing and discouraging; gradually realization was dawning that the characteristics of the new medium of transmission could not be equated to that of a conductor cable, and with this came the depressing thought that for all anyone knew, it might fail completely at any time.

For the second time Marconi was in a quandary as to how to deal with the Press. The threat to the cable companies had roused intense interest and speculation as to the prospects of the Marconi Company, the future of which would undoubtedly be enhanced by a favourable Press demonstration. But, under the circumstances, could optimism be justified?

When on December 14 good strength signals were received over the two-hour test period, Marconi decided, rather against his better judgement, to gamble on the circumstance. He elected that the first message denoting the opening of the transatlantic wireless service should be sent the following night.

Good fortune was with him; conditions on the night of December 15 were excellent and Dr Parkin, *The Times* correspondent at Glace Bay, composed the first wireless message ever to be sent across the Atlantic by a member of the public. Addressed to his paper, it ran:

TIMES, LONDON. BEING PRESENT AT TRANSMISSION IN MARCONI'S CANADIAN STATION HAVE HONOUR SEND THROUGH TIMES INVENTOR'S FIRST TRANSATLANTIC MESSAGE OF GREETING TO ENGLAND AND ITALY. PARKIN.

The following nights were equally good for transmission and advantage was taken of this to send the following messages:

HIS MAJESTY THE KING. MAY I BE PERMITTED BY MEANS OF FIRST WIRELESS MESSAGE TO CONGRATULATE YOUR MAJESTY ON SUCCESS OF MARCONI'S GREAT INVENTION CONNECTING CANADA AND ENGLAND. MINTO. (Lord Minto, Governor-General of Canada.)

LORD KNOLLYS BUCKINGHAM PALACE LONDON. UPON OCCASION OF FIRST WIRELESS TELEGRAPHIC COMMUNICATION ACROSS ATLANTIC OCEAN, MAY I BE PERMITTED TO PRESENT BY MEANS OF THIS WIRELESS TELEGRAM TRANSMITTED FROM CANADA TO ENGLAND MY RESPECTFUL HOMAGE TO HIS MAJESTY THE KING. G. MARCONI GLACE BAY.

GENERAL BRUSATI ROME. OCCASIONE PRIMA TRANSMISSIONE RADIO-
TELEGRAPHICA TRANSATLANTICA INVIO CONQUESTO TELEGRAMMA
TRANSMESSO ALTRAVERSO LO SPEZIA DEL NUOVO AL VECCHIO
MONDO DEYOTTO OMAGGI A SUA MAESTA IL RE. GUGLIELMO
MARCONI.

In order to ensure that all four messages were received satisfactorily
and that they should be released simultaneously they were held back at
Poldhu until they had been cross-checked. Release took place on
December 21.

A limited service was started; daylight hours were taken up with
experimental work and transmissions effected at night whenever conditions permitted. It would be idle to pretend that the cable companies
had any real competition. Relatively few messages were sent, and time
spent in sending repetitions was considerable. But the potential threat
to the cable interests was plain enough.

On January 14 Marconi left Glace Bay for the American station at
Cape Cod, which was now completed. The distance between the
Canadian and American stations (600 miles) was found to be too great
for daylight working but at the time of the initial tests satisfactory
signals were exchanged at night.

On January 18 some two thousand words were transmitted from Cape
Cod including a special message to Glace Bay for retransmission to
Poldhu. The message, from the President of the United States, read as
follows:

HIS MAJESTY KING EDWARD THE SEVENTH (BY MARCONI'S TRANS-
ATLANTIC WIRELESS TELEGRAPH) IN TAKING ADVANTAGE OF THE
WONDERFUL TRIUMPH OF SCIENTIFIC RESEARCH AND INGENUITY
WHICH HAS BEEN ACHIEVED IN PERFECTING A SYSTEM OF WIRELESS
TELEGRAPHY I SEND ON BEHALF OF THE AMERICAN PEOPLE MOST
CORDIAL GREETINGS AND GOOD WISHES TO YOU AND ALL THE
PEOPLE OF THE BRITISH EMPIRE.
THEODORE ROOSEVELT. WHITE HOUSE WASHINGTON.

It so happened that conditions were so good on that particular night
that the transmission intended for Glace Bay was picked up direct by
Poldhu, thus making history as the first wireless message received in
England direct from the U.S.A.

This achievement, which naturally attracted considerable public
attention, was severely tempered by the circumstance that King
Edward VII's reply was sent by cable. The reason for this was curious.

It so happened that King Edward's message was handed in on a Sunday when the Mullion* Post Office telegraph station was closed. It was therefore impossible to send the telegram overland to Poldhu until the Monday morning, and the Company felt that the delay occasioned would have been discourteous to the King. It was therefore decided to send the message by cable on the Sunday.

This unfortunate sequel was remedied as far as possible by an explanatory letter from the Company's Managing Director, Mr Cuthbert Hall, which was published in *The Times*, but it did not prevent detractors from seizing the chance to assert that over-extravagant claims had been made on behalf of the transatlantic service.

That the service was unreliable was undeniably true, but no specific claims had been made to the contrary. True, there was an element of *suggestio falsi* in the publication of the messages, in that it could be inferred that communication was consistently possible. On the other hand the Marconi Company was carrying out the experiments as an expensive private venture (apart from the Canadian Government aid) and it was essential to continue them if the problem of unreliability was to be solved.

Nevertheless in spite of another bitter-sweet climax the Company benefited by it. Congratulatory messages from the King of England and the King of Italy were followed by votes of thanks from the Italian Senate and the Italian Chamber of Deputies. *The Times* published a letter of congratulation to the British people received from the acting Premier of Canada. Marconi himself was awarded the Italian Order of Merit and his Company received a welcome order from Italy for the installation of high power and other stations.

But back on the experimental front it soon became painfully clear that plans for a full-scale public transatlantic service were premature and that more development work was essential. Accordingly, when Marconi left Cape Cod for England on January 22 the three stations involved closed down temporarily and the Italian cruiser *Carlo Alberto* was released from her special duties. There was a temporary resurrection of the service when the London *Times*, in a praiseworthy attempt to further the cause and at the same time to emphasize its journalistic pre-eminence, pressed the Marconi Company to initiate a news service from Canada for the use of the paper. As preliminary tests which began on 20 March 1903 gave great promise for four nights in succession, a limited Press Service was inaugurated on the 28th. It was doomed to

* Mullion, Cornwall, the nearest Post Office telegraph station to Poldhu.

have a brief life; on April 6 misfortune struck at the Glace Bay station, where a heavy silver thaw deposited an extra load of one inch of ice on the antenna, which broke under the strain, putting the Canadian terminal station out of action.

Yet in spite of this sorry postponement to Marconi's dream, much valuable data had been gleaned. The syntonic system of operation had proved itself, although handicapped by the circumstance that no portable apparatus had been devised to measure the wavelength of the transmission and to aid the tuning of the receiving station to resonance with it. More information was being collated every day about the design of antennas, coupling transformers and circuits and also upon the practical design of masts and towers.

Other problems still remained unsolved, notably the reason for the increase in signal strength after nightfall and indeed the overall mystery of why signals followed the earth's curvature in apparent defiance of well-established laws of physics.

Naturally, theories were put forward to attempt to account for this curious behaviour. Marconi himself suspected solar influences (which was correct) but he did not follow this up and it was left to Heaviside (Great Britain) and Kennelly (U.S.A.) to suggest what eventually transpired to be the correct solution. Both made the hypothesis that at a certain height above the earth's surface a layer of ionized atmosphere existed which was serving to bend the wireless waves back to earth again. These suggestions were put forward in 1902 but did not gain universal acceptance for many years; in fact it was not until the 1920s that the theory was proved to be correct.

Although in 1902 the full significance of the influence of wavelength upon transmission conditions had not been fully appreciated, Professor Fleming had advocated the use of longer wavelengths for transatlantic work on the grounds of their greater diffraction and this policy was experimentally adopted. The Glace Bay and Cape Cod stations were designed to transmit on wavelengths in the region of 2,000 m. whilst in May 1902 the wavelength of Poldhu was increased to about 1,100 m.

As a result of the relatively successful performance of the Glace Bay station, which had a power input of 75 kW, it was realized that for reliable two-way transatlantic communication, Poldhu's power of 25 kW would have to be substantially increased. The Cape Cod Station, which was designed to work with Glace Bay and not across the Atlantic, was so far employing only about 10 kW of its rated 25 kW.

Even at this time, when all controversy as to the feasibility of transatlantic signalling by wireless had been silenced by events, Marconi still had critics to contend with. It was frequently asserted that the powerful land stations necessary for transatlantic working would swamp the more useful ship-to-ship and ship-to-shore stations, putting them out of action. To exorcise such statements, Marconi asked Dr Fleming to carry out special tests and demonstrations at Poldhu.

This Fleming did in his characteristically thorough way, using the high power Poldhu transmitting equipment as the potential 'blaster' while short range communication was being attempted between a typical Marconi ship's installation which was contained in a hut some 100–150 yards distant, and the Lizard station six miles away.

To remove all possible shadow of doubt about the experiment, Fleming prepared eight messages of the ship-to-shore type and eight of the kind sent across the Atlantic, four of these being in cipher. He then sealed the messages and arranged that the transmission of a transatlantic type of message should be synchronized with the sending of a ship-to-shore message between the two local stations. The envelopes were to be opened only immediately before transmission time.

At the Lizard two receivers were connected to the same antenna but tuned to the respective wavelengths of the high power and 'local' transmitters at Poldhu; each picked up its correct message without interference and printed it via a Morse inker. Not once was a mistake made. To prove that the main Poldhu station was transmitting at high power similar receivers were installed at Poole, 150 miles away. Here the receiver which was tuned to the low power transmission's wavelength was silent (as was to be expected) but the other receiver recorded the 'transatlantic' message.

This demonstration, which took place in March 1903, publicly underlined the syntonic system's ability to operate under the most severe conditions and effectively silenced those who had doubted. Some months later a similar test was witnessed by Admiralty officials; on that occasion naval observers were at the 'local' station watching the reception of independent messages at the same time as high power signals from Poldhu were being received by other naval observers aboard the *Duncan* at Gibraltar.

Although this book is devoted to an account of the work of the Marconi Company (which has meant up to 1903, virtually the story of Marconi himself) it will not, it is hoped, be inferred that all the developments in wireless telegraphy were coming from this source. Such would be far from the truth. In Britain such workers as Sir Oliver Lodge, Dr

Muirhead, W. Duddell, H. H. Taylor, A. C. Brown, C. R. Nelson, Capt. H. B. Jackson, R.N., and others were responsible for much useful development work.

Some of the German scientific workers such as Professor A. Slaby, Professor F. Braun and Count von Arco have been mentioned earlier. Others included Professor P. Drude, Doctors Wehnelt, M. Abraham, M. Wien, A. Oberbeck, V. Bjerknes, E. Aschinass, J. Zenneck, G. Seibt, B. Schafer, W. Schloemilch, A. Neugschwender and J. Donitz; all made important contributions to either theory or practice in the field of wireless.

In the United States practical contributions were being made by such investigators as Professor R. A. Fessenden, Dr Lee de Forest, Dr J. S. Stone and H. Shoemaker, and important theoretical studies by Professors Trowbridge and Pierce, J. E. Ives, C. A. Chant and others.

France was another stronghold of investigation with such names as Professor Poincaré and Branly, M. M. Blondel, C. Tissot, Captain Ferrié, Ducretet and Turpain. In Italy Professor Righi was the leading authority and in Russia, Professor Popoff. The Japanese were reported to have brought their practical knowledge of the subject 'to a high state of perfection'.

As an instance of the intensity of foreign research effort mounted in those early years, it may be of interest to record that Shoemaker of the U.S.A. filed over forty patents relating to wireless telegraphy between 1901 and 1905. It will be seen therefore, that the Marconi research team of those days had no time to rest on its laurels. It was fortunate indeed that its leader was young and possessed of an almost fanatical energy which fused his little band of immediate associates into a highly efficient spearhead.

8

Progress and Problems

From 1895 until the turn of the century the predominant activities within the fledgling Company were those of research and demonstration. This was *force majeure*, for the apparatus was limited in its capabilities and the civilized world with its network of telegraph lines and cables was not yet conditioned to accept this new-fangled device of Marconi's.

One of the chief obstacles to gaining sources of revenue lay in the monopolistic powers conferred on the British Post Office by the Telegraph Acts of 1868–9 which prohibited the Marconi Company from instituting a competitive inland message-carrying service. Such a service, had it been possible, would have been an invaluable 'shop window' for potential customers from overseas.

As a result of this impasse, other possible sources of income had to be considered, of which the shipping interests seemed to provide the best immediate prospect. As has already been related, this brought about the formation of the Marconi International Marine Communication Co. Ltd. on 25 April 1900.

But the mere act of forming a second Company was no panacea, for the Post Office monopoly extended not only over the confines of the British Isles but beyond them to the three-mile limit. It was thus impossible to inaugurate a straightforward legal communication service between ship and shore, whereby ship owners could purchase wireless apparatus and use it for an exchange of intelligence between their vessels and Marconi coastal stations for a given fee per message, for this contravened the Post Office monopoly in the matter of sending messages for commercial gain.

Accordingly the Company had to adopt a stratagem, whereby the Marine Company entered into an agreement with a shipping company to install wireless transmitting and receiving apparatus aboard ship on a rental basis. The sum agreed covered not only the maintenance of the equipment and the cost of the messages, but also the services of a Marconi sea-going operator, who, although subject to the general ship's discipline, remained throughout an employee of the Marine Company. By this means messages could be exchanged with other shipping fitted with Marconi apparatus and with the Marconi wireless stations which were being erected along the British coastline, as no direct charge was made for the handling of the intelligence.

The first order for the installation of wireless telegraphy aboard a British ship came from the Beaver Line (later merged in the C.P.R. Line). The vessel, the *Lake Champlain*, sailed from Liverpool on 21 May 1901, establishing contact with the Holyhead and Rosslare shore stations on the outward journey and with the newly-opened station at Crook-haven also, on the voyage home. The *Lake Champlain* later exchanged messages with the *Lucania*, the first Cunarder to carry wireless. The *Lucania*'s installation was an advance on that supplied to the *Kaiser Wilhelm Der Grosse* and the *Lake Champlain* in that it employed the new syntonic (tuned) circuit of the type which had been christened 'Tune A', operating on a wavelength of about one hundred metres.

Curiously enough, one of the first major orders for ground wireless stations came from the Antipodes; not from the mainland of Australia or even New Zealand, but the Hawaiian islands, where the Inter Island Telegraph Co. had been formed.

Up until 1 March 1901 when a public wireless telegraph service between the five principal islands in the Hawaiian group had been inaugurated, there had been no telegraphy in the area, so in addition to carrying out the installations on Oahu, Kauai, Molaki, Maui and Jawaii, the Marconi engineers had to prepare the General Orders for running the system as a business.

This order was a foretaste of the pattern of systems engineering which became a tradition of the Company, for not only did the contract call for the supply and installation of the stations but also for their operation and maintenance. More significant still, the Company contracted to train Hawaiian operators, teaching them the Morse code and sufficient electrical theory and practice to enable them to service the equipment themselves in the fullness of time. It is a procedure which has been followed to this day.

The Hawaiian installations gave valuable experience to the Marconi engineer-operators in the field and to the designers at home. One very useful lesson was learned when out of the five installations carried out, three were found to be incapable of providing satisfactory ranges. The mystery deepened when, upon testing individual sections of the equipment, no fault could be found.

In the end, Andrew Gray (then a senior engineer at Chelmsford, later to become the Company's first Chief Engineer) had to go to the islands to investigate. He found that the wire guys supporting the masts were the source of the trouble; because of the close relationship in lengths between the top set of mast stays and the antenna itself, the stay-wires were absorbing an excessive amount of energy. As weather conditions made it undesirable to use hemp guys, Gray solved the problem by breaking the wire guys into short lengths by the insertion of dead-eyes and rope lanyards. This became standard Marconi practice.

The 'General Orders' referred to earlier were in due course issued to the Hawaiian operators in the form of a printed booklet. This was the forerunner of the Marconi book of General Orders which was the manual of procedure for controlling the Company's ship-to-shore traffic.

In the United States the *New York Herald* sponsored a project to equip the Nantucket lightship with Marconi wireless telegraphy. This installation was carried out in August 1901, together with that of a station at Siasconset on Nantucket island. The *New York Herald* thus became the first newspaper to own and operate a wireless station.

In September of that year the *Campania* became the second Cunarder to be fitted with 'Tune A' and emergency plain antenna. Later in the month the third, *Umbria*, was also equipped, and, toward the end of 1901, *Etruria*.

In those early years it was the custom for the installing engineer to sail with the ship as its operator; as a consequence many of the early ships' operators later became prominent figures in wireless circles. One such was the engineer-operator of the *Umbria*, Charles Samuel Franklin, famous for the short-wave beam.

On 26 September 1901 the Marconi Company's prospects were considerably brightened by the news that the Lloyd's Corporation had awarded them a contract for the installation of wireless apparatus in ten of the Lloyd's signal stations. With such an internationally famous organization publicly demonstrating its faith in Marconi wireless equipment the prospects for further sales to maritime interests strengthened considerably.

The French liner *La Savoie* was the next to be fitted, the order having been placed with the Brussels office of the Marconi International Marine Communication Co. This installation was completed before 2 November 1901.

Just before this a Belgian associated Company came into being when on October 26 the Cie de Télégraphie sans Fils (Belge) was formed to develop and operate the Marconi system on the Continent. Two sister ships of the *Savoie*, namely *La Lorraine* and *La Touraine* were the first to be fitted with wireless through this Company.

In England, the next Cunarder to be equipped was the *Philadelphia*, with which installation, it will be recalled, Marconi succeeded in confirming that transatlantic working was possible. The *Philadelphia* sailed on her epoch-making crossing on 22 February 1902; a month or two later she became the first ship to be fitted with 'Tune B' equipment which operated on a wavelength of 270 m. instead of the 100 m. of the 'Tune A' sets. The immediate effect of this increase of wavelength was to extend the standard ship-to-shore working range from seventy miles to approximately 150 miles.

One of the more out-of-the-way 'firsts' that can be credited to the *Philadelphia* is that the first game of chess to be played via the medium of wireless communication was contested between a team recruited on this vessel and one aboard the *Campania*. This pastime subsequently became popular with ships at sea.

The years 1901–3 were exciting ones for the Company. On the research side an immense amount of real progress had been made, culminating in the first attempts at transatlantic working on a commercial basis. On the sales side, optimism seemed justified for there was every sign that the doldrum period was past. By the end of 1902, seventy ships had been equipped with wireless and twenty-five land stations had been erected.

On 24 April 1903 another continental bridgehead came into being when the Cie Française Maritime et Coloniale de Télégraphie sans Fils of Paris was founded. This organization took over the French liner contracts from the Belgian Company and in July obtained an award for three further installations, namely for *La Bretagne*, *La Champagne* and *La Gascogne*.

With the growth of orders there had naturally come a commensurate growth in the engineering and commercial organization of the Company. In the earliest years, an electrical engineer who joined the small band of brothers had to have specialist training in the new art; as this was of necessity acquired in the field it inevitably brought him into personal contact with Mr Marconi. With the birth of the factory at Hall Street, Chelmsford in December 1898, the situation became more formal. Various departments came into being; a condenser (capacitor) and winding shop; a carpenters' shop; a mounting shop and a machine shop,

A. A. CAMPBELL SWINTON.
ELECTRICAL ENGINEER.

Telegraphic Address
"DYNAMIS. LONDON."
Telephone Nº 3147.

66, Victoria Street,
London. S.W.

March 30 th 1896.

Dear Mr Preece.

I am taking the liberty of sending to you with this note a young Italian of the name of Marconi. who has come over to this country with the idea of getting taken up a new system of telegraphy without wires. at which he has been working. It appears to be based upon the use of Hertzian waves. and Oliver Lodge's coherer. but from what he tells me he appears to have got considerably beyond what I believe other people have done in this line.

It has occurred to me that you might possibly be kind enough to see him and hear what he has to say and I also think that what he has done will very likely be of interest to you.

Hoping that I am not troubling you too much.

Believe me.

Yours very truly,

A. A. C. Swinton

W. S. Preece Esq. C.B.

Guglielmo Marconi
101 Westport Rª
Bayswater Bologna

i. Letter of introduction to William Preece

2. Marconi and early apparatus, 1896

3. Post Office officials with Marconi's apparatus
at Bristol Channel demonstration, 1897

4. Poldhu antenna system erected for the transatlantic experiment of 1901

5. The wireless cabin of the *Lusitania* (*c.* 1912)

6. Sound broadcasting; the 2LO transmitter at Marconi House, London, 1922

7. Marconi's yacht *Elettra*

under the overall supervision of Mr E. T. Priddle, the first Works Manager.

In July 1899 Dr Erskine Murray left the experimental establishment at the Haven, Poole, Dorset to take charge of the technical work at the factory. When Erskine Murray resigned in 1900 to take up a post at University College, Nottingham, he was succeeded by Dr W. H. Eccles, one of whose many subsequent claims to fame was his work upon the oscillating crystal (1910 and onwards) which can be regarded as the forerunner of the tunnel diodes re-invented comparatively recently. Dr Eccles resigned in 1901 to become Head of the Department of Mathematics and Physics at the South Western Polytechnic, Chelsea.

There had also been changes at the Company's Head Office at 28, Mark Lane, London. Mr H. Jameson Davis, Marconi's cousin, who had agreed to become the first Managing Director on the Company's formation, had done so only on the understanding that he should resign as soon as it was firmly established. Accordingly he had relinquished his position in August 1899 and Major Flood-Page had become Managing Director. Until this time, Marconi had been personally consulted upon all inquiries, had given his instructions and Jameson Davis had delegated members of the staff to deal with them.

The Company was now growing vigorously, to a point where this simple form of control was deemed inadequate, and, before his departure, Jameson Davis had delegated the control of technical staff movements to one of his senior engineers. The outbreak of the Boer War, however, took this engineer, G. L. Bullocke, to South Africa with five other senior men, and as a consequence the new Managing Director found himself in technical control of the Chelmsford Works as well as having to deal with the increasing spate of technical inquiries. To shed the load somewhat, Flood-Page appointed a Manager, Mr H. Cuthbert Hall, who took the post early in 1901. At the same time Mr E. A. N. Pochin, a well-qualified industrial electrical engineer, assumed responsibility for the technical control of the Company.

Inevitably there were teething troubles with this arrangement. The new administrative régime struck at the very roots of the 'band of brothers' spirit of the original organization and was resented by those who had been in the Company since its birth; these pioneers, not unnaturally, did not take too kindly to the concept of taking orders from what they regarded as a bureaucracy, and probably did not over-exert themselves to be helpful.

The situation was made more difficult by the geographical disposition of the Marconi personnel. Unlike most industrial organizations, they were not under one roof but scattered far and wide; at the Haven, the Needles, Chelmsford, the coastal stations and abroad; a virile, independently-minded body of men who, while unswerving in their personal loyalties to Marconi himself, were not nearly so amicably disposed towards the rather nebulous 'They' of Head Office.

A brave new world was being born; a world in which the application of advanced physics to engineering was presenting an entirely novel set of problems for immediate solution. An intricate and contentious patent situation was developing which demanded first-hand knowledge to steer the Company through the shoal waters. A realistic plan for the staffing and overall control of the growing ship-to-shore traffic was also urgently needed.

Last, but not least, of the problems which beset the Company in the first years of the twentieth century was the purely financial one. The prolonged transatlantic tests had dwindled the cash reserves to a degree which was all the more alarming because no prospect of establishing a profitable service between the Old World and the New was in sight. Neither were the ship-to-shore services as yet proving remunerative. At the same time there was a growing demand for apparatus which was intermediate in power between the short-range ship-shore installation and the high-power transatlantic equipment. For this a potentially profitable market existed, provided that the apparatus could be quickly and efficiently developed.

These, then, were some of the hazards which beset the Company at this time. In June 1901, Major Flood-Page resigned as Managing Director (although continuing in an advisory capacity for a further fourteen months) leaving the control of the Company in the hands of Mr Cuthbert Hall, although the latter was not formally appointed Managing Director until August 1902.

With these multifarious problems on his shoulders, Cuthbert Hall's position was not one to be envied. Fortunately for him, the hour produced the man in the form of Andrew Gray, a senior engineer of the Company who was at the time in America. In October 1901, Gray was recalled to take over full technical control from Pochin, with the title of Chief of Staff.

This promotion of Andrew Gray was a wiser one than anyone perhaps realized. Gray, who had already proved himself a very able engineer, was not long in making his presence felt in his new appointment. Here at last was a man at Headquarters who talked the language the engineers understood; who ruled with the proverbial rod of iron but who recognized outstanding ability when he saw it and encouraged it by all the means in his considerable power. His presence revitalized the engineering side of the Company and in so doing removed much of the intolerable load from Cuthbert Hall. During his long years of service, he at all times served the Company faithfully and well, becoming a world figure in electronics and a truly great Chief Engineer.

Just prior to Andrew Gray's appointment, another decisive step had been taken by the setting up at Frinton, Essex, of the first school for the training of probationer Marconi engineers and others. This institution subsequently moved to Chelmsford to become Marconi College, which is in vigorous existence to this day, justifiably proud of its claim to be the world's first wireless college.

During the following month (October) training classes in Marconi techniques were started at Chelmsford for the instruction of the otherwise qualified men who joined the staff as wireless operators. This scheme was extended in the following year when a building was erected at Waterloo, Liverpool, to house a school, a repair shop, office and operating room. This establishment (irreverently christened the 'Tin Tabernacle' by its early occupants) continued as the main gateway through which, for many years, Marconi operators passed to the oceans and the four quarters of the globe.

In parentheses it is perhaps a matter for surprise that, at a difficult period in the Company's finances, these expenditures should have materialized when retrenchment might have seemed more prudent. The training establishments were in fact an implementation of Guglielmo Marconi's personal policy, which in the simplest terms might be stated as building for a future in which he had an unshakeable faith.

Against the back-drop of reorganization the commercial pattern of Company activity was proceeding much the same; many demonstrations and a few sales were still the norm. For example, the first ship-to-shore demonstration of wireless to be seen in Holland took place on 28 April 1902, when the Dutch cruiser *Evertsen* was fitted with 'Tune A' and 'Tune B' equipment and a shore station was erected at Scheveningen, near The Hague. Duplex transmission was effected between this station and the cruiser fifty miles away at sea, official messages being sent to Queen Wilhelmina and the Dutch ministers.

A somewhat similar demonstration was given to the Colonial Premiers who were in London for the coronation of King Edward VII. For this the pleasure-steamer *Koh-I-Noor* was chartered and fitted with wireless apparatus; as the vessel with the official party aboard steamed down the Thames, continuous communication was effected with the Marconi stations at Chelmsford, Frinton, Dovercourt and North Foreland, the trip culminating in a visit to the latter station.

The year 1902 also saw a revival of War Office interest in military portable stations and official tests were carried out between stations at Chatham and Maidstone, as a result of which transportable wireless stations were used in the British Army manœuvres of 1903. These employed demountable umbrella-type antennas, syntonic transmitters and magnetic detector reception.

The army installations at this time were carried by horse-drawn general service wagons; in this connection it is interesting to note that two years before this Guglielmo Marconi was experimenting with transportable equipment housed in self-propelled vehicles. For this purpose a steam-driven Thornycroft wagon fitted with omnibus-type coachwork was purchased. Syntonic apparatus was fitted, using a 25 ft. collapsible zinc cylinder on the roof as a radiator, the earth system consisting of a wire net. Numerous tests were carried out with this vehicle in the neighbourhood of the Haven and also in the Chelmsford area and on at least one occasion the equipment received signals over a range of thirty-one miles.

This, the world's first transportable self-propelled station, anticipated events, for in 1904 the automobile displaced the horse-drawn wagon in the Italian Army manœuvres; on that occasion a syntonic ship's set was used in the vehicle, the antenna being an umbrella type with wires radiating from a central 20 ft. pole to a ring of shorter poles. Operating under field conditions, two such stations maintained contact over a range of twenty miles.

Although Marconi engineers who operated and maintained these equipments did not know it at the time, they were the pioneers in what in later years became an important branch of the Company's business, the Field Station department which specialized in the fulfilment of Army requirements.

9

The Growing Competition

Although the state of the art as it existed in 1903 had convinced everyone that signalling across the Atlantic by wireless waves was an accomplished fact, it was still not sufficiently advanced to support a reliable commercial service. Nevertheless, it had given the cable companies much food for thought, and the burden of their thoughts was that they might well be the reluctant chief participants at a modern Belshazzar's feast. Were the days of the cable telegraph numbered?

For informed opinion the advice of Sir William Preece (he had now been knighted) and Professor Oliver Lodge was sought and the answers they gave provided more than a crumb of comfort.

Said Sir William: 'Causes of disturbance which may or may not be remedied in the future are at present existent, and fatal to the establishment of a practical and reliable system of commercial wireless telegraphy. I am therefore very clearly of the opinion that submarine cable enterprise has nothing to fear in a commercial sense from the competition of etheric telegraphy.'

Professor Lodge backed this opinion by saying: 'To the best of my belief submarine cables will for a long time be pre-eminent for the purpose of long-distance telegraphy. It is manifest that wireless or open methods cannot compete in point of secrecy or certainty with closed or cable methods, and can only compete with them in point of speed and accuracy by aid of great improvements and new inventions involving little less than discoveries.'

These pronouncements were, in the light of the knowledge existing at the time, sober statements of fact, although Sir William's opinion that the cable interests had nothing to fear proved, in the years which lay ahead, to be far too dogmatic. That the 'causes of disturbance' that were fatal to the establishment of a reliable service were there was all too true. Neither, as Lodge pointed out, could wireless telegraphy compete in terms of secrecy with a cable system, despite the advent of syntonic tuning (which it must be remembered owed a very great deal in its conception to Lodge himself).

The cardinal point which Preece in particular failed to evaluate sufficiently was Man's ingenuity. It had been overlooked that only ten years before it had seemed impossible to harness etheric waves for practical communication purposes at all; that, when the first painfully slow signals were tapped out, the lack of speed was held to be a fatal handicap – which it would have been had not ways and means been found to speed it to a point where it was comparable with the cable's forty words per minute. It had been forgotten, too, that when transatlantic wireless was first mooted it was calculated (correctly, too, according to all known data) that masts 200 miles high would be needed on either side of the Atlantic. And last but not least there had been the dire prediction that high-power wireless stations would blanket out all others. In the face of these it was rash of Preece to dismiss the competitive potential of wireless telegraphy as being of no consequence to the cable interests.

Nevertheless, the two pronouncements – sincere as they undoubtedly both were – did much to make the shareholders in the cable companies sleep sounder of nights and provided nothing in the way of reassurance to those of Marconi's Wireless Telegraph Company.

In addition to the cable companies' natural determination to resist encroachment by all means at their disposal, the Marconi Company also found it beset on its own ground. For about this time the skirmishing shots were fired in a long-drawn-out struggle with German wireless interests.

The background to the story is both political and commercial. The German Government had quickly realized that wireless telegraphy would prove an invaluable ally in the event of war as a means of communication between the colonies which made up the German Empire, for, unlike Britain, Germany's possessions were not for the most part linked to the home-land by cable. Furthermore, cables were too vulnerable; nothing was more certain than that, with the British Navy in command of the seas, one of its first acts if hostilities broke out would be to sever such German-controlled cables as existed. On the other hand, having gained a lead in wireless communication, Britain had no intention of losing it, and was in a very strong position by reason of the fact that nearly all the master-patents were at that time owned by the Marconi Company.

On the commercial plane there was also a strong divergence of interests. In Germany, the Telefunken Company, backed by the very powerful Algemeine Elektricitats Gesellschaft and a formidable group of scientists, had, since the end of the nineteenth century, been making strenuous efforts to capture world markets in wireless apparatus with its Slaby-Arco-Braun system. The Marconi Company were not only contending for these markets but carrying the 'war' to the 'enemy's' front door-step by trying to influence German mercantile interests to use Marconi installations.

One of the biggest bones of contention was the official Marconi policy of discouraging ships fitted with their apparatus from communicating with those equipped with foreign installations.* Harsh as this ruling might seem at first thought, it had reason on its side because the Company was the only one providing a complete ship-to-shore service, and to allow participation in this was to provide rival Companies with shore facilities to the upkeep of which they did not contribute.

This sore had come to a head early in 1902 when Prince Henry of Prussia sailed for New York in the Marconi-equipped *Kronprinz Wilhelm*, for which event arrangements had been made to demonstrate to the Prince the simultaneous reception of two different messages by means of syntonic apparatus.

The demonstration was a complete success, the messages being duly received from the Lizard and the Poldhu stations. The Prince was further impressed by the amount of traffic passing between shipping and the shore in the coastal waters of Britain and the U.S.A.

Prince Henry returned from New York in the *Deutschland* belonging to the same shipping line but equipped with Slaby-Arco-Braun equipment, and could not fail to note that the ship did not contact either the Nantucket station, the Lizard or indeed any Marconi station on the home run.

The climax came when the liner reached Germany. Accusations were made against the Company which alleged that out of pique (because an original Marconi installation aboard a German ship had been followed by the use of another make of apparatus in sister ships), the Marconi stations had deliberately jammed the *Deutschland*'s wireless. This was, in fact, totally untrue; on the contrary, those stations had received specific orders to reply to any transmission from the German vessel because of the distinguished passenger she carried.

Although at this distance of time it is impossible to establish the truth of the matter, there is no doubt that at that time the German equipment

* With one important exception; namely, a call from a vessel in distress.

was not proving particularly successful and it is likely that on that run the *Deutschland*'s wireless was either partially or wholly out of action because of a technical fault. Certainly the apparatus was removed from the ship shortly after.

The *Deutschland* incident was symptomatic of the tension which existed between the two nations and the two wireless Companies, British and German, at that period. With the Marconi Company in possession of most of the master patents, the German organization had perforce to devise methods of transmission and reception which bore sufficient similarity to certain of the British apparatus as to constitute possible grounds for legal action. Unfortunately for the Marconi Company, its resources were too slender to dissipate upon the hazards of foreign litigation and so the situation had to be endured, but it did nothing to lessen the hostility.

The alleged non-co-operation of the Marconi stations with the *Deutschland* stung Germany into calling for an International Wireless Telegraphy Conference on the grounds that it was for the general benefit of mankind; this duly took place in Berlin on 4 August 1903, with Germany, Great Britain, Austria, Hungary, Spain, Italy, Russia, France and the United States of America taking part. The outcome provided a setback to the Marconi Company, for it was there resolved that the delegates should make a recommendation to their respective governments that it should be obligatory for all coastal wireless stations to transmit and receive messages to and from all shipping. It was further resolved that there should be a pooling of all technical information necessary for the purpose. The British and Italian delegations accepted the protocol with reservations but agreed to pass on the recommendations to their governments.

While this commercial 'war' was being fought, orders continued to come in. On 29 January 1903, an agreement was entered into between the Marconi Company and the Italian Ministry of Posts and Telegraphs for the building of a high-power station at Coltano, some 175 miles from Rome, for which the King of Italy gave the land. Monopolistic rights were conferred on the Company for a period of fourteen years, and this, together with the £32,000 contract for the station, gave a much-needed fillip to the Marconi order book.

In May 1903 Marconi visited Rome to receive the honour of the freedom of the city. Whilst there he was invited to dinner at the Quirinal where the German Emperor was staying as the guest of the King of Italy. The Kaiser made no attempt to disguise his sentiments over the

Marconi Company's struggle with the Algemeine Elektricitats Gesel-lschaft when he remarked over dinner:

'Signor Marconi, you must not think that I have any animosity against yourself, but I do object to the policy of your Company.'

On 18 July 1903, royal interest in wireless telegraphy was again officially shown, this time in Britain, when the Prince and Princess of Wales visited Poldhu.

The following week came another valuable (and long-sought) order when, on 24 July, an agreement was signed between the Marconi Company and the British Admiralty for the general use of the Marconi system in the Royal Navy for a period of eleven years. Under that agreement the Company granted the Admiralty full use of all patent rights and the exclusive use of a high-power station for twenty minutes per day, priority over all messages and the supply of all apparatus. The financial terms included the sum of £20,000 with £1,600 royalty fee for the thirty-two existing marine stations and £5,000 a year over the eleven-year term.

The orders gave Guglielmo Marconi renewed encouragement to pursue his dream of a commercial transatlantic service, and so on the experimental front long-range tests were again the main item. Experience was drawing the researchers farther and farther from the extremely short wavelengths of the earliest wireless sets to very much longer wavelengths, for empirical findings seemed to indicate clearly that the formula for success was longer wavelengths + higher power = longer ranges (it was in fact a wrong road taken, as was to be shown twenty years later, but in the light of scientific knowledge in 1903 this could not be foreseen).

Thus we find that extensions were made to the Poldhu antenna to make it into a multiple 'T' array with an operating wavelength of over 2,000 m. After initial tests carried out in conjunction with a new receiving station at Broomfield, Chelmsford, Marconi sailed for New York on 22 August 1903 on a three-fold mission.

The first of these was accomplished aboard ship, the *Lucania* when, before representatives of the Admiralty, the Italian Navy and the Press, it was shown, for the first time, that the vessel could be in constant communication with land – either the Old World and the New – with a useful overlap in mid-Atlantic, when simultaneous reception of both could be effected. This was no academic exercise. It had an important secondary purpose, namely to show that a ship's newspaper could be produced which would give the passengers the important news of the day just as if they had been on shore. It was this demonstration which paved the way for the production of the *Cunard Bulletin*, the first regular ship's newspaper, in the following year.

The remaining two projects were widely dissimilar, but both merited the undivided attention which Marconi could not, or rather in one instance did not want to give. This was a legal action against the American inventor Dr Lee de Forest for alleged infringement of patent rights; the second concerned improvements to the apparatus at the Glace Bay station, for which Marconi had planned an extension to the antenna system and the installation of a 150 kW generator. It is not difficult to guess where Marconi's heart was, but the legal action could not be ignored and so perforce he had to alternate between New York and Glace Bay for the period of this visit. Then another important assignment from the British Admiralty called him back to England.

This consisted of a further series of tests to establish that Poldhu could be reliably received by a wireless station at Gibraltar and by ships *en route* to The Rock. For these tests the seaborne trials were carried out aboard the *Duncan* which sailed from Portsmouth on October 24. Despite damage to the ship's antenna during a storm in the Bay of Biscay, messages were reliably received up to a maximum range of 600 miles during the daytime and over the full 850 miles at night.

Increasing pressure on the part of the Press and general public was being brought to bear upon the shipping lines to equip their vessels with wireless apparatus. Two incidents, in particular, occurred in the course of 1903 to illustrate in graphic fashion that maritime wireless equipment was no toy. In January of that year the American liner *St Louis* broke down at sea, becoming long overdue; as the ship carried no wireless her disappearance became a complete mystery, causing distress and anxiety not only to the shipping line authorities but also to the relatives of all on board – a situation which was only relieved when at last the ship limped into port.

On 8 December 1903 the Red Star liner *Kroonland* suffered a steering gear breakdown when 130 miles west of the Fastnet Light, but having wireless equipment, her captain was able to inform the owners of the ship's predicament and to receive instructions from them. Even more important, nearly all the passengers were able to get in touch with friends and relatives and to reassure them.

The year had been one of ups and downs. Although the Company's declared policy of restricting its maritime message-carrying service to Marconi-equipped ships and shore stations had been quashed at the

Berlin Conference, this reverse had not significantly affected orders, which had continued to come in at a rate which, although leaving something to be desired, nevertheless held promise of a greater volume for the future.

The establishment of a regular transatlantic service had still not come to pass, but here, too, the signs were hopeful that, by using longer wavelengths and higher powers, the goal might be attained in the not too distant future.

In matters of research, and notably by the advent of the magnetic detector as a commercial production, the Marconi reputation had been kept above that of the ever-increasing foreign competition, although the latter was of such a character that it permitted no respite; no breathing space.

For Guglielmo Marconi himself the year ended happily with the award of an honour from the Czar of Russia; he was created a Knight of the Order of St Anne, a distinction which was indicative of the esteem in which he was already held by the world at large.

Further Struggles and Achievements

The magnetic detector was already proving to be a great asset to the Company by reason of the greatly increased speeds in reception which it permitted. The coherer, which it deposed, had been developed into a reasonably reliable performer, but its Achilles heel was its slow speed; this shortcoming was inherent, because, after the passage of every wave-train, the filings had to be restored to their former sensitive condition by tapping or otherwise physically loosening the metal particles.

In view of this limitation the transmission speed had to be slowed accordingly. Thus we find that under good conditions a transmission speed of not much better than ten words per minute was the best which could be hoped for although somewhat higher speeds had often been recorded during experimental tests. At ten words per minute, wireless telegraphy could never hope to compete with cable telegraphic speeds.

The magnetic detector put an end to this era of cable supremacy by boosting wireless speeds to match those obtained over line telegraphy systems. It also made the Marconi apparatus much faster in operation than any on offer by the Company's commercial rivals.

An interesting instance of this occurred when the leading Dutch newspaper, the *Handelsblad*, arranged with the Company for the transmission to Holland of a Stock Exchange News Service. Accordingly a station was built at Amsterdam and communication was maintained with a similar station at Broomfield, near Chelmsford. Transmissions from the English station were sent at thirty words a minute and received in Holland on a magnetic detector. As the messages were mainly in the form of numerals and abbreviations, traffic at this speed was a remarkable achievement.

On this occasion Company enthusiasm outran discretion, for after the service had been in satisfactory operation for some time it was argued that as permission to operate it had been granted on an experimental basis, it could be regarded as a demonstration circuit, and therefore there could be no harm in showing its capabilities as a two-way channel to interested parties. The Dutch station accordingly began to give this a truly liberal interpretation by accepting telegrams for England at the rate of 8 cents a word; a move which, although it pleased the Dutch public, not unnaturally incensed the Dutch Posts and Telegraphs authorities.

At this point an element of comedy enters, for in order to bring legal pressure to bear upon the erring Company, proof had to be obtained that such telegrams did, in fact, pass to England, so attempts were made to intercept the messages. This was easier said than done; the Maas Lightship became an official interception post, but, alas, its coherer receiver could make nothing of the thirty-words-a-minute transmissions and the Marconi Company would not provide a magnetic detector to be the instrument of its undoing.

The next move was to call in the Dutch Army wireless experts to intercept the messages, but this proved useless also. Finally, in desperation, a new and fully-equipped station was set up by the newly-born Netherlands State Radio. At first this fared no better than its predecessors, but at length, with specially selected coherers and highly skilled operators, a record of the Marconi transmissions was obtained which, although far from perfect, was sufficiently good to enable the Dutch Government to take action to restrict the service within the experimental limits allowed.

This then, was some measure of the technical advance provided by the magnetic detector when it was introduced into general service. In a branch of science which is noted for rapid advances, it held its place for an astonishing length of time; *Maggies* are known to have been in service up to the early 1920s.

On the broader front of research, transatlantic experiments were quietly pushing ahead. The Poldhu station had been re-equipped with new transmitting plant and a fore-and-aft 'T' antenna radiating on a longer wavelength than ever before (4,250 m.). As an alternative to the equipping of a transatlantic liner with special apparatus, with all the inevitable publicity that this would bring, it was decided instead to build a receiving station within the British Isles, as far from Poldhu as was possible so that the signals would travel by a shorter route but under the more difficult conditions occasioned by the overland nature of the path. In this way work could be pushed ahead out of the glare of publicity.

A suitable site was selected at Fraserburgh in N.E. Scotland and a receiving station built there. Tests conducted between Fraserburgh and Poldhu, a distance of 550 miles, showed considerable promise, for it was found that reception was possible using only 1 kW of energy at the transmitter.

In view of this success there was no option but to revert to tests aboard a transatlantic liner. On 7 May 1904, Marconi sailed on the *Campania* with long-range checks as the main objective, but the results were insufficiently good – 1,200 miles by day and 1,700 miles by night.

Marconi now had to come to terms with the realization that he was not a free agent, but the servant of his Company's shareholders. Had he been the former he would without doubt have sunk every penny he could lay hands upon in the building of a mammoth super-power station operating on a very long wavelength in a gamble to provide a full-scale commercial transatlantic service. But he was not his own master in this, as he well knew, for his Company was in no financial position to shoulder such a heavy expenditure on a venture which might not come off.

It was indeed a bitter blow to have to call off further tests, knowing as he did that his protagonists would be dismayed and his opponents jubilant. But there was, as he saw it, no other rational course; accordingly, he released the Poldhu and Glace Bay stations for service as revenue-earning assets in a new project, the Marconi transatlantic news service to shipping, contenting himself with a decision to choose a new site for the Glace Bay station; one which would permit the erection of an antenna which would radiate on a longer wavelength than the present one could.

After signing a formal agreement with the Cunard line for the regular supply of news to their ships on the transatlantic run, and after further tests, the service was officially inaugurated on 4 June 1904, when the first *Cunard Bulletin* was published aboard the *Campania*. Although this was not the first ship's wireless newspaper (it may be recalled that a single issue of the *Transatlantic Times* was published aboard the *St Paul* in November 1899) it was the first one to appear regularly day after day and provided not only a much-appreciated service to passengers but a useful piece of publicity for the Company.

Several significant events took place almost simultaneously about this time. One of these was the Russo-Japanese war, which began in February 1904. At the invitation of the Russian Government the Marconi Company sent out field stations comprising spark coil transmitters powered from batteries and petrol engine generators, and coherer receivers. These were demonstrated near St Petersburgh by four engineers who elected to go on this errand.

Later, low-power stations were built at St Petersburgh, Vishni Volechok and Vladivostok. Each consisted of a transmitter coupled to an antenna system which was supported between four 150 ft. wooden towers and powered by an oil engine and generator. The receiving equipment consisted of both coherers and magnetic detectors.

One of the installation engineers was C. S. Franklin. In describing his experiences in those early days he recalled that he and his colleagues were not equipped with suitable clothing to combat a Russian winter and, at the onset of bad weather, cabled Head Office for a supply of warmer clothing. The engineers' feelings can be imagined when they read the cabled reply which said simply 'Work harder!' Despite this, the clothing did arrive.

On another occasion, at the commissioning of one of the stations, priests arrived to bless the equipment, but unfortunately some of the holy water, which was being liberally sprinkled, short-circuited the high tension supply and with a lurid flash the station went off the air to the consternation of all, particularly the priests.

But, mishaps such as these apart, the station worked well and the Russian Army authorities expressed themselves as thoroughly satisfied. (Later, in 1906, further stations were built at Reval and in Finland). At sea, however, the Russian Navy had no such opportunity for satisfaction, for it suffered a crushing defeat by the Japanese at the battle of Tsushima in May 1905, a circumstance which was attributed in part to the failure of their wireless communications. It is recorded in the Marconi archives (not perhaps without some satisfaction) that the equipment for the Russian Navy had been supplied by a rival firm.

C. S. Franklin, who has been mentioned earlier, made his first notable contribution to wireless telegraphy whilst on service in Russia, for it was from here that he sent home sketches and drawings of the first disc capacitor. Here is an instance of an invention which has been in constant usage ever since that time. The disc (or variable) capacitor enormously simplified the adjustment of the receiver-tuned circuits of the day and Franklin gave it an even greater value by constructing a compact assembly of three coupled tuned circuits, variable both in wavelength and coupling, and, moreover, ganged for simplicity of operation. The multiple tuner was patented in 1907. In conjunction with the magnetic detector it was adopted as standard equipment for ship-to-shore service and remained so for many years.

February 1904 saw the introduction of an extremely good idea in the form of Communication Charts which were thereafter issued on a

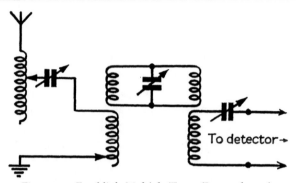

Figure 10.1 Franklin's Multiple Tuner (Patented 1907)

monthly basis from Headquarters. These superseded an innovation of the previous year, a sailing list of ships fitted with Marconi apparatus. Each of the new charts gave the tracks of wireless-equipped ships sailing across the Atlantic during that particular month and from this the approximate position of every ship could be ascertained on any given day, as their respective sailing times from British or New World ports were known in advance. By this simple but ingenious means the operators at sea could always determine which ships were within range. This tabulation system was subsequently extended to cover other oceans and continued for some years until eventually the range of ships' installations improved to the point where there was little further need for the charts.

In May 1904, the Canadian Marconi Company* was busy fulfilling a Canadian Government contract for the supply and installation of eight coastal stations for shipping and commercial telegraph traffic work on a licence and royalty basis.

In July of that year the most powerful radio station in the world at that time began operation when Guglielmo Marconi performed the official opening ceremony of the Italian station at Coltano. It was a highly efficient installation which served to raise the Company's prestige throughout the world and in the Mediterranean area in particular. Communication was effected with Italian East Africa, a distance of 2,238 miles, to the considerable satisfaction of the Italian Government.

The following month saw the inauguration of a fast wireless telegraphy service between Bari in Italy and Antivari in Montenegro, to link Italy to the Balkans. On August 2 this, the first international wireless telegraph service under State control, was officially put into service, communicating over 130 miles of sea.

* More correctly, Marconi's Wireless Telegraph Co. of Canada, formed in 1903. The title was changed to Canadian Marconi Company, 12 June 1925.

August was also a significant month in quite another direction for it saw the passing of the Wireless Telegraphy Act, 1904, although the Act did not actually come into effect until 1 January 1905. This to some extent regularized the Company's position in regard to ship-to-shore traffic in areas around the British coastline. Prior to that date the Postmaster General had forbidden commercial signalling from the coast within the three-miles limit; also up to that time any foreign operator could erect a wireless station on the coast of the British Isles, whereas no complementary rights existed for a British company to do this on foreign soil.

The Wireless Telegraphy Act made it compulsory that any organization desiring to build a wireless station in Britain had first to obtain a licence from the Postmaster General. The Company's stations were at once licensed for a period of eight years and thereafter were officially recognized as proper vehicles for the passage of messages between ship and shore. From 1 January 1905, messages for ships were accepted at British Post Offices for transmission via the coastal stations of the Marconi Company.

The first meteorological forecasts to be prepared from information obtained by wireless from ships at sea were begun about this time. The *Daily Telegraph* was the first newspaper to employ this method and came to an arrangement with the Marconi Company whereby all ships on the North Atlantic run which were equipped with Marconi wireless should supply bulletins giving data on the weather. This foresight gave *Daily Telegraph* readers a weather information service which was much more up-to-date and accurate than had hitherto been possible.

By December 1904, the Company had in operation some sixty-nine land stations and one hundred and twenty-four ship stations as tangible evidence of the growing appreciation of the value of wireless telegraphy as a medium of commercial and military communication. But the most important event of the year (although it was not recognized as such until many years later) took place in a quiet laboratory, when the opening of a cupboard symbolically opened the door to a revolution in wireless communication and to diversification into all those highways and byways of manufacture which make up the electronics industry. For in 1904 the thermionic valve was born.

I I

The Invention of the Diode Valve

It will be recalled that in 1899 Guglielmo Marconi acquired the services of Dr J. A. Fleming as technical consultant to his Company. Never did he make a better investment, as witness Fleming's brilliant work on the original Poldhu station at the time of the great transatlantic experiment.

Fleming was that unusual mixture of brilliant scholar and gifted practical engineer who had risen via various professorial chairs to the post of Professor of Electrical Engineering at University College, London. Sometime a pupil of the great Clerk Maxwell, he accepted the consultancy and brought great enthusiasm to bear upon the problems with which Marconi confronted him from time to time.

At the time under discussion, the year 1904, Fleming turned his attention to the devising of a new form of detector. One reason for this was purely personal; he had long been afflicted with deafness and the condition was growing worse, making it impossible for him to hear a morse sounder in action and difficult to distinguish the clicks in an earphone. A detector which would give a visual indication would prove very useful to him. There was, however, a more general need, for the magnetic detector, although a great advance upon the coherer, was susceptible to the influence of strong static discharges, which could temporarily paralyse its operation.

Fleming first experimented with chemical rectifiers with no great success. It was at this point, in October 1904, that in casting around in his mind for possible alternatives, he remembered a curious incident which had occurred twenty-two years earlier when in 1882 he had been an electrical adviser to the Edison Electric Light Company of London.

At that time the early electric lamps had been plagued with a short filament life and a discoloration of the glass envelope. Edison was working on these problems in his laboratory at Menlo Park and so also was Fleming in London. Both agreed that the deposit on the glass was

106

an accumulation of carbon which was thrown off from the filament. Various expedients were tried in order to overcome this, one of which (first tried by Edison) consisted of a coating of tinfoil over the inside of the glass envelope in the area of maximum discoloration. It was hoped that by charging the tinfoil electrically, the carbon particles would be repelled to the filament.

To Edison's surprise, when the tinfoil was connected via a galvanometer to the positive side of the d.c. filament supply, a small current was registered as flowing from the filament to the foil; but when the latter was connected to the negative supply, no current at all flowed.

Edison did not pursue this matter, being preoccupied with improving the life of his electric lamps, but he recorded the incident and his discovery, known thereafter as the Edison Effect, became, after verification, a scientific curiosity and no more.

This was the incident which Fleming recalled in 1904. He had duplicated the experiment in 1882 and indeed one or two of the special lamps still lay in a laboratory cupboard. Hastily Fleming brought one to the bench and connected a supply voltage across the filament. He then connected the tinfoil to one side of the secondary winding of an oscillation transformer via a galvanometer, and the other side of the winding to the negative side of the filament's d.c. supply.

The result was exactly that which he had hoped for. When a small spark transmitter was switched on in the laboratory, the waves, reaching the receiver, were transferred as alternating currents to the transformer secondary winding, then rectified by the experimental lamp. When the foil was positive with respect to the filament a current flowed and was registered by the galvanometer. On the reverse cycle no current flowed. Fleming had found the visual detector he was seeking.

In the twenty-two years which had elapsed since the original discovery, considerable improvements had been made in the manufacture of lamp filaments. Fleming's next step was to arrange for the construction of a modern (1904) lamp with a filament which was encircled by a metal cylinder. This performed even more convincingly than the original and so Fleming lost no time in patenting the device (Patent No. 24,850).

Thus on 16 November 1904, the thermionic valve was born. Fleming wrote to Guglielmo Marconi telling him of his discovery and added as an afterthought 'I have not mentioned this to anyone yet as it may become very useful'.

Just how useful it was going to be, Fleming at that time had no idea;

neither had Marconi, but he saw enough potential in the device to order it to be put into production. Fleming christened his invention the oscillation valve; he used the term 'valve' as descriptive of its one-way action (the terminology continues in Britain to this day) and 'oscillation' as indicative of its sphere of activity and not in any sense of being able to generate oscillations, which of course it could not.

The Fleming oscillation valve (or diode, as it is called today) did not in itself emerge as a device that brought profit to the Company. On the contrary, it cost Marconi dear by reason of the extensive litigation which followed when the celebrated American inventor Dr Lee de Forest announced his amplifying triode or Audion, a couple of years later. But more of this in due course.

Neither did the oscillation valve supersede the magnetic detector, for it was not quite so sensitive as the *Maggie* and certainly not so robust. It was, however, not so susceptible to the effects of heavy static discharges and was, largely for this reason, often used as a standby to the magnetic detector.

Fleming continued as a consultant to the Marconi Company almost up to the time of his death on 18 April 1945, at the advanced age of ninety-five. Over the years he had continued to contribute valuable research papers and inventions and had received full recognition in the broad field of electronic engineering by awards of the Gold Albert Medal of the Royal Society of Arts, the Faraday Medal of the Institution of Electrical Engineers, the Kelvin Medal and the Franklin Medal. In 1929 he was knighted for his valuable services to science and industry.

In assessing the highlights of Sir John Ambrose Fleming's career, many would hold that the invention of the thermionic diode was his greatest achievement; this is possibly so from the standpoint of its effect upon civilization, but for sheer engineering brilliance, his work upon the first high-power station at Poldhu must surely rank at least as its peer. Perhaps, when all is said and done, his work as Professor of Electrical Engineering at University College, London, was of greatest overall value, for many hundreds of radio engineers were trained by him, in due course to take their places as leaders in the field of electronics and to make their own contributions to the sum total of knowledge.

Fleming packed into a lifetime as much labour as could reasonably be expected from any four men. A brilliant theoretician, a very capable practical instrument maker, a first-class lecturer and an author of textbooks which became standard sources of reference for engineers the world over – somehow, Fleming found time for all these and other activities, and upon each was stamped the hallmark of immaculate, lucid reasoning. When he died, full of years, he had had the satisfaction of seeing a world industry grow from those crucial experiments carried out in 1904.

12

The Directional Antenna

Early in 1905 the then Managing Director, Mr H. Cuthbert Hall, decided that a factory in London was advisable and the Works equipment was accordingly transferred from Chelmsford to a large four-storey, three-wing building at Dalston in North London. In this new factory, not only was the Company's wireless equipment manufactured, but also a temporary entry was made into another promising new industry, for at this period the Company began the mass production of ignition coils for automobiles.

It will be recalled that the Wireless Telegraphy Act of Great Britain which was passed in August 1904, became effective on 1 January 1905. This event was of considerable importance to the Company for it rationalized its position with respect to the G.P.O. by defining with clarity the legal position in regard to the handling of commercial messages via the agency of wireless telegraphy. Up until this time the Company had conducted its ship-to-shore traffic in the British Isles on rather a grace-and-favour basis, in the uneasy feeling that a sharp change in the political wind could bring disaster. The new Act, by the granting of licences to transmit and receive, brought a stability to the Company that was reflected all through the organization.

By this time wireless telegraphy was becoming recognized by the world's shipping companies, not only as a useful asset to commercial trading but also as a form of insurance for their passenger-carrying vessels. To the timid passenger there was a wealth of reassurance in the sight of a ship's wireless antenna, providing as it did, the implicit promise of continuous communication either with the shore or with other vessels in the vicinity, and, accordingly, ships so equipped were in demand, particularly on the North Atlantic run. The latest leading shipping company to have wireless installations aboard its fleet had been the White Star Line, the *Oceanic* being fitted in January 1905, with the *Baltic*, the *Cedric*, the *Celtic* and the *Majestic* following in quick succession.

With the passing of the Wireless Telegraphy Act the organization of ship-to-shore traffic could push ahead in an atmosphere of confidence. Much of its success was derived from the leadership of Andrew Gray who was in technical control of the service and had nursed it through its infancy to the point where it was a thoroughly reliable service to the shipping lines and their passengers.

On the experimental side of the Company's activities, research at this time was mainly concentrated on the development of the Fleming oscillation valve and upon Marconi's personal dream of the establishment of a regular transatlantic service.

It will be recalled that in May 1904 a decision had been taken to select a new site for the Glace Bay station, with the main objective of acquiring enough land area to build a much larger antenna system. However, legalities intervened and possession of the selected site was not obtained until November of that year.

Throughout the hard winter months the engineers and labourers toiled, dismantling the equipment, the buildings, the masts and everything useful at the old station and re-erecting them on the new site some five miles distant and about three and a half miles inland.

The antenna system now consisted of an umbrella of two hundred wires with the original four towers in the centre, from which the wires

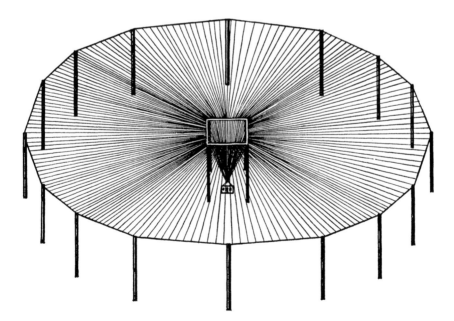

Figure 12.1 Glace Bay Antenna, 1905 (inner towers not shown).

ran laterally to two concentric rings of 180 ft. masts, eight in the inner circle and sixteen in the outer (Fig. 12.1). Provision was also made to extend the diameter of the umbrella still further if required, by means of an outer circle of forty-eight poles, each 50 ft. high. The diameter without this extension was 2,220 ft. and this could, by the means described, be brought to 2,900 ft. A special earthing system was also fitted. By May 1905 the station was in a state of readiness for the carrying out of test transmissions, Marconi himself visiting the site to supervise the tuning process. This completed, he sailed for Liverpool on the *Campania* to test the effective transmission range.

The improvement recorded was good – reception up to a distance of 1,800 miles in daylight, a fifty per cent increase on that obtained with the original Glace Bay station – but it was not considered good enough by Marconi who had had expectations of reception all the way across the Atlantic. Tests were continued in conjunction with the Poldhu station and in June 1905, two-way communication was effected in full daylight, the wavelength being approximately 3,660 m.

This was good news, but it was overshadowed by the importance of a discovery which Marconi had made while carrying out the tests at Poldhu. He had found that an antenna wire laid upon the ground could give stronger reception when its free end was pointing away from the transmitting station than when it was pointing towards it. A series of tests showed that this was no freak; the antenna (if the wire could be so called) exhibited definite directional properties. Further experiments showed that 'inverted L' antennas also behaved in this way provided that the horizontal part was several times the length of the down lead. It was further found (as might be supposed) that the directional effect was equally apparent with a transmitting antenna of this type.

This was a discovery of profound importance. Hastily, the information

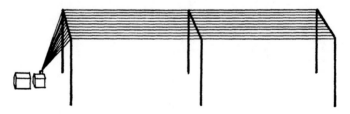

Figure 12.2 Marconi's 'Bent Aerial' (Antenna), providing directional transmission and reception. (Patent registered 18 July 1905.)

was sent to the Glace Bay station with instructions to lower three-quarters of the umbrella antenna, leaving only the segment facing away from England in circuit. Signals received at Poldhu improved considerably.

The so-called 'Bent Aerial' (antenna) not only constituted a significant advance in terms of ranges obtained but was also simpler to construct than the inverted cone and the umbrella types which were in common usage at the time. Marconi lost no time in taking out a patent for the horizontal directional antenna, this being registered on 18 July 1905.

This success allowed Marconi (as representing the research arm of the Company) to apply sufficient leverage to the Board of Directors to persuade them that a more powerful European station was necessary if the dream of a reliable commercial transatlantic service was to become reality. At first it was intended to rebuild Poldhu but it was soon realized that the site was not large enough to contain the long antennas contemplated, and in considering alternatives, the west coast of Ireland was an obvious contender. At that time of course, the whole of Ireland was under British rule; furthermore, a site there offered a shorter Atlantic path. So Ireland was decided upon.

On 25 July 1905, Marconi and two assistants left Cork for Cashel in County Galway and carried out receiving tests in that area. A site was chosen at Clifden and, with characteristic enthusiasm, work on clearing the ground and constructing buildings was in hand by October.

In December a demonstration of directional working was given to Naval authorities, using a vessel cruising off the Cornish coast and transmitting signals from various bearings. This was the first augury of wireless direction finding, which in vastly improved form was to play such an important part in World War I, a decade later.

13

More Inventions and Discoveries

It is a rather curious fact that for nearly ten years after the invention of wireless telegraphy, the engineers of the day possessed no portable test instrument which was capable of checking the wavelength of the signals.

This situation was rectified in 1905 when Dr J. A. Fleming developed the first portable wavemeter, or 'cymometer' as he called it, which enabled the operator to read the frequency (or wavelength) of any energized radiator to which it was coupled, directly from a scale on the instrument; the correct reading was indicated by a maximum brilliancy in a neon tube which was in circuit. Not the least remarkable aspect of this device was its simplicity of operation; the inductive and capacitative variable elements were controlled by one adjusting knob – one of the earliest examples of ganged tuning, although not the first, for C. S. Franklin had embodied a ganging principle in his multiple tuner a year earlier.*

On the commercial side of the Company's activities at this period was the welcome contract from Trinity House to equip five more lightships with wireless telegraphy. The *Sunk* lightship installation was completed in September 1905 and the *Gull* and *South Goodwin* in January 1906. The *Cross and* off Yarmouth was completed in July 1906.

Towards the end of 1905 the Australian Government became interested in the establishment of wireless communication between the mainland and Tasmania and also to some of the outlying islands. The undersea cable to Tasmania in particular was unsatisfactory as the rugged nature of the sea bottom in Bass Strait was constantly fracturing it. A mission was sent to Australia and demonstration plant was installed to communicate across the 230 miles from Port Lonsdale, near Queenscliff and East Devonport, Tasmania.

The two stations began operation in June 1906 and proved satisfactory in service. In November the first working demonstration of wireless in New Zealand was given between a station erected in the grounds of the

* Although developed in 1904 it was not patented until 1907.

New Zealand International Exhibition at Christchurch and a similar station some miles away.

No immediate orders resulted from these demonstrations as discussions were postponed until the termination of a Colonial Premiers' Conference later in the year. At this conference it was proposed to discuss the projected use of wireless communications in the Pacific in conjunction with the implications of the 1906 International Conference on wireless which took place in October. This conference, which was held in Madrid, ratified the main proposals of the 1903 Berlin conference, namely that all coastal wireless stations should receive from, and transmit to, all shipping regardless of the type of apparatus which the vessels were using. The British Government, with its control over British wireless stations established by the passing of the Wireless Telegraphy Act of 1904, agreed to the proposal as did all the other countries involved.

In retrospect, it was eminently the right decision to take; unfortunately it deprived the Marconi Company of its trump card as a brief review of the position will show:

Up until this time the Marconi Company had painstakingly built up a large number of shore stations, both at home and overseas, to handle the message traffic to ships equipped with the Company's apparatus and to no others except in an emergency. These stations, which far outnumbered those of its commercial rivals, were a strong inducement to the shipping lines to sign a contract for the Marconi wireless service whereby the sea-going equipment was hired complete with trained operators, thereby providing an 'all-in' arrangement for the efficient working of which Marconi's were entirely responsible.

With the signing of the agreement, the Marconi shore stations were no longer sacrosanct to those ships using Marconi apparatus. Henceforth, any ship might use them without contributing liability or expense. As a consequence the shipping lines were now free to use any form of wireless apparatus they cared to choose and still make full use of the Marconi shore stations.

Behind the political scenes, this decision was a triumph for the Telefunken Company, who had easily the most to gain under the new arrangement. But even though the Marconi Company spoke vehemently against the new provisions when a House of Commons Select Committee considered the matter in March 1907, the provisions of the Convention were confirmed by a majority vote of one. On the larger canvas of the struggle for power between Britain and Germany it was a distinct score for the latter.

A further recommendation by this International Conference was that the distress call CQD ('CQ' – phonetically 'seek you' – meaning calling all stations and 'D' for 'Danger') should be superseded by SOS. It should perhaps be noted in passing that these letters do not stand for anything specific, despite popular belief to the contrary. The letters were adopted as being the easiest to send and the most distinctive to decipher. Although the recommendations came into force in 1908, the CQD distress call continued to be used at times for some years after SOS became official.

In 1906 another setback occurred when the Company, by now confident of its ability to provide long-distance communications in any part of the world, put forward to the British Colonial Office its first proposal for a British Imperial Wireless scheme in which communications between Britain and the Dominions were to be effected by means of 1,000 mile wireless links. Such a scheme was, however, far too revolutionary for its time and was rejected. Nevertheless, the idea survived and was to bear fruit nearly two decades later.

Yet the year was by no means entirely filled with reverses. The British Post Office, after ten years of indecision, decided that it was time that its communication system included wireless telegraphy, and accordingly began to fill in gaps where overland wires or submarine cables were impracticable.

A case in point was the Outer Hebrides. In May 1906 the Post Office placed a contract with the Marconi Company for a wireless link between Loch Boisdale, South Uist, and Tobermory, Mull. Another wireless station was built for the Post Office at Bolt Head, South Devon.

Meanwhile the construction of the Clifden station in Southern Ireland was proceeding apace. It embodied every new and proven device known to the Marconi engineers. The antenna system was of the recently-developed directional type, aligned for maximum radiation towards Canada and operating on a wavelength of approximately 6,666 m. (actually 45 kHz).

The transmitting equipment also differed radically from that previously employed. The type of capacitor which had been employed at Poldhu used glass plates as the dielectric separating the metal plates; this method had been none too satisfactory and for Clifden and its sister station at Glace Bay it was decided to use air as the dielectric between the plates of the capacitor. A large building to house this giant capacitor was built and the metal plates were suspended at a separation distance of twelve inches from each other. This capacitor proved to be more efficient electrically than its predecessors and, because air is a self-healing dielectric, an accidental arc-over between plates had no serious consequences and caused only momentary interruption to the service.

The generating plant used was also a complete innovation. This provided an output of 300 kW direct current at a maximum potential of 20,000 volts. The direct current served to charge banks of secondary storage cells; in all, 6,000 cells each of forty ampere-hour capacity were used to give a potential of approximately 12,000 volts. These cells were grouped in relatively small banks and suspended in stands from the ceiling by means of insulators. Electrically operated switches isolated the battery into sections of a potential low enough to be handled without risk to personnel.

This system, which superseded the alternator method used at the Poldhu station eventually enabled both Clifden and Glace Bay* to operate for sixteen hours out of the twenty-four without recourse to the main generator.

When using the cells only, a working voltage of between 11,000 and 12,000 volts was obtained and when working with batteries and generator together the voltage could be increased to 15,000 volts.

Another important development which was taking shape in 1906 was the disc discharger, for which a patent was taken out in September 1907. To see this invention in its true perspective it is necessary to recall something of the state of the art of wireless telegraphy at the time.

Stations were becoming much more numerous and this situation raised the problem of co-station interference. Whilst it is true that the syntonic or tuned system had been the master-stroke in the minimizing of this, it could not be wholly effective because of the heavily damped oscillations produced by the conventional spark gap, which produced radiations over a wide band of frequencies and thereby flattened the tuning. If, therefore, some means could be found to produce continuous oscillations instead of highly damped wavetrains, the receivers desiring to pick up this transmission could be tuned precisely to this frequency; more important still, a slight readjustment of the receiver-tuned circuits would be sufficient to lose this transmission and to receive another on an adjacent wavelength or frequency. As matters stood with a transmitter using the conventional spark-gap the receiving station might alter its tuning very considerably and still be unable to get rid of the transmission.

The apparatus first devised is shown in Fig. 13.1. A metal disc A,

---

* Glace Bay used the Poldhu alternator method until fire destroyed the transmitter in 1909. It was then rebuilt to the Clifden design.

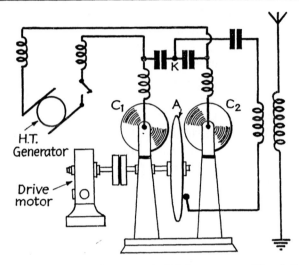

Figure 13.1 Marconi's Rotating Disc Discharger, 1907. (Timed disc)

insulated from earth, is rotated at a very high speed. Adjacent to this disc are placed two other discs C_1 and C_2 (called polar discs) and these also can be rotated at high speed. These polar discs have their peripheries very close to the edges of the middle disc (A).

Two capacitors in series (K) have their free terminals connected to the polar discs – one terminal to each – and the capacitors are also connected via suitable inductances to the terminals of a high-tension d.c. generator. The middle disc (A) is connected to the mid-point of these series capacitors via an inductance and capacitor, the inductance being coupled to an antenna.

When the high tension power was supplied with the discs stationary, an ordinary arc was established across the small gaps between the polar disc and the middle one. But when the three discs were rapidly rotated a discharge passed which Marconi described as 'neither an oscillatory spark or an ordinary arc', and continuous oscillations having frequencies of up to 200 kc/s resulted.

It is perhaps appropriate to pause and consider at this point whether Marconi, in producing a continuous wave type of oscillation, had not put himself in possession of a practical form of wireless telephony. But, in fact, the generation of continuous waves was no new achievement. It had been shown by Duddell in 1900 that a carbon arc is capable of producing continuous waves, and several pioneers, notably Poulsen, had experimented, with limited degrees of success, with the problem of using such waves as a carrier of telephony. Two obstacles proved almost insuperable, namely the generation of an oscillation which was sufficiently stable in frequency and amplitude, and the difficulty of devising a suitable and convenient means of modulating the carrier wave.

So, for these reasons, it is no occasion for surprise to find that Marconi, although he had found a new way of generating continuous waves, was not sidetracked into experimenting with wireless telephony. He no doubt realized that, had he done so, the main problems still needed to be solved, and he accordingly kept to his original project, although others within the Company were keeping an eye on wireless telephony as will be seen. But with the development of the disc discharger something of a

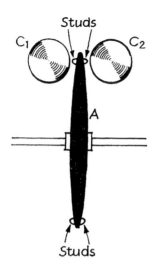

Figure 13.2 Detail of Modified Discs, producing musical note.

contretemps occurred. Although Marconi had succeeded in achieving the ideal waveform for the maximum degree of selectivity to be obtained at the receiver, the unmodulated carrier would of course be inaudible in the earphones and interrupting it via a morse key would not produce a signal which was readily recognizable. The new discharger clearly had to be modified. The solution was simple and elegant. Instead of making the middle disc with a completely smooth surface it was provided with copper studs fixed at regular intervals in its periphery and placed transversely to its plane (Fig. 13.2). The studs were arranged so as almost, but not quite, to make contact with the polar discs in passing. This arrangement serves to interrupt the continuous wave periodically and so make the signal audible when received on a magnetic detector or diode detector. By the use of a suitable number of studs a musical note is produced at the receiver which is in strong contrast to the rasp of a conventional spark gap and is much more easily read through static interference.

So, during the months of 1906, the station at Clifden grew, dwarfing Poldhu in its size, which was that of a fairly big factory. The turbines which were to drive the generators were provided with steam from peat-fired boilers, and a unique feature of the huge installation was the Marconi Light Railway which transported the stacks of peat from the bogs one and a half miles away to the furnaces. On the other side of the Atlantic, Glace Bay was also being equipped with the new types of transmitting equipment. The project was no small strain on the Company's financial resources and one can readily imagine the qualms of the Board of Directors as Marconi poured hard-earned money into what must have appeared to be a highly speculative venture.

Few of them, however, lost any sleep over a device which was announced at the end of 1906. This was the carborundum detector, discovered by General Dunwoodie of the United States Army; a simple device indeed but one which promoted the first practical awareness of the existence of solid substances which did not obey Ohm's Law, and which soon led to the development of a variety of forms of crystal detector which were to challenge the supremacy of the magnetic detector in no uncertain manner. During the years to come many varieties of crystal detector were to make their appearance, some good, some bad, some indifferent. But although this type of detector at its best was sensitive and was not so susceptible to static interference as the magnetic detector, its lack of robustness enabled the *Maggie* to reign supreme for many years.

It was true that the Company had a 'second string' detector in the Fleming diode, but this, in the rudimentary state of the art at that time, was certainly not robust and not quite so sensitive as either the crystal or the magnetic detector. It did, however, permit fast operation and on demonstration was shown to be capable of handling one hundred words per minute.

Another cloud on the horizon, although no bigger than a man's hand, was a valve patent by Dr Lee de Forest in 1906, which added a third electrode to the existing diode and which was alleged to provide means of amplifying weak signals. At that time no clear idea of the exact function of this third electrode seems to have existed and in any event the device would not have provided amplification with the external arrangement as shown in the patent application. The following year, however, de Forest took out another patent and this time the valve (tube) and its associated circuits had practical possibilities. Undeniably, the de Forest 'Audion', as its inventor called it, had little to offer in the way of amplification and was a temperamental performer in that often for no apparent reason its third electrode (nicknamed the gridiron and shortened to grid) seemed to fulfil no function at all. But equally undeniably, in its day the Audion could provide a little amplification, which the Fleming diode could not.

The Marconi Company grew alarmed. That tiny cloud which had appeared innocuous enough in 1906 had become a menacing overcast in the space of a few months, for it was realized that in all probability the Audion's principle, if developed along the right lines, could provide a key device for the future.

It therefore became vital to the Company's interests that the introduction of the third electrode or grid should be considered as a variant of the diode patent and not as an invention in its own right, and legal proceedings were instituted to defend this position. The decision to go to law was one in which the Company had little option, and at first all seemed well, for the validity of the Fleming valve as a master patent was upheld in a United States court. In the event, however, the litigation cost everyone concerned a great deal of time and money and only the lawyers grew fat. The decision was overset by another Court and action and counter-action dragged on for years. The issue was not settled finally until the 1920s and even then was in the nature of a truce.

The costs of these early actions were ones which neither the Marconi Company nor de Forest could afford to lay out. The irony of the early lawsuits lay in the fact that the fight was over what at the time was a worthless device, for it was not until 1913–14 that advances in valve technology made the triode into a worthwhile commercial proposition.

Another development in embryo form at this time was the wireless telephone. Since 1900, when Duddell discovered that an arc was capable of generating continuous waves, various experimenters had investigated the problem of modulating such waves with speech frequencies. Several workers, notably Fessenden, Poulsen and Koepsel had succeeded in radiating telephony transmissions, but the essential obstacles, namely a satisfactory method of modulation, and the distortion created by the impurity of the continuous waves, were still unsolved.

In 1906–7, H. J. Round of the Marconi Company, who was subsequently to play a major part in the development of British broadcasting, entered the arena. Round, after obtaining First Class Honours at the Royal College of Science, had joined the Company in 1902 when he was sent to America (where incidentally he had as an office junior a youngster by the name of David Sarnoff, now President of the Radio Corporation of America and an internationally famous figure). During his stay in America and after his return in 1906, Round, between other assignments, experimented with arc telephony transmitters to such effect that in 1908 he was able to demonstrate the transmission of intelligible speech over a distance of fifty miles. The quality, however, was far from good, and the practical wireless telephone had to await a fundamental new discovery in connection with the triode valve in 1913, a development in which Round was again to figure prominently.

14

The Transatlantic Service Realized

Early in 1907 the Company was called on at short notice to render aid to the British Post Office, when the hundred-mile cable between Guernsey and the mainland was fractured and Marconi's were asked to install a temporary link. This was promptly done and the traffic was handled by wireless until repair was effected. A station having the new type of directive antenna was then installed at Jersey for the War Office.

A contract to fit the luxury steam yacht *Iolanda* with the most up-to-date design of ship set provided an opportunity to redesign the standard ship's equipment completely. This was an important step forward, for the new design eliminated the old laboratory type of apparatus with its Leyden jars and induction coil. In its stead the $1\frac{1}{2}$ kW shore set was modified to derive its input power from the ship's electricity supply and provided three possible transmission wavelengths, namely 300, 450 and 600 m. This equipment, designed by Andrew Gray, became the standard shipboard installation for several years to come.

By mid-1907 the Clifden station was completed and some preliminary tests had been carried out. Marconi, during those summer months, was alternating between the two terminals of the transatlantic circuit, Clifden and Glace Bay, supervising the final adjustments. It was a nerve-racking time. So much money had been poured into the construction of these giant stations that the effect on the Company, should a satisfactory transatlantic service not materialize, could scarcely be contemplated.

On 15 October 1907, zero hour arrived. A number of notabilities on either side of the Atlantic had been invited to hand in inaugural telegrams, and there was a strained silence at the Clifden station as, at 11.30 a.m. precisely, the duty operator set his hand to the key, tapping a message from Lord Avebury to the *New York Times*. The engineers must have been vastly relieved as a congratulatory message was received from Glace Bay by way of reply.

All day long the messages passed as traffic between the stations.

Transmission conditions were perfect. The transmitters and receivers worked without a hitch. In all, 10,000 words were sent and received. The engineer in charge of Glace Bay expressed the feelings of all when he wrote:

'Only those who worked with Marconi throughout these [past] four years realize the wonderful courage he showed under frequent disappointments, the extraordinary fertility of his mind in inventing new methods to displace others found faulty, and his willingness to work, often for sixteen hours at a time, when any interesting development was being tested. At the same time the Directors of the Marconi Company showed wonderful confidence in Marconi, and courage in continuing to vote the large sums necessary from year to year until success was finally achieved.'

It was a moment of triumph for all concerned and in no circumstances was it better earned. But life rarely offers the perfect fruit of success and this occasion was no exception. The worm in this case was the land line between Glace Bay and New York which provided 800 miles of trouble for the new service by being almost permanently overloaded with traffic. The practical consequence was that although the messages from London were received at Glace Bay without significant loss of time, the delay in onward transmission to New York over the land line could amount to as much as twelve hours. By contrast, the transocean cable came from Europe direct to New York and its messages suffered no comparable delay.

That the wireless circuit could do as well if given the chance was proved by a test carried out by the *New York Times* in which the land-line was cleared for a short space of all traffic other than that from the wireless station. During that period messages filed in London were received in New York within ten minutes of their despatch.

By 8 February 1908, nearly 120,000 words had been transmitted and the traffic had been extended to Montreal and London by land lines linking Glace Bay with Montreal and Clifden with London. The South Wellfleet (Cape Cod) transmitter was improved by the installation of a Poldhu-type twelve-stud disc discharger which was later increased to twenty-four-stud.

The year 1908 saw the beginnings of a new era of re-evaluation and consolidation of Company strengths, with strenuous attempts made to repair breaches in its structure. For the future looked none too rosy; the original impetus of technical achievement had stabilized; the Marconi Company was no longer a small brotherhood of engineers but a growing commercial organization with shareholders who naturally wished to see some return for their investments.

A considerable setback had been experienced when a Select Committee of the House of Commons decided, by a majority of one, to ratify the 1906 International Convention on Wireless Communication at Sea. This, which became operative in 1908, destroyed the Marconi Company's virtual monopoly of sea-going and ship-to-shore traffic. From this time forward the merit of the equipment alone would decide shipowners whether British or foreign wireless apparatus should be installed on their vessels. Even at best the market was not over-large, for the shipping lines were in business to make money also and were not too eager to lay it out for the installation of equipment which, although potentially valuable in an emergency, might well never have to figure in such a situation. In short, although fresh ships were being fitted, the rate was nothing like as great as had been anticipated.

In March 1908, Mr Cuthbert Hall, the Managing Director, resigned, and at the request of the Board Marconi took over his duties until a suitable appointment could be made. He had as his aides Mr H. Jameson Davis and Major Flood-Page, both ex-Managing Directors of the Company.

Financially, the Marconi Company was making heavy weather. The transatlantic wireless service, although it had satisfied Marconi's ambition by being a technical triumph, was running at a loss and hampered by the land-line delays mentioned earlier. On the production side, the large four-storey Works at Dalston had proved something of a white elephant, being quite unsuitable for the needs of the Engineering Department. At that time the Company, in order to supplement its relatively small income from wireless equipment, was undertaking the mass production of automobile ignition coils and this was the mainstay of the Dalston Works. Unfortunately the motor industry had slumped and with it the orders for ignition coils. So the Dalston Works was also losing money.

Much as Marconi wished to press on with his experiments his presence was needed on the administrative side. A policy of retrenchment was the only rational course. The Dalston Works was closed down and eventually disposed of, and the original factory at Hall Street, Chelmsford which, providentially, was still held on a 20-year lease, was re-opened. Further development of the ignition coil business ceased. Shortly after, the Company increased its capital to £750,000 by the issue of 250,000 Preference Shares at £1 each.

At the same time, no opportunity was lost to try to open up new overseas markets wherever possible. Such a prospect was in mind when a Russian firm of wireless manufacturers was taken over, and, on 8 October 1908, the Russian Company of Wireless Telegraphs and Telephones was formed.

There now occurred an incident which illustrates how near the Company was to financial shipwreck; it also demonstrates the loyalty to Marconi which existed amongst his engineering staff.

Earlier in the year Marconi had succeeded in redirecting attention to the possibility of linking the British Empire by means of wireless, and this had been augmented by a letter written to *The Times* newspaper advocating 'Imperial Wireless Communications'. This had been written by Mr R. N. Vyvyan, a senior engineer of the Company, who had recently been appointed Superintending Engineer.

Vyvyan, who had been actively involved in the transatlantic work, obtained Marconi's permission to pay a visit to South Africa in an endeavour to get business. The permission, however, was conditional, the stipulation being that Vyvyan should pay his own expenses unless he returned with orders. The fact was that the Company had no spare funds to lay out against problematical returns such as this.

Vyvyan accepted the condition and in the following year visited South Africa, where he interviewed General Botha and General Smuts. It transpired that both had read his letter to *The Times* and were enthusiastic in their support of the project. Vyvyan sold the South African Government two stations on the spot, one for Durban and the other for Slangkop, Cape of Good Hope. On his return to England he received his expenses.

In January 1909 a sea tragedy occurred which, had it not been for the existence of wireless, would have resulted in heavy loss of life. On the 22nd of that month the White Star Line *Republic* (15,000 tons) collided in dense fog with the Italian ship *Florida* when twenty-six miles southwest of Nantucket.

The *Republic* carried only one wireless operator, who was off duty at the time of the collision. On scrambling to his wireless cabin he found it partially wrecked, with the main power supply to his equipment cut off, but switching to the emergency battery supply he sent out the (old) international distress call CQD. Siasconset, the nearest land station, picked up the call and re-radiated it to wireless-equipped shipping in the area.

By this time the *Republic*, which had had by far the worst of the en-

counter, was in a bad way; accordingly her 460 passengers were transferred to the *Florida*, severely overcrowding her. Meanwhile the distress
signals had been received by the sinking vessel's sister ship, the *Baltic* and
also by the *Touraine*. The *Baltic*, over 200 miles away, steamed through
fog at twenty-two knots, reaching the disaster area within twelve hours.
With the *Republic's* wireless operator providing rough bearings, the
Baltic located her, arriving just as the fog lifted. At night, and in a torren-
tial rainstorm, 1,690 passengers (the total from both ships) were transferred to the rescue liner.

The *Florida* was escorted to port but the *Republic* sank later that day.
The total casualties amounted to five, all killed as a result of the collision.
The rest of the passengers and crew owed their lives to the wireless
installation, the courage of the Marconi operator, Jack Binns, and the
seamanship displayed by the captain and crew of the *Baltic*.

Another set-back for the Company occurred in the autumn of 1909
when the public wireless service between Clifden and Glace Bay was
interrupted by a serious fire at the latter station. The transmitter and the
receiving apparatus were completely destroyed although the power
plant, which was housed in a separate building, was unaffected.

Work was immediately put in hand to restore the service with all
speed. At the same time opportunity was taken to modernize the transmitting equipment by providing high tension d.c. generators and an
h.t. battery of 6,000 cells to the same general pattern as at the highly
successful station at Clifden. A departure from previous practice was,
however, made with the receiving apparatus which was installed in a
building half a mile away from the transmitter, with a separate antenna
system for incoming signals. Another innovation was the remote control
gear installed in the receiver building, whereby the transmitter would be
run up or shut down by remote control (a method, incidentally, which is
still common practice today). Work went on through the winter months
and the new Glace Bay station opened for traffic on 23 April 1910.

Another activity within the Company which anticipated modern
practice was the study of the effects of wind pressure upon antenna
masts at different heights above ground level. Around this period (1909),
an intensive study of various designs of mast structure was initiated under
the supervision of Andrew Gray, the Chief of Staff. Wooden structures
had been abandoned in favour of steel and experiments were carried out
to assess the relative advantages and disadvantages of lattice and tubular
types of structure, whether they should be stayed or self-supporting and
whether they should be insulated from the ground or not.

Finally the Engineering Department under Andrew Gray evolved a design of sectionalized tubular wire-stayed mast, sections of which in model form were tested in the National Physical Laboratory's wind tunnel. Full-scale sections were subjected to a series of rigorous tests, including tests to destruction. Not until the mast had survived stresses and strains which were far in excess of anything likely to be experienced in the field, was the design accepted. The first 200 ft. mast was erected at the Chelmsford Hall Street Works in 1909. A year later, masts of this type ('Gray' masts, as they were called) were used overseas for the first time, on which occasion they were erected in an Amazon jungle. So successful did the 'Gray' mast prove that the type was for many years the standard for medium- and high-power installations. Later, the design was modified to provide 400 ft. and 450 ft. masts and these proved equally satisfactory.

In addition to the South African orders obtained by Vyvyan the Company received a most welcome contract from the Admiralty for three complete stations, one at the Admiralty itself, one at Hornsea and the third at Cleethorpes. These were to be used for purposes of centralized Fleet control.

In December 1909, Marconi lectured at the Royal Academy of Science, Stockholm, in connection with the award of the Nobel Prize for Physics which he shared with Professor Braun, chief technical consultant to the Telefunken Company.

So ended 1909. All in all, a trying year, as had been its predecessor. Two years of triumph alternating with misfortunes and near disasters. A period of financial touch-and-go, when the decisive factor was in all probability the magic which, in the lay mind, had become associated with the name of Guglielmo Marconi. The move of appointing him Managing Director upon the resignation of Cuthbert Hall was an astute one, both for its calming influence on the shareholders and for turning his zeal aside temporarily from research to the resolute pruning of his Company's dead wood which was to result in more vigorous growth for the future.

I5

The Commercial 'War' with Germany

Gradually over the first decade of the twentieth century the Marconi Company grew in size and, inevitably, in the complexity of its administration. In the early formative years its aims might be summarized as 'Invent, patent, develop and sell'. It was as simple as that – provided that the inventions were forthcoming, as indeed they were. Because of the newness of the art, sales were mostly on a 'one-off' basis, signifying that the customer was trying out the ultra-modern mode of communication. Only a small clerical staff was necessary and for the most part the engineers were also the salesmen.

But with the establishment of the usefulness of wireless telegraphy and the increasing complexity of the equipment, orders increased in size and value, with complete systems or chains of stations tending to replace the isolated 'one-off' order. Gone were the days when an engineer, carrying out an installation, would order his mast from a local timber yard and have it fashioned on the spot. Now, when the next order might require a dozen tubular steel masts, the sections had to be on hand against the contingency. Such a situation, multiplied by a hundred in different directions, called for careful forward planning. Contracts had to be carefully committed to paper and a considerable amount of correspondence entered into. With the growth of its engineering, operative and administrative staffs the Company was inevitably losing some of its flexibility.

Another significant change had taken shape in the gradual growth of competition. In Britain itself the Company had no serious challengers, but in the United States the American Marconi Company was experiencing serious opposition from the United Wireless Company, which controlled over five hundred ship installations and seventy land stations.

In Europe, various wireless companies were in the field, by far the most formidable of which was Telefunken,* that redoubtable German

* Literally 'spark at a distance' or 'far spark'.

organization which had on more than one occasion in the past been a thorn in the flesh.

Although the Marconi Company had, over the years, acquired a large number of master patents, it was known that these were being infringed by other companies. Unfortunately, legal action over such matters is liable to be more expensive than ignoring the infringements and the Company had no surplus finance to dissipate in long-drawn-out wrangles in the Courts.

Differences of opinion over the attitude to be taken over patent infringements had been one of the causes contributing to Cuthbert Hall's resignation in 1908, for Hall had hesitated to take a firm line on the issue. Marconi, who had succeeded him as Managing Director, had been too busy dealing with crisis after crisis and, furthermore, was impatient to return to the freer life of research. He and his co-directors had for some time been looking for someone capable of taking over, but the desired attributes of energy, business acumen, intelligence linked with imagination and the requisite degree of aggressiveness were not easy to find.

At last a choice was made in the person of Godfrey C. Isaacs who in January 1910 became joint Managing Director and after a probation period took over full responsibility in the following August.

Godfrey Isaacs, from the onset, left no one in doubt about his intentions. He intended to enforce the Company's patent rights at all costs. One of his first actions was to institute proceedings against the British Radio Telegraph and Telephone Company for infringement of the 'Four Sevens' (Pat. No. 7777) of 1900 which covered the principles of tuning. Judgement was given in favour of Marconi's in March 1911.

Encouraged by this success the American Marconi Company in 1911 took action on similar grounds against the United Wireless Company and the Clyde Steamship Company; in the following year this case also ended in a verdict for the Marconi Company. Shortly afterwards, the United Wireless Company was absorbed into the American Marconi organization, bringing with it the seventy shore stations and the five hundred shipping installations referred to earlier.

But by far the biggest problem which confronted Godfrey Isaacs was how best to deal with the commercial menace offered by the German Telefunken Company. This organization, like Marconi's, offered a ship-shore service as an important part of its activities and also, like Marconi's, had grown in size and importance over the years. With their interests conflicting at every turn, it is scarcely surprising to find that the incessant struggle for markets which was going on behind the scenes should sometimes manifest itself in ill-will in public.

The situation was particularly difficult for the Marconi Company for, whereas it was only backed by strictly limited private capital and no sort of government aid, its rival had, in addition to a substantial State subsidy, the resources of the German banks behind it; and used these powerful weapons to the very best advantage. As a consequence, wherever a Marconi representative went in an attempt to interest a foreign government in wireless communication, it was found that German high-power salesmanship and diplomatic support had already been hard at work, usually to good effect. The predicament gave birth to a descriptive phase 'The Telefunken Wall'.

Not all the battles were lost however. In 1910 the Marconi Company was trying to interest the Spanish Government in its system, but unfortunately the Spanish authorities had already granted a concession for the erection of a wireless station to a French Company, although it was true that a tangible outcome was unlikely.

Marconi's had a much more ambitious plan than just one station. Theirs was a scheme to cover the whole country with a network of wireless stations which would provide both internal and external communications.

In the latter months of 1910 Marconi and Godfrey Isaacs went to Madrid to assay the situation at first hand, only to find that not only had they to contend with the French Company but that the ubiquitous Telefunken Wall hid their goal from view. The Spanish technicians were already Telefunken-minded and their Army and Navy were Telefunken-equipped.

Godfrey Isaacs persuaded the Spanish authorities to appoint a Technical Commission to report on the relative technical merits of the three competitors. The outcome of this was that the Commission found against the French Company and also against the Telefunken system. It also found against the Marconi proposal but only on the ground of cost, as well it might, for the Marconi project visualized a string of high-power stations at Aranjuez, near Madrid, Barcelona, Cadiz, Teneriffe, Las Palmas and Vigo as a means of serving not only the Iberian peninsula but also the Canary Islands, Italy, England, all Atlantic shipping and the two Americas.

Isaacs had realized that the Spanish Government would not agree to the huge cost involved, and by the time the decision was made he was ready with another proposal, whereby the Government could acquire the system without it costing them a single peseta. This could be done, he said, by granting wide and generous concessions to a Spanish company which would be formed to exploit the Marconi patents for the purpose of implementing the scheme.

The Spanish Government agreed, and as a result the Compania Nacional de Telegrafia sin Hilos, financed by the Marconi Company, came into existence on 24 December 1910. Construction of the stations went on for the next eighteen months and the complete network was inaugurated officially by King Alfonso on 19 May 1912. The King awarded Guglielmo Marconi the Grand Cross of the Order of King Alfonso XII.

This private war between Marconi's and Telefunken was, in Cuthbert Hall's time, fought behind the scenes, albeit with no quarter asked or given. The time had now come when a firm stand must be taken before the rest of the world. But first there were two distinct aspects of the situation to be considered, namely the Company's maritime interests, particularly within Germany itself and in its neighbouring countries, and the more general question of how best to breach the 'Telefunken Wall' in matters of general communications.

First, the maritime situation. The Marconi Company had made many attempts to gain a solid footing within Germany itself and two of the big German shipping lines, Hapag and Bremer Lloyd, were Marconi equipped, but most of the others carried Telefunken apparatus, so that there was little prospect of further Marconi contracts in these directions.

Despite the 1906 International Wireless Convention, which had been ratified in 1908, Marconi's were still boycotting messages – other than emergency calls – between their stations and those which did not use their apparatus. This was a considerable nuisance to Telefunken in particular, because the considerable volume of German shipping using the English Channel was unable to communicate with the British coastal stations. In German waters, however, the embargo was a two-edged sword, for Marconi-equipped vessels (and these included the two German shipping lines Hapag and Bremer Lloyd) were without general access to the Telefunken shore stations and most of the German shipping.

In short, the position was stalemate and the need for diplomacy was being recognized by both sides. The situation reached crisis point for the Marconi Company when, in 1910, the German Government declared that henceforth no foreign wireless apparatus would be permitted aboard German vessels.

At that time the Compagnie de Télégraphie sans Fils of Brussels was the licensee for Marconi patents in Germany, Austria and certain other countries in Europe. The German decree meant that the Belgian Company would have to remove all Marconi apparatus from German ships and would lose all hope of any further business in that direction.

There was only one sane course open, namely negotiation with the Telefunken Company. In due course an agreement was reached whereby a new German Company was formed in which the Belgian and Marconi Companies held a forty-five per cent interest and the Telefunken Company the remaining fifty-five per cent. The new organization, the Deutsche Betriebsgesellschaft für Drahtlose Telegraphie (D.E.B.E.G.) took over the wireless business of the entire German mercantile marine, with the resources of the hitherto rival systems for ship-to-shore and ship-to-ship signalling to be pooled and operated on a basis of full intercommunication.

Subsequent to the formation of D.E.B.E.G., which came into being on 14 January 1911, the Austrian Government took the same line as the Germans had done. It was then further agreed that the Austrian ship stations should be transferred to D.E.B.E.G. and that the new Company's sphere of action should be limited to dealing with German and Austrian shipping; foreign vessels which carried German or Austrian wireless apparatus should be within the province of the Belgian Company alone. This, the final phase of the agreement, did not come to conclusion until 1913, when the Belgian Company structure was reconstituted whereby Telefunken, Marconi and a Belgian banking consortium each held one-third of the total shares. The Company was renamed the Société Anonyme International de Télégraphie sans Fils (S.A.I.T.).

It is pertinent to record that upon the outbreak of World War I in 1914, the German interests in the Company were liquidated and its centre of operations temporarily removed to Marconi House, London. The Company still flourishes today as a valued associate of the Marconi Company; it is now known as 'S.A.I.T. Electronics'.

In retrospect, considering the weak bargaining position of the Marconi Company in 1910, this maritime agreement provided terms which were more than equitable to the British organization, providing early proof that in the person of Godfrey Isaacs a man of strength had been found to handle the complex commercial aspects.

So much then for the maritime communication struggle with the Telefunken Company. There still remained the general communications 'war' which was being waged all over Europe and in various other areas, and in this connection matters were approaching flash point with accusations of patent infringements being hurled from both sides.

This time Isaacs decided upon a show of strength. But first he consolidated his ground; an approach was made to Sir Edward Grey the Foreign Secretary, who, although unable to duplicate the powerful backing which the German Government was affording the Telefunken Company, nevertheless promised much needed aid from British Embassies abroad to counteract in some measure the powerful position of the German Company.

In considering the Company's patents position it did not take Isaacs long to discover that an Achilles heel existed in the matter of the all-important 'Four Sevens' tuning patent of 1900. This weakness, which was by reason of a complementary patent held by Sir Oliver Lodge, was eliminated by negotiation with that eminent scientist, which resulted in the Lodge-Muirhead patents being acquired by Marconi's and Sir Oliver himself becoming a scientific adviser to the Company.

The stage was now set as far as it might be. Isaac's first offensive against Telefunken was mounted by a legal action for infringement of the 'Four Sevens' patent against Siemens Brothers, acting in England for the Telefunken Company. In November 1912 it was announced that the validity of the patent was admitted by the German Company and that arrangements had been made whereby the dispute was ended.

But bigger game was afoot. At that time the Australian and New Zealand Governments had placed contracts with the Australian Wireless Company Ltd. (which was Telefunken-owned) for the construction of powerful coastal wireless stations. As the equipment for use in these installations was considered to infringe Marconi patents, Godfrey Isaacs took the bold course of sueing both the German-owned Company and the Australian Government. The outcome was that the High Court of Australia made an order (later confirmed by Lords of Appeal in London) authorizing a right of inspection of all wireless telegraphy plants in Australia, the inspections to be carried out by the Marconi Company.

This situation was resolved amicably in 1912 when agreement was reached between the contestants whereby a new Australian Company should be formed which would purchase the interests of the Marconi Company and the Telefunken Company throughout the continent. This Company had a capital of £140,000, with Marconi's holding one-half of the shares, the Australians some £62,000 worth and Telefunken about £8,000 worth. Thus, complete control of wireless in Australia passed into Australian and British hands. The Company, registered as

Amalgamated Wireless (Australasia) Ltd., has gone from strength to strength through the years and today is a highly valued associated Company of the Marconi organization.

These and other commercial agreements with the Telefunken Company did much to ease the Marconi position in the matter of making sales in various parts of the world. Turkey and Rumania became customers; the Greek Navy 'went Marconi' and in March 1912 an important provisional contract was signed by the Portuguese Government and the Company for the supply of five stations at the Azores, Madeira, Cape Verde Islands, Lisbon and Oporto. The function of these stations was to unify the Portuguese metropolitan and overseas terrain and to complete a network of wireless communications over the South Atlantic.

Mention must be made at this point of a man who played a vital part in the long-drawn-out 'battle' with the German Company. This was the Marquis Solari whose personal association with Guglielmo Marconi dated back to 1901, since which time until 1906 he had represented the Italian Navy at many of Marconi's demonstrations. In 1906 Solari joined the Company as its representative in Italy and quickly proved his value, not only as an engineer (he held a degree in electrical engineering) but as a salesman and negotiator. To Solari must go much of the credit for securing those vital contracts from Spain, Turkey, Rumania, Greece and Portugal, his commonsense eloquence and technical expertise often swaying a verdict Marconi-wards when the customer had been all but committed to purchase elsewhere.

An agreement signed in 1912 by the Telefunken Company and the Marconi Company ended the litigation over patents that had cost so much in time and money and provided for an exchange of patents, past and future. This happy ending to an otherwise unhappy phase was to prove beneficial to both Companies in the following year and after World War I.

Today both Companies are liable to find themselves as rival contenders for contracts, and when this happens the struggle is fierce, the award going sometimes to one, sometimes to the other. But, thanks to the lessons learned the hard way in the first decade of the century, keen commercial rivalry is no longer confused with vindictive animosity. The wounds have long since healed and a common respect is now the keynote of the relationship.

16

Momentous Events

Concurrent with the battle of the 'Telefunken Wall' there were momentous events on the home front.

Godfrey Isaacs, fulfilling his function as the long-awaited new broom, made many changes and innovations before he had been long in the Managing Director's chair. One of these is worth recording as an instance of tall oaks growing from little acorns. This was the inauguration in October 1910 of what in effect was an embryo Publicity Department, a private Company called 'The Marconi Press Agency Ltd.', the object of which was to disseminate to the general public items of wireless interest gleaned from the reports of engineers and operators in various parts of the world.

By the early months of 1911, so much information was being garnered that it was decided to publish it in the form of a monthly illustrated journal. *The Marconigraph*, as it was christened, was the first periodical in the world to deal exclusively with wireless matters. It was an immediate success; its growth and ever-widening scope led, in April 1913, to a change of title to *The Wireless World* as being more indicative of its editorial content.

Today, *The Wireless World* still ranks among the foremost of the electronics journals. Although it passed from Marconi ownership in 1925, it was with genuine pride that, in 1961, the Marconi Company was able to congratulate the journal upon its Golden Jubilee.

Guglielmo Marconi, once more back on engineering and research, was busying himself with improvements at the Glace Bay and Clifden stations. By September 1910 the transmitting wavelength at Clifden had been increased to 6,000 m., and Marconi, accompanied by H. J. Round, who was rapidly making a name for himself as a very capable engineer, sailed for Buenos Aires aboard the *Principessa Mafalda* in order to carry out range tests *en route*.

This exercise was not merely for the purpose of testing the new Clifden wavelength. It had a much greater significance, for with transatlantic wireless telegraphy now a matter of commercial routine, Marconi had replaced his old dream with a new one – the establishment of a chain of stations linking the British Empire and the world. The signal ranges obtained as the *Principessa Mafalda* steamed southward confirmed his every expectation – 4,000 miles by day and 6,775 miles by night.

The success was confirmed a year later when the 500 kW station at Coltano, Italy, was brought into service. Marconi was able to demonstrate to the King of Italy when he visited the station on 19 November 1911, that the station could communicate with Clifden, Glace Bay and the station at Massaua in Italian Eritrea, 2,400 miles away over sea and land. By the following month the Italian long wave receiving station at Ancona was taking telegraphic traffic from Poldhu at the rate of 5,000 words per hour.

The range of performances obtained *en route* to Buenos Aires provided impressive and tangible data upon which to base a proposal for an Imperial Wireless Scheme. This project was discussed at the Imperial Wireless Conference which took place in May 1911; the Empire statesmen were duly impressed and decided that an Imperial Wireless system should be created, but that it should be State owned.

In the Autumn of 1911, the Marconi Company began serious negotiations with the Post Office, from which emerged a tender which called for the erection of any desired number of long wave high-power stations at a cost of £60,000 per station, this cost to include all apparatus for duplex working. In addition to the payment per station there was to be a ten per cent royalty on the gross traffic receipts over a period of twenty-eight years.

By the end of the year Godfrey Isaacs and his directors had every reason to contemplate the prospect for the future with lively satisfaction. Inquiries and orders were flowing in; the Telefunken 'war' had abated to a truce which was honourable to both sides and the Imperial Wireless project seemed to be progressing very favourably in the Company's direction. All the signs were present to indicate the long-awaited boom in Company business.

Godfrey Isaacs determined to be ready when it came. For some time past, expansion of the Works at Hall Street, Chelmsford, had been taking place, but was insufficient to meet the demands of the present, let alone the future.

Isaacs decided that the time was opportune for the building of a new Works, designed on modern lines, equipped with the latest and best in the matter of tools, apparatus, test rooms and laboratories. He laid the proposal before the Board in terms of the utmost urgency, reminding them that in June an International Radiotelegraphic Conference was to be opened in London and that a visit by the delegates to inspect the new premises would be of inestimable value.

One tends to regard that long-ago era as one of leisurely progress; against this background the facts concerning the building of the new Works come as something of a shock. In January 1912 they existed only in the imagination of Godfrey Isaacs. By February, the Board of Directors had been converted to the cause, the site (one of ten acres, formerly the Essex County Cricket Ground) had been acquired and by the tenth of that month the site had been pegged out. Seventeen weeks later, despite the intervention of a building strike, all the workshops and laboratories were functioning. The changeover from the Hall Street premises to the new factory was accomplished over one weekend; by the Monday morning, Hall Street was silent and empty and the New Street Works humming with activity. The International Radiotelegraphic Conference delegates made their tour on 22 June 1912 and were vastly impressed. That evening, at the Savoy Hotel, London, the Directors were hosts at a banquet given to their four hundred guests, and on June 30 the delegates visited Poldhu as part of a weekend programme. The visit to this country terminated in a garden party at 'Eaglehurst', the Marconi private residence on the Solent.

Concurrent with the building of the new Works, Godfrey Isaacs also decided that new Headquarters premises in London were imperative, since the staff in the existing building, Watergate House, had long since overflowed into Durham House, and both buildings were now congested.

At that time the Gaiety Restaurant and its associated block of luxury flats were tenantless; an offer was made by the Company to the owners, the London County Council, and the terms of a ninety-nine-year lease agreed upon. The necessary structural alterations were completed in short time and on 25 March 1912, Marconi House, in the Strand, was formally opened.

On Sunday 14 April 1912, the greatest peacetime marine disaster in history occurred, when the *Titanic* of 46,328 gross tons struck an iceberg while on her maiden voyage from Southampton to New York and foundered within three hours. The circumstances of this tragedy have been so thoroughly documented that it is unnecessary to repeat them here, except in so far as they affected the future organization of wireless communication at sea.

While it is true that wireless telegraphy was the instrument whereby

712 people were saved that night, it is equally beyond dispute that 1,517 of the ship's company were lost, and this in spite of the fact that the sinking occurred in view of another vessel, the *Californian*, which steamed on without realizing what had occurred and (although equipped with wireless) without intercepting the distress calls put out by the stricken liner.

Whilst all sections of the public were generous in their praise of wireless telegraphy in general, and Mr Marconi in particular as the media of salvation for the rescued, the maritime authorities were profoundly shocked over various aspects of the sinking of the allegedly unsinkable *Titanic* and a series of exhaustive official inquiries was instituted. These revealed some disquieting circumstances.

One of these was that at 7.15 p.m. on that Sunday evening, the *Californian* wirelessed a warning that icebergs were in the vicinity. Similar messages were sent by at least three other ships in the area. The *Titanic* acknowledged all these but still steamed on at high speed. At 10.30 p.m. the *Californian's* wireless reported that she was surrounded by ice and had stopped. The *Titanic* acknowledged, but brusquely added 'Shut up. I am busy with Cape Race' (the Newfoundland shore station).

At 11.40 p.m. the *Titanic* struck an iceberg and a hole estimated at 300 ft. in length was torn out of her side beneath the waterline. The bulkheads failed to limit the flooding and she was doomed. Ten minutes later, Phillips, the senior wireless operator, was instructed to send distress signals.

By a master-stroke of irony, the *Californian* was now within sight of the sinking vessel, but did not receive the signals as her only wireless operator, having been on continuous duty for sixteen hours, had turned in. Again, because of the angle between the two ships the *Californian* did not recognize the lights as those of a liner and although the watch reported the firing of rockets, these were not identified as distress signals. It also transpired that both ships had tried to communicate by means of Morse lamp, but that neither had seen the others' messages, although the night was clear.

The *Titanic's* CQD's and SOS's – she sent both forms of distress signals – were first picked up by the German steamer *Frankfurt* which was 153 miles away. Almost at the same time the *Carpathia's* wireless operator reported the emergency to his captain and was able to give the stricken liner's position. Immediately the *Carpathia*, which was fifty-eight miles away, altered course to the rescue.

Here again, chance played its part, but this time as a beneficiary, for the *Carpathia*'s only wireless operator, although officially off watch, had returned to his equipment and was putting out some routine traffic calls, including some to the *Titanic*. At 12.20 a.m. the distress calls were received. Before long at least six ships were steaming towards the disaster area.

At 2.20 a.m. the *Californian*, which for some time past had been watching the lights of the unknown vessel grow steadily dimmer, noted that they had vanished, the optical impression being that of a ship getting under way and receding into the darkness. The watchers were not to know until it was too late that they had witnessed the end of the 'unsinkable' *Titanic* and that all around them the black sea was dotted with hundreds of human beings struggling for life. Another two hours were to elapse before the *Carpathia* arrived and began to take aboard survivors. Among the 1,517 lost that night was Jack Phillips, the senior wireless operator, who remained at his post to within a few minutes of the ship foundering. McBride, the second wireless operator, who showed equal devotion to duty, was eventually picked up after one and a half hours in the sea.

The official inquiries also brought to light another circumstance which, although it had no bearing on the actual rescue operation, might well have done. The drama which by daybreak had been enacted on the high seas had encouraged numerous American amateur operators to attempt to participate – possibly with the best of intentions – but the practical effect was to clutter the wavebands to such a degree that they became a babel of sound from which it was impossible to decipher messages.

Ultimately out of stark tragedy some good emerged. The investigations into the disaster showed that while wireless telegraphy in itself had emerged before the world as an invaluable means of saving lives at sea, the overall system – that is, the ways in which it was employed – left much to be desired, and machinery was set in motion to improve matters.

These were finally implemented at an International Conference on Safety of Life at Sea, held in London. On 20 January 1914, representatives of sixteen nations signed an agreement which embodied seventy-four Articles relating to the improved safety of shipping in numerous directions, among which was the employment of wireless telegraphy.

It was, for instance, laid down that all merchant ships which carried fifty or more persons must be equipped with wireless. (Although certain exceptions could be made, this effectively made the carrying of a wireless installation compulsory for most ships other than small coasters or local craft.) A classification of shipping was drawn up; those in certain categories had for the future to maintain a continuous watch system with their wireless apparatus. Minimum range requirements were laid down for the apparatus and emergency equipment having an independent power supply which was capable of working for at least six hours, was demanded.

The continuous watch stipulation meant that all vessels within the categories laid down had henceforth (actually a year's grace was given) to carry at least two operators, or one operator and a 'certified watcher'. It was recognized, however, that some form of continuous watch was desirable on all wireless-equipped ships and this question had been raised at the Board of Trade inquiry into the loss of the *Titanic*. Marconi, who had been called to give evidence, suggested two possible courses whereby this might be achieved. One was to give a member of the crew sufficient instruction to enable him to recognize an emergency call and to place him on listening watch whenever the wireless operator was off duty so that he could raise the alarm.

The second possibility, he said, was one upon which he had already carried out experiments which had enabled him to regard the project as feasible. This was to devise apparatus which would automatically ring an alarm bell whenever a distress call was received on the unattended apparatus. The auto-alarm system eventually came to be approved and adopted, but not until the end of World War I.

Another lesson learned from that night of April 14–15 was that much more rigid control of transmissions must be effected in order to avoid a repetition of the chaos brought about by amateur operators. The allocation of particular wavebands for specific purposes was instituted with no unauthorized encroachments permitted.

Yet another indirect benefit was the inauguration of new thinking on the problem of dealing with the iceberg menace in the North Atlantic. For some time past an Ice Patrol had been maintained by the United States Coastguard service, the technique being to locate an iceberg and then destroy it with high explosive, but because of the huge size of some of the 'bergs this had met with only limited success.

As a result of the Board of Trade inquiry the *Scotia*, equipped with Marconi wireless, left Dundee on 8 March 1913 with orders to patrol the North Atlantic sea lanes to report the positions of all icebergs encountered. The technique proved so successful that the Ice Patrol was reorganized as a wireless reporting service, with the United States assuming responsibility for its operation. It is worthy of record that since that time no ship on the North Atlantic run has been lost through collision with icebergs, and that today's comprehensive Atlantic weather reporting service is the logical extension of ideas which began as a result of the sinking of the *Titanic*.

17

'The Marconi Scandal'

It will be recalled that the dawn of 1912 saw the Company in high hopes of being awarded the contract for the Imperial Chain of wireless stations. When, in March 1912, the tender was signed, it seemed that nothing could prevent the fulfilment of Guglielmo Marconi's greatest dream.

But then came a serious obstacle. Because the project involved telegraphic communication it came under a Standing Order which had to be approved and ratified by the House of Commons. At first, in view of the urgent need for wireless links throughout the Empire, it was considered that the act of ratification would be a mere formality; in the event, this proved to be far from the case.

The situation which resolved was an extremely complex one, of which only the briefest account can be given here.* The background was that of a long and bitter feud between the Liberal Government of the day and the Tory Opposition; a time of unparalleled storms and emotions in the House. Racial hatred was also a contributory factor, for three of the leading figures in the drama which was to follow were Jews. When not only public spending but the taxpayers' private purse became major issues, an explosion was inevitable.

Over the months from August 1911 to April 1912 Marconi shares, which at that time were on public offer, rose from £2. 8s. 9d. to £9. 0s. 0d. About the time of the signing of the tender, in March, ugly rumours began to circulate. In the House of Commons, much was made of the fact that while the Marconi Company had publicized the signing of the tender, the Postmaster-General, Sir Herbert Samuel, had blocked all discussion. Why, it was asked, were the terms so favourable to Marconi's? Could it be related to the fact that Godfrey Isaacs' brother, Sir Rufus Isaacs, was the Attorney-General and that they and Sir Herbert Samuel were Jews? Many decided that there was indeed a strong odour of corruption.

In the City, gossip was virulent for a different reason, for the spectacular

* Those who wish to read a full account are recommended to *The Marconi Scandal* by Frances Donaldson (Rupert Hart Davis).

rise in the value of Marconi shares had been followed by a fall and this had been echoed by a boom in new shares issued by the American Marconi Company, and a similar drop in value. Before long the two sets of rumours, namely, that concerning corruption on the part of the Ministers of the Crown and that of the shameless 'rigging' of the stock market became widespread. The more the public heard of the affair, the stronger became the feeling that the contract for the Imperial Wireless Chain should not be placed with the Marconi Company.

The matter was first brought out into the open by Wilfred Ramage Lawson, a journalist who wrote a series of articles in *Outlook* attacking the Company and the Government. This was soon followed by a similar series in *Eye-Witness*, a journal edited by Cecil Chesterton, brother of G. K. Chesterton, and before long every newspaper in the country was discussing the 'Marconi Scandal' as Chesterton christened it. So serious did the outcry become that a Select Committee was appointed by Parliament to investigate the whole affair. This met for the first time on 25 October 1912.

This Committee confined itself broadly to the task of excavating the paylode of truth from the mountain of political rumours and a qualified technical committee, known as the Parker Committee, was convened to advise upon the engineering issues. The chief task of this group was to assess whether the Marconi tender had been accepted on merit or whether rival systems such as the Telefunken, the Poulsen Arc, the Goldschmidt alternator, or the Alexanderson alternator could provide superior performance.

Shortly after the appointment of the Parker Committee, Godfrey Isaacs sent a document to the Select Committee asking that, in view of the expense of keeping engineers idle, and the mounting cost of material, his Company should be allowed to regard the tender as no longer binding in law.

The Parker Committee presented its report on 30 April 1913 and came down wholeheartedly in favour of the Marconi system which, it advised, was the only one of which it could be said with certainty that it was capable of fulfilling the requirements of the Imperial Chain.

The Select Committee first called various journalists who had been particularly outspoken in their criticisms. One of these, Leonard Maxse, appeared on February 12. Two days later the French journal *Le Matin* misquoted what Maxse had said in evidence, stating that he had imputed that Mr Herbert Samuel, the Postmaster-General, had entered into an arrangement with Sir Rufus Isaacs, the Attorney-General, who was the brother of Godfrey Isaacs, the Managing Director of the Marconi Company. The report went on to say that, according to Mr Maxse, all three had bought shares in the Marconi Company before the Imperial Chain negotiations were opened and had sold them at a considerable profit when the Company's tender was agreed by the Post Office.

This was the first time a specific accusation, naming personalities, had been made in print, and Sir Rufus Isaacs was quick to take advantage of it. He called upon the London editor of *Le Matin*, as a result of which an apology and full retraction was printed in the journal's issue of February 18. Despite this, a writ for libel was issued on behalf of Sir Rufus Isaacs and Mr Herbert Samuel.

The action, which was conducted for the plaintiffs by Sir Edward Carson and Mr F. E. Smith, brought the Marconi case back into the headlines again. In his speech Sir Edward denied that Sir Rufus had ever dealt in shares in either the British, Canadian or Spanish Marconi Companies, but admitted that six weeks after the Imperial Chain tender had been made public the Attorney-General had bought 10,000 shares of the new issue of the American Marconi Company and had subsequently sold 1,000 of them to Mr Lloyd George (then Chancellor of the Exchequer) and 1,000 to Lord Murray. These shares had since depreciated in value, and constituted an investment loss for all three.

Although *Le Matin* did not defend the action and had agreed to pay the costs, the victory was a hollow one. The *London Star* went on the streets with a placard: 'MARCONI LLOYD GEORGE SENSATION'.

The Select Committee went about its task with extreme thoroughness, taking the evidence, not only of journalists, but of almost everyone concerned. The witnesses included Sir Rufus Isaacs, Mr Lloyd George, Mr Herbert Samuel, Godfrey Isaacs and another Samuel brother, Harry, Hilaire Belloc and Mr Marconi.

From this gallery there had been one notable absentee, Cecil Chesterton, editor of the *Eye-Witness* (formerly edited by Hilaire Belloc) until its bankruptcy, after which he became editor of the *New Witness*.

Chesterton's history in connection with the Select Committee was a curious one for he had on several occasions appealed to it to take his evidence, but for some time without success. In view of this he had publicly suggested that a good reason existed for the Committee's tardy behaviour. Perhaps encouraged by this, the next issue of the *New Witness* publicized its contents by means of placards proclaiming 'Godfrey Isaacs' Ghastly Record'. Sandwichmen paraded these posters in front of the House of Commons and the Marconi headquarters. The outcome was that Cecil Chesterton was summoned to appear at the Old Bailey on a charge of criminal libel, the date of the trial being fixed as May 27.

On April 28 he was called before the Select Committee, but excused himself on medical and legal grounds. The Committee decided by members' vote not to call him and so Chesterton never came before them as a witness.

His trial at the Old Bailey was in relation to two distinct libels. One was that Mr Godfrey Isaacs, Sir Rufus Isaacs and Mr Herbert Samuel were three corrupt men who had connived at a corrupt contract. The second alleged that Godfrey Isaacs had been guilty of criminal offences in connection with certain companies of which he had been director, for which offences he would go to prison if his brother did his duty. There were in all, six counts in the indictment.

After an exhaustive trial, the jury found Cecil Chesterton guilty on five of the six counts, and the judge sentenced him to a fine of £100 plus the costs of Godfrey Isaacs' case, which were in the region of £1,500. Chesterton himself had withdrawn his allegations against the Isaacs brothers and Mr Herbert Samuel during the course of the trial, and so the three principal participants in the upheaval had at last had their names cleared in a Court of Justice.

Nothing so convincing emerged from the reports (there were three) of the Select Committee, which were concerned with the propriety of conduct of the politicians involved in the case, notably Sir Rufus Isaacs (Attorney-General), Mr Herbert Samuel (Postmaster-General), Mr Lloyd George (Chancellor of the Exchequer) and Lord Murray (Government Chief Whip until August 1912 when he resigned), all of whom, with the exception of Mr Herbert Samuel, had taken part in transactions in shares of the American Marconi Company.

Regrettably, although foreseeably, the verdict became a Party issue. The Majority Report, defending the Liberal cause, cleared the Ministers of all blame, and this became officially the Report of the Select Committee. But the Tory element of the Committee also made public their report, whilst the Chairman, to add to the confusion, published his original draft which had been amended out of all recognition by members of his own Party, the Liberals.

The Minority (Tory) Report, while clearing the Ministers concerned of the charges of corruption and misuse of privileged information, gave the opinion that the Attorney-General, the Chancellor and the Chief Ministerial Whip had acted 'with grave impropriety' and censure was likewise placed on the part the Postmaster-General played in the affair.

This ludicrous situation made it inevitable that there should be a debate in the House, and in due course it took place, on the following resolution, framed by the Opposition:

'That this House regrets the transactions of certain of His Majesty's Ministers in the shares of the Marconi Company of America and the want of frankness displayed by Ministers in their communications on the subject to the House.'

The debate took two days; the battle was fought all over again and, predictably, the House divided. The Government won with a majority of 78, the resolution being defeated by 346 votes to 268.

So officially the Marconi Scandal ended, although two further Committees of Inquiry were to present reports. One was on the conduct of various jobbers and stockbrokers, who were severely censured for their handling of the introduction of American Marconi Company shares into the Stock Market. The second, which was a Select Committee of the House of Lords, investigated Lord Murray's part in the affair. While acquitting him of the charge of dishonourable conduct, there was a strong opinion expressed that those who held public office should on no account speculate in stocks and shares.

Then when it seemed that the Marconi Scandal would retire from the front pages of the newspapers another big lawsuit served to keep it there. In summing up the Isaacs v. Chesterton libel action the judge had suggested that there might be a claim by shareholders in the British Marconi Company against Marconi and Godfrey Isaacs to share in the profits made by their transactions in American Marconi Company shares.

A test case on behalf of the shareholders was begun, but was quickly settled out of court. Although the explanations given by the defendants (Godfrey Isaacs, Harry Isaacs, Marconi and the stockbroking firms concerned) were accepted by the court, one of the jobbers concerned had offered to pay £4,000 towards the costs, whereupon the case was withdrawn.

From all this political turmoil the Marconi Company, as a Company, emerged with colours tattered but still flying. It had been established in the Courts of Law and by Parliamentary findings, that there had been no shadow of corrupt communication between members of the Company and Ministers of the Crown. The Parker Report had stated plainly that the Marconi system was at that time the only one which could with certainty fulfil the requirements of the Imperial Chain. Now with the vital issues settled, more tranquil times might predominate.

The Company was not without its wounds however. Guglielmo Marconi was embittered at the reflections which had been cast upon it. A heavy financial loss had been sustained by the suspension of activities pending the various hearings and although a new agreement and amended contract between the Postmaster-General and the Company was signed on 30 July 1913, and ratified by the House of Commons on August 7, this was cancelled by the Post Office on 30 December 1914 because of the altered circumstances arising from the war with Germany and her allies. By that time work on the stations in India, in Egypt, and those at Leafield and Devizes in the British Isles had been partially completed.

The cancellation was a heavy blow indeed. The Company had not only spent £140,000 of its own money on the enterprise but had turned down other valuable contracts in order to erect the stations with the utmost speed. In an attempt to cut its losses to the minimum, negotiations were opened with a view to establishing some degree of compensation, but this matter too was put in abeyance by the exigencies of war. As it turned out, the incidence of the Marconi Scandal was destined to delay the Imperial Wireless Scheme for another decade.

18

Further Advances in Technology

Amid all this unpleasant political upheaval, technical progress was still being made. The diode valve was beginning to replace the magnetic detector in some installations, or alternatively was being fitted as a standby. From 1911 onwards some naval vessels and various shore stations were fitted with 3 kW and 5 kW tuned spark-transmitters based on Marconi's synchronous disc discharger patents of 1907–9, these providing not only a more powerful signal but one which gave a musical note and therefore was more easily read through static interference.

Static, or rather its elimination, was the target for much research during those years and various devices were patented to minimize its effect on reception. Marconi's method of using balanced antenna circuits in conjunction with Fleming diodes was patented in 1909. In the following year C. S. Franklin patented a rejector valve circuit with the same end in view and H. J. Round followed this with a different circuit using balanced carborundum crystals in place of diode valves. This was the most successful of the three, but did not eliminate static interference entirely.

Round's compact portable wavemeter of 1908 had also proved a success and was widely used as a successor to Fleming's cymometer which was much bulkier and could not be so easily tuned over a wide range of wavelengths as Round's equipment. Professor Fleming, who was never one to suffer rivals gladly, wrote a tart letter to Mr Marconi complaining that 'these young men read my books and then pretend to make inventions'.

Another extremely useful invention of Round's was a device to measure the rate of decay of the damped wave trains radiated by the Marconi stations. This 'Decremeter' which was patented in 1909 provided a tunable pick-up circuit and press-button switches that enabled a thermo-couple and galvanometer detector to be used to measure the rate of change of slope to the tuning curve, from which the decrement of the transmission could be found.

Direction finding was another field in which considerable research was being carried out. Hertz in his original experiments had demonstrated the directional effect obtained by using an open loop of wire as a receiver. Various proposals had followed through the years, notably those of S. G. Brown in 1899, A. Blondel in 1903 and F. Braun's valuable work of 1904–6.

Marconi's discovery of the directional properties of the long horizontal antenna was made in 1905, and was followed a year later by a direction finding system which employed a number of horizontal radial antennas connected to a magnetic detector and earth through a rotating switch, the strongest signals being received by the antenna pointing at 180° to the transmitter. This system was later used by the Royal Navy.

H. J. Round also carried out experimental work using loop or frame antennas in 1905–6 and, by means of adding an open wire produced a heart-shaped polar diagram, but this important development was not followed up at the time. The most successful method devised at this period (actually in 1907) was that devised by E. Bellini and A. Tosi. Their method employed two vertical triangular antennas, each open at the apex and crossed at right angles, with a radiogoniometer (consisting of two fixed field coils and a rotatable search coil) connected in circuit.

The Bellini-Tosi patents were purchased by the Marconi Company in February 1912. Dr Bellini joined the technical staff as a consultant and rapid development work followed, to which C. E. Prince and J. G. Robb made important contributions. Tests carried out aboard *Eskimo* between Hull and Oslo, and others on the *Royal George* between Avonmouth and Montreal demonstrated the potential value of this equipment to shipping.

The thermionic valve was also subjected to considerable development work from 1910 onwards. The introduction of the grid by Dr Lee de Forest in 1906–7 at first conferred only marginal practical benefits, as the principles of efficient triode operation were only imperfectly understood and the amplification factor, as a consequence, was insignificant. It was at first believed that the presence of gas ions was an essential factor in producing a unidirectional current flow, but in 1912 Dr Langmuir of the (American) General Electric Company and other research workers proved this to be a fallacy and high-vacuum valves, which for the first time provided a reasonably predictable common standard of performance between valve and valve, were being experimentally produced.

Considerable improvements were also made to valve cathodes,

whereby a more copious emission of electrons could be provided. In 1913 H. J. Round devised a three-electrode gas-filled ('soft') valve embodying an oxide-coated filament (the filament acted as the cathode in early valves) which, although tricky to operate to best advantage, was a sensible improvement on anything which had been designed previously. In Germany, the improved Lieben-Reisz valve had made its appearance.

It had been common knowledge for some considerable time past that if a microphone is connected in circuit with a telephone earpiece and both suitably energized, a clear musical note will be emitted when the two devices are brought into close proximity to each other, the note being produced by action and reaction between microphone and earpiece. Various workers in 1912-13 were considering whether it was possible to produce an analogous condition with the improved triode valves.

C. S. Franklin, returning from a visit to Germany with samples of the Leiben-Reisz valve, brought back the news that Alexander Meissner of Telefunken had claimed to have found a way of making this type of valve act as a generator of continuous-wave oscillations. This information was at once exciting and alarming because both Franklin and Round were on the threshold of similar discoveries. Unknown to any of them, Armstrong in the United States was working on parallel lines.

In the event, Meissner won the race, taking out a patent on 9 April 1913. C. S. Franklin's patent was registered in June; Armstrong's in October and H. J. Round's in May 1914.

This situation needs some qualification however. Without wishing to detract from Meissner's brilliance as an engineer, it is on record that the apparatus he used was very inefficient. The Wehnelt cathode used in the Leiben-Reisz valve lasted only a few minutes in the circuit and the power output was very small. (Nevertheless, it is also on record that he achieved telephony over a distance of 36 km with it.)

Franklin's patent related only to the use of controlled positive feed back as a means of improving receiver signal strength, although the wording of his application makes it clear that he knew of the valve's properties as a generator.

Round, although legally almost a year behind Meissner in terms of a patent, had in fact given a demonstration of valved radio telephony between Marconi House in the Strand and the Savoy Hotel in 1913. The circuit he used was much more efficient and embodied an important innovation, notably that of a grid capacitor with a high resistance shunted across it, and of a resistance in the anode circuit to limit the

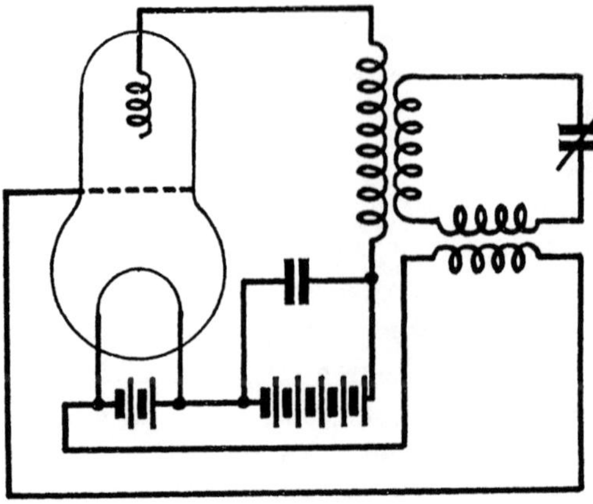

(a) *A. Meissner's Circuit of 1913*

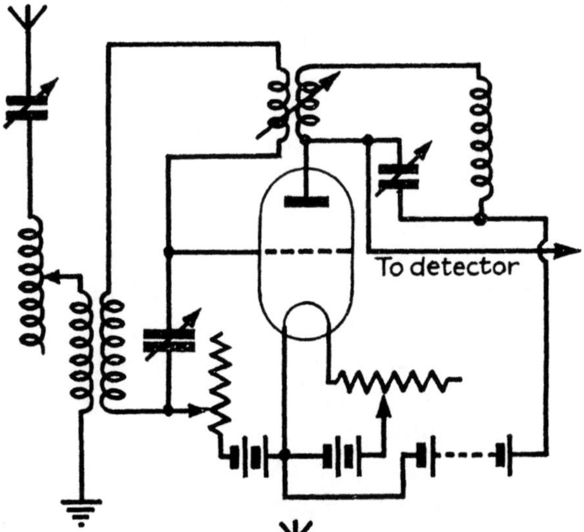

(b) *C. S. Franklin's Circuit of 1913*

The application is that of an amplifier with negative feedback but the patent specification shows clearly that Franklin knew that the circuit would oscillate.

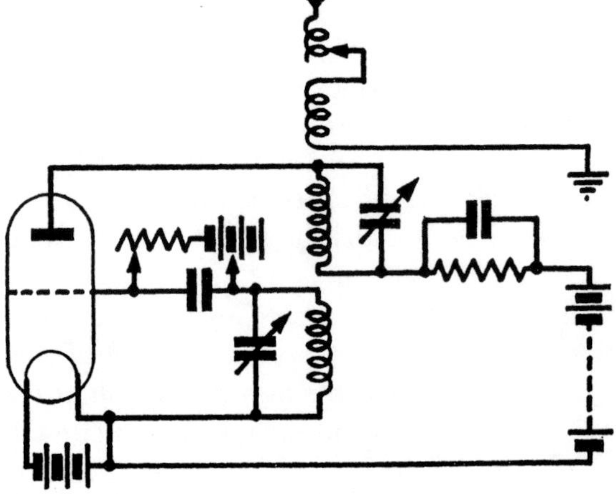

To detector

(c) *H. J. Round's Circuit of 1914*

Round had publicly demonstrated this circuit's use for radio telephony in 1913.

Figure 18.1 The Triode Valve as a Generator

current flowing through the valve, thereby preserving it from the effects of excessive ionization.

.   .   .

Although in the matter of commercial wireless telegraphy operation a commutator method of duplex working which enabled another station to break in on the transmission had been adopted in 1908, this had its limitations insofar as it did not permit the simultaneous transmission and reception of two messages, one from either end of the circuit.

An important step forward was made in 1911, when a separate directional ('bent') antenna system was installed at Letterfrack some seven miles from Clifden. This consisted in essentials of two antennas, one of which was aligned for maximum reception in the direction of North America and the other was arranged for minimum pick-up in this direction. With both stations transmitting (one on either side of the Atlantic), both the Letterfrack antennas received signals from the local station (Clifden), but one in addition received the transatlantic transmission. By connecting these two groups of signals in antiphase in a common circuit and with suitable adjustment, the two sets of local signals were nullified, leaving the distant signals clear of the local interference. This work, which was carried out by R. N. Vyvyan and C. S. Franklin, under the direction of Marconi, speeded operations very considerably. With similar arrangements on the far side of the Atlantic, simultaneous working from both terminals was possible, with a traffic limit increased by four times.

The Glace Bay station was modified in 1911 by the replacement of the 212 ft. wooden towers by 250 ft. Gray-type steel masts and in 1912 a new receiving station in the Louisberg area was begun, coming into operation in 1913.

A further improvement in the transatlantic service was effected in 1912 when a photographic method of recording signals, devised by C. S. Franklin, was put into service. In this equipment S. G. Brown microphone relays were inserted in the detector circuit and the strengthened signals impulsed an Einthoven string galvanometer. The movement of the galvanometer opened a slot and thereby exposed a photo-sensitized tape to a light beam. The tape passed through a series of developing, fixing and drying baths and in under three minutes emerged, showing the signals as morse characters on the tape. This device remained in use for some years.

Franklin also introduced a method of recording the signals on phonographic cylinders about this time. This was the first step towards automation for it enabled one operator to supervise a simultaneous intake of messages from several receivers at one time, for later transcription. It also effected a very considerable increase in the traffic rate, for signals could be transmitted at high speed for recording on the cylinders, which, on removal, could be played back at low speed for transcription purposes.

Another notable improvement brought about at this time – again by Franklin – was the design of a high tension magnetic relay incorporating a high pressure air blast for quenching the spark. This significantly increased the permissible keying speed and was so successful that relays of this type were to be widely employed over the subsequent ten years after which the valved high-power transmitters which then came into operation made the air-blast relay unnecessary.

By 1912, enough experience had been gained in transatlantic working to enable an analysis of the system to be carried out. One obvious fact was that although the Company possessed alternative channels, one to Canada and one to the United States, there was no doubt that the bulk of the traffic, and therefore the most profitable financial return, was provided by the American circuit.

Another factor for consideration was the unpalatable truth that the wireless circuits compared unfavourably with the cable circuits in terms of reliability of service. This was not because of any inherent defect in the wireless apparatus; it was the old trouble of long and inefficient landlines between the terminal stations and the centres of population. It stemmed from the fact that the terminal sites had been originally chosen with the object of making the path between them as short as possible, which had meant building them on the coast regardless of how remote they were from the ultimate destination of the messages.

With the passage of the years technological improvements had provided enough reserve signal strength to permit a longer service path to be used, thereby shortening the landline to obvious advantage. It was thereupon decided to build new stations (one transmitting and one receiving) on the mainland of the British Isles and that the American Company should build similar stations near New York. In Britain, Caernarvon in North Wales was chosen as the transmitting site while the receiving station was to be at Towyn, twenty miles further south. In the United States equivalent stations were planned at Tuckerton and New Brunswick, 60 miles apart in the state of New Jersey.

Work was put in hand in 1912, and by March 1914 the British stations were all in commission. In the U.S.A. the stations were also virtually completed by July 1914, when tuning and testing was begun, but the outbreak of war interrupted progress as the Marconi engineers were hurriedly recalled to England.

The period 1912–14 was one in which intense interest in the implementation of international wireless links was demonstrated. In November 1912, the Norwegian Government placed a contract with the Company for a transatlantic station intended for direct communication with the new transatlantic stations which were being built near New York. Again the war intervened and this station (at Stavanger) did not come into operation until 1919.

It had also been agreed by London and New York that the American Marconi Company should establish terminal stations for a 2,100 mile trans-Pacific service between San Francisco and Honolulu. Work on these was begun in 1913 and by September of the following year was at the 'test and tune' stage, when a fracture in the underseas cable between the two centres resulted in the wireless link being brought into service before its official inauguration date. Immediately on official completion, further work was put in hand to extend the service to Japan; this was at the instigation of the Japanese Government. The service, which was inaugurated on 27 July 1915 by an exchange of messages between the President of the United States and the Mikado, was operated by the Marconi Company.

On 9 October 1913 another dramatic instance of the value of wireless telegraphy to shipping occurred when the passenger ship *Volturno* bound for the U.S.A. from Rotterdam, caught fire in mid-Atlantic. The Marconi wireless operators on board sent out distress signals which were picked up by numerous vessels, the first of which, the *Carmania*, arrived on the scene within four hours, closely followed by the *Seydlitz* and the *Grosser Kurfurst*. Heavy seas prevented the transfer of passengers and crew on that day, and by dawn the following day the burning *Volturno* was ringed by no fewer than ten rescue ships. One of these, the tanker *Narragansett* pumped oil on the water, whereupon passengers (mostly immigrants) and crew to a total of 521 were ferried to safety. A further 136 who had panicked, perished, but had it not been for wireless telegraphy and the superb seamanship exhibited by all concerned, the whole of the *Volturno*'s complement would almost certainly have been lost.

The *Daily Telegraph* of October 15, in commenting on the news, paid a glowing tribute to Guglielmo Marconi and remarked acidly on the indifference exhibited by those in a position to award national honours to such men.

In 1913 the Company secured licences from both the British and Spanish Governments to maintain direct wireless services between the two countries. For this purpose the Poldhu station was enlarged and regular traffic began between this station and the Canary Islands.

In December of that year the Trans-Oceanic Telegraphy Company was incorporated, with a capital of £200,000 for the purpose of establishing a wireless service between the United Kingdom and the United States. A telegraph office was opened at 1, Fenchurch Street, London, which communicated direct with Caernarvon so that when that station came into operation early in 1914 a new service was opened to the New Brunswick (New York) station. The service was considerably speedier than anything which had been possible before because of the elimination of the unreliable landlines referred to earlier.

.   .   .

At this point in time when the Great War was shortly to signal the end of an era, it might be opportune to refer to labour relations as they existed within the Company.

While it would be idle to pretend that an ideal state of harmony reigned, such friction as did exist was not the traditional circumstance of workers versus the boss, but rather that of the engineering element versus what was regarded as Head Office bureaucracy. Marconi was the boss, and one who drove his men hard, but never so hard as he drove himself. He had a disconcerting habit of demanding the seemingly impossible, but would throw off his coat and work day and night alongside the man charged with the task until the project, whatever it was, was completed. This the engineers understood.

As for the other side of the coin, it must be remembered that many of the original brotherhood of engineers had now attained senior status. They remembered the arduous, yet informal, early days and did not appreciate the 'red tape' edicts which are inevitable when a Company becomes sizeable.

This attitude, although perfectly understandable, was not altogether just, for 'Head Office' was, on the whole, well-meaning. As an example of this, in those far-off days when exploitation of the working class was the rule rather than the exception, we find that in April 1913 the

Company established a retiring age and a Contributory Pensions Fund, in association with a Benevolent Fund.

A further instance is shown by the specifications for the housing of engineers at the Belmar (New York station) where a 45-bedroom hotel was built to accommodate the unmarried employees, equipped with a luxurious lounge and a smoking-room, and a number of private sitting-rooms. A 12-acre vegetable garden supplied fresh produce and a French chef was in charge of the catering arrangements, in a kitchen equipped with the latest devices, including refrigeration. The married operators had four-bedroomed cottages and the senior engineers and their families lived in spacious bungalows.

The grounds were landscaped, with ornamental gardens overlooking a river and the Atlantic; woodlands provided shooting facilities and the streams an abundance of good fishing. In short, the managerial policy was years ahead of its time, which is perhaps one reason why the Company has an astonishing record in long-service employees, with a strong family tradition in which it is not uncommon to find three generations at work in the organization.

19

Wireless at the Outbreak
of the Great War

The years 1910–13 had been tumultuous indeed for the Marconi Company, but those who looked forward to more settled times were sorely disappointed. For Britain, and indeed much of the world, was moving inexorably towards the horror of the Great War.

Paradoxically, while diplomatic relations between this country and Germany were steadily worsening, the private Marconi-Telefunken 'war' had been succeeded by a period of peaceful co-existence in which exchanges of technical information backed up by bi-lateral visits of interest were the order of the day.

But the halcyon days were limited in number. At the end of July 1914, a Marconi delegation of senior engineers visited Berlin and were afforded the usual friendly courtesy and generous hospitality by their German hosts. Their programme included visits to various factories and research establishments associated with the Telefunken Company, with a grand finale in the form of an inspection of the high-power station at Nauen, at which 200 kW high-frequency alternators and massive new antennas had recently been installed. The complete equipment was shown to the British party which shortly afterward left to take the night boat home.

Immediately they left the station, Nauen closed down its normal commercial operations and the military, who had been awaiting the visitors' departure, took over control.

On the following morning, July 30, a wireless signal from the British Admiralty sent the Grand Fleet, which that summer had staged a mighty review off Spithead, away to its battle stations all over the world.

On 1 August 1914 the use of wireless was forbidden to all other than British ships while in territorial waters, and on the following day the Government took control of all wireless messages. On August 3 the Admiralty prohibited the use of wireless telegraphy on all merchant ships in territorial waters and all amateur experimental stations were closed down, with arrangements made for the gear to be impounded. Across the North Sea, Nauen sent out an ominous call to all German merchant shipping on the high seas to make for the nearest German ports, or, if too far away, for a neutral port.

German troops had entered France on August 2, and on August 4 Belgium was invaded. At 11 p.m. the British ultimatum to Germany expired and the two countries were automatically at war. Wireless signals were sent to all units of the Grand Fleet 'Commence hostilities against Germany'. Poldhu stuttered the declaration of war far and wide.

One of the first acts of war was to cut the German undersea cables and, with this done, Nauen became that country's sole means of telegraphic communication with the outer world. This station, at the time the most powerful transmitting station in the world, at once opened up traffic with another new German giant at Kamina, in Togoland, with Windhoek in S.W. Africa and with German stations which had been built in the U.S.A., pouring out propaganda on a 24-hour basis. Every single message transmitted throughout the war – in all, some eighty million words – were intercepted by special staffs of Marconi operators and passed on to the appropriate Government authorities.

Immediately on the outbreak of war the Marconi Works was taken over by the Admiralty. The Clifden–Glace Bay transatlantic circuit was allowed to continue its function as a commercial station, but with interruptions and a change of wavelength to handle Naval traffic. The control of Caernarvon and Towyn passed into the hands of the G.P.O. and later to the Admiralty, the Company operating them for the Government. Stations for the interception of German wireless transmissions were hurriedly pressed into service at the Hall Street experimental station while New Street factory was put under high pressure to meet the demands of the armed services.

Trained wireless operators were in great demand and in this respect an interesting sideline of the Company's peacetime activities unexpectedly bore fruit. For some time past Marconi's had been stimulating the interest of wireless amateurs by offering prizes for competitors in examinations and by making Morse practice sets available, an innovation which had created great interest in wireless among young men, many of whom had enrolled as learners. Now the Company's offices were open day and night, enrolling new recruits, instructing them and finally examining them.

The R.N.V.R. was desperately short of operators, not only for naval vessels but also to man the Marconi equipment which had been installed in dirigibles. As merchant ships reached port, the Marconi wireless operators were taken off and transferred to the Royal Navy. But this, while providing experienced men for the Fleet, in turn created a shortage in the Merchant Navy; the deficit was made all the more acute by the need to provide a much greater number of ships with wireless apparatus (until 1914 only ships of more than 1,600 tons carried wireless and these for the most part had only one operator). The Company undertook to find a further 2,000 operators to augment the 3,000 already serving on merchant ships, for which purpose class-rooms at King's College and Birkbeck College were made available to ease the overload of trainees upon Marconi House.

The price of Government procrastination in sanctioning an Empire Wireless Chain was now apparent to all. The lack of such a system fell most heavily upon the Admiralty which perforce had to perform hurried replacements of existing low-power shore stations with others of medium or high power. The high-power Imperial Scheme station at Abu Zaabal in Egypt, which had been partially constructed in peace-time, was now urgently needed and Marconi's were ordered to complete it and to get it into operation as a top priority. There was no time to post working drawings so constructional details of the power house and transmitting-room floors were telegraphed to Egypt; steam generating plant was collected from various parts of England, and this, together with all the units comprising a 100 kW transmitter, were transported to the site. Within one month of demand, the apparatus of the emergency station was installed and the British Isles and Egypt were in continuous wireless communication.

The Navy and Empire forces meanwhile, had been doing everything possible to even the situation. On August 9 the German wireless station at Dar-es-Salaam was destroyed and on the 12th a station at Yap in the Caroline Islands, South Pacific. On the 24th the Germans themselves blew up Kamina, Togoland, to prevent it being taken over. The Royal Australian Navy captured the Samoa station on August 29 and followed this with Nauru in the Marshall Islands and Herbertshihe on the island of New Pommern. The Duala station in the Cameroons was seized on September 27 and on November 9 the Japanese occupied Kiauchau and its wireless station. The last powerful station of what was intended to be the German Imperial Chain, Windhoek, in German East Africa, fell on 12 May 1915 to a military force sent by the Union of South Africa.

Before the war was many weeks old the first of the 348 Marconi men who were subsequently to die before peace was declared had tapped their last messages. These were the wireless operators of the *Aboukir*, *Hogue* and *Cressy*, early casualties of the war at sea.

In those tense, early days of the war, one thing was very certain. Wireless was no longer the experimental toy of the Boer War; it was now vital and indispensable, and the gaps in communication which existed in 1914 were a sore trial to the Navy in particular, which had the unenviable task of hunting down and destroying elements of the German Fleet which were at large in the vast expanses of the South Atlantic and the Pacific. After the near-annihilation of Admiral Cradock's force at Coronel and in the same month – November – as Admiral Sturdee left Plymouth to avenge the defeat, the Admiralty placed a contract with the Company to install and man thirteen long-range rotary discharger stations in various parts of the world. The first of these was erected on Ascension Island, mid-way in the South Atlantic. Others followed at the Falkland Islands, Bathurst, Ceylon, Durban, Demerara, Seychelles, Singapore, St John's, Aden, Hong Kong, Mauritius and Port Nolloth. All equipment, with one exception, was on site and in most instances in operation by June 1915, a circumstance which brought congratulations from the Admiralty.

The exception was the Falkland Islands installation. Some idea of the work involved in constructing such a station may be gathered from the following details:

On 7 March 1915, the *Ismailia* sailed for the Falkland Islands carrying 4,500 tons of gear for building roads, and reinforced concrete buildings, the components for seven 300 ft. steel masts, all the wireless apparatus, and two hundred men. Her decks were loaded with coal and she also carried sheep for rations. Six weeks later the *Freshfield* followed, having been fitted out as living quarters for the party, and carrying sufficient provisions to last the men for eighteen months.

Four miles of light railway track were laid from the harbour to the site in four months and the station was brought into service in the last quarter of 1916.

There are, in the histories of the Great War, innumerable instances in which wireless telegraphy played an important role in tactical movements and in providing communication when no other means was possible. But, in the early days of the struggle a new weapon, wireless direction-finding, had been developed, and by 1916 chains of these secret stations were in wide use, initially by the Army in France, but from 1915 onwards by the Admiralty also.

L

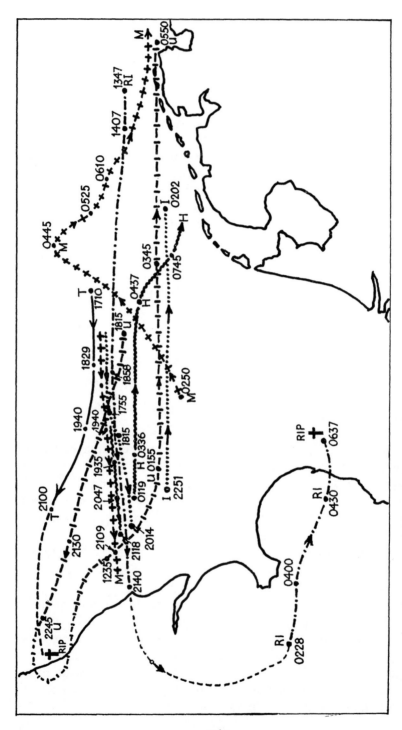

Figure 19.1 German Zeppelin raids plotted by Marconi D.F. Stations, 27–28 November 1916

The direction-finding equipment, which used soft 'C' valves and a modified Bellini-Tosi directional system, had been developed by H. J. Round of the Marconi Company just before the war. It was not long before news of Round's work came to the notice of the War Office and, on the outbreak of hostilities, he was seconded to Intelligence and was ordered to provide an initial two stations for service in France. This was speedily done and following their success a large network, covering the entire Western Front, evolved.

The Admiralty also demanded similar stations to be sited in the British Isles, with the object of obtaining bearings from transmissions from enemy submarines and it was not long before similar networks were being built to maintain watch not only for submarines but also for Zeppelins and German surface naval vessels. By 1916 the coastlines of Britain were covered by networks of such stations. Naval vessels were also fitted experimentally with d.f. equipment, one of Round's inventions in connection with this being the quadrantal error corrector.

Although the German Navy was aware that some form of direction-finding device was in use it had no idea that Round's valve amplifiers were any further advanced than its own. As a consequence the German warships, when in their own home waters, used low-power wireless telegraphy quite freely, supremely confident that the signals could not be picked up in Britain. In fact continuous bearings were being taken on all such vessels.

The general naval situation during the first two years of the war was an irksome one for the Admiralty, for the Germans were in the habit of making brief forays into the North Sea but were always in home waters again before the Grand Fleet could effect an interception.

Then on 30 May 1916, the d.f. stations reported that a German warship lying at Wilhelmshaven, 300 miles away, was being unusually prolific with her wireless signals. That same afternoon it was further noted by the stations that the vessel had left Wilhelmshaven and was now lying in the River Jade about seven miles away from her original station (this was shown by a change in bearing of less than one and a half degrees).

The Admiralty reasoned from this information that the German warship was about to put to sea and that the incessant chatter of her wireless telegraphy had constituted sailing orders to other warships. It was the opportunity that had been long awaited, providing the chance to get into a favourable position in time to make an effective strike. The Grand Fleet was ordered to sea with all haste and to make for the German Bight.

On the following day the Battle of Jutland was fought. The secret of how the German Fleet was brought to battle was kept until the end of the war. Then in 1920 Admiral Sir Henry Jackson,* who had been First Sea Lord in 1916, disclosed that the man primarily responsible for the historic encounter was Captain H. J. Round, M.C.

The Army, too, made considerable demands upon the Company. In August 1914, the Chief of the Marconi Training School at Broomfield, near Chelmsford, was seconded to the War Office and charged with the organization of a large-scale training school at the Crystal Palace for the instruction of officers and engineers of the allied forces in the use of wireless in the field. At the same time a Field Station development section at the Works was re-formed as a separate department in order to meet the ever-increasing needs of the armies overseas.

At the start of the war the possibilities of wireless telegraphy in the field were far from fully appreciated. No separate organization existed; men from various units were detailed to attend to such wireless equipment as existed in addition to their normal duties, and even the most *avant-garde* of senior officers were prone to look upon wireless as possibly a useful adjunct to visual and line signalling, with its main sphere of use confined to communication between cavalry and H.Q.

Thus, a day or so after the British Expeditionary Force landed in France, its total self-propelled mobile wireless force consisted of a single lorry fitted with a wireless transmitter and receiver. By the time of the first Battle of the Marne (September 1914) the force had expanded to ten units.

But by October 1915 the war of movement had ended and the advent of trench warfare brought to an end the limited role which wireless telegraphy had played as a means of communication between cavalry units and H.Q. In its stead an urgent new requirement arose, namely the need for corps H.Q. to be fully informed on a continuous basis of the situation obtaining in the front line. This was speedily organized by adopting a relay system consisting of a power buzzer in the front line feeding to a 50 watt mobile spark set which in turn was in contact with a 120 watt spark set further back towards base. The ultimate link was a $1\frac{1}{2}$ kW light motor set which was well within range of H.Q. Much of the output of the Chelmsford Works was at this time devoted to the provision of such sets.

In December 1914, the first two direction-finding stations were

* Sir Henry Jackson pioneered wireless telegraphy in the Royal Navy and made many notable contributions to its practical employment.

shipped to France, the equipment for each station being contained in two lorries and one car. The lorries carried 70 ft. demountable masts, the Bellini-Tosi direction-finding apparatus and Type 16 Marconi receivers, the latter employing a crystal detector and a 'Round' soft valve audio frequency amplifier. The wave-range covered was about 400–2,000 m.

The two stations were erected for tests at Blendecques, near St Omer, on December 16 and a few weeks later (1 January 1915) one station was moved to Abbeville to form a base line from there to Blendecques. From that date, weekly maps were produced for G.H.Q. Intelligence showing the latest positions of German Army wireless stations of all types. Later the range and accuracy of d.f. reception was extended by shifting the two stations to the base line Amiens–Calais, with land line communication to G.H.Q. The records provided by these stations included the movements of Zeppelins, the changes in position of German trench stations and later the location of enemy aircraft.

On 2 January 1915 the importance of wireless in the British Army was recognized by the establishment of a Wireless Signal Company as a unit in its own right.

By the following month the original crystal sets used by the Army for message-interception purposes were being replaced by 'Round' valve receivers, which, by reason of their amplification properties gave a vast increase in the number of interceptions of enemy signals. The enemy also was effecting improvements, notably by changing the spark sets originally employed to types embodying continuous wave transmission. On the Allies' side of no-man's-land the 'Round' valve sets were quickly modified to intercept C.W. and so the grim game of chess went on.

A considerable step forward was made in 1915 when the brilliant work of Irving Langmuir of the United States, and other workers, on the production of high-vacuum tungsten filament valves was published. This method of construction gave greatly improved stability and made possible the production of valves which possessed uniform characteristics. This had an immediate effect on British and French valve production; in France, the work carried out under the direction of Colonel – later General–Ferrié, resulted in a superior type of valve which, after the war, became well known as the 'French' valve.

As the war progressed and the value of direction-finding stations became thoroughly proven, large numbers of such installations were built for the Army and used in France and other areas of conflict. With the growth of experience in the use of these, valuable technical knowledge was being acquired. K. W. Tremellen, a very able Marconi engineer, noted in 1915 that directional readings taken during the day were different once night had fallen, a phenomenon which was thereupon christened 'Night Error'. By 1917 sufficient of the theory of some of the causes of errors in the reading of aircraft bearings had been established and F. Adcock, working with Tremellen, had devised an antenna system which gave a considerable improvement in accuracy. The first rotating frame d.f. equipment to be used in France was set up in February 1917. The antenna consisted of a large single loop slung from a triatic between two 30 ft. masts and rotated by a motor-car steering wheel. Several of them were soon in operation, their chief function being to locate wireless-equipped German aircraft as they flew over the front line, sending gun-ranging messages. The stations operated on the then 'short waves' between 70 and 150 m. Such was their success that as many as eleven German spotting planes were brought down in one week on the bearing information supplied.

(In connection with research into improvements in bearing accuracies, T. L. Eckersley, F.R.S., a brilliant mathematician of the Marconi Company, who in 1917 was working with the Royal Engineers in Cairo, produced a valuable research report on errors in the original system, a paper which was complementary to Adcock's research in France.)

From the two d.f. stations originally shipped to France in 1914 very large networks were built up, and by the end of the war each of the five armies had its own chain of stations.

Very early in the war, indeed, almost as soon as the pattern of movement had given place to the stalemate of trench warfare, it had become evident that the Germans were tapping the Allied front-line telephone systems. Both the French and the British devised ways and means of returning the compliment and by 1916 a three-valve amplifying equipment was in service which could pick up messages transmitted via the earth up to a distance of 5,000 yds.

Ever since 1911, when a Canadian, J. D. A. McCurdy, in a Curtiss biplane flying over Long Island had succeeded in sending a message to the ground via a Marconi spark transmitter in the cockpit, the Company had been carrying out considerable experimental work in air-to-ground (and ground-to-air) communication. A successful airborne transmitter had been designed by R. D. Bangay of the Company's Field Station Dept., but the more difficult problem of reception in the noisy cockpits of the early flying machines had not been satisfactorily solved at the outbreak of war.

Like the British Army, the Royal Flying Corps entered the war with only a very limited appreciation of the role of wireless; it is on record that the first R.F.C. units which embarked for France in 1914 possessed one airborne spark transmitter and one ground-based receiver between them.

In the following month Captain Lewis of the R.F.C. took a transmitter in his machine and succeeded in communicating with a ground station sited near an artillery battery. This experiment under conditions of actual warfare proved that in principle wireless could provide a great time-saving improvement on the then existing method of reconnaissance, which was for the observer to make sketches of what he saw over the enemy lines and for the information to be dropped over the British batteries as ranging aids.

Shortly after the outbreak of hostilities the R.F.C. took over the Marconi experimental establishment at Brooklands, Surrey, and R. D. Bangay and the rest of the Marconi staff there were seconded to the Corps.

The major handicap to the wholesale adoption of wireless in aircraft was the very limited load capacity of the machines and the weight of the wireless apparatus.

A significant step forward was taken early in 1915 when the first of an improved series of receivers and airborne spark transmitters was shipped from the Marconi Works for service in the R.F.C. in France. These equipments were rapidly brought into use for the purpose of co-operation between spotting aircraft and ground batteries and immediately proved their value. To speed up this development, qualified wireless engineers were given commissions in the R.F.C. and the Marconi experimental section at Brooklands was turned into a wireless training school for pilots. The school was in the charge of Major C. E. Prince assisted by Captain Whiddington and Captain Furnival – all Marconi engineers.

At the same time the heavier-than-air reconnaissance system was extended to sea warfare, both for the spotting of submarines and for general observation purposes, thus supplementing the work already being carried out by wireless-equipped dirigibles, aboard which the weight of the equipment had not been such an acute problem. The German cruiser *Konigsberg* was sunk in the Rufiji River in German East Africa as a result of information passed back from a spotting aircraft to British warships.

Thanks to intensive development, by the end of 1915 the Marconi

Company was manufacturing a transmitting set for aircraft which weighed only twenty pounds. Constant improvement was also being made by aircraft manufacturers in the matter of the weight-lifting capacity of the machines.

At the outbreak of war, Prince, working at the Brooklands experimental establishment, was developing a continuous wave valve transmitter for airborne use. From this the idea of a telephone set was but a logical step, but one which presented many obstacles before its practical realization. In the summer of 1915, however, success was achieved when speech from air to ground was obtained at Brooklands over a range of about twenty miles using a wavelength of 300 m. (the trailing antenna was 250 ft. in length). For ground-to-air communication wireless telegraphy was used.

Air-to-ground telephony was not, however, generally employed during the war, but an urgent demand arose for one-way inter-aeroplane communication. The reason for this was tactical, the objective being the control of a fighter squadron by its leader when on patrol or in combat. Telephony was essential, not only for speed of command, but also because the pilot of a single-seater fighter could not manœuvre his machine and operate a morse key at the same time; the use of telephony in larger aircraft would also permit the employment of observers who were not trained as wireless telegraphists. Prince and his staff worked desperately to evolve a practical system.

20

The Great War (continued)

By 1916 all three armed services were depending heavily upon wireless. In the great offensive of June 1916 it was often the sole means of communication between aircraft, artillery and infantry, mobile wireless stations following the infantry and the R.F.C., keeping divisions in touch. Paratroops were first employed in 1916 when Belgian soldiers, who in civilian life had been marine wireless officers, were asked to volunteer for special duties. After parachute instruction and a period of training by Marconi's, these men were dropped into enemy territory with small sets manufactured by the Company strapped to their backs, their task being to transmit intelligence from behind the German lines.

Early in 1916 the Company carried out the first valve transmitter tests between an aircraft and units of the Royal Navy. These took place at Scapa Flow, a Short seaplane carrying the transmitting equipment which included a 1,000-volt high tension battery slung under the aircraft. *Calliope*, a light cruiser, was the first warship to be fitted with the complementary equipment and six months' trials followed. These proved so successful that seventy-five ships of the Grand Fleet were equipped with valve sets of similar design. At the same time the Company was heavily engaged in equipping seaplanes for U-boat patrol work.

By 1917 the importance of this use for wireless brought into being the Marine Observers' School (R.N.) at Eastchurch, where many Marconi men were on the teaching staff. This was also the case at the R.N.A.S. Training Station and, later, at Cranwell.

In 1917 dirigibles were still in use for military purposes and more were under construction. At Howden Station in Yorkshire the Company fitted No. 9 Rigid with a valve transmitter, the first valve set ever installed in such an airship. (Because of the huge envelope containing highly inflammable gas, spark sets were considered to be more dangerous.) Subsequently all dirigibles were Marconi-equipped and must have exhibited a curious contrast in methods of communication, for not only was wireless carried, but carrier pigeons also.

By late 1917 the R.F.C. had taken delivery of night bombing aircraft which was capable of a range of a hundred miles and these were fitted with Marconi continuous wave sets. The use of these bombers worried the German military authorities to the point where substantial rewards were offered for all parts found from Allied machines.

At about the same time continuous-wave telegraphy transmission was introduced into the R.F.C. ground networks and telephony took up its inter-machine function in the air. The new tactics which this system of squadron control made possible came as an unpleasant surprise to the German Air Force whose losses mounted rapidly.

The Allied effort in terms of air warfare was now in top gear and gaining ascendancy over the enemy. From the school at Brooklands a weekly output of thirty-six fighter pilots emerged, fully trained in the use of the wireless telephony equipment and in the essential art of clear articulation under the noisy conditions of aircraft in flight. In 1917 the R.F.C. Wireless Experimental station, then under the direction of Captain J. M. Furnival, was transferred from Brooklands to Biggin Hill.

Shortly afterwards a flight of No. 39 Squadron was transferred from North Weald to Biggin Hill to form the nucleus of the London Defence Squadron (No. 141). At this time a further important development, two-way telephony between aircraft, was coming off the production line and the Wireless Officer of this Squadron, F. S. Mockford, had the task of equipping the aircraft and training the crews of No. 141 Squadron in the use of this new aid.

Another significant technical advance was also made in 1917 when Major Prince developed 'choke control' for telephony modulation of aircraft transmitters. This method, which had been suggested by H. J. Round in 1914, provided greatly improved speech quality. It was demonstrated to the General Staff in the same year and in 1918 was put into large-scale usage by what had now become the Royal Air Force, the equipment being known as the 'Mark II choke controlled telephone set'.

By the end of the war, the Royal Air Force had 600 aeroplanes fitted with wireless apparatus, operating in conjunction with 1,000 ground stations, the force being manned by over 18,000 wireless operators.

It may be wondered what Guglielmo Marconi was doing during these momentous years. As an Italian subject, Marconi was technically a neutral until 24 May 1915, when Italy declared war on Austria.

In March 1914 he had been in Italy where he, together with H. J. Round and K. W. Tremellen as assistants, carried out the first wireless telephony experimental tests on the high seas. The apparatus was installed on the Italian warships *Regina Elena* and *Napoli* and communication was established between the two up to a distance of forty-five miles.

The equipment was designed by H. J. Round and incorporated his 'soft' type C valve. The valve telephony set used in the Italian tests was so successful that several were built for demonstration and sale in the U.S.A. and elsewhere.

In January 1915, Guglielmo Marconi took his place in the Italian Senate. Returning to England shortly after, he was presented with the Albert medal by the Royal Society of Arts on April 13.

At the end of April he left Southampton by the *Lusitania en route* to the United States, where he was required to give evidence in a lawsuit between the American Marconi Company and the Atlantic Communication Company, a subsidiary of the Telefunken organization.

Whilst in America on that occasion he inspected a new device which interested him greatly, the first design of Alexanderson's high frequency alternator, which, rated at 50 KVA at frequencies between 25 and 50 Kc/s, promised to be a significant new development for use in high-power wireless stations.

On May 24 when Italy declared war, Marconi announced to the American legal authorities that he proposed to go immediately to Italy to serve his country. The case was accordingly adjourned.

At this time German authorities in New York had issued a public warning that the *Lusitania* would be torpedoed on entering British waters. There was also a strong rumour that plans were afoot to capture Guglielmo Marconi. The United States and, indeed, much of the world were profoundly shocked to find that the German announcement was no idle threat, when, on May 7, the *Lusitania* was torpedoed off the Old Head of Kinsale, Ireland, with heavy loss of life. The plot to capture Marconi – if it ever existed – did not succeed. He was not aboard the *Lusitania*; instead, travelling incognito, he sailed on the *St Paul* and arrived in London without incident on 31 May 1915. He proceeded to Italy where he was immediately appointed to the Army General Staff as a Lieutenant in the Engineers, in charge of the organization of the Army Wireless Service.

This, however, was by no means the extent of his duties. A parallel appointment to the Naval Electrical Equipment Committee enabled him to ensure that the latest improvements in wireless communication were available to the Italian Fleet. In addition he acted as consultant to a long distance wireless service which was being organized between Coltano and St Petersburg, a project which was vital to the joint Italian and Russian cause as no other means of telegraphic communication existed between the two countries. Earlier in the month a wireless telegraph service between Italy and Spain had been inaugurated. All the stations concerned used Marconi apparatus, and on this new service the newly created Lieutenant had also to keep a watching brief. In fact, Marconi was no newcomer to modern warfare for he had been at Tripoli in 1911-12 when the Italians were in conflict with the Turks. In 1915, however, operations were on a much vaster scale and he saw active service on the Isonzo and at Monte Grappe.

In December 1915 Marconi accompanied General Cadorna to a meeting of the allied commanders at Marshal Joffres Headquarters and returned to Italy with new ideas for the application of wireless to military needs.

One notable result was brought about because of the increasing congestion of the wavebands in the Mediterranean area. With a view to easing the situation for the Italian Fleet, Marconi, assisted by C. S. Franklin, turned his attention in 1916 to what were then regarded as ultra short wavelengths (about two metres) as a possible source of additional channels of communication. These wavelengths had been neglected since the turn of the century when empiric research had pointed (it seemed conclusively) to the use of longer wavelengths and high powers as the only means of achieving long-distance working. As a result it was universally believed that the ultra short waves held no practical promise.

Marconi was now not concerned with long ranges; his immediate objective was inter-ship communication over optical distances, using ultra short waves as a means of freeing the conventional wavelengths for other traffic.

To this end C. S. Franklin designed a spark transmitter to operate on a wavelength of about two metres (spark was employed because no valve of the period would oscillate at such a wavelength). The associated antenna radiated in the focal plane of a cylindrical reflector composed of metal strips resonating at two metres. The receiving equipment consisted of a similar antenna and reflector coupled to a carborundum detector circuit.

Pleased as Marconi was at the success of the experiment he did not fully realize at the time the historic significance of the occasion. It was historic because it marked the turning point in a long road which, ever since 1901, had been signposted 'Long wavelengths and high power' as the only means of reaching the goal of long ranges. The 1916 experiments marked a return to the hitherto neglected wavelengths which Marconi had used in his first developments of wireless communication. By using a reflector the power, instead of being broadcast in all directions (or over a wide area) was now being concentrated into a beam. The work carried out in Italy, although in itself concerned only with short-range working, paved the way for further work on the short wavelengths and eventually led to the evolution of the beam system which is still, after over forty years, the backbone of the world's long-range wireless circuits.

On behalf of the Italian Government, Senatore Marconi visited the United States in 1917 where on June 6 he received the honorary degree of D.Sc. from the University of Columbia. As a sidelight on the visits, recruitment of men for wireless duties in the United States Force, soared wherever he went.

Meanwhile, the war dragged on in mud and blood to its close and a wireless message, the first open act of war, was also the last.

At 5.40 a.m. on 11 November 1918, W. H. Chick, a special duty wireless operator at Marconi House in the Strand, intercepted the long-awaited message sent out from the Eiffel Tower station by Marshal Foch. The message ran:

> 'Les hostilites seront arretees sur toute le front a partir du onze Novembre onze heures (heure française).
> Les troupes alliees ne dispasseront pas jusqu' a nouvelle ordre la ligne atteinte a cette date et a cette heure.'
>
> 'MARECHAL FOCH'

Among the hundreds of wireless operators who were tuned to Eiffel Tower's familiar grunting was Guglielmo Marconi in his apartment in Rome. One can imagine the emotions of the man who had in his youth foreseen wireless as a means of saving life and who, until his death, never ceased to look upon it as a potential means of promoting peace and understanding between the nations.

On 21 June 1922 Mr Godfrey Isaacs unveiled a memorial plaque in Marconi House, Strand, to the 348 men of the Marconi Companies who lost their lives in the war, the bulk of whom were sea-going wireless operators of the Marconi International Marine Communication Company. The plaque, which many years later was moved to the entrance hall of a new Marconi building at Chelmsford, bears the words:

'THEY DYING SO, LIVE.'

PART TWO

21

The Post-War Scene

With the signing of the Peace Treaty of Versailles in June 1919 and its coming into force on 10 January 1920, the war-weary nations, after the five longest years in history, began the struggle towards rehabilitation and peaceful commerce.

It is a sad commentary upon human nature that scientific knowledge increases at a much faster rate when the goal is the destruction of fellow human beings. The Great War had been no exception and in no area of science had it been more marked than in wireless. From a mere 'useful adjunct to visual signalling' it had grown to be a vital factor upon which the armies, navies and air forces had relied to an ever-increasing degree.

The key component in this transformation scene had been the thermionic valve. In 1914, valves were hand-made, fragile, unpredictable, indifferent performers. The vast strides made during the war years, notably in the evolution of more efficient and robust cathodes, the introduction of high-vacuum techniques and the growth of expertise in manufacture, saw the valve emerge in 1919 as a relatively robust, stable performer with a useful amplification factor (at least, at audio frequencies) and capable of being manufactured in quantity to close tolerances in characteristics. This in turn made possible the design of new circuits and permitted applications which were impossible in 1914.

The return to the Company of the large number of its engineers who had been seconded to service with the armed forces, emphasized the need to resume without delay the exploration of commercial markets which the war had interrupted. A great deal of research was needed in order to channel the techniques and experience which had been gained into forms suitable for these markets. And research meant the expenditure of time and money, neither of which could easily be afforded.

Money, in particular, was in short supply. Although the Imperial Wireless Scheme was still afoot in that the contracts of 1913 had been superseded by a new Government offer two years later, and had been accepted by the Company, no draft contract had been forthcoming.

The Government also owed the Company large sums of money for its war work, notably in respect of the stations which had been commandeered, together with their staffs, and for the interception of some eighty million words from the enemy's fixed and portable stations and his immense volume of traffic in cypher which was in Russian, German, Italian, French and Rumanian.

For the handling of this mammoth task and in recompense for the commandeered stations, the Post Office offered payment at the rate of one and one-fifth pence per word. This was refused as constituting little more than out-of-pocket expenses. Upon the Government's refusal to arbitrate, the Company took its case to the Courts of Petition of Right, where, after a two days' hearing, judgement was given in its favour.

The question of settlement terms showed a sharp divergence of opinion. The Post Office contended that the contract was worth £47,000 whilst the Arbitrator, Mr Justice Lawrence, placed it at £1,200,000. Eventually a cash payment of £590,000 was made. This settlement, although welcome in comparison to the original offer, was quite insufficient to cover the Company's current and future financial requirements, and the situation had to be met by a new issue of shares. The capital was increased to £3,000,000 by this means in November 1919.

The period which followed saw an intensive commercial programme initiated, the outward sign of which was the formation of a large number of subsidiary and affiliated Companies at home and abroad. No fewer than nineteen were constituted between 1918 and 1923.

At the same time other associated Companies were overhauled and extended. The Russian Marconi Company had sadly been lost in the revolution but in Spain the Compañia Nacional de Telégrafia sin Hilos (formed in 1910) was developing its services at a rapid rate. In France the Compagnie Française Maritime et Coloniale de Télégraphie sans Fils, which handled all French maritime signal business, merged with the Compagnie Universelle de Télégraphie et de Téléphonie sans Fils to become the Compagnie Générale de Télégraphie sans Fils, formed in Paris on 5 February 1918.

The thermionic valve designs of the Marconi Company had, until 1919, been commercially manufactured for the Company by the Ediswan Company with very satisfactory results. By that time the production of valves required so much special treatment and the demand was so heavy that an agreement was reached to pool the valve interests of Marconi's and the General Electric Company. The new organization, first known as the Marconi-Osram Valve Company was registered on 20 October 1919; the name was abbreviated to the M.O. Valve Co. one year later. Production of the valves was at the Osram Works at Hammersmith, London.

These and other activities represented a determined attempt to set the Company on its feet in a post-war world after five years' all-out participation in the war effort. The effort was timely, for the international outlook in the commercial field was now entirely changed. Prior to 1914, wireless companies were few, and serious competitors could be counted on the fingers of one hand. Not so in 1919, for the spread of hostilities throughout the world had not only brought the rapid advance of technologies to all the major participants but had also, by reason of the imperative nature of the demand for equipments in huge quantities, seen the creation of a large number of new manufacturers and also the growth of tiny pre-war organizations into companies of considerable size.

One benefit which the war had brought to Europe was the relaxation of a stranglehold on the manufacture of triode valves. The issue was basically that of whether the de Forest triode was a master patent in its own right or merely an improvement (albeit a very important improvement) on the Marconi-Fleming diode. Lawsuits over this began in 1911 and had gone on interminably as the judgement of one Court was overset by another, thus beginning the wrangle all over again.

The issue was, of course, so important that neither the Marconi Company nor de Forest could afford to admit defeat, in spite of the fact that the costs of litigation were as a bottomless pit and only the lawyers were profiting from it. The situation in 1914 was that the Marconi Company would not permit the public sale of any version of the de Forest valve, while de Forest retaliated by prohibiting the use of the third electrode, or grid, in any valve manufactured by companies other than his own.

The exigencies of war broke this stalemate in Europe, where the contestants felt free, in their respective national interests, to develop the triode valve without regard to civil patent laws. In the U.S.A., however, which was still neutral, the litigation continued and spread, involving not only de Forest and the American Marconi Company but also Langmuir, Armstrong, Dr Arnold of the American Telephone and Telegraph Company and others.

But in other respects the American national interest was furthered by neutrality. The European war created profitable new markets and also provided opportunities for entry into world markets which had hitherto been dominated by the European manufacturers.

This encouraged the rapid growth of American wireless manufactories from an insignificant size to a point where they became serious rivals to the American Marconi Company.

This organization had, until 1914, been manufacturing marine wireless equipments and transoceanic stations in moderate quantity. The outbreak of war in Europe brought a massive demand for all types of equipment, so that the factory at Aldene, New Jersey, had to be enlarged. Simultaneously, new designs of spark equipment had to be formulated and thermionic valve techniques had to be investigated. Almost overnight the American Marconi Company became a great manufacturing firm.

Upon the declaration of war, the Company's high-power and coastal stations were taken over by the United States Government, and the rental system for shipping abandoned in favour of outright purchase. The coastal stations, with one exception (Galveston) were eventually purchased by the United States Navy.

By the end of the war, technical progress had been such that it was evident that the existing Marconi spark method of transmission was on the way out in favour of either arc, radio-frequency alternator or – more in the future – thermionic valve transmission, all three of which provided continuous waves in place of the damped wave-trains of the spark systems. This situation presaged a crisis, for the patents to cover a complete continuous wave communication system were divided between several companies, and none of them could legally operate a radio circuit which embodied all the new developments.

Under the auspices of the U.S. Navy a merger was proposed between the General Electric Company of America (which held the patents of the successful Alexanderson alternator) and the American Marconi Company, with its fundamental valve and other patents and its expertise in wireless manufacture and operation. This was manifestly advantageous to both parties, except for a sting in the tail for the British-held company, brought about by the U.S. Government's insistence that the new company should be national in character and not affiliated with any foreign organization.

The British Marconi Company was in no position to fend off this proposal. In low financial water pending the receipt of payment for its war work and with heavy financial commitments of its own, it was quite unable to finance the proposed big expansion programme of the

American Marconi Company. It had no alternative therefore but to discuss terms and eventually agree to the sale of its holdings. Thus, on 17 October 1919, the Radio Corporation of America came into being.

This, however, was by no means the end of the affair, for other essential patents were still in rival hands. Again, the United States Navy acted as an intermediary, finally bringing about an agreement between all relevant parties for a full interchange of patent rights. In this way the Radio Corporation of America became possessed of the rights to the fundamental Marconi patents and those appertaining to the Alexanderson alternator, the de Forest patents on the triode valve, the Westinghouse patents of Fessenden and Armstrong relating to the principles of heterodyne, regeneration and feedback, and the Pickard patents on crystals and other detectors (these being owned by the United Fruit Company). In short, R.C.A. was placed in possession of a completely workable modern system of wireless communication, and the extensive practical experience to go with it. Truly, an unassailable position.

No mention of the Radio Corporation of America would be complete without reference to its organizing genius, David Sarnoff. In the year 1900, Sarnoff, then nine years old, arrived in the U.S.A. When he was fifteen he entered the service of the American Marconi Company as an office boy, and it was soon clear, by his application to the mastery of the theory of wireless telegraphy and his zeal in carrying out experimental work in his spare time, that more was to be heard of this remarkable young man. It is on record that at the time of the *Titanic* disaster, Sarnoff, by then a first-class wireless operator, worked without rest for three days and nights, handling an enormous flow of news traffic.

By 1916 he had risen to the position of Contracts Manager and it was in that capacity that he put forward a startling proposal to his General Manager. In view of the advance which wireless telephony had made since the outbreak of the European war he suggested that transmitting stations should be built for the purpose of broadcasting speech and music and that what he called 'a radio music box' should be manufactured for sale to the general public. 'This device,' said Sarnoff, 'must be arranged to receive on several wavelengths with the throw of a switch or the pressing of a button. The radio music box can be supplied with amplifying tubes (valves) and a loudspeaking telephone, all of which can be neatly mounted in a box. . . .'

Radio for entertainment. An unheard of, revolutionary idea, and as part of it, a vision of a radio receiver much as we know it today. The top management mulled over it, with its breathtaking implications, and its stupendous risks, not the least of which was the impossible valve (tube) situation as it then existed. The plan was still under active consideration when, in 1917, the United States entered the war, whereupon it was shelved for the duration.

Today David Sarnoff has lived to see, not only his dream envelop the world, but black-and-white and colour television as well. And in so doing he has realized a personal dream also, for the emigrant office-boy later became Chairman of the mighty Radio Corporation of America.

22

The Start of Sound Broadcasting in Britain

In view of Sarnoff's proposal for the setting-up of an entertainment sound broadcasting organization in 1916, it is surprising to find that on both sides of the Atlantic the enterprise, when it did come to pass, started by accident.

Yet such was the case. In the United States in 1919, Dr Frank Conrad of the Westinghouse Company, in carrying out range tests with a telephony transmitter, began to broadcast a few phonograph records as a variant to speech transmissions. To his surprise he received a large number of letters asking for more, mostly from ex-service personnel who had been connected with wireless during the war and had built crystal receivers to keep in touch with commercial transmissions. In sheer self-defence Conrad found himself putting on two phonograph recitals a week.

An election was coming along. Hastily, Westinghouse authorized Dr Conrad to build another transmitter and this, by a monumental effort, was made ready for election night. The election results were broadcast to an audience which now amounted to several hundred, and the innovation was widely publicized. As a result it was decided to transmit regular programmes in the hope of creating a new market for components and complete receivers, a speculation which succeeded beyond measure, aided as it was by the easement in the thermionic valve patent situation which was coincident with the start of the service.

In this way broadcasting began in the United States, from a station whose call-sign KDKA has since become famous the world over.

In Britain a somewhat similar situation occurred, except for one marked difference, namely that in Britain the control of all wireless transmissions was vested in one authority – the Post Office.

The beginnings of the British story go back to the year 1906 when

H. J. Round, at the time an ex-employee of the American Marconi Company (he had been sacked in an economy drive), carried out private experimental work on Marconi premises and produced an arc wireless telephone. (Professor R. A. Fessenden, a Canadian working in the U.S.A., was also carrying out wireless telephony experiments at this time, but using a high-frequency alternator as a carrier source. Neither man knew anything of the other's activities.)

Round, fortunately for the Company as it turned out, was quickly reinstated and shortly afterwards returned to the parent Company in England, where he continued his telephony experiments and demonstrated his apparatus to Guglielmo Marconi, whose personal assistant he became.

Some account of Round's pioneering work on the development of the thermionic amplifying valve and his subsequent war career has already been given. The year 1919 finds him back in civilian life with the Marconi Company, which, with an extensive background of experience in military wireless telephony, was anxious to put this to whatever commercial usage might come to hand.

Round's first task was to develop more powerful transmitting valves, which he did most successfully in the form of the MT1's and MT2's. In March 1919, under his direction, a wireless telephony transmitter was built at Ballybunion, Ireland, and this, although only of $2\frac{1}{2}$ kW input power, became the first European telephony station to be heard on the other side of the Atlantic.

A Marconi engineer, W. T. Ditcham, was the broadcaster on this occasion. The wavelength used was the comparatively long one of 3,800 m.

The significance of this transatlantic telephony broadcast was not so much the spanning of the Atlantic, which had in fact been done four years earlier, in 1915, when the American Telephone and Telegraph Co., in association with the Standard Electric Co., had transmitted speech from Arlington to the Eiffel Tower station, Paris. Its importance lay rather in the tremendous advance in valve and circuit technique, for, whereas the Arlington transmitter had employed over 300 valves, the Ballybunion station used only three main valves, namely two MT1's as oscillators and a third as modulator.

In January 1920, a rather more powerful telephony transmitter (6 kW input) was put into operation at Chelmsford and this was followed a month later by one rated at 15 kW input. The usual range tests were carried out using this transmitter but, bored with the continual recital of the names of railway stations (an established practice for speech tests) Round and Ditcham pressed into service a number of Company employees with musical talent.

Thus it came about that the first broadcast artistes in this country were from the Chelmsford area. For the record, they were a Mr White (piano), Mr E. Cooper (tenor), Miss Winifred Sayer (soprano), Mr A. V. Beeton (oboe) and Mr W. Higby (cornet). Two hundred and fourteen appreciative reports came in from experimenters and ships' operators, the greatest range being 1,450 miles.

In spite of the interest aroused by the concerts, the official Company view was that the future of wireless telephony lay in commercial speech transmission. In furtherance of this policy a wireless telephony news service was inaugurated from the Chelmsford station on 23 February 1920 – the first of its kind in the world.

But soon opinion began to veer somewhat, particularly when the Dutch experimental station PCGG, using Marconi apparatus, began its concerts from The Hague on April 29, and were so enthusiastically commented upon by British and Continental amateurs.

The novelty of broadcast entertainment had not gone unnoticed by the newspapers and it was in fact the enthusiasm of the *Daily Mail* which helped to change the original scepticism of the Company to a point where a second (and harder) look was taken at the possibilities of entertainment broadcasting.

This point came when, under the sponsorship of the newspaper, it was arranged that Dame Nellie Melba, the famous Australian prima donna, should visit the Chelmsford Works and give a concert.

The great day, 15 June 1920, duly arrived, and with it Dame Nellie at Chelmsford. In the preceding few weeks, everything possible had been done to improve the acoustics of the 'studio' and the quality of the microphone and circuit characteristics. Melba was shown the transmitting equipment and then the towering antenna masts, the engineer in charge of the tour explaining that it was from the wires at the top that her voice would be carried far and wide. 'Young man,' exclaimed Melba, 'if you think I am going to climb up there you are greatly mistaken.'

Suitably reassured, on that summer evening Dame Nellie stood up in front of the microphone (a telephone mouthpiece with a horn made of cigar-box wood fastened to it), and at 7.10 p.m. a preliminary trill came to listeners' ears as the engineers established the best distance between singer and microphone. There followed for the fortunate few who possessed receivers, her magnificent renderings of 'Home Sweet Home', 'Nymphes et Sylvains' and the 'Addio' from *La Boheme*. In response to the applause of her local audience she gave an encore consisting of 'Chant Venitien' and 'Nymphes et Sylvains', ending the concert with the National Anthem.

The following days and weeks left no doubt about the triumph. Congratulatory letters poured in from all over Europe, from Persia and one from as far afield as St John's, Newfoundland. Reception at the Eiffel Tower station was so strong that gramophone records were made of Melba's voice.

Wireless telephony had had its first major test as a medium of entertainment; a gruelling one indeed in view of the range of sound frequencies covered. It had succeeded beyond all reasonable expectations, but even so there were those within the Company who measured the success in terms of educating the public to the fact that, unlike wireless telegraphy, the new wireless telephony enabled two unskilled users to exchange messages over considerable distances. But for the less conservative element the Melba broadcast brought hope of an entirely new field of activity although no one was quite sure at this time where it would lead.

For the more immediate future, the development of the telephony news service was a much more promising target, and a first-class opportunity to demonstrate this service was at hand in the form of a delegation to an Imperial Press Union conference which was to sail from Liverpool on July 20 *en route* to Ottawa.

Hurriedly the co-operation of the Canadian Pacific Ocean Services was sought and permission was granted to install a 3 kW telephone/telegraph set aboard the *Victorian*, the ship in which the delegates were to travel. A 6 kW telephone transmitter was installed at Signal Hill, Newfoundland, and the liner *Olympic* was fitted with a $1\frac{1}{2}$ kW cabinet telephone set. The Marconi station at Poldhu had for some little time past been transmitting a telephony news service via a 6 kW installation and this could be supplemented by programmes radiated from the 15 kW Chelmsford transmitter; Poldhu and Chelmsford used a common wavelength of 2,800 m.

As the *Victorian* steamed towards Canada the Press delegates were provided with morning and evening issues of a special newspaper, *The North Atlantic Times*, edited by Arthur Burrows, the Marconi Publicity Manager, from material derived from Poldhu, and were entertained by musical programmes from Chelmsford, these being reproduced by loud-speaking telephones on board. On July 26 the concerts were still being received when the *Victorian* was 2,100 miles from Chelmsford – easily a record for shore-to-ship telephony.

The *Victorian* was also transmitting gramophone records and these concerts were picked up by operators on many liners and by the *Olympic*'s telephony set. Two-way conversations between the *Victorian* and the *Olympic* took place over distances up to 570 miles, while two-way telephony was established between the *Victorian* and the Signal Hill station at a range of 650 miles. On July 25, when the ship was 300 miles from the Canadian shore, greetings were exchanged between the Premier of Newfoundland and Lord Burnham, leader of the delegation. Altogether a very impressive series of demonstrations, and given to the very people who could, via the Press they represented, give wireless telephony the maximum publicity.

Demonstrations of the broadcasting of news items from the Chelmsford station to newspaper offices in Sheffield, Preston, Newcastle and Belfast, and also to Norwegian, Danish and Swedish journals, were given during July and August 1920, reception in all cases being effected via 6-valve receivers used in conjunction with frame antennas. Telephone subscribers in the Scandinavian capitals were able to enjoy a unique experience in July when Lauritz Melchior, the famous Danish tenor, broadcast from Chelmsford; the concert was received on the other side of the North Sea and, by special arrangement, the telephone exchanges in the Scandinavian capitals were connected to the receiving stations, thus enabling their subscribers to listen to the concert.

It is salutory to recall at this point that whereas in the United States no overall controlling authority existed, the Chelmsford transmissions were only possible by reason of the approval of the Postmaster-General, who had – and still has – absolute authority over wireless stations within the British Isles. Thus the Marconi licence to transmit was only granted for experimental purposes and so nothing in the nature of a programme of entertainment could be radiated as such. This was singularly unfortunate because it was becoming clearer every day that entertainment broadcasting was rapidly gaining favour with the American public and that the U.S.A. would be making a strong bid for world markets in receivers and broadcasting transmitters. It was therefore vital that Britain should be in a position to demonstrate her knowledge and skill in the new art to as many foreign countries as possible.

It was at this critical point, and just as the concept of entertainment broadcasting was sweeping the U.S.A. like a forest fire, that the British

Post Office acted. It withdrew the Marconi licence completely on the ground of 'interference with legitimate services'.

At this time an increasing number of amateur telephony stations were coming into being, officially licensed by the Post Office, but subject to severe restrictions upon their operation, including a limitation of output power to ten watts.

The amateurs were incensed at the closure of the Chelmsford station as this had been a valued yardstick, transmitting on a precise wavelength at a declared power and using the best techniques in the light of the knowledge of the period.

An application by the Marconi Company to renew transmissions as a means of mollifying the amateurs was refused by the Postmaster-General on the grounds that to grant the request would make it impossible to refuse similar requests from other manufacturers. It was hinted that the application would be reconsidered if it came from the amateurs themselves.

The Wireless Society of London held a conference with the provincial and suburban Amateur Wireless Societies (later all were amalgamated into what is now the Radio Society of Great Britain). The conference took place in March 1921 with Dr J. Erskine Murray as its President. It was agreed to ask the Postmaster-General to authorize the Marconi Company to recommence transmissions, and this resolution was put into effect.

The months dragged by. Then at last came word that permission was granted, but for continuous wave morse transmissions only. Nine months had now passed and with every day resentment mounted within the Wireless Societies, which culminated in a petition signed by the Presidents of sixty-three amateur societies, asking for the reinstatement of professional transmission in Great Britain

This time the Postmaster-General relented. In a letter dated 13 January 1922 he stated that he had now authorized Marconi's Wireless Telegraph Co. to establish a station, subject to certain conditions.

These, it soon transpired, did not err on the side of generosity. Firstly, the power must not exceed 250 watts; secondly, transmission time must not exceed one half-hour per week; thirdly, the station must close down for three minutes in every ten while the engineers maintained a listening watch on its own wavelength for instructions to close down completely if interference was being experienced by other services. It was the electronics equivalent of the man with the red flag in front of horseless carriages.

During the interval of total cessation of transmissions the Marconi

Company had formed an Aircraft Department in anticipation of another new market, namely airborne wireless telephony, when civil aviation got under way. A Development Section was established at Writtle, near Chelmsford, and housed in a large wooden hut.

Upon the news that telephony broadcasting was to recommence (if such a pittance as a half-hour per week could justify this description) the Writtle Development Section were asked to rig up a suitable transmitting station, and this was speedily done under the direction of Captain P. P. Eckersley. The circuit used was almost identical with that of a standard Marconi telephone set of the time, the transmitter feeding a four-wire antenna 250 ft. long and 110 ft. high, and originally radiating on a wavelength of 700 m., although this was soon changed to 400 m. to avoid a clash with one of the harmonics of the G.P.O. station at Leafield.

Whilst construction was going on, thought was also given to the provision of programme material for the weekly half-hour which had been scheduled for Tuesday evenings between 8 p.m. and 8.30 p.m. This task was also undertaken by P. P. Eckersley.

On 14 February 1922 the country at large received a belated valentine at eight o'clock in the evening in the form of the first radio entertainment broadcast from that wooden hut at Writtle. The call-sign 2-MT, or in telegraphese, 'Two-Emma-Tock' brought joy to the hearts of the amateurs who had won the battle against Authority, and the programmes brought even more joy. For P. P. Eckersley proved to be (even to his own surprise) a natural broadcaster with a complete irreverence for that sinister device the microphone, which was to strike terror in thousands of others. His handling of the weekly half-hour was delightfully informal and his listeners loved it, the letters of appreciation multiplying every week.

It is probable that Eckersley never enjoyed himself more than when he was compère, actor-manager and a soloist at Two-Emma-Tock; at least, this was the impression his spontaneous humour gave his listeners. The general atmosphere of the transmissions is typified by the theme song used for signing-off, which was sung to the tune of 'Parted', a song then much favoured by concert artistes. There were various versions of which one was:

> C.Q.!* The concert's ending
> Loud squeals the heterodyne
> You must soon switch off your set
> I must soon switch off mine.

* C.Q. is the wireless telegraphic code signal for 'calling all stations' ('seek you').

Stay for one fleeting moment
Tuned to the last degree
C.Q.! The concert's ending –
Ending from 2MT.

(accel) How can we keep it going
    Valves blue and engine hot?
(cresc) C.Q.! The concert's end-ed
f.f.   I wish we could scrap the lot!
(rall.p.p.) I wish we could scrap the lot.

Yet it would be wrong to suppose that Two-Emma-Tock represented nothing more than thirty minutes of frivolous nonsense. Far from it. The transmissions provided amateurs with invaluable checking references and the programme content itself contained in embryo certain patterns which were followed later; for example, the first radio play was produced (Cyrano de Bergerac) – the single microphone handset being passed from player to player as the lines demanded! – and a rudimentary 'Children's Hour' was evolved.

23

The Formation of the B.B.C.

Shortly after 2-MT began transmissions, another permit was received from the G.P.O., this time authorizing the establishment of an experimental station at Marconi House in London. The permit, received by the Company direct, allowed it to transmit speech for a maximum time of one hour daily using a radiated power of not more than a hundred watts. Musical items were not allowed at first, but after a while this restriction was removed and the maximum permissible power was increased to $1\frac{1}{2}$ kW.

This station was allocated the call sign 2LO. The transmitter (designed by Round) and its associated studio, were housed in a room at the top of Marconi House and began operation on 11 May 1922.

The programmes were officially demonstrations and, as such, were not publicly advertised; those listeners who were on the Company's mailing list were notified in advance by post. The demonstrations were arranged for the benefit of audiences at some institution; a hospital, a wireless society, a private garden party and similar organizations or functions at which receiving sets were installed by the Company for the occasion. Each transmission was the subject of a special Post Office permit. (Later, some of the evening programmes were announced editorially but mention of the Marconi House station was forbidden.) The wavelength was 360 m.

The man in administrative charge of these activities was A. R. Burrows (later to become the well-loved 'Uncle Arthur' of the B.B.C.). Some idea of the rudimentary nature of the broadcasting system can be gathered from his early reports to the Management:

'The new arrangement of microphones and switches ... is not a good one from the stage-management point of view. With the singer facing the piano it becomes necessary for the M.C. who is checking the singing to go right round in front of her, using the long lead and the headphones for this purpose. This practice has two defects:

1. That other artistes have a most unfortunate habit of tripping over the 'phone leads and nearly breaking the M.C.'s neck.
2. That before the M.C. can return to the switches at the end of a performance the singer has often passed a remark on her performance which becomes audible all over the country. With fresh artistes each night we are bound to have these asides unless the switches are immediately at hand to the M.C.'

From the outset, the 2LO transmissions were markedly more sober than those originating from 2-MT Writtle, meticulous care being taken 'never to offend anyone' for fear of having the licence revoked. This outlook was not lost upon the irrepressible P. P. Eckersley, and the Writtle programmes took every opportunity to poke fun at 2LO's self-conscious sobriety. It must have been galling for Burrows to receive letters requesting him *not* to transmit between 8 p.m. and 8.30 p.m. on Tuesday evenings so that the programme should not clash with that from Writtle!

But although an average 2LO concert programme of that time would be rated as dull indeed by today's standards, there were nevertheless some broadcasting highlights, notably the running commentary on the Lewis-Carpentier fight on May 11 (the opening day for transmissions), the broadcast made by Georges Carpentier on behalf of the British Legion on June 20; reports on the King's Cup air race on September 7 and 8, and the speech made by the Prince of Wales to the Boy Scouts of Great Britain following the great Scout Rally at Alexandra Palace.

As was to be expected, the inauguration of broadcasting in Britain by the Marconi Company brought a host of applications for similar permits from other manufacturing companies – to be precise, twenty-three in all. It was thereupon stated by the Postmaster-General that to grant individual licences on such a scale would be to invite broadcasting chaos. His proposed solution was that the interested parties should form a consortium to create a single broadcasting authority, with which the Post Office would be pleased to treat.

The proposal was put to the manufacturers' representatives on May 18. The manufacturers thereupon formed a committee of seven with the President of the Institution of Electrical Engineers as Chairman. Negotiations were started with the Post Office and Sir William Noble, a retired Chief Engineer of the Post Office, was then elected Chairman of a committee empowered to inaugurate a single broadcasting company.

On October 18 the scheme was explained to two hundred manufacturers to which membership of the company would be open. The

British Broadcasting Company Ltd. was instituted, being formed by six of the big manufacturers, namely the Metropolitan Vickers Co., the Western Electric Co., the British Thomson-Houston Co., the Radio Communication Co., the General Electric Co., and Marconi's Wireless Telegraph Co. The capital was £100,000 in £1 shares, and any bona fide manufacturer was eligible to join by depositing the sum of £50 and taking up one or more shares.

These shares bore a fixed cumulative dividend of seven and a half per cent per annum on the paid-up capital. Any profits in excess of this percentage were to be devoted to the improvement of programmes or the reduction of receiving licence fees.

Revenue was to be derived from two main sources:

1. A tariff of approximately ten per cent paid by the member manufacturers on all receiving sets and certain accessories sold by them. Protection was afforded the member Companies by an embargo being enforced for two years on all foreign-made receivers or others not approved by the Post Office.
2. Half the ten shilling licence fee paid by listeners.

A committee of the founder-members was entrusted with the formation of the new Company and on 14 November 1922 this committee took over responsibility for the evening transmissions of news and other items from the London station 2LO. The official registration of the British Broadcasting Company took place on 15 December 1922.

The infant Broadcasting Company grew apace. On the day after the advent of 2LO under the new régime, the Birmingham station 5IT came into service from the G.E.C. Works in that city, as also did the Manchester station 2ZY, located at the Metropolitan-Vickers Works there. These were followed by the Newcastle station 5WO on December 24, the Cardiff station 5WA on 13 February 1923, the Glasgow station 5SC on March 6, Aberdeen 2BD on October 10, Bournemouth 6BM on October 17 and the Sheffield relay station 6SL on November 12, with other stations planned to follow.

Of the nine original transmitters, seven were of Marconi manufacture. These were 'Q'-type transmitters, fitted with independent drives to ensure frequency stability. The modulation was choke controlled, maximum permissible modulation being approximately eighty per cent. The studios employing Marconi equipment used Sykes-Round microphones which were a vast improvement on the original telephone handset type. The new medium of entertainment continually posed new problems in transmission and as these arose new techniques were evolved to master them, Captain H. J. Round being particularly prolific in new inventions at this time.

The sale of licences boomed to such an extent that the Post Office was unable to deal with them fast enough, and wholesale evasion of licence and royalty fees (the latter being payable per valve by amateur constructors) took place. In March 1923 the total number of licences issued was 80,000, but the numbers of receiving sets in use were estimated at four to five times that figure. Less than a month later the Post Office issued the following licence figures: Broadcasting: 87,661; Experimental: 35,285; Experimental awaiting attention: 33,000; users of home-constructed receivers evading licence, at least 200,000 more.

Foreseeing to some extent the opening of an entirely new market, namely that for domestic receivers, the Marconi Company had, in 1922, created a 'Marconiphone' Department, the task of which was to take over the activities of the Marconi Scientific Instrument Co. and to design, manufacture and sell domestic receiving equipment which complied with Post Office specifications and tests, thereby qualifying for the B.B.C. authorization stamp which was carried by all such receivers. The sets were at first made at the Chelmsford Works.

The first to receive Post Office approval was the 'Crystal Junior'. This incorporated 'spade tuning', an idea of C. S. Franklin's, in which a flat solenoid and a copper sheet could be moved relative to each other to vary the solenoid's inductance and so tune the set.

This was followed shortly after by the 'V1', a single valve detector with positive feed-back from anode to control grid to provide reaction or regeneration. This set was designed by P. W. Willans, another notable engineer of the Company.

The third in the series was the 'V2', designed originally by C. S. Franklin, although later models incorporated further improvements by H. J. Round. In its final form it incorporated an h.f. stage and detector in a reflex circuit, with reaction applied. The V2 was for a long time the most sensitive receiver on the market and the first to incorporate automatic bias.

In December 1923, the Marconiphone Company was formed to take over the activities of the Marconiphone Department; as the domestic receiver production capabilities at Chelmsford proved to be inadequate in view of the demand, mass production was started at the Sterling Telephone Company's Works at Dagenham, although the research and design work was still continued at Chelmsford.

Earlier in the year, on 17 January 1923, the Marconi station 'Two-Emma-Tock' at Writtle had made its final bow to a regretful circle of enthusiasts. It closed down with full honours, its mission accomplished. And more than accomplished, for in addition to providing an extremely useful reference station for the original body of amateurs, it had created an enthusiasm for broadcasting that was destined to make it into the greatest mass medium for entertainment and instruction that the world has ever seen. In its short and hilarious career it laid the foundations of the age of broadcasting.

It is worthy of note that of the original small band of development engineers who devised and ran those riotous half-hours, Captain P. P. Eckersley became the first Chief Engineer of the B.B.C.; Noel (later Sir Noel) Ashbridge became the B.B.C.'s first Technical Director; B. N. MacLarty became Head of the B.B.C. Designs and Installation Department, and R. T. B. Wynn also became a Chief Engineer of the B.B.C. On his retirement from the B.B.C. in 1952, Sir Noel Ashbridge became a Director of the Marconi Company, while B. N. MacLarty returned to the Company in 1947 and later (1954) became Engineer-in-Chief.

It would be inappropriate to leave the period 1920–22 without some small comment on the Post Office attitude towards the formative period of entertainment broadcasting.

Without doubt the G.P.O.'s embargo on telephony transmissions in 1920 delayed the advent of sound broadcasting in this country and thereby gave American interests (which were not subject to this kind of restriction) a valuable lead in their bid for world markets. In this connection it is tempting to accuse the Post Office of excessive officialdom. In fairness, however, it must be remembered that very few in those days foresaw that entertainment broadcasting would become the tremendous force that it is today, and, as far as the G.P.O. was concerned, it meant the allocation of precious wavelengths for the benefit of a tiny band of enthusiasts who had made a hobby of wireless telegraphy and who now wished to experiment with telephony, urged on (it was darkly suspected) by little more than the thrill of hearing voices in their headphones in place of the more impersonal Morse code.

The whole thing could so easily have been a nine days' wonder. In the event it was not, but thanks to the Post Office's rigid control, its growth and expansion was logical and orderly, in marked contrast to the chaotic state of the wavebands which then existed in the U.S.A.

In short, the role of the Post Office was that of an over-zealous and stern guardian rather than that of a wicked uncle.

In April 1923 the B.B.C. acquired premises at No. 2 Savoy Hill, London, and studios were built there to take over from those at Marconi House. These incorporated the results of many of the researches into studio acoustics which were carried out by Captain H. J. Round, including the 'echo box' facility of his devising.

June 1924 saw the inauguration of the Chelmsford 5XX high-power long wave station which gave coverage to a large part of the country and was particularly appreciated in remote areas where reception from 'city' stations was unreliable and subject to fading. The new station was an immediate success and plans were put into operation for the building of an even more ambitious long wave station of 25 kW radiated power (subsequently increased to 30 kW) situated at Daventry, near the geographical centre of the country. This took over the 5XX call-sign and came into operation in July 1925. The Chelmsford station thereupon acquired the call-sign 5GB and continued to operate on high power but on the medium waveband and on an experimental basis.

In March 1925 the $1\frac{1}{2}$ kW transmitting equipment at Marconi House, London, was superseded by a new 6 kW Marconi 'Q'-type transmitter situated on the roof of Selfridge's store in Oxford Street. This station took over the call-sign 2LO, and continued to radiate programmes to the London area until 1929 when on October 21 the Brookman's Park station took over. Brookman's Park heralded an important new phase in technical policy, being the first-fruit of a brilliant concept by P. P. Eckersley, the B.B.C.'s Chief Engineer. The 'Regional Scheme', as it was called, envisaged the abandonment of the multiplicity of relatively low-powered stations of which many had been built throughout the country, in favour of approximately half the number of high-power 'twin' stations. These stations, each embodying two sets of transmitters operating on different wavelengths, were to provide alternative programmes over a very much larger service area than that covered by the single station which it was to supersede. The scheme's success is measured by the fact that it was still in use in 1965.

On 20 July 1925 the Postmaster-General announced in the House of Commons that a committee was being set up to consider the future of broadcasting and in particular the situation which would arise at the end of 1926 when the British Broadcasting Company's licence expired. Almost exactly a year later the main findings of the Crawford Committee were officially accepted by the Government. Of these, the most fundamental change was to be the reconstitution of the B.B.C. from a Company to a Corporation, with the granting of a Royal Charter.

Accordingly, on 31 December 1926, the British Broadcasting Company ceased to exist, and the British Broadcasting Corporation took its place with John (soon to be Sir John and later, Lord) Reith, who had been its first General Manager, still at the helm, but now as the Corporation's Director-General.

Thus, on the last day of 1926, the wireless manufacturing companies ceased to be directly responsible for broadcasting in this country. The four short years of the existence of the British Broadcasting Company had seen an amazing progress in growth and in the state of the art. In December 1922 the staff of the B.B.C. numbered four. By 1925 it had risen to 552. The army of listeners had grown from a few thousand to over two millions. The technology had advanced almost beyond measure, as also had the art-form of broadcasting. The Broadcasting Company had played an indispensable part in the evolution of the new medium, bringing as it did its technical expertise and a guarantee of continuance at a time when the financial revenue from licences was very small. The 'Big Six' Companies had borne all the financial risks and had received no direct rewards of any consequence. Indirectly, of course, the sponsorship of the B.B.C. had been responsible for the phenomenal growth in demand for both capital and domestic equipment, and in this respect the manufacturers had no reason to complain.

24

Sound Broadcasting 1925–1939

The economic blizzard which swept the world in the 1920s and early 1930s spared but few and the Marconi Company was not of that fortunate minority. The effects of the storm will be a recurring theme over several subsequent chapters but we are concerned here with its effect on the Company's broadcasting business.

With the formation of the British Broadcasting Corporation, Marconi's reverted to the role of a manufacturer whose products were on offer to the Corporation in open competition with others; in other words, orders for broadcasting transmitters and studio equipment were dependent on such factors as quality and competitive price. On the domestic receiver side, the Company possessed no background of experience in the consumer market and, furthermore, the delay occasioned in issuing receiving licences, referred to earlier, had brought contract cancellations to the newly-formed Marconiphone Company and represented losses which it was ill-equipped to withstand.

Matters came to a head in the Company generally when Godfrey Isaacs retired in February 1925, only to die on 17 April. The full repercussions of this blow are dealt with in Chapter 27; suffice it to say for the moment that his place was taken by the Rt Hon. F. G. Kellaway, a former Postmaster-General. Under Kellaway's direction a policy of severe retrenchment came into being. Reductions in staff, reductions in salaries and changes in departmental structures became the order of the day, some of them justifiable, but others less so. In 1928 a works costs accountant was appointed to overhaul the costing methods used in the factory with, it seems, singularly unfortunate consequences; H. M. Dowsett, then Assistant Technical General Manager, describes them as 'resulting in a flood of forms, printed literature, a considerable increase in clerical staff and a brave attempt at standardization which lasted for eighteen months; then, as the system demonstrated its unsuitability for application to the changing requirements of the Marconi business, a halt was called to its further application.'

With the appointment of a new Works Manager, B. St J. Sadler, in July 1929, the better features of the costing procedure were retained, but in general the old 'model shop' principles of manufacture were resumed. A halt to retrenchment – temporary as it turned out – was called; an extension to the main bay of the Works was built, together with a new building for high-power broadcasting transmitters, an additional power house building and a large garage.

But the economy axe was again to fall, with the Marconiphone Company as the sacrificial victim. From the engineering standpoint there seems no good reason why the amputation should have taken place, for the receiver designs were excellent, the patent position was good, much useful research was being carried out and although losses had occurred as mentioned earlier, sales were recovering and the market steadily expanding. The decision can only have been reached partly because the Company in venturing into the consumer market had departed from tradition, but more particularly because the sale of Marconiphone would bring in some badly needed cash. At all events the die was cast. Marconiphone had to go.

The background to the sale, or rather to the purchaser, is interesting.

A few years earlier, the tremendous impact of broadcasting as a means of home entertainment had dealt a crippling blow to its predecessor, the acoustic gramophone, so much so that it was widely believed that the end of the gramophone industry was in sight.

Unexpectedly, reprieve, and ultimately salvation, came from the wireless industry and in particular from H. J. Round, then Chief of Research at Marconi's. As part of the development of new electronic techniques, Round devoted himself to the problem of the electrical recording of speech and music, and in 1926 he had patented such a process which had been acquired by the Vocalion Record Company. Gramophone records made by this method were so markedly superior to those of the old acoustic process as to be sensational, particularly when used in conjunction with the electric pick-up and amplifier of 1925 which Round had designed for the British Brunswick Company. The death of the acoustic system had been brought about with these devices but simultaneously they provided the first gleam of hope of revival for the gramophone record industry.

In Britain at that time the two big contenders for the sale of gramophones and records were, respectively, The Gramophone Company ('His Master's Voice' and other labels) and the Columbia Graphophone Company, the former being a subsidiary of the Radio Corporation of

America. David Sarnoff of R.C.A., on learning that the Marconiphone Company might be coming on to the market, astutely decided that a merger of H.M.V., Marconiphone and Columbia interests would place the resultant Company in a very strong position in both the broadcasting receiver and the recording fields.

Negotiations began, first for the Marconiphone Company, which on 31 December 1929 passed to the possession of R.C.A., together with the Marconi Company's holdings in the M.O. Valve Company which had also fallen under the retrenchment axe. The purchase was added to the assets of The Gramophone Company which now had the right to use Marconi and R.C.A. receiver patents and permitted it the use of the trade mark 'Marconiphone' and the copyright signature 'G. Marconi' on domestic receivers. The Marconi Company was precluded from trading in domestic broadcast receivers for a period of twenty years under the terms of the agreement.

With the passing of the Marconiphone Company to another organization, a considerable number of Marconi engineers and salesmen went also. Probably the most valuable single asset which Marconi's lost in the deal was Isaac Shoenberg who had been a Marconiphone director and Chief of its Patent Department. Shoenberg left to join the research staff of Columbia Graphophone.

With phase one of the operation completed, Sarnoff successfully negotiated to bring Columbia Graphophone into the R.C.A. fold. The new company was named Electric and Musical Industries Ltd. Isaac Shoenberg became its Director of Research and it was he and his brilliant team which developed the video section of the Marconi–EMI television system which was adopted for use in this country in 1936 (see Chapter 31).

It would be idle to pretend that the inclusion of the name 'Marconiphone' and the Marconi signature in the sale was a wise move on the part of the original owners. It has always caused confusion and even today it seems to be widely believed that a financial link exists between E.M.I. Ltd. and Marconi, which is not the case. What was particularly irksome at the time was that the name 'Marconi' which had hitherto only appeared on equipment made under 'model shop' conditions should now be applied to mass produced apparatus. In fairness, however, it must be admitted that the use of the trademarks was perfectly valid and, indeed, logical for Guglielmo Marconi had been offered and had accepted the Presidency of the new E.M.I. organization. The receipt at Marconi House of the occasional domestic receiver query and even

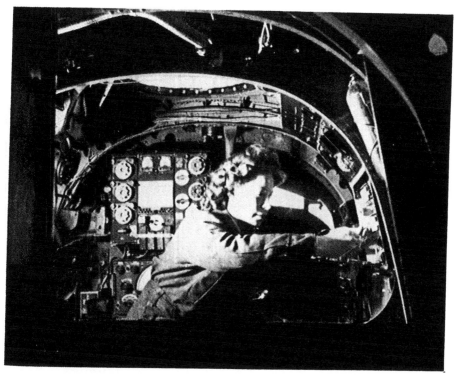

10. Routine maintenance in a wartime bomber aircraft. In the background can be seen the Marconi transmitter-receiver T1154/R1155, of which over 80,000 were manufactured

11. A war-battered Marconi undulator (for dealing with high-speed Morse signals) comes in for overhaul

8. Marconi transmitters at the B.B.C.'s Brookman's Park broadcasting station, 1929

9. Wartime airborne radar picture of Nordhausen compared with a conventional map of the area. The picture was taken at night

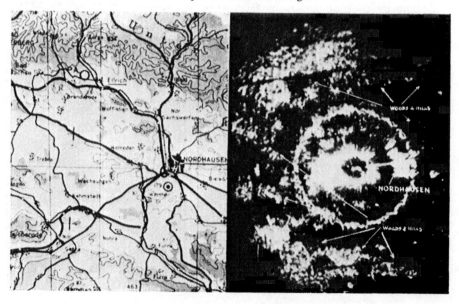

12. The world's first tuned circuit is shown inside the output stage of a modern transmitter

13. The central control positions at the G.P.O. radio station at Rugby

14. The control console at the B.B.C. television station at Crystal Palace

15. 500 kW, 50 cm radar type S264A with SECAR secondary radar antenna mounted on top

requests for window-dressing materials shows that the misapprehension still lives after nearly forty years!

The broadcasting transmitter side of the Marconi Company's business continued to make satisfactory progress. In 1927 the B.B.C. decided to initiate experimental short-wave broadcasting to the Empire and the Company was commissioned to build a transmitter at the Chelmsford Works, where it operated under the call sign of G5SW. The Brookman's Park station – which also used Marconi transmitters – took over the London programmes in October 1929 and other important contracts matured between these dates.

On 7 July 1929 a historic occasion occurred when the thanksgiving service for the recovery of King George V from a serious illness was broadcast not only to the nation but to the Empire. The service was transmitted from London to Bodmin, Cornwall, by landline. There it was fed into the Marconi-Mathieu multiplex beam circuit and received at the terminal near Montreal, Canada. From Montreal it travelled via landline to various Canadian broadcasting stations while the Canadian beam system passed signals across the Pacific to La Perousse, Sydney, Australia whence they were broadcast throughout the Antipodes.

By 1930 Round and Franklin had advanced the design of broadcast transmitters to a remarkable state of efficiency. In Europe the trend was toward high-power transmission as used so successfully by the B.B.C. Switzerland, for example, ordered a 60 kW transmitter of the type used at Brookman's Park; other countries followed suit.

By this time broadcasting had captured the public's attention in no uncertain fashion. Listeners' licences in Britain had passed the 3,000,000 mark and the same upward trend was evident in many countries all over the world.

But the growth of broadcasting brought problems in its wake. The wavebands were getting congested and International Conferences were called to discuss ways and means of avoiding co-station interference. One prime requisite of maintaining order was that each station should remain stable on its allotted wavelength, and this was at first no easy task, involving constant vigilance on the part of the Broadcasting Authority and manual retuning as necessary, until means of automatic control were devised.

There were in 1931 three methods of automatic control in commercial use. One was the tuning-fork method while another employed a quartz crystal to maintain stability of transmission. The third was the Franklin master-oscillator. This employed a capacitor/inductor circuit of special design which automatically adjusted itself for any change in temperature.

The Marconi Company pioneered the piezo-electric quartz crystal for the frequency control of high-frequency oscillators. As early as 1926 a crystal oscillating at about 94 kc/s had been tediously cut by hand, a process which took one week to complete. By 1931 the art had progressed considerably and in that year a v.h.f. transmitter was fitted with a crystal having a zero temperature co-efficient, the first of its kind in Europe. The success of this was immediate and within two years at least twenty-two European broadcasting stations were modified for crystal control. This innovation brought with it real frequency stability.

On 12 October 1931, on the occasion of the 439th anniversary of the discovery of America, an interesting and historic application of wireless took place when Guglielmo Marconi pressed a transmitting key in Rome and thereby flood-lit the great statue of Christ the Redeemer which had been erected on the summit of the Corcovada Mountain dominating Rio de Janeiro. The signal from Rome was sent over landline to the great Coltano station, whence it was transmitted by beam to the Brazilian Wireless Telegraph Company's station near Rio. From this station it again travelled via landline to the base of the mountain to operate flood-lighting switchgear for the unveiling ceremony.

In November 1931 a high-frequency broadcasting and wireless telegraph and telephone station at Vatican City was officially inaugurated by His Holiness the Pope, who, on that occasion, conferred on the Marchese Marconi* the Grand Cross of the Order of Pius, Vatican City State.

In 1932 the first permanent Empire broadcasting station was officially put into operation at the B.B.C. station at Daventry. The transmitters were Marconi-built and broadcast programmes to Australia, South Africa, West Africa, India and Canada.

Empire broadcasting on a regular basis brought with it the problem of time-differences in various parts of the world, which made it necessary to record many of the programmes for transmission at a suitable hour. As the gramophone of that period permitted only a short period of playing time an alternative method was sought and found in the Marconi-Stille apparatus which was the forerunner of the modern tape recorder. This was extensively used by the B.B.C. and other broadcasting authorities.

In February 1933 the Marconi 60 kW broadcasting station at Athlone in the Irish Free State was officially opened, although it had come on the

* Marconi had been created Marchese in the previous year.

air at very short notice in the previous June to broadcast news of the Eucharistic Congress which was held in Eire that year. Other broadcasting installations completed in 1933 included those at Osaka, Bratislava, Bucharest, Lwow, Reykjavik, Trieste, Florence, Bari, Viborg, Wilne, Monte Ceneri, Buenos Aires and Cape Town.

In June 1933 Marchese Marconi spoke from the Board Room at Marconi House, London, over the G.P.O. transradio (Argentina) circuit, in which country his words were re-broadcast from the new 20 kW Radio Excelsior broadcasting station near Buenos Aires.

An outstanding event of 1934 was the opening of the B.B.C.'s new 'National' long-wave broadcasting station at Droitwich. This employed what was then regarded as a super-power transmitter rated at 150 kW into the antenna. This was supplied by the Company, which also in that year was building 150 kW broadcast transmitters for Lahti (Finland), Bod (Rumania) and Motala (Sweden). Before delivery their power output was increased still further, the Lahti transmitter having an output of 220 kW on site.

These stations were supplied in 1935 together with several of smaller power, notably two for Hyderabad and five for Afghanistan. In September of that year Marchese Marconi, accompanied by the Marchesa, inaugurated the Radio Tupi broadcasting station, some twenty-two miles from Rio de Janeiro, which was equipped with a 10 kW medium-wave transmitter, the first of several of its type to be exported to Brazil.

In 1936 a medium-wave 50 kW crystal controlled broadcasting transmitter was installed at Tallinn, Esthonia, and a 35 kW short-wave installation was supplied to Nanking, China. At Santa Palomba, Rome, a 500 kW installation was also completed.

The steady increase in radiated power which occurred over the years is indicative of the rate at which technological progress, and in particular that which was applied to transmitting valve design, was progressing.

By 1936 the Marconi Company and its subsidiaries and associates had been granted no fewer than 800 patents. Marconi broadcasting transmitters were in service at 180 stations in 32 countries.

25

The Imperial Wireless Scheme Again

In view of the size and importance of the Company's Broadcasting Division today, it is difficult to realize that in 1921 it only existed in part of a wooden hut at the Writtle outstation. Few saw the future as differing significantly from that of the Company's past history, namely the further development of commercial and military communications.

Thus, after the 1914–18 war, the first task was to pick up the threads and to press ahead with various communication schemes as the Marconi lifeline. Plans for a European network of wireless communication were revised and the establishment of several of the subsidiary Companies mentioned earlier was an integral part of the scheme.

Post Office licences to operate wireless telegraph services between Britain, France, Spain and Switzerland were obtained in 1919 and in the following year land was acquired at Ongar, Essex, for the erection of a centralized transmitting station for these circuits.

At first legal delays impeded construction, and the station was not ready when an urgent call came from the Government to provide an alternative high-speed channel between London and Geneva in time for the first assembly of the League of Nations which was to take place at the Hotel Victoria, Geneva, in November 1920, as it was quite certain that the existing line and cable telegraph system would be unable to cope with the spate of words.

Accordingly in October 1920 the Company erected an emergency transmitting station in the Jura hills at Place Belle Air and a receiving station at Chien Bourg, near Geneva. The transmitter (of about $1\frac{1}{2}$ kW rating and operating on 3,000 m.) and the receiver were both remotely operated from a Central Telegraph Office at the Hotel Victoria. The London terminal was at Fenchurch Street from which the high-power transmitting station at Caernarvon and the receiving station at Towyn were remotely controlled. The circuit came into operation in time for the historic opening session of the League of Nations.

Further to speed the flow of traffic a 6 kW transmitter at the Chelmsford

Works and a temporary receiving station at Witham, ten miles from Chelmsford, were also pressed into service. It was on this auxiliary equipment that a most useful invention, the absorber keying of continuous-wave transmitters, was evolved; this was commercially developed and first came into use at Ongar in 1922.

These circuits closed down temporarily at the end of 1920, having fully satisfied the Press demands made on them. The Swiss station was then transferred to the Berne area, with the transmitter power increased to 10 kW, and throughout the summer of 1921 a regular high-speed duplex service was maintained between London, Berne and Paris, for the requisite stations had also by this time been established in France.

By the autumn of 1921 the Ongar station was well under construction, together with a receiving station at Brentwood, Essex, and a large Central Telegraph Office in Wilson Street, London. The last-mentioned later became known as Radio House.

In February 1922 the Swiss Marconi Company (later known as Radio Suisse) was formed and the pioneer stations at Berne were reconstructed on the Ongar and Brentwood models. In the early summer of that year, Ongar, Brentwood and Radio House took over the continental circuits and some transatlantic traffic.

This turned out to be providential timing for in July 1922 the huge transatlantic station at Clifden was completely wrecked by Irish irregulars as part of their struggle for Home Rule. The loss of the station, while a serious financial blow to the Company, did not seriously interrupt traffic for any length of time as the load could be transferred to Caernarvon, Towyn, Ongar and Brentwood. The Clifden station was never rebuilt; it had in fact outlived its usefulness, for transmitter, receiver and radiator improvements had removed the necessity for having a station so far West. Its ruins still remain in that remote Irish bog-land as a monument to a great pioneering enterprise.

The Brentwood and Ongar stations represented, in 1922, the ultimate in wireless communication and held the world's speed record for 'paid words' for many years (fifty-eight words per minute).

The three transmitting antennas at Ongar, the basic design of which was carried out by T. L. Eckersley, the brilliant mathematician brother of P. P. (Broadcasting) Eckersley, each consisted of two 4-wire cages suspended from two 300 ft. lattice towers. The high-speed transmitters and independent drives were designed by Round, Ditcham and Mogridge.

At Brentwood, the transatlantic receiving antenna was supported in square formation on four 200 ft. towers; the six receivers, each tuned to a different transmitting station, were fed simultaneously from one antenna. The antenna for the Continental circuits was supported on 96 ft. towers.

Seven underground telegraph circuits and seven underground telephone circuits connected Brentwood to Radio House, with extensions to Ongar. Tone signalling over the telephone lines replaced the Wheatstone duplex circuits and their d.c. signals, thanks to the development work of three other Company engineers of note, namely G. M. Wright (who later became Engineer-in-Chief), S. B. Smith and J. Brown.

The services provided by these stations were soon in full-scale use by the public for traffic with Paris, Berne, Barcelona and the Canadian and United States stations. A highly successful demonstration was given to the Industrial Group of the House of Commons on 27 June 1923. In that year the Towyn station became redundant and was dismantled, the traffic being taken over by Brentwood. The Caernarvon station was operated by remote control over landline from Radio House, London.

In parallel with these important commercial communication developments other and even more ambitious projects were under way, namely the resurrection of the long-delayed Imperial Wireless Scheme.

In 1919, with a wealth of long-distance communication experience behind it, the Company put forward a new proposal to the Government to establish direct wireless communication between Britain, South Africa, India and Australia. These countries were to be linked by long-wave, high-power transmitting stations, with lower powered stations feeding into these arteries from outlying areas.

Under the chairmanship of Sir Henry Norman, a new Select Committee was appointed to investigate the proposals. Its report was issued in May 1920 and the findings were adverse, the Committee being against any suggestion that a private company should be given even the semblance of a monopoly. Instead, it proposed that a chain of stations should be built at intervals of approximately 2,000 miles along the route but that these should be run by the Post Office. The first two stations in the chain, said the Committee, should be Leafield and Cairo, which the Post Office had taken over in 1914 and where Poulsen arc transmitters were now (1920) being installed. The remaining stations should be built and operated either by the British Post Office or the corresponding P and T Authorities in the Dominions. The Norman Report brought a highly unfavourable reaction from Australia, where Amalgamated Wireless (Australasia) Ltd. submitted a proposal to provide a high-power station for direct communication with England and a service of feeder stations covering the whole country. The

Australian Government, which had disliked the Norman Report concept of placing their country at the far end of a vulnerable set of links, the disruption of any one of which would sever Australia's link with Britain, decided to adopt the A.W.A. proposal.

In South Africa too, grave dissatisfaction was expressed with the existing and proposed order of things but India and the other Dominions held aloof. The climax came when the British Parliament in debate refused to accept the suggestions put forward in the Norman report.

Despite this head-wind of opinion the Post Office Poulsen Arc installations at Leafield and Cairo had been pushed ahead as the first link in the proposed chain. This was unfortunate, for the service provided was erratic and of outdated performance. The Poulsen Arc transmitter at Leafield became extremely unpopular in various continental countries as its prolific output of harmonics resulted in the jamming of their services.

At the Imperial Conference held in 1921 the Post Office scheme based on the Norman Report was damned with faint praise and was put out of its misery shortly after by Mr Winston Churchill (then Colonial Secretary) who, as Chairman of the Imperial Communications Committee, refused to have anything further to do with its outmoded proposals.

The Marconi Company took no part in any of these public discussions, but stood aside, conscious that it held a high trump card in the store of theoretical and practical experience at its disposal. In respect of the practical aspect, realization had come in 1918, when the 200 kW 'timed spark' disc transmitter at Caernarvon, operating on 14,000 m., and with an antenna system which could be used for directional radiation towards New Brunswick of the Antipodes, had transmitted telegraphy messages direct to Sydney, Australia. A further important development had been the installation of a 200 kW Alexanderson high frequency alternator at the station in 1920 as an addition to the timed spark equipment. Even more momentous, however, was the construction at Caernarvon of a 100 kW transmitter which employed thermionic valves (fifty-four in all). This transmitter, designed and built under the supervision of H. J. Round, was highly successful. In November 1921 it established communication with Australia, and on December 4, at the Company's invitation, the *Daily Mail* sent the first Press message direct to its correspondent in Sydney.

A certain amount of data as to field strength measurements had already been acquired, but much more was necessary. Field strength measuring

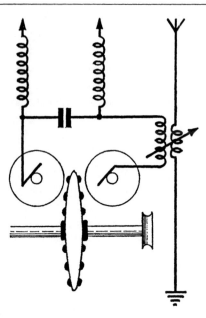

Figure 25.1 Marconi Timed Disc. The studded disc revolves in synchronism· with the alternator supplying the power for the circuit

equipment was designed and the first well-shielded signal generator ever made formed part of it. Godfrey Isaacs authorized that the further acquisition of data should proceed with urgency and almost regardless of expense.

In 1921–2–3 various expeditions consisting of trained men and the new equipment were despatched to all quarters of the earth. One went to Brazil, another to South Africa and a third to New Zealand and later Australia. Others were sent on long-distance voyages or to far countries. All took scientific checks on field strengths received at all hours of daylight and darkness, and during all seasons, from all the high-power long-wave stations then in existence.

With the possession of this data, and the practical long-distance demonstrations given by the Caernarvon station, the Company's strength in the field of high-power, long-range transmission was unassailable, for no other organization had anything comparable to offer. Where others could only offer a system and hope for the best, Marconi's alone could guarantee a service from foreknowledge.

By the beginning of 1922, Godfrey Isaacs was in a position to fire the first shot in a new campaign. This took the form of a cable to the Government of South Africa. 'We will', it said at our own expense erect within eighteen months in South Africa on a suitable site selected by mutual consent, a wireless station capable of maintaining wireless communication with England and elsewhere if necessary, and run such a station efficiently . . . As an alternative we offer to erect stations and to maintain wireless telegraphic connection with the Union Government on the same basis as that approved by the Australian Government.

This offer produced a cabled inquiry to which the answer was

. . . We wish to state that we do not ask for a monopoly but we shall need all inland telegraph facilities and we shall give the Government rights to take over such a station on reasonable terms.

The proposal brought matters to a head in South Africa. For some weeks alternatives were debated in the Union Parliament but at length, under the guidance of General Smuts, judgement was given for private enterprise. On 6 September 1922 an agreement was signed authorizing the Company to erect a high-power station. This agreement offered the Union 'all the benefits of private enterprise plus all the advantages of State control of profits and rates for transmission'. It contained a clause whereby the Company undertook that the station should be used as an integral part of any Empire Wireless system with priority given, as far as possible, to communications with other stations of such a system.

This was very heartening news for the Company; two of the most important areas of the British Empire, Australia and now South Africa,* were to be Marconi-equipped for long-distance wireless communication. But the outcome in other quarters, notably India, was extremely doubtful and although Canada was in favour of leaving wireless communication to private enterprise, the British Post Office had other ideas and were making every effort to achieve them.

For two years past the Post Office had been proposing to effect wireless communication with India, using the Cairo station as a half-way stage, being unable to recommend direct communication in one hop. Now the tactics were changed and they were suggesting the erection of a vast single station in Lincolnshire which was to communicate direct, not only with India but with South Africa and Australia also. The proposal included provision for England to supply the money for the Indian station. This new suggestion aroused much criticism at home and also seems to have been unpopular with the Indian commercial community and the general public.

* The Company's interests in S. Africa were looked after by the Wireless Agency Ltd., registered 1919. This Company became Marconi (South Africa) Ltd., in 1948.

In February 1923 the British Government appointed another Committee to report on the whole subject. The report was soon available, and recommended that the Post Office should own and directly operate all stations in this country for communication with the various parts of the British Empire, with the exception of Canada, in which connection private enterprise might operate on a competitive basis with the State. Private enterprise was to be encouraged to establish services to other places outside the British Empire.

Heartened by this report the Post Office began the construction of a high-power station at Rugby which was to operate on a very long wavelength and was to be so designed that it did not infringe Marconi patents and apparatus.

Simultaneously the Marconi Company pressed ahead with a contract from the Australian Government to build a super-station which had been tendered for via Amalgamated Wireless (Australasia) Ltd. This was to be of 1,000 kW power, with an antenna system supported on twenty steel masts each 800 ft. in height. In South Africa also, matters were moving. The Wireless Company of South Africa was registered in 1923 to implement the concession obtained earlier to operate a wireless station for overseas communication, and preliminary work was going ahead at Klipheuval, near Cape Town.

In England the Empire Press Union was urging a statement of Government policy, a demand which seemed to be fulfilled when in March 1923 Mr Bonar Law announced the Government's decision to issue licences to private enterprise for the purposes of communication with the Dominions, Colonies and foreign countries. There was, however, a rider. This stated that in the interests of national security there should be a wireless station in Britain which was capable of communicating with all the Dominions and this should be owned and operated entirely by the State. It was to be used for both services and commercial messages. The pronouncements were received with much satisfaction both at home and throughout the Empire. It seemed that at long last everybody knew where they stood.

Alas for hopes! Two new Postmasters-General followed each other in quick succession, each with different ideas. Under the second, Sir Laming Worthington-Evans (the first was Sir William Joynson Hicks), a decision was taken to inaugurate a vast pooling arrangement between private enterprise (in practice, the Marconi Company) and the Post Office for the co-operative development of the Empire Wireless Scheme. Services were to be conducted through stations provided by Marconi's and the Government in agreed proportions, and it was proposed that for a start the Company should provide two stations and the Post Office one, in addition to the already existing Marconi station at Caernarvon and the G.P.O. station at Leafield. Maintenance was to be the responsibility of the party providing the station. Revenue was to be divided between the parties in proportion to the effective power of the stations for which they had been responsible. All the stations were to be manned by G.P.O. operators, a proportionate part of the costs and overheads being charged to the Company. The rates charged for messages were to be agreed between the parties, with the general aim of making them lower than equivalent cable rates.

The proposals were doomed to failure from the outset as the respective interests of the Post Office and the Marconi Company were too conflicting to hold out hope of complete agreement. For example, the Post Office insisted that the entire service should be run by their own officials, over which the Marconi Company would have no jurisdiction whatever, a situation which, from the Company viewpoint, was far from equitable. There were further points of difference also and by September of that year (1923) deadlock had been reached, to the bewilderment of the Empire countries whose arrangements were already being implemented and whose representatives were about to meet at an Imperial and Economic Conference in London. The Conference was able to do little to provide a solution.

At the beginning of 1924 a change of government brought yet another Committee to consider the Imperial Wireless Service. This Committee, under the presidency of Mr Robert Donald, chairman of the Empire Press Union, did not call for any evidence on behalf of the Marconi Company. Its report, presented to Parliament on February 28, put forward two main recommendations, namely:

1. That the Post Office should own and operate all wireless stations in Great Britain which communicated with the Empire, with a partial exception in the case of Canada, for which a service run by private enterprise already existed.
2. That private enterprise should be free to develop wireless communication with foreign countries which were not within the British Empire.

With regard to the first proposition a rather curious suggestion was made by the Committee. '*To ensure success,*' it ran,

'*nothing should be left undone in the way of improved business organization so as to put the Post Office on equality with a private corporation. The administrative head of the wireless and associated services should be able to act promptly in all matters of business and the normal routine should be modified to enable this to be done.'*

Two months went by, and the Donald Committee's recommendations were still being debated in Parliament, when a brand new crisis came to a head within the Marconi Company itself, a crisis which was profoundly to affect Britain and the Empire also.

For some years past Marconi and some of his engineers had been investigating a puzzling skip-distance phenomenon which occurred when short waves of the order of one hundred metres were employed. The signal strength of such waves, in accordance with natural physical laws, attenuated rapidly beyond the rim of the horizon, and for this reason the short waves had been neglected for many years as useless for long-distance working. Over a few years previous to 1924 it had been noted, however, that these waves were, on occasion, reappearing at locations hundreds of miles away from the transmitting station.

This circumstance was subjected to considerable experimental work within the Company and a fuller account of this will be given in the following chapter. Suffice it to say for the moment that by 1924 the riddle of the behaviour of these short waves had been solved to the point where it was considered that a system of reliable long-distance communication might be evolved from it. It challenged the long-held concept of 'long wavelengths plus high power equals long ranges', with its corollary of stations of vast size and expense; for experiments had shown that equally long ranges could be achieved with the hitherto neglected short waves employing comparatively small stations which would use only a fraction of the power of the long-wave giants.

This realization put the Company in a dilemma, not so much in connection with the British Government as with the two Dominions, South Africa and Australia, both of which had awarded contracts to Marconi's for the erection of super-power long-wave stations; contracts which at the time had been entered into in all good faith as representing the best – indeed the only – technical solution to long-distance communications; contracts which were even then being implemented. Now, to hand, the Company had a revolutionary new concept which promised to outmode these giants even before they were completed.

The situation was made even more acute by the fact that the short-wave project was still in the experimental stage; enough had been done to convince Marconi and his associates that a practicable system could be evolved, but this was a far cry from being able to offer a fully-engineered system.

The issue resolved itself into one of principle. The easy way out would be to engineer the new system at comparative leisure and in secrecy, letting the existing long-wave situation take its course. Then, after a few years, when the giant Australian and South African stations (and perhaps others) had been built, the short-wave system could be unleashed. All would be perfectly legal; at the time the long-wave contracts had been placed the super high-power stations were the only certain means of achieving the desired ends.

But such a course was considered as breaking faith with the customers concerned, namely the Australian and South African Governments. The losses which would be incurred if the short-wave system fulfilled the expectations placed in it could only be minimized by an immediate open declaration, without waiting for full-scale practical tests under service conditions.

The decision to inform all interested parties was taken. It was done in the full awareness of the serious consequences it could have for the Company. Performance specifications and guarantees would have to be given based on theoretical calculations alone, and the penalty for failure would probably be bankruptcy. But the decision was taken, for better or for worse, rather than fracture the Company/customer relationship of good faith.

Thus it came about that two months after the publication of the Donald Committee's recommendations and while the vexed questions of the ownership and operation of the home stations were still being debated, the Company placed before the Empire Governments their proposal to achieve the specified performance of the original long-wave contracts by means of short-wave stations which would beam the signals to destination with a fraction of the power which had previously been necessary. The costs of the new stations were likewise to be only a fraction of those of the old.

The new offer was in the nature of a bombshell; nevertheless, Canada, Australia and South Africa quickly decided in favour of giving the new system a trial. But these decisions could only be fully implemented if Britain, as the nerve centre of the Empire scheme, agreed also.

The British Government prevaricated, not without reason, for whereas with the Dominions the issue was the straightforward one of reliable message traffic from point to point over long distances, Britain's requirements were more complex. Apart from the problem of private enterprise or State ownership of the stations, it was foreseen that in an emergency a broadcasting type of station which could simultaneously reach all units of the Royal Navy in all parts of the world would be invaluable, and this the proposed short-wave system with its highly directional beam, could not do. Furthermore, expert unbiased opinions were stating that the beam system would prove to have very limited hours of operation and could therefore be only used for deferred traffic. Others, going to the opposite extreme, expressed fears that the new system would be so efficient as to put the cable companies out of business, thus depriving the country of her world-wide submarine cable network, an asset of great strategic importance.

At length, however, faced with the Marconi Company's offer of co-operation in any agreed scheme, whether long-wave, high-power or short-wave beam, state-owned or run by private enterprise, and with Canada, South Africa and Australia placing contracts for beam stations, the British Government finally announced its decision on 2 July 1924.

The short-wave system was to be adopted. The naval strategic aspect was taken care of by pressing ahead with the super-power long-wave Post Office station at Rugby. For the rest, the main recommendations of the Donald Committee were to be followed in the matter of state ownership and operation of all stations in Britain which were in communication with the units of the Empire, while private enterprise was to be licensed to provide services to countries outside the Commonwealth. The Government further agreed to co-operate in the trials of the new beam system. A new Committee, again under the chairmanship of Sir Robert Donald, was appointed to recommend ways and means of improving the business organization of the Post Office.

The Government's decision to co-operate in the trials of the short-wave system was given force by its approval of an agreement by the Marconi Company that, as the contractor, it should build an initial beam station for communication with Canada. If this proved successful, the system could be extended to communicate with South Africa, India and Australia.

Considered in detail, the terms of the agreement provided a severe test of the Company's resources as examination of some of the clauses will show.

The price to be paid for the first station was to be the capital cost, plus five per cent establishment charges and ten per cent contractors' profits, the maximum figure not to exceed £35,120. The Post Office was to pay the Company a royalty of six and a quarter per cent of gross traffic receipts so long as any Marconi patents essential for the working of the station were in use.

The penalties were severe. The station had to be completed within twenty-six weeks of the site becoming available and the Government would only be liable for an initial payment if certain minimum guarantees were fulfilled during a seven-day demonstration. The payment was then to be fifty per cent of the cost. If the station succeeded in meeting the guarantees for a further six months under Post Office operation, a further twenty-five per cent was to be paid, with the final balance of twenty-five per cent payable after a further six months' satisfactory working.

These figures were such as to provide no profit from the actual building of the station; if there was to be a profit it would come solely from the traffic receipt royalties. To qualify for any payment at all, messages had to be exchanged with the Canadian station seven days per week for at least eighteen hours per day (duplex) at a speed of not less than one hundred words per minute in both directions.

Stringent as these conditions were, the price of failure was even higher. If the station failed to win Post Office approval during the stipulated period, it had to be cleared from the site entirely at the Marconi Company's expense and any payments already made were to be refunded to the Government.

The terms were accepted. In doing so the Company took an unprecedented gamble with a system still in the development stage, that is to say, with several major technical problems still to be solved. It was an act of faith in the abilities of three men: Guglielmo Marconi, the driving force; C. S. Franklin, the brilliant architect of the new system and R. N. Vyvyan, then Chief Engineer, who would be responsible for the building of the stations to Franklin's specifications, to an almost impossibly rigorous time schedule.

The work of these men is discussed in the next chapter.

26

The Short-Wave Beam System

Although the original experiments carried out by Guglielmo Marconi were conducted using centimetric waves, it was not long before he realized that the known physical laws governing the propagation of electromagnetic waves were being fulfilled and that he could expect line-of-sight ranges and no more. Accordingly he began to employ higher masts and longer wavelengths in an effort to increase his ranges to the maximum. To his surprise, he began to achieve distances which were greater than could be accounted for by theoretical physics. Greatly encouraged, he pushed on to even longer wavelengths and found the ranges extending still further, stretching to a hundred miles or more.

The transatlantic experiment of 1901, in which he used a wavelength of about 350 m. and high-power transmission, set the world of physics by the ears, for the distance spanned could not be accounted for by any or all of these measures and it seemed for a time – at least to those who accepted Marconi's claim – that the laws of electromagnetic wave propagation might have to be modified. Even when Oliver Heaviside put forward his suggestion of the bending of the waves by ionization in the upper atmosphere it was long regarded by many as merely a plausible attempt to prop up a badly sagging theory. In fact, it was not until the 1920s after brilliant confirmatory work by Appleton, Breit and Tuve, T. L. Eckersley and others that the ionized layer theory gained universal acceptance.

But in 1901, Marconi was not disposed to worry unduly over purely theoretical considerations. The waves were travelling distances of 2,000 miles and that was all that mattered to a young man who bore the responsibility of a Company on his shoulders. Let the physicists wrangle; his task was to push on to purely practical ends, namely the realization of a commercial system of message-carrying, and this he proceeded to do by following the road opened to him by the transatlantic experiment, the highway of longer wavelengths and higher powers for even longer ranges.

It was, as Marconi subsequently came to realize, a wrong road. But he and his competitors all took it and even now, with hindsight, it is difficult to blame them for following the most promising lead in their race for supremacy and leaving the apparently unprofitable short waves severely alone.

Not until 1916 did Marconi return to this universally neglected field, when a requirement materialized from the Italian Navy for a short-range method of intercommunication between units of the fleet. Marconi brought C. S. Franklin to Italy and together they evolved experimental apparatus operating on a wavelength of two metres. Such a short wavelength, they reasoned, would limit the signals to quasi-optical ranges, thus preventing any eavesdropping by an enemy well down over the horizon. A further advantage accrued from this choice of wavelength, for by using a reflector of quite manageable size the signals could be radiated in the form of a directional beam thereby concentrating the carrier wave's power in one desired direction. This not only provided a maximum of received signal strength at the desired receiving point, but provided an additional factor of secrecy.

As no valve of the period would oscillate at anywhere near two metres, Franklin devised a spark circuit operating in compressed air for the experiments. Some highly promising results were obtained; an interesting side-issue to the main theme was that reflections from objects in the path of the signals were noted (these had of course been observed by Hertz in the 1880s, but the circumstance had ever since dwelt in the limbo of the physics text books). Marconi's practical mind reacted characteristically to this rediscovery and led him to predict the possibility of what today is known as radar.

In 1917 Franklin continued the short-wave experiments, first at Caernarvon and then at Inchkeith and Portsmouth. These were sufficiently advanced by the end of the war to enable him to go to Marconi with a proposition that the apparatus should be tested between London and Birmingham, using a wavelength of fifteen metres. Marconi was sceptical of the chances of success on this wavelength and Franklin, reminiscing in later years, recalled that his Chief backed his opinion with a five-pound wager.

Despite his belief that the signals would not get through, Marconi permitted Franklin to go ahead. In fact, the experimental link proved highly successful and Marconi parted with his five pounds with good grace.

Coincident with the work on the Hendon–Birmingham link,

Franklin's colleague, Captain H. J. Round, was carrying out independent wireless telephony tests between Southwold and Holland on a wavelength of one hundred metres, and both he and Franklin found that on occasion reports were received of the reception of their signals from quite long distances, although no consistent pattern emerged. Sometimes the long-range signals appeared; sometimes not.

These random long-distance transmissions were backed by reports from quite another source. The emergence of wireless telegraphy and telephony from the war years had seen a great increase in the number of amateur experimenters – many of them ex-servicemen who had been connected with wireless during the war – and to these the Post Office allocated wavebands which lay outside the broadcasting bands, some of them in the despised regions below 200 metres. These amateurs, working with only the few watts permitted them, were also reporting the occasional long-distance contact, sometimes even from the other side of the Atlantic, but with no degree of regularity.

Marconi, impressed by the strength of signal along the 97-mile Hendon–Birmingham link with only 700 watts input, and mindful also of these erratic long-distance paths which the short waves were spanning, determined to experiment on a larger scale.

By this time Franklin and Round had solved many of the problems attendant upon the use of thermionic valves at wavelengths between fifteen and one hundred metres and could design transmitters which provided very useful powers. Marconi delegated Franklin to the task of establishing an experimental short-wave site at Poldhu and of building a transmitter of 12 kW input, together with a parabolic reflector. In conjunction with the latter, various antennas could be tested and the waveband from ninety-seven metres downward explored.

At the end of 1919, Marconi had purchased an ex-enemy steam yacht, the *Rovenska* of 700 tons and had re-named it *Elettra*. This had been fitted out as a floating laboratory and in it he was wont to spend much of his time. The yacht was now pressed into service as the receiving terminal at which the Poldhu short-wave transmissions could conveniently be monitored from various parts of the world.

It was decided to begin the work at a wavelength of ninety-seven metres. At Poldhu, Franklin had built an 8-valve transmitter and also a half-wave antenna for this wavelength. Aboard *Elettra* the normal wireless equipment was supplemented by short-wave receiving equipment and a special antenna, all designed by G. A. Mathieu, another very able Marconi engineer. No reflector was used at the receiver because of space limitations, but this omission carried with it the assurance that whatever signals were received and whatever the ranges recorded, they would be considerably better when a fixed station with a reflector was erected.

Tests began on 11 April 1923, with the Poldhu reflector in action (it could be brought into service or taken out as required) and orientated to direct the beam in a south-westerly direction. The *Elettra*, which had been lying off Falmouth, steamed away, heading down the west coasts of France, Spain and Portugal, then via Gibraltar, Tangier, Casablanca, Funchal, Madeira and finally on to St Vincent in the Cape Verde Islands.

At first the signals attenuated as the yacht left Falmouth well behind; then after several hundred miles they began to increase in strength. At Cape Verde, the farthest point of the voyage, the signals at the best period during the night were much more powerful than those being received on the yacht's standard installation from the Post Office long-wave high-power station at Leafield. This despite the proximity of high mountains and the fact that only 1 kW was being radiated from the Poldhu station. The range at this point was 2,230 nautical miles and quite obviously the signals were reaching to much greater distances. But Marconi's presence was required in London, so the yacht had to turn for home.

The most detailed observations had been taken on the voyage; recordings of signal strength, times of fading, the degree of natural static present and so on, sometimes with the Poldhu reflector in service, sometimes not. The first data relating to long-distance communication on short waves had been taken.

A preliminary analysis of these produced some extremely interesting, if puzzling information. It exploded the then widely-held belief that daylight communication on such a wavelength was erratic and limited to short distances, for even although signals were much weaker during daylight hours, nevertheless ranges up to a maximum of 1,250 nautical miles had been established. What was not known at the time was that of the various wavelengths under consideration the experimenters had inadvertently picked the worst for daylight reception. One thing, however, was very clear; in some way the signal strength was connected with the altitude of the sun.

The tests conducted with and without the use of the reflector had not shown such a disparity in recorded signal strengths as had been antici-pated from the previous experimental work on the Hendon–Birmingham link. This was rightly attributed to the inefficiency of the parabolic reflector, and Franklin set to work to redesign this part of the equipment.

To sum up, the Cape Verde experiment in its overall implications was highly encouraging. Marconi felt that they were on the brink of an entirely new era in wireless communication and ordered that further research should be pressed forward with all speed. Accordingly, the Poldhu transmitter was re-designed to give a radiated output of about 17 kW and further tests, this time on 92 m., were carried out across the Atlantic, using receiving equipment installed aboard the *Cedric*. No reflector was used at Poldhu; nevertheless the daylight range was found to be 1,400 nautical miles with very strong signals receivable at New York after dark.

At the same time, Amalgamated Wireless (Australasia) Ltd., had been briefed to maintain a listening watch and reported the amazing news that clear signals of good strength were being received at Sydney from 5 p.m. to 9 p.m. GMT and also from 6.30 a.m. to 8.30 a.m. From Canada came reports that the signals were being received for about sixteen hours out of the twenty-four. These results were so impressive that Marconi decided to attempt to telephone to Australia, still using the ninety-two metre wavelength and no reflector. This was success-fully carried out on 30 May 1924, when good-quality speech was received at Sydney direct from Poldhu.

It will be appreciated at this point just how great was the dilemma in which the Marconi Company found itself in connection with the Imperial Wireless scheme of long-wave high-power stations. Was it justified in continuing with the construction of the South African station in view of these startling performances of the short-wave beam? And yet the beam was purely experimental; no one knew for certain that the ranges accomplished were not freak propagation effects. Between the apparatus at Poldhu and a fully-engineered system there was a gulf fixed, which in the normal way would take from five to ten years to bridge.

As has been related, the critical decision was taken to offer the beam system despite the enormous risks that were inherent in the situation.

A new series of tests were carried out between Poldhu and *Elettra*, covering the 92, 60, 47 and 32 m. wavelengths and from these it was established that over long distances the daylight range increased as the wavelength decreased. In October 1924, tests were carried out on 32 m. with Montreal, New York, Rio, Buenos Aires and Sydney, using a power of only 12 kW. Messages were received at those cities even when the whole of the radio path was in daylight, and reception was at that date possible in Sydney for twenty-three and a half hours out of the twenty-four.

This was heartening news, for it meant that the service could be carried on a shorter wavelength than had originally been contemplated and this in turn meant an antenna and reflector system of smaller and more manageable proportions.

The observations made during these experiments enabled a firm decision to be made regarding the wavelengths of the various beam stations; the information was provided in the nick of time, for mast construction at some of the new stations had already begun. These were at Bodmin for transmission to Canada and South Africa; near Bridgwater for the receiving station for those areas; a site near Grimsby, for transmission to India and Australia, with the receiving station at Skegness, while for transmission to New York, Buenos Aires and Rio, a site was chosen near Dorchester, with the receiving station at Somerton in the neighbouring county of Somerset. Corresponding stations in the overseas countries concerned were also under construction, with the Canadian station as a priority.

Meanwhile, Franklin had three formidable tasks ahead of him, namely the engineering of the experimental transmitter into a form for commercial sale; the design of antenna systems to radiate on the various wavelengths demanded and, last but not least, there remained the problem of how to convey the energy from the transmitter into the antenna system without undue loss. When it is remembered that virtually no practical experience of short-wave design existed, giving no precedents upon which to build, and that the work had to be completed within weeks, some idea can be gained of the weight of responsibility which rested upon the shoulders of Franklin and his team. In the event, the design of the transmitter was so good that over forty years later one or two at least are known to have still been in full service. One of the major teething troubles was in the thermionic transmitting valves of the day which, at the high frequencies used, developed faulty seals and, through this, excessive grid and anode currents. Larger seals were introduced and this provided an even more perplexing problem, for whereas some of the new valves behaved well, others, apparently identical, gave considerable trouble.

The mystery was eventually solved when it was found that impurities in the glass were causing the losses and accordingly a power valve was designed in which a copper anode itself formed the envelope, cooling being effected by oil circulation. These were christened CAT valves

(Cooled Anode Transmitting). The power amplifier of Franklin's transmitter used two such valves connected in push-pull.

A stable drive was provided by a valve drive taking less than 100 watts; its output was then amplified in three successive stages. At first, the transmitter was designed to tune to any wavelength between twenty and sixty metres, but this was subsequently altered to fifteen to forty metres. Absorber keying was employed, thus eliminating the use of a spacing wave, a panel of valves being used to absorb the energy during signal intervals. In all cases where different wavelengths had to be employed for day and night signalling, duplicate drives and associated circuits were provided, making it possible to change wavelength in about ten minutes.

For beam stations using two discrete wavelengths, a 5-mast system was employed, each mast being 287 ft. high and spaced 650 ft. apart. This enabled an antenna system 1,300 ft. wide to be used for each wavelength. These antennas, when erected at the beam stations, were aligned with great care to ensure that they were at right angles to the shortest great circle route to destination. As compass bearings were insufficiently accurate, the installation engineers had to be instructed to take fixes on the sun or on certain stars to provide the correct orientation.

The Franklin beam array consisted of a multiplicity of vertical antenna wires, cut to resonate at half the desired wavelength, with similar wires spaced behind them at a specific distance to act as reflectors by reinforcing the signal strengths in the forward direction and cancelling it to rearward. The length of the line, relative to the wavelength, determined the horizontal beam width while the vertical beam width was restricted by stacking units above one another to form a curtain array.

The desired angle of elevation of the beam was found by experiment to be between ten to fifteen degrees from the horizontal for ranges of 2,000 miles or over. Franklin overcame the natural tendency of a half-wave vertical antenna to give maximum radiation at an angle of forty-five degrees by introducing phasing coils between each half-wave section to bring each antenna into phase. (This was later simplified by giving the array a zig-zag form to provide a non-radiating phase reversing device.)

Careful design of such a system can give a great concentration of energy and serve to direct it at an optimum angle of elevation for reflection from the ionized layers which surround the earth. But no matter how efficient the transmitter and the antenna may be when considered as isolated units, the design effort is wasted if the feeder system transferring the power from the one to the other is ill-conceived.

This was the third problem which faced Franklin, for no one had ever designed a transmission line to convey such power at such a high frequency; furthermore, the situation was rendered far more difficult by the fact that it was no simple dipole antenna which had to be fed but a large number of separate antenna wires, each one of which had to be supplied in phase with the supply to every other.

Franklin solved the problem brilliantly, the key factor in his success being his invention of the concentric feeder – the forerunner of the familiar coaxial cable of today. The feeder, as finally designed, took the form of concentric copper tubes, air-insulated from each other by porcelain spacers; the inner tube was the conductor and the outer one was earthed. The structure was carried on iron supports about four feet apart, driven into the ground.

The feeder line was brought to the centre of the antenna system and then branched off symmetrically to two points. Each of these two points fed two further symmetrical branches, and these in turn were branched, the process continuing until every antenna wire was catered for.

Provided that careful attention is paid to the absolute symmetry of the branches, it will be seen that the physical length of the conductor from each antenna wire back to the central distribution point will be the same for each radiating element. Slight differences in electrical length can be compensated by the use of matching transformers at each tee joint.

Such was Franklin's solution; today it would be regarded as straight-forward engineering, but in the 1920s, with absolutely no precedent to guide him, it was brilliant design, carried out at astonishing speed.

A human sequel to this is on record. Franklin telegraphed the good news of his overcoming this last main obstacle to Headquarters in London and received word that Marconi was on his way to Poldhu. On the following day he arrived, but to Franklin's chagrin made only the briefest of stops, departing after a few words to visit friends in the vicinity and without witnessing a demonstration. Superficially, Marconi's off-hand approach had every appearance of bad psychology; in fact, it was a measure of his faith in Franklin.

Concurrently with the work on the transmission aspect, the receiving equipment was being designed by G. A. Mathieu. This took the form of a single r.f. stage and demodulator with further stages of a.f. amplification as necessary. Because at that time the problems of frequency drift at the transmitter had not been wholly solved, the receiver's tuned stages were designed with a fairly wide band-pass characteristic in order to minimize the need for receiver adjustment. Limiting circuits were also introduced to offset as far as possible the fluctuations in received signal strength brought about by the ionospheric reflecting layers.

With the design of both the transmitting and the receiving apparatus completed, the main burden of responsibility shifted to the Company's Chief Engineer, R. N. Vyvyan, whose task it was to co-ordinate the manufacture of the various units of the system in fully engineered form and to supervise its installation in a race against the clock.

On 18 October 1926 the British terminals of the Canadian circuit at Bodmin and Bridgwater were officially handed over to the Post Office for test purposes and for communication with the Canadian transmitting and receiving stations which had been built at Montreal and Yama-chiche. The circuit passed its preliminary acceptance easily, proving conclusively that it was possessed of a greater traffic-handling capacity than any other long-distance wireless telegraph circuit in the world. Later developments, such as the simultaneous transmission of two or more services on the same antenna without mutual interference, and the inauguration of methods of multiplex working with a mixture of telephony and telegraphy services, were to increase the traffic potential still further.

Further stations followed in rapid succession; all were extremely successful. The Australian Company, for instance, had guaranteed their Government an average traffic capacity of 20,000 words per day in either direction. In the event, the capacity proved to be over three times this amount.

The Australian circuit was opened on 8 April 1927; the South African service on July 5; the Indian on September 6. In a single week in December 1927 the total number of words carried by the four beam circuits was at a rate which would total 34,840,000 words a year.

The British stations, built for the Government, were operated by the Post Office. The Dominion stations were operated by local Companies in which the Marconi Company had substantial interests.

In this fashion Guglielmo Marconi's dearest ambition namely, to provide a world-wide system of wireless communication, was realized. The idea which had thrust down its roots after the transatlantic experiment of 1901 had taken a quarter of a century to come to fruition. For Marconi, now fifty-three, it was the end of an era; the last battle in which he was in the forefront. From that time onward he spent much more time cruising in his yacht *Elettra* which he had converted into a floating laboratory. He was still experimenting, it is true, but during the latter period of his life he entered much more into a social life which had hitherto taken second place.

For the Marconi Company the adoption of the beam system was a great triumph, although one in which prestige was predominant over financial gain. The great gamble had come off, but the terms of the contract were such that the actual cost to the Company exceeded the amounts which it received, and the hope for ultimate profits lay in the traffic receipts. Just how little or how much these were going to amount to, no one knew.

The Company's foreign competitors had naturally been watching proceedings with close attention. At first there had been considerable scepticism as it was widely believed that on encountering the ionized layers the beam would be scattered in all directions and thus lose its most valuable property. The explosive success of the system changed this attitude overnight to one of considerable alarm as it was suddenly realized that the technological approach to long-distance working was completely changed. Everyone had now to manufacture short-wave beam systems or go out of business, and must do so in the face of the several years' lead acquired by the Marconi Company. At least two of the main competitors purchased Marconi beam transmitters, antennas and receivers and set their research teams the task of producing equivalent equipments without infringing the Marconi-Franklin patents.

One particular source of personal satisfaction to Guglielmo Marconi was the gloom which the success of the beam system had cast over the world's cable interests, for Marconi's aversion to these was akin to that attributed to the devil for holy water. But the last shot in the cable versus wireless war had by no means been fired, as Marconi was soon to discover.

27

The Cable and Wireless Merger

Thus, in the early 1920s the Company had covered itself in glory in two distinct fields, namely sound broadcasting and world communications. Unfortunately, in business, glory is not a satisfactory substitute for cash – and in terms of cash, Marconi's was in very bad shape.

In 1921 several of the subsidiaries had made heavy weather and had to be assisted financially by the parent Company. The large claims upon the Government for war services were still unmet. In 1922 the Clifden transatlantic station had been blown up by Irish patriots in the course of the Rebellion and its career as a valuable source of revenue was ended, although this was mitigated by the employment of the Caernarvon station to carry the full transatlantic service.

In the broadcasting field the delay occasioned in issuing licences in 1922 caused contract cancellations to the newly-formed Marconiphone Company and this brought serious losses.

By 1923, debts due from associated companies amounting to £1,059,262 had to be written off. The compensation from the Government for wartime manufacture was still not forthcoming, while the rapid expansion of Company activities into fields other than commercial and military wireless communication called for the sinking of more and more capital in order to finance it.

Matters came to a head in February 1925, when Godfrey Isaacs was forced to retire owing to ill-health. At that time the composition of the Board included four financial experts, three technical experts and five good linguists (the latter being important in view of the Company's extensive overseas business). Six of the Board members held executive posts.

Opinions may differ as to the true assessment of Godfrey Isaacs' worth to the Company, depending upon the standpoint adopted. Certainly he gave of his utmost in the Company's service; his first-class financial brain stood it in good stead time and time again by finding the money to finance various costly but necessary research programmes and by encouraging the development of new applications in the art of electronics. In these respects he loyally backed Guglielmo Marconi's concept of a Company as an innovator first and foremost, with the matter of providing shareholders' profits a secondary consideration. He was also largely responsible for the unofficial world intelligence service which the Company provided during the Great War, and which was so valuable to the Allied cause.

On the other hand he was an almost compulsive litigator whose successes in this field were counterbalanced by protracted and indecisive lawsuits, notably those concerning thermionic valve patents. Certainly these had to be contested, but it would have been to the financial advantage of all parties to have settled out of court. He had also tended to push the Company too fast and too far, relying upon his undoubted financial genius to see him through. There were, at the time of his death, Marconi interests in some sixty concerns, scattered through twenty countries of the world.

Godfrey Isaacs was succeeded by the Rt Hon. F. G. Kellaway, who had been Postmaster-General in the post-war Asquith Government and had subsequently joined the Marconi Board in 1922.

To his new post, Kellaway brought a wide experience of chairmanship of Government committees, acknowledged qualities as a diplomatist and conciliator and a capacity for firm decisions. He was, however, no technician, no linguist, and his experience of commercial finance was limited in comparison with that of the late Godfrey Isaacs.

In June 1924, that is, prior to his acceptance of the Managing Directorship, Kellaway had been chairman of a finance committee set up within the Company to control the aspects of policy and finance. Its first decision had been to stop further investments in all concerns not properly connected with Company business. The next steps were to reorganize those with profit-earning capabilities; to concentrate on the manufacture, sale and installation of sound broadcasting material within the framework of one Company; to press ahead with the Beam project and to secure from the Government a general licence for telegraphic services throughout the world. Shortly after these resolutions were passed, Godfrey Isaacs' ill-health forced him to resign.

By January 1925 a statement which had been prepared for the finance committee showed that more capital was urgently needed. Accordingly, in the following month, an issue of 500,000 additional shares was made, which brought in the sum of £663,000.

But worse was to follow, for the draft accounts for 1925, prepared by a new deputy accountant and submitted in May 1926, disclosed that the

Company had written off, or had written down, sundry assets to the total of £3,000,000 during the preceding two years and that a further £1,000,000 was now required. In the light of this alarming news an outside firm of accountants was called in to make a searching investigation in collaboration with the auditors. This report, which took six months to prepare and ran to some four hundred pages, showed, as related earlier, that the Company's interests were much too diversified.

At an Ordinary General Meeting of the shareholders held on 15 March 1927 with Marchese Marconi in the chair, Kellaway was able to report that remedial action taken had resulted in the Company making a trading profit of £150,000 in 1925. He stated that the Board proposed that the nominal value of the one pound Ordinary Shares should be reduced to ten shillings; this would put the Company immediately on to a dividend-paying basis and permit it to build up a substantial reserve fund. He further proposed that upon such a reduction of capital taking effect, the capital of the Company should be increased to its former amount of £4,000,000 by the issue of 3,250,092 new shares of ten shillings each. These resolutions were carried, together with that for a reconstitution of the Board.

The new Board, unlike the one which was operative during the latter phase of the Godfrey Isaacs' régime, was almost wholly financial in its composition. The only technical member and its only competent linguist was Marconi himself. With this one exception, therefore, the Board was unfitted to judge any aspect of the Company's business but cost. The situation worsened still further in July 1927, when Guglielmo Marconi resigned from the chairmanship in favour of the Rt Hon. Lord Inverforth, one of the newly-elected members of the Board, a move which freed him to devote his whole time to the scientific and engineering aspects of the Company's work. Marconi now became an ordinary director, acting as Technical Adviser to the Board.

The financial operations to which reference has been made were efficacious in wiping off the major part of the Company's outstanding debts, while rigorous pruning of dead wood by Kellaway had already curtailed the trend towards over-expansion and brought the trading aims more clearly into view.

With the Company now on a much sounder financial footing and with bright prospects in several areas of the electronics field, notably in the beam communication system, it was singularly unfortunate that another crisis blew up in which the Board's weakness in technically-orientated Directors became very apparent.

The crisis originated not as a crisis for the Marconi Company, but in the ranks of the cable interests. For the past thirty years wireless had been challenging the cables in terms of world communication, without decisive result. It had been a ding-dong struggle, with technical improvements on one side or the other giving temporary advantages, but not for long. In the first years of the 1920s, advantages and disadvantages of the two systems were such as to place them on approximately equal footing.

The evolution of the beam system overset this equilibrium, both in the comparatively low cost of the short-wave wireless stations and the high operating speeds which they provided (100–250 words per minute, depending on conditions, compared with 35–100 words per minute over a cable route). While many of the cable links had the advantage of being able to pick up or drop off messages at certain points *en route* (for example the London–Singapore cable could collect or drop out traffic automatically at about a dozen points between the two terminals), the beam system provided a more economic method of communication over really long distances, such as England to Australia, but without the drop-out facility.

It will be seen from this that the two systems were now complementary, the cable interests providing a better service over medium distances and the beam giving a cheaper wordage rate over the long-distance circuits. Overall, the advantage lay with the beam system and this was reflected in the tremendous rate in growth of traffic it experienced; some of this was new business but a considerable proportion was acquired at the expense of the cable companies. Wherever the two systems operated in competition the cable interests lost revenue at an alarming rate and by 1927 nearly half of their traffic had gone over to the beam. As the cable interests were already being heavily subsidized by the U.K. and Dominion governments and could expect no more direct monetary aid from these quarters it will be clear that they were in real trouble.

Although the battle was being fought by two private enterprises, the British and Dominion Governments were interested parties because of the value to the Empire of an efficient cable network, particularly in time of war. Thus it came about that representations by the Dominion Governments caused the calling of an Empire Government Conference in January 1928, at which all the cable and wireless interests involved explained their individual positions. Behind the scenes, approaches had been made which resulted in a meeting between Sir William Plender on behalf of the Associated Cable Companies and Sir Gilbert Garnsey on behalf of Marconi's. Their brief was to try to find an equitable basis for a merger, after which a joint report could be submitted to their respective Boards.

The Empire Conference had a hard nut to crack in view of the complex of governmental and financial interests involved and the situation would be considerably eased if the two principal antagonists could find a basis for agreement. The old political controversy over control by Government or by private enterprise also loomed large in the background. So, effective discussion at the Conference awaited the outcome of the joint report.

On March 16 the report was issued to both Boards. It recommended an arrangement for the fusion of interests through the medium of a holding company, dependent upon an agreement, satisfactory to both parties, being made with the Governments of the U.K. and of the Dominions. The proposed arrangement as detailed in the report distributed the voting power in the merger company in the proportion of 56·25 per cent to the Cable group and 43·75 per cent to the Marconi Company.

Regarded with hindsight, this agreement was astonishing in view of the fact that the Marconi Company's position was so strong. It had saved the British Empire millions of pounds by the introduction of the beam system. The service was proving efficient and because the Company had supplied the system at less than cost price it had every right to expect to be allowed to recoup itself over the years from the profits accruing from traffic receipts. These and other factors make it incredible that Marconi's should consent to become a junior partner; this point will be discussed later.

In the light of the merger proposal the Empire Conference issued its recommendations on 27 July 1928. These were duly debated in the House of Commons and approved on August 2. They were, in brief, that a merger company should be formed to combine the respective interests of the cable and the Marconi Groups. The formation of a separate communications company was proposed to which both parties would sell, broadly speaking, all their communications assets in return for shares. The communications company would thus segregate in one organization the 'communications aspect', leaving with the merger company the investments of the cable group and the Marconi Company's manufacturing and other non-traffic undertakings. The report recognized that the adoption of the proposals would involve the transfer also of the Post Office Beam installations and staffs if the scheme were to prove successful. Naturally, the Government would have the right to assume control of the entire system in times of national emergency.

Upon the publication of the Conference report, political temperatures ran high in both the Press and Parliament, but in December the proposals became law by the passing of the Imperial Telegraphs Bill, the merger scheme having been previously approved by the Governments of Canada, Australia, India and South Africa.

On 8 April 1929 two new companies were registered under the titles of Cables* and Wireless Ltd., and Imperial and International Communications Ltd. The former had for its object the acquisition of the stocks, shares, debentures and other obligations of The Eastern Telegraph Co. Ltd., The Western Telegraph Co. Ltd. and Marconi's Wireless Telegraph Co. Ltd.

The objectives of Imperial and International Communications Ltd. were to acquire the whole of the traffic undertakings and physical assets, patent and traffic rights, licences and so on of the same group of companies and their subsidiaries, together with those of the Pacific Cable Board (including those relating to the West Indian Cable and Wireless System operated by that Board), the Imperial Transatlantic Cables and the lease (for twenty-five years) of the Beam wireless installations then being operated by the Post Office. The undertakings, assets and liabilities of Electra House Ltd. (Moorgate) were also included.

The directors of the new companies were identical under the leadership of Mr J. C. Denison-Pender and Mr F. G. Kellaway as joint Managing Directors of both companies. Lord Inverforth was President of Cable and Wireless Ltd. and Sir Basil P. Blackett Chairman of Imperial and International Communications Ltd. The name of I. and I.C. Co. Ltd. was soon changed to 'Cable and Wireless Ltd.', the original of that name having its title changed to Cable and Wireless (Holding) Ltd.

Thus the life-long ambition of Guglielmo Marconi, the establishment of a Marconi-controlled Imperial Wireless Chain, ended almost as soon as it had been realized by the beam system. The struggle which had begun in snow and storm on the headland at St John's, Newfoundland, more than a quarter of a century before, was over. For by the formation of the two new companies, the Marconi Company ceased to be directly involved in the transmission of messages as a source of revenue; its role was from then onward limited to the areas of research, invention and manufacture.

* Originally plural; later changed to singular.

The merger was a grim reminder that a Godfrey Isaacs was no longer at the helm. At the outset, the Company had had almost everything in its favour in matters of dictating terms. The success of the beam system was such that in a year or so's time the cable interests would have been virtually out of business, particularly as the Marconi organization had an ace up its sleeve in the form of facsimile and picture transmission.

There was, it is true, the larger canvas of national interests. From the Empire point of view it was highly desirable that communications traffic should be controlled by one body and equally undesirable that the cable network should deteriorate. One would like to think that patriotic sentiment influenced the Marconi Board of Directors to surrender the Company's freedom of action and to agree to its becoming a junior partner in an organization in which cable interests predominated. The real reason, not nearly so palatable, lies in the technical weakness of the Board, for of its twenty-two members only one (Marconi himself, now an ordinary director) had any experience of the Company's technical business.

But the decision had been made, and without doubt it gave Great Britain and the Empire the finest system of world communications ever to exist under the control of a single body. It was at this point, when the skies of Empire communication seemed to have cleared, that the winds of change threatened to produce a fresh storm.

When, in 1923, the Bonar Law Government had ruled that a State-controlled station should be built for the purpose of communicating with the whole Empire, the Post Office had pressed ahead with its long-wave high-power station at Rugby. A short-wave station had also been built there with which a radio telephone service with New York (and from there by landline to Canada) was maintained. In 1929 a landline service to Paris and Berlin had been inaugurated, from which capitals the messages were transmitted by radio to Argentina. Experiments were being carried out to communicate with Australia direct.

At the time of the Imperial Conference it had been assumed that after the merger and the formation of Cable and Wireless Ltd. as a private company, the Post Office would make use of the short-wave beam for telephony as well as telegraphy as the system had proved capable of providing channels for both simultaneously. But when Cable and Wireless Ltd. offered its services to the Post Office, stating that it was in a position to provide direct telephonic communication with Canada, South Africa, Australia, India, Egypt, Argentina, Brazil, Siam and other countries, the Post Office made it quite clear that they had every intention of developing an entirely independent wireless telephony network with the Rugby station as the centre of the system.

This issue, although it did not provoke any major conflict, was not finally settled until after World War II when the Commonwealth Telecommunications Conference of 1945 recommended the acquisition of the services in the United Kingdom, the Dominions and Rhodesia by the Governments concerned, and the establishment of a unifying Commonwealth Communications Board. In the United Kingdom this was implemented by the Government in the Cable and Wireless Act of 1946.

It is of interest to note that the value of the beam system was heavily emphasized in November 1929 when a vast upheaval on the bed of the Atlantic broke ten of the twenty-one cables. No significant disruption of communications resulted, for the cable traffic was switched without hitch to the short-wave beam.

28

Wireless and Aviation to 1939

In the *Army and Navy Illustrated* for 22 July 1899 appears an account of the first use of wireless in aviation. This was a demonstration by Marconi's to the Army authorities at Aldershot, whereby a transmitter installed in a captive observation balloon could be used to send signals to a receiver in a much smaller balloon some few miles away. The intelligence was received by the ground staff via a wire from the receiver to the ground.

Although the experiment appears to have been very satisfactory, nothing further was done to develop it and it is not until 1907 that a rather similar series of attempts is recorded. These were carried out by Lt. C. J. Aston, Royal Engineers, who by 1908 was receiving good signals from a ground station while travelling in a free flight balloon some twenty miles distant from the transmission.

In 1910 the first use of wireless in an air-sea rescue operation took place. The occasion was the flight of the Wellman airship *America* on October 15 of that year.

The *America*'s programme was an ambitious one; nothing less than the crossing of the Atlantic. A Marconi operator, Jack Irwin, signed on as one of the crew and installed his transmitting and receiving apparatus in a 27 ft. lifeboat slung beneath the main car of the airship.

Four days after the start of the adventure, the airship was well off her desired course, sometimes rising to an altitude of 11,000 ft., sometimes plunging almost to wavetop height. It was decided to come down into the sea and Irwin, the operator, was ordered to transmit messages to this effect. The descent was then safely accomplished and the lifeboat launched, the crew being picked up by the Royal Mail steamship *Trent* which had received Irwin's signals. In this fashion the first air-sea rescue was effected with the aid of wireless.

(Irwin seems to have had a charmed life, for he subsequently signed on as Marconi operator aboard a new airship, the *Akron*, but was not on the vessel when on 2 July 1912 it exploded in flight, bursting into flames and killing the crew of five.)

In 1911 also, the British dirigible *Beta* was equipped with Marconi wireless apparatus at the order of the War Office; a range of thirty miles was established during its transmissions.

According to an interviewer quoted in the *Dublin Daily Express* of 4 November 1911, Marconi was having serious thoughts of designing an aircraft. Although no details exist, he is stated as endeavouring to produce a machine capable of vertical take-off.

One thing he realized quite clearly at this time was that a heavier-than-air machine would only be able to make an efficient use of wireless telegraphy when designs were sufficiently advanced for an aircraft to carry at least two people – one pilot and one to operate the wireless.

The first recorded use of wireless between an aeroplane and ground was on 27 August 1910 when a Canadian, J. D. A. McCurdy, tapped out a wireless message from a Curtiss biplane 600 ft. up over Long Island, U.S.A. The signals were received at a range of one mile. Exactly one month later Robert Loraine, the actor, flying over Salisbury Plain, England, transmitted signals to the nearby Larkhill experimental ground station. The instruments used in all the experiments mentioned were Marconi spark transmitters and magnetic detectors.

Shortly after, investigations into the possibilities of airborne wireless were begun at the Royal Aircraft Factory at Farnborough, Hampshire. Similar work was also carried out at Brooklands Aviation Ground in Surrey, using a Flanders monoplane with a Marconi timed spark trans-mitter installed. This transmitter, powered by a 6-volt battery, was designed by R. D. Bangay of the Company's Field Station Department.

The part played by the Company in developing airborne wireless telegraphy and telephony during World War I has been described in Chapter 19. By the end of the war tremendous technological progress had been made and further improvements were coming at such a rate that quite a number did not come into full production until after the armistice. Notable among these was a 5-valve set designed by Whid-dington which was ten times as sensitive as those in use by the R.A.F. at the end of the war.

With the coming of peace, the Company was faced with the problem of how to re-employ those engineers who, as specialists in aviation wireless, had been on military service. In common with many other industrial organizations it had to learn the art of beating swords into ploughshares. It was decided to create an Aircraft Department in anticipation of a demand for wireless for civil aircraft.

The war years had seen the evolution of the aeroplane from a frail bamboo-and-fabric machine to a sturdy dependable means of missile delivery, and it was seen that the heavy bombers could, with a reasonable amount of modification, be converted into passenger-carrying aircraft. But the heavier-than-air machine had a formidable rival in the dirigible, which also had obvious potential for civil use. By mid-1919 both forms of air transport had succeeded in crossing the Atlantic – the aeroplane, a Vickers Vimy crewed by Alcock and Whitten-Brown, and the airship, the R.34. Both carried Marconi wireless equipment.

The first passenger-carrying service using aeroplanes was operated by the R.A.F.'s No. 86 Communication Wing, using two converted Handley Page HP 0/400 bombers, each equipped to carry six passengers. These machines had Marconi wireless telephony installations. The aircraft, christened respectively *Silver Star* and *Great Britain* did valuable pioneering work on the Paris air route, including the first night passenger service to France. The service was discontinued in October 1919.

Before its termination however, private-venture civil airlines were being planned and two, in fact, were in operation. On 25 August 1919, the first day on which scheduled civil flying was permitted, the world's first commercial scheduled service was inaugurated by Aircraft Transport and Travel Ltd., operating from Hounslow Heath aerodrome to Paris. On the same day Handley Page Transport Ltd. began operation, but on an *ad hoc* basis. This Company began regular services to Paris on September 2 and extended its operations to Brussels on September 24. The flights were made from Cricklewood aerodrome, Hounslow Heath being used only for Customs clearance purposes.

The first civil aircraft wireless *telephony* installation to go into operational service was a Marconi type AD 1/S set fitted in the DH42 machine G–EALU belonging to Aircraft Transport and Travel Ltd.

The Marconi Company collaborated with Handley Page Ltd. by fitting AD 1 sets in the aircraft and by installing and manning a ground station at Cricklewood for communication purposes. This station was the only ground station ever to be operated under a private licence in the United Kingdom.

In that year (1919) an important demonstration of the value of airborne radio was made when the Handley Page G–EALX (a converted 0/400 bomber) took off from Cricklewood on an experimental flight to Paris. With H. C. Van-de-Velde as operator, telephonic communication was established with Chelmsford and then with Lympne aerodrome on the Kentish coast when at a distance of seventy-five miles from it. While out over the Channel, Van-de-Velde was able to report to Cricklewood that they had just passed their sister ship G–EAMA on her homeward flight.

The Hounslow aerodrome, at which the Air Ministry had established the world's first civil airport, relinquished its status as London's air terminal to Croydon in 1920. To the order of the Air Ministry a Marconi ground station was installed at Croydon. This consisted of a 100-watt CW/ICW telephony transmitter and a type 55 Bellini-Tosi direction-finding receiver. It was the first station of its type to provide remote control of the transmitter from the receiver building. The transmitter was shortly afterwards replaced by one of 1·5 kW output; this was designed by P. P. Eckersley.

The position of Wireless Officer in charge of the airport's equipment was a civil appointment by the Air Ministry; it was held for some ten years by F. S. Mockford, who, after this period, joined the Marconi Company, eventually becoming its Commercial Manager. Mockford devised the early operating procedure and the examination syllabus for PMG licences for air wireless operators. He was the first examiner and contributed to the building up of International Regulations relating to the use of wireless by civil aircraft; in addition, he and his staff devised quick means of direction-finding triangulation. In 1922 he was respon-sible for the first attempts at the 'talking in and down' of aircraft in conditions of bad visibility. It was Mockford who originated the Mayday distress call.

In a reminiscence of these early days, Mockford throws an interesting light on some prevalent attitudes of the times:

At the end of the war [he writes] the public were far from regarding the aeroplane as a device which could go from A to B safely and regularly. It was looked on as an eccentric form of travel at best.

Those early airlines – the world's first – had therefore either to go bank-rupt, which they usually did, or induce people to pay heavily for the chance of getting from London to Paris a little earlier, of being deposited in a cornfield at Beauvais or of having to sit dejectedly for hours or even days at the airport of alleged departure.

To the pilot, radio was a new-fangled, unappreciated box of tricks. To the air line proprietor, a waste of pay-load and maintenance cost. An early regulation came along to make the carriage of wireless compulsory, but it did not say that it must be in working order. Almost anything could delay a departure except the Marconi engineer's plea for a moment to look over the gear. . . .

It was in these circumstances that the Marconi Company – which was quite alone then – set about developing a reliable two-way telephony communication and direction-finding service with the co-operation of the Air Ministry Civil Aviation Department and Signals Branch which operated the airport stations. The aircraft gear had to be pilot-operated and had to work over one hundred miles – something vastly ahead of the wartime achievements of the Air Force.

Headway was remarkable and the early hostility of the pilot was overcome. There was now just a chance of being picked up if the flight ended in the English Channel. And then came the first time when a pilot got a d.f. bearing, understood it, believed it, and found Croydon through the fog. Faith was born and the pilots and ground operators began to work together towards extracting the utmost from this radio aid to safety. . . .

The Design and Development section of the Company's Aircraft Department was established in a large wooden hut erected at the edge of an open field near the village of Writtle, Essex. Here the AD2, a pilot-operated radio-telephone equipment, was developed for use with the aircraft of Handley Page Transport and of Air Transport and Travel. This equipment provided a reliable range of more than one hundred miles.

It was, incidentally, in the hut mentioned above that the pioneer experimental broadcasting station 2-MT Writtle was built, as described in Chapter 22.

In 1920 the Company acquired a DH6 aircraft for experimental work, this machine being the first private plane to receive a wireless licence from the P.M.G. It was also the first aircraft to be fitted with a completely screened ignition system. This important contribution to aviation radio technology, removing as it did most of the aircraft-generated interference to the radio signals, was developed under the supervision of H. C. Van-de-Velde.

The practice of using a Company aircraft as a flying test-bed is still maintained. The DH6 was replaced in due course by an Avro G–BAJ which in turn was superseded by a Bristol Fighter G–EB10. This was followed by a Viking GA–HOP. The present (1968) aircraft is a Piaggio P166, GAPWY.

Sir Samuel Instone of S. Instone & Co., coal exporters and ship-owners, had long shown a lively interest in civil aviation and a private air service for the conveyance of that Company's staff and documents on the route Cardiff–Hounslow–Le Bourget had come into operation in 1919. In May 1920 these operations were converted into a public service between London and Paris. Instone Air Line was incorporated in

December 1921; later, in August 1922, the London–Cologne route was added.

In August 1921 Sir Samuel Instone was able to make the first telephone call in history from a private number on the ground to an aircraft in flight – Vickers G–EASI of Instone's fitted with an AD2 – with the co-operation of the G.P.O. and the Croydon ground station.

By 1922 more airlines had come into existence and the AD2 was well established, being in use by Handley Page Transport, Daimler Air Hire (formerly Aircraft Transport and Travel), Instone Air Lines, SNETA (forerunner of Sabena), KLM and others.

Another piece of aeronautical wireless equipment which came into service at this time was the airborne direction-finder. It will be recalled that the ground direction-finding stations operated by taking bearings in triangulation upon the aircraft's transmission, the pinpoint 'fix' so obtained being transmitted from a ground station to the aircraft by wireless telephone. The airborne direction-finder made it possible for the aircraft's navigator to provide his own 'fix' by obtaining bearings on two or three fixed communication stations, identified by their call signs and therefore having known positions. The bearings so obtained could then be plotted on a chart to give the aircraft's position. Such a piece of equipment was particularly useful when travelling by routes which were remote from any ground d.f. stations.

The equipment, which had been in an experimental stage during the latter part of the war, had, by 1922, been put into production as the Type 14 Aircraft Direction Finder. A unit principle of construction was adopted; the four main units consisted of:

a. The antenna system, consisting of two loops, one running fore-and-aft and the other secured across the wings, at right angles to the first.
b. The direction-finder unit, consisting of four fixed coils connected to the antenna system and a search coil which could be rotated within the fields of the fixed coils (the goniometer arrangement).
c. The tuning unit, consisting of an r.f. transformer, a phasing resistance, an antenna inductance and a 'd.f. sense' switch.
d. The amplifier unit, comprising eight valves (six r.f. amplifiers, a rectifier and an a.f. amplifier).

The approximate weight of the type 14 was thirty pounds.

A significant change in British civil airline policy occurred in 1923, when the four private-venture companies were amalgamated into the state-aided Imperial Airways Ltd., a decision which followed the recommendation of the Hambling Committee, set up to inquire into the future of British civil aviation. In the same year the Marconi Company decided to amalgamate the Aircraft and the Field Departments. The union, henceforth known as the Field and Air Division, had Captain Furnival as its Chief, with H. C. Van-de-Velde as his Deputy. The development work was transferred in the following year from Writtle to Croydon aerodrome, where it was under the direction of A. W. Whistlecroft.

Thus ended what might be described as the early pioneering period of civil aviation in this country. Both the airline operations and the airborne wireless development had been carried out by private enterprise and in very much of a hand-to-mouth manner, for passengers were few and money at a premium.

It is of interest to note that the Marconi Company, following the practice of its maritime organization, did not sell its wireless apparatus to an airline, but instead provided a complete service at a standard rate per flying hour on a sliding scale determined by the number of machines equipped and the number of flying hours. It provided the apparatus, installed it, maintained it, supplied all spares and expendable stores and trained the airline personnel in its operation. No charge was made for unsatisfactory communication if occasioned by faulty equipment.

The trials and tribulations of those early days – both technical and financial – had its reward in giving Britain the leadership in civil aviation. No foreign airline possessed such an advanced system of airborne communication and navigational aids.

With the formation of Imperial Airways, civil flying entered its second phase, which was one of steady expansion and development of air routes consequent upon the growth of public support, the design of machines which were airliners in their own right (as distinct from modified bombers) and the ever-increasing ranges and speeds which were achieved. The increased ranges and speeds in turn stimulated rapid development in airborne and ground wireless apparatus, for not only had increased ranges of telephonic contact to be provided, but swifter means of obtaining d.f. information had to be sought, particularly in respect of the airborne direction-finder.

The next decade was remarkable for its trail-blazing flights; Captain Hinchcliffe, Captain Courtney, Major Kingsford Smith, Colonel Lindberg, The Hon. Mrs Victor Bruce, Miss Amelia Earhardt, Miss Amy Johnson, Mr J. Mollinson, Sir Alan Cobham and others contributed a mass of invaluable data to the world of aviation by their epic flights. With many of these pioneers the Marconi Company was associated through the provision of wireless equipment and on several occasions the apparatus was instrumental in saving lives.

The airship never proved to be a serious competitor of the aeroplane, for although various attempts were made to design dirigibles for passenger-carrying service, Germany was the only nation to meet with success; indeed, the transatlantic crossings by the *Graf Zeppelin* seemed at one time to be tipping the scales, but two major airship disasters, the destruction of the British R101 and that of the German *Hindenburg* wrote *finis* to the challenge.

The extension of the British air services, first to the bounds of Europe and then beyond, to the Empire countries, led to an investigation of the possibilities and also the limitations of the short or high frequency (h.f.) waves as a means of communication for aircraft. (In this the pioneer work of Round and Franklin provided a sound basis for the modified circuits which were necessary for airborne usage.) Experimental work was carried out in 1927-8 and this proved remarkably successful; in December 1928 Cairo reported reception of h.f. telephony conversations from an airliner flying over England – easily a world record for airborne transmission.

In March 1930 another new service, air-sea rescue, was inaugurated. This had its origin in the work of the National Lifeboat Institution, which adapted the new Dover lifeboat for the purpose. The vessel, embodying every modern device, was fitted with two 375 h.p. engines, making her the fastest ship of her class in the world. For air-sea rescue work she carried Marconi equipment in the form of a trans-receiver (type XBM1) which was so constructed that it was impervious to the action of sea-water. Soon after, other vessels of the N.L.I. were similarly equipped, including those at Stornoway and St Peter Port, Guernsey. The large organization built up by the R.A.F. during World War II was a direct development from the pioneering work of the N.L.I.

In 1932 Marconi's carried out tests on behalf of the Air Ministry and Imperial Airways Ltd. in order to determine the most suitable wireless equipment for the new *Atalanta* type of aircraft used on the Cairo–Capetown air-route. It was a necessary condition that continuous two-way communication must be maintained between the aircraft and one or other of the widely-spaced ground stations during the trans-African crossing.

After six months' experimental work carried out by Marconi engineers flying over the route, a design of transmitting and receiving equipment covering the dual wavebands of 40–89 and 500–1,000 m. was evolved. The fully engineered equipment, the type AD37a/38a, fulfilled its range obligations, not only to the maximum demand of 1,300 miles, but also under normal conditions permitted communication with the G.P.O. station at Portishead when the aircraft was over the White Nile nearly 5,000 miles away. Norddeich, Germany (5,000 miles) and Coltano, Northern Italy (4,000 miles) were also contacted and news messages received from Miami Beach in the U.S.A.

By the end of 1932, orders were placed to equip four of the *Atalanta* class airliners with the AD37a/38a transmitter-receivers.

By this time the demand for civil airline wireless equipment had become considerable and was rapidly accelerating in growth. As a consequence, the Company decided to create an Aircraft Wireless Establishment as a separate entity in which the development, design and manufacture of aircraft equipment could be carried out under one roof. Hackbridge, Surrey, was chosen because it was within easy reach of Croydon. The factory, in Wandle Road, Hackbridge, was a two-storey building with a floor space of 6,000 ft.

The establishment was responsible for every phase of design, testing and final engineering up to the final model stage, when it was passed to the Chelmsford factory, together with drawings, for quantity manufacture. Captain J. M. Furnival was in charge at Hackbridge at its inception in 1935.

In that year the additional risks undertaken by engineers during airborne tests of wireless equipment were underlined by the death of Major B. S. Benning, a promising young engineer who was killed when the Company's experimental aircraft crashed. Three years later the crash of a hired machine put Captain Furnival in hospital for a long while; the Company's star test operator, T. A. Valette, was badly injured and died the following year, while the pilot, Captain Bailey, was also badly injured. Fortunately, since 1938, the Company's air testing has been free from serious accident.

In 1936 a promising new phase of commercial aviation began when the *Canopus*, the long-range flying boat built at Rochester for the Empire service, came into service with Imperial Airways and made an inaugural flight to the Mediterranean. This aircraft was the forerunner of twenty-seven others which did much to make trans-oceanic air travel the commonplace circumstance it is today.

The *Canopus* was fitted with Hackbridge-designed equipment (type AD57a/58a) covering the short and medium wavebands and, in addition, carried an airborne direction-finder and homing equipment. The Marconi screening harness for aircraft electrical systems had been further improved at Hackbridge and was now impervious to petrol, oil and water, thereby eliminating a potential source of fire and engine trouble. The Pegasus engines of the flying-boats incorporated this harness.

In the following year, 1937, the Empire flying boat *Caledonia*, undergoing its preliminary trials, made a non-stop flight from Southampton to Alexandria carrying the latest type of aircraft wireless equipment, the Marconi type AD67a/6872b. The sister aircraft *Cambria* made a round-Britain flight shortly afterwards as part of her trials, and exhaustive tests of the wireless equipment were carried out with success on both occasions.

In July of the same year *Caledonia* carried out her first Atlantic crossing, keeping in touch with stations on either side of the ocean all the way, using wireless telegraphy on the medium waveband.

The growing responsibilities of Imperial Airways Ltd. made it imperative that this organization should look to the future. At the beginning of commercial aviation, the pilots had been recruited from the R.A.F. fully trained in the handling of heavy bombers. Now, with new generations of aircraft in operation, the bomber/airliner flying techniques had diverged considerably. Accordingly, Imperial Airways opened a school at Croydon Aerodrome for the training of pilots and wireless operators. This came into service in 1935. In the matter of training wireless operators, the co-operation of the Marconi Company was invited, as a result of which H. T. Sayer, a highly experienced senior engineer, was appointed as Chief Wireless Instructor.

In the following year the Marconi Company opened its own aircraft wireless instructional establishment at Wallington, Croydon, to which its staff at Croydon transferred. Marconi's Air Radio Training School, as it was known, provided instruction for pilots and radio officers of Imperial Airways, the curriculum leading the trainee to the taking of the Air Operator's Certificate. A scheme was also put into operation for selecting good marine operators from Marconi personnel and giving them a free course. This built up a body of operators who were qualified both for marine and air duties. The school also accepted outside students and overseas air forces took advantage of this, notably the Egyptian Air Force which sent a number of men for training. The courses were also open to staff from other airline companies.

The ever-increasing air speeds kept the Company continually on its toes to provide new marks of equipment which were not only as reliable as they could be made – a few minutes 'off the air' could now be vital – but which were simpler to operate and therefore faster in providing information to the pilot.

One significant step forward had been made in 1930 with the AD18 transmitter, the first to embody control by master-oscillator. Even earlier, the first airborne direction-finding equipment, the type AD14, had made the aircraft independent of ground d.f. stations thus enabling it to fly on routes which did not have such stations. The airborne d.f. had been considerably improved over the years but the obtaining of a bearing by this means still involved the pilot or navigator in no fewer than thirteen visual, manual and vocal operations; as a consequence, although practice and dexterity could reduce the time taken, by the time a 'fix' had been obtained in one of the faster airliners it was already some distance further on from the indicated position.

In answer to this problem the 'Marconator' was evolved. This provided a very considerable simplification, reducing the number of operations to three and providing a direct read-out of the true bearing from a cursor on the D.R.* compass scale. The entire operation was reduced to one of twenty to thirty seconds' duration.

Following J. M. Furnival's accident in 1938, L. A. Sweny was appointed Manager of the Hackbridge Works, continuing in this capacity until the outbreak of war in 1939 when that Works was put on a war footing under R. Telford, and L. A. Sweny transferred to Chelmsford as Manager of the Aircraft Department.

* Distant Reading.

29

Developments in Marine Equipment
to 1939

Although the story of the development of wireless equipment for maritime use is properly within the province of the Marconi International Marine Company, this organization was, until 1962, housed at the Marconi Works at New Street, Chelmsford, and the equipment was manufactured there.

The use of wireless aboard ship had grown very considerably during World War I and by 1920 only the smallest vessels were without it. This situation, while it was clearly desirable, brought certain problems. One of these concerned the smaller categories of vessels in which only one radio officer was carried, for he obviously could not be on watch for twenty-four hours a day and yet a distress call might be received at any time.

A partial answer to this problem was to train one or two members of the crew to recognize an SOS call when they heard it; this was effective up to a point, but precious time could be consumed before the radio officer was roused to decipher the rest of the message and establish the whereabouts of the ship in trouble.

Experiments were carried out in the Chelmsford laboratories which gave birth to the Marconi 'Auto-Alarm' or Distress Call Device. This operated as follows:

The ship in difficulties transmits her call, an internationally recognized signal consisting of three four-second dashes with one-second intervals. This is received by the Auto-Alarm on a small vessel (the equipment is permanently switched on) and amplified so as to operate an alarm bell on the bridge and another in the radio officer's cabin. The equipment is designed to respond to that particular signal and to no others. The first demonstrations with this set were given in 1920.

Another development in the use of wireless at sea also occurred in 1919–20 when the Company designed and installed wireless telephone sets for use on whaling vessels or other ships which were at sea for long periods with no professional wireless engineer aboard. These sets were designed for simplicity and to withstand rough handling in the extremes of weather encountered in the Antarctic Circle.

The success of these equipments encouraged the Company, or rather one section of it, to specialize in whaling ship installations and equipment for polar duties. In 1923, the whale factory ship *Sir James Clark Ross* was fitted with a Marconi installation especially designed to cater for her special purposes. She needed very powerful wireless since she operated at distances far remote from her base; it was soon found that the range of her equipment was far greater than had been stipulated and in 1925 this ship made the first-ever short-wave communication across the Pacific Ocean to San Francisco, 8,000 miles distant. Shortly afterwards many whaling ships were fitted with the Company's short-wave wireless equipment.

In August 1924 a small expedition under the direction of a Marconi engineer, M. B. Hunter, left Hull for South Georgia where a wireless station, a laboratory, living quarters and stores accommodation were erected. This station provided a valuable asset to the whaling companies over the years.

A very thorough study of the problems which were peculiar to the whaling industry was undertaken from 1925 onwards. In that year another small expedition was sent to the Antarctic especially for this purpose. As a result of this first-hand observation the Whaler telephone set (Type XMC1) was designed. This had a power of 100/150 watts into the antenna and could be used by personnel who had no knowledge of wireless technology; it was an immediate success because it was absolutely right for the job and the environmental conditions. Large orders flowed in from the various whaling companies. The XMC1 was followed by two smaller sets, the XMD1 of 50/60 watts and the XMB1 with a power of 30/35 watts.

On 24 February 1928, the whaling mother ship *Southern Queen* struck an iceberg after her whalecatchers had been dispatched for the day, and were out of sight. Although the ship began to settle quickly her radio-telephone recalled the whalecatchers which arrived fifteen minutes after the mother ship had gone down. The crew were rescued from the boats, to which they had taken.

When Sir Douglas Mawson sailed for the far South in *Discovery* in 1929, complete Marconi equipment including a $1\frac{1}{2}$ kW quenched spark transmitter and a ship's receiver were installed. A Moth aircraft carried on deck was also Marconi-equipped. By such means the expedition was able to keep in continuous touch with civilization.

In the commercial marine world wireless had long since proved indispensable. A significant step forward in safety at sea had been taken in 1914 when the *Aquitania*'s lifeboats were installed with Marconi wireless apparatus. Other ships followed suit but the carrying of such equipment was entirely at the discretion of the shipping companies until the loss of the *Trevessa* in 1923, on which occasion its two lifeboats were lost for twenty-three and twenty-five days respectively. This disaster hastened legislation to make the carrying of wireless in lifeboats compulsory. It came into force on 1 July 1925, and by April 1926 Marconi's had fitted 171 such sets.

The mention of wireless in conjunction with piracy may seem a couple of centuries out of period, but it is a fact that in 1925 the Company introduced an anti-pirate installation for the benefit of coastal shipping in Chinese waters, where piracy was rife. This consisted of a $\frac{1}{4}$ kW quench spark transmitter fitted with an automatic keying device. This, together with a power supply, was housed inside a fireproof safe. By closing a switch the safe automatically locked and the transmitter was put into operation; the operator was thus freed to take a hand in the defence of the ship, while even if the pirates gained access to the wireless room they could not readily destroy the apparatus which was spreading the alarm far and wide. The pirates quickly realized that to attack a ship so equipped was to court swift capture and as larger numbers of their prey invested in such installations, so the menace of piracy dwindled.

The early 1920s saw the gradual introduction of wireless telephony aboard passenger liners and smaller vessels. The *Olympic* was equipped with a Marconi telephony transmitter in May 1923 and three months later the *Lorina*, a cross-channel packet owned by the (then) Southern Railway, made history by effecting the first conversation between a telephone subscriber in London and a cross-channel steamer. In February 1925 the Marconi Marine Company installed duplex wireless telephony equipment on the Southern Railway's *Princess Ena*, when telephone subscribers in Bournemouth, Glasgow and London held conversations with passengers. These were the beginnings of the ship-to-shore telephony service which will be referred to later.

Wireless telephony for trawlers was also introduced in 1925 and has proved an invaluable service over the years. (The conversations between trawler skippers materially extended the vocabulary of those who happened to be experimenting on those wave-bands around this period.)

The passing of an era came in 1927 when the general replacement of all spark apparatus by valve transmitters was ordered. Thereafter, the journalistic cliché 'the wireless crackled into life' which is still to be found today, passed into the realms of fiction. The early induction-coil spark sets which even by 1910 were beginning to be superseded by generator-powered equipment, were long since consigned to museums. Now the superseder was outmoded to take its place among the historical relics. The transition from electrical to electronics had arrived.

On shore also, maritime wireless telephony was making considerable headway. By 1929 over thirty Marconi wireless telephony stations were in service, linking lightships and lighthouses to the shore.

The first ship to be equipped with short-wave wireless telephony equipment was the *Majestic*, aboard which a large cabin was devoted to the posting of the latest London and New York stock-exchange prices; from this room passengers could transact business via the telephony service with the same ease as if they were on shore. The Marconi Marine Company carried out this installation in 1929, together with others for the White Star line, thus providing the ships' passengers with the means of telephonic communication with either hemisphere throughout the Atlantic crossing. In the following year a regular radio-telephone service, with a fixed scale of charges (£4. 10s. od. for the first three minutes and an additional £1. 10s. od. per minute thereafter) was instituted between the *Homeric* and Britain or the United States.

In 1932 a further advance in maritime communication was the completion of a chain of radio telephone stations around the coasts of Britain. These, by means of their overlapping service areas, enabled modest telephony installations aboard small ships to keep in two-way contact with the shore up to a range of 300 miles. As the sea-going equipment permitted inter-ship conversation, messages could be relayed to a vessel well out of direct range of contact with the shore.

But the use of wireless was by no means confined to the transmission and reception of routine or emergency messages. Since 1912 the provision of regular transmissions of time signals and weather information had become international practice. The time signal service from shore stations gave the master of a vessel a positive check upon his chronometer and thereby a more accurate means of determining his longitude.

In 1912 also, the *Mauretania* had pioneered the use of the Marconi-Bellini-Tosi direction-finder, and this aid to marine navigation was reintroduced for use by the Merchant Service after the war, but only gained slow acceptance, despite its greatly improved performance. Once again it took a near-disaster to bring home the importance of the equipment when, in 1921, the Norwegian steamer *Ontaneda*, drifting helplessly off the Newfoundland banks, was located by the Marconi direction-finding equipment carried by the *Fanad Head*. This created a profound impression and by 1923 the d.f. apparatus was being adopted by Cunard, Canadian Pacific, Elders and Fyffes, the P. and O., Royal Mail and Red Star and White Star lines, among others.

The importance of the direction-finder must be assessed in relation to other navigational equipment of the period. Whilst it is true that by the 1920s the gyro compass had superseded the standard compass in large naval and commercial vessels, all other shipping had to rely upon the standard compass, an instrument subject to various forms of error. The wireless d.f. equipment provided such ships with a means of checking their positions.

That the possibility of error was no myth is substantiated by various incidents of the time. Such a one occurred in the winter of 1926 when the British cargo vessel *Antinoe* encountered a 100 mph hurricane when in mid-Atlantic which battered the ship so severely that her Master was forced to send an SOS followed by what he believed to be the ship's position. On picking up the signals the *Roosevelt*, which was equipped with American wireless apparatus, changed course and steamed to the position given, only to find an empty waste of ocean. Fortunately the *Antinoe* had not foundered; that much was certain because her wireless signals were still being received. But where was she?

Fortunately also the *Roosevelt* was equipped with d.f. apparatus and by using this to 'home' on the *Antinoe*'s transmissions the helpless vessel was located, listing at an angle of thirty-five degrees and slowly sinking, at a point nearly sixty miles from her stated position. All hands were rescued.

By coincidence, while the *Antinoe* rescue was in progress another British ship, the *Laristan*, was also in dire trouble. Her rescuer, the *Bremen*, was directed to her by means of the Marconi-Bellini-Tosi d.f. equipment carried by the Canadian Pacific ship *Montnairn*. The *Laristan*'s actual position was 26 miles distant from that calculated by dead reckoning.

Such incidents emphasized in the most forceful manner possible the value of the direction-finder as a navigational aid, although of course its primary function was to obtain bearings upon known shore stations and thereby provide a 'fix'. The provision of direction-finding equipment on all ships of 5,000 tons burden and over was made compulsory in July 1931.

Parallel with the development of this sea-going navigational aid was that of the short-wave automatic beacon. The first of these, designed by C. S. Franklin, was erected at Inchkeith, Firth of Forth, in 1921, and operated on four metres using a rotating antenna with a parabolic reflector. An improved version was erected at South Foreland in 1923–4, upon which further development work was done. A successful demonstration of this six-metre beacon was given in the Spring of 1928, but short-wave equipment of this type did not come into general usage. The Company also developed medium-wave beacons of both the fixed and rotating type from 1923 onwards.

Another device which operated for the greater safety of mariners was the remote control of fog signalling apparatus which was first demonstrated in 1932. By transmitting a train of pulses at a recurrence frequency of sixty per minute, a special receiver installed at the fog signalling station actuated the fog horn. A transmission at a pulse recurrence frequency of forty-six per minute switched it off. By this means control could be effected from a convenient point many miles away.

Depth sounding was yet another development which has brought great benefits to the marine world. Following upon the work on sonic waves carried out by the Admiralty for the detection of submarines in the First World War, the Marconi Company and others pursued this line of investigation in the 1920s. In December 1930, the Marconi Sounding Device Co. was formed using the patents of Professor Langevin, notably the special form of quartz oscillator which he had developed.

The first Marconi Depth Sounder was tested aboard the trawler *Umberto Lupi*, cruising off the East African coast. Various sonic frequencies were tried; it was found that ultrasonic frequencies could be made much more highly directional than the sonic type. From these beginnings emerged, over the years, the range of echo-sounding equipments now marketed by the Marconi International Marine Co. for a wide variety of applications.

30

Special-Purpose Wireless Communication; Pictures by Wireless

In giving some account of the new developments in the years immediately following the 1914–18 war – developments brought about as a result of improvements to the thermionic valve – it should be emphasized that these were going on against a background of conventional communications orders.

Typical of these were a chain of twenty-four spark stations in Angola (1918), a number of arc stations for China (1918) and, in the following year, spark stations for several Portuguese colonies and for Spitzbergen, Bear Island and Northern Norway. Others included wireless links to the Fiji Isles and a large number of portable stations for China, Spain, Portugal, Brazil, Italy, Peru, India, Greece, Canada, Holland, Rumania, Siam and Mexico – all these in 1920. In that year also, two wireless telephony stations, one at Horton and the other at Oslo, were installed together with the first wireless telephone service in Gambia.

At the same time it was clear that, with the further development of the thermionic valve, more and more applications would become apparent. Accordingly, in 1922 we find the (then) not inconsiderable sum of £40,000 being set aside for research purposes; these included a series of probing exercises designed to evaluate various potential markets.

One such possibility was the application of wireless communication to police work. The first recorded instance of this had occurred in 1910 when Dr Crippen, who had murdered his wife, was apprehended as a result of wireless messages sent to Scotland Yard by the captain of the *Montrose* who rightly suspected that one of his passengers was the wanted man.

In 1920 the Company developed a small (for that time) but very efficient 'portable' receiver with which experiments were carried out between Marconi House, London, and various locations in Essex, where a police officer, with the receiver incorporated in a suitcase, was given the task of receiving 'emergency' calls. The experiments proved very successful.

In 1925 at the International Police Conference held in New York, an extensive demonstration was staged to show the various ways in which wireless could aid the police, and as a result of this many police forces in various parts of the world began to use such equipment. From this stemmed the present international police system of rapid inter-communication and co-operation in catching criminals and the employment of wireless-equipped patrol cars which now forms so vital a part of modern police organization.

Another possible application of wireless communication which was actively investigated in the early 1920s was its use by railroads. This again was not entirely new, for in 1914 the Company had carried out a series of experiments between moving trains and a fixed station at Wannamaker Buildings, New York City. These preceded an installation for the Delaware Lachawanna and Western Railroad, which thoroughly proved its efficacy during a great blizzard which swept over the region in March 1914. Trains stranded at remote points were located by wireless and put in touch with rescue parties.

In 1923 the Canadian National Railways experimented with the provision of wireless programmes on their transcontinental services. These were so successful that the Canadian Government eventually built twelve broadcasting stations for use with their train services. These stations extended from Montreal to Vancouver.

In 1924 a number of tests, under the supervision of the Radio Society of Great Britain, were carried out in this country between King's Cross, London, and Newcastle-upon-Tyne. These proved that a two-way service was feasible between a moving train and a fixed terminal station, but no practical use was ever made of the idea, no doubt because the relatively short distances of British train journeys do not warrant such an innovation.

·　　　·　　　·

Another 'probing' operation which met with far more success was also carried out at this time. In December 1924 the Caernarvon station participated in the first experimental wireless transmission of still pictures between England and the U.S.A. The method used was that of R. H. Ranger of the Radio Corporation of America; it was based on the exploration of the picture to be transmitted by a beam of light, the modulation of the reflected light being converted to electrical signals by a photo-electric cell. The point-by-point exploration was effected by mounting the picture on a rotating cylinder, which was traversed by the light beam. At the receiving end a similar cylinder rotated in synchronism; this was achieved by the use of tuning fork control at both transmitter and receiver.

Such a method is not true facsimile; even at best the reproduction was not better than inferior half-tone reproduction where a coarse screen has been used. It was also too slow for Press work. Nevertheless, it was a promising start and the system was put into operation after some improvements had been made, and was used commercially as from 1926. The service was between Radio House, London (the Company's main telegraph station at that time) and New York, and vice versa.

A considerable range of material was copied across the Atlantic, including cheques, wills, contracts, blueprints and specimen signatures. This photo service was carried by the short-wave beam. It soon became clear, however, that the system had its limitations, particularly in respect of the amount of detail which could be transmitted and in the length of time taken to send the picture. The latter circumstance made the cost of transmission prohibitive for all except the most important and urgent cases. It was equally clear that the system did not lend itself to development to the standards desired and so a decision was made to attempt an entirely new approach.

At the same time, development had been taking place in the field of super high-speed morse telegraphy, with considerable success. In this, a beam of light passing through the punched holes of a Wheatstone tape were directed on to a photo-electric cell, the varying output of which was used to actuate the transmitter and thereby send morse signals as represented by the holes punched in the tape. At the receiver the signals were recorded on a dictaphone wax cylinder run at high speed; on completion the cylinder was re-run at a lower speed for translation of the messages by a Creed telegraph printer or a recording undulator. In 1927, demonstrations were given at which speeds of 3,000 words per minute were achieved.

Certain aspects of this development, including a revival of interest in the Kerr cell as a high-speed shutter for polarized light, had considerable implications for facsimile work. As a result, in 1929 the Company were able to put an entirely new device on the market, the Marconi-Wright*

* Developed by G. M. Wright, later to become Engineer-in-Chief.

facsimile apparatus, which was demonstrated on 3 November 1929 before a large gathering of Press representatives. A transatlantic transmission was affected from a beam station at Rocky Point in the U.S.A. and was successfully received at the beam reception station at Somerton, Somerset.

This was true facsimile; documents and Press material of all kinds including photographs could be transmitted across the Atlantic at high speed – three minutes was an average time for a photograph. The equipment could be run continuously so that an entire newspaper might conveniently be sent between countries. By 1934 the state of the art had developed to the point where Cable and Wireless Ltd. were able to inaugurate a facsimile service between England and Australia, using the Marconi system. This service was inaugurated on October 16 of that year. A few days later not only documents and photographs were transmitted but motion-picture film also. On October 23 the winners of the England-Australia air race reached Melbourne. Film of the arrival was transmitted from Australia to England via the short-wave beam service and was being shown in British cinemas only a few hours after the pilots stepped out of their machines.

There was, however, a maggot in the apple. This lay not in the equipment itself but in the transmission medium, in the form of the ionospheric layers; these do not remain constant in height or in density and so produce fading effects. Another imperfection lies in the circumstance that the radio signals reflect from more than one point in the ionosphere and so they arrive at the receiver having travelled over more than one path; those travelling over a longer route are sufficiently delayed in time to distort the waveform of the original. Under such conditions the received signals, whether they be in speech, telegraphic or picture form, are correspondingly mutilated.

This problem has been energetically attacked over the years and various devices, notably diversity transmission and reception and automatic error detection and correction equipment have been evolved which reduces the ill effects to a minimum.

Another aspect of the beam system which was being developed from 1926 onwards was multiplex signalling, whereby the carrier wave could be sub-divided into discrete channels each carrying separate messages simultaneously. While the Cable and Wireless merger was taking shape the first demonstration of multiplex working across the Atlantic was given, using the Marconi-Mathieu method which permitted the simultaneous transmission and reception of one telephone message and two telegraphic messages. Earlier than this, on March 1, a duplex test had been made, during which Sir Robert Donald, Chairman of the British Imperial Wireless Telegraph Committee had held a telephone conversation with Mr David Sarnoff, Vice-President of the Radio Corporation of America. The respective Vice-Presidents of the Canadian Bell Telephone Company and the Canadian Marconi Company also participated. Two telegraphic channels were in operation at the same time.

These were most important developments, for not only was a considerable economy in frequency allocations effected but the cost of adapting the beam stations for duplex and multiplex operation was relatively small.

31

Television

The concept of the transmission of visual images over greater-than-optical distances is very much older than that of transmitting signals via wireless waves, pre-dating it by almost a hundred years. By the beginning of the nineteenth century various proposals were being put forward, most of them of no practical value because of the multiplicity of wires demanded between transmitter and receiver, but by 1842 Alexander Bain had devised a chemical telegraph which foreshadowed a workable system. This was followed in 1847 by Bakewell's model which recognized the need to dissect the picture into elements and reconstruct it at the receiver, a fundamental principle of television to this day. By 1867 the art of picture transmission had advanced to the point where a commercial service was put into operation in France, although with only qualified success.

The key to the problem of moving picture transmission had been discovered in 1839, when Becquerel the elder produced the first crude photo-voltaic cell. No practical use was made of this however and it was not until 1873, when Willoughby Smith of the G.P.O. published a paper on the photo-conductive properties of the metal selenium, that the attention of experimenters was drawn to the possible significance of photo-electric phenomena.

Two years later, G. R. Carey of the U.S.A. proposed a method of transmitting and receiving moving pictures by the utilization of a mosaic of selenium cells at the transmitter and a corresponding number of electric lamps at the receiver, but Carey was defeated (like the early still picture workers) by the large number of wires needed to connect the transmitter and receiver. Other experimenters followed the same general lines as Carey and met with a similar lack of success.

Senlacq of France was probably the first to see clearly that the image must be scanned; a suggestion to this effect was made by him in 1878. Then in 1884, Paul Nipkow, a German engineer, produced on paper what subsequently proved to be the first workable method of moving picture transmission. This employed a scanning disc at the transmitter which rotated in synchronism with a similar device at the receiver, the scanning operation being effected by a spiral of holes through each disc.

Unfortunately, Nipkow's apparatus needed two items more before it became capable of producing recognizable pictures. These were a less sluggish cell than selenium and an amplifier to intensify the very weak currents the apparatus would produce. Neither had been invented and so Nipkow's device remained undeveloped for nearly forty years.

In 1889 another German, Professor Weiller, proposed another form of scanning, the mirror drum system, which was also destined to be resurrected after more than forty years on the laboratory shelf. It could not, at the time of its proposal, produce pictures because it, too, suffered from the same inherent deficiencies as the Nipkow apparatus. Others tried, with the same negative results until, with the problem seemingly insoluble, interest in the subject waned. A practical system of television (the word was coined by a Frenchman, Perskyi, in 1900) was to remain a pipedream for many years.

Nevertheless work was going on in apparently unrelated fields which was to prove of immense importance to television. The cathode ray oscilloscope, developed by Karl Braun from the previous work of Plucker, Hittorf, Crookes and others, was gradually being improved, notably by Fleming's focusing coils and the Wehnelt hot cathode. In 1905 the researches of Elster and Geitel produced a much faster light-sensitive cell than the selenium type. Fleming's thermionic diode of 1904 and the introduction of a third electrode, the grid, by Dr Lee de Forest in 1907, were eventually to provide the essential amplifying device which early experimenters lacked.

In 1907 the Russian scientist, Professor Boris Rosing, revived interest in television by building an experimental equipment which used mirror drum scanning at the transmitter and a cathode ray tube as a means of picture display at the receiver. It is believed that, despite the lack of a signal amplifier, crude pictures of geometrical shapes were produced at the receiver, but the use of a selenium cell inhibited any display of movement.

A very significant step forward was made in the following year when A. A. Campbell Swinton, a well-known electrical engineer – the same man who introduced the young Marconi to William Preece of the G.P.O. – wrote a letter to *Nature* in which he proposed a television system which was to use a cathode ray tube at both the transmitter and receiver. Campbell Swinton did this without knowledge of Rosing's

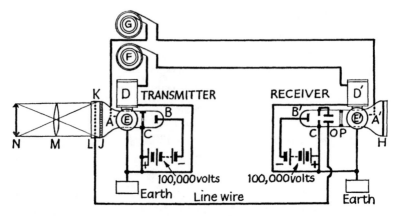

Figure 31.1 Campbell Swinton's Proposal for a Television System, 1911

experiments of the year before. Three years later, as President of the Röngtgen Society, he gave a detailed account of his proposed system, the fundamental principles of which are those in use throughout the world today.

Campbell Swinton's proposed apparatus was never built however, and again interest in television languished. It is worthy of note that television had never been visualized as anything more than that of a closed circuit system using a wire conductor as the medium of transmission from one point to another. The first proposal to harness radio waves as a carrier for picture signals was made by A. Sinding-Larsen in 1911; a remarkable proposal indeed, since no one had up to that time produced light, shade and movement in a television picture even on a closed circuit basis, while the only continuous wave carriers available were those produced by the arc method or by r.f. alternator.

The discovery in 1913 of the thermionic triode's properties of continuous-wave generation made Sinding-Larsen's proposition much more feasible – except of course that no one had as yet produced television picture signals – but the Great War brought any significant experimental work in this field to a halt. At the end of the war, however, with sound radio and thermionic valve amplifiers relatively commonplace, it was not long before various experimenters began to turn their thoughts toward television. Among these were D. Mihaly (Germany), J. L. Baird (Britain) and Herbert E. Ives, C. F. Jenkins, P. Farnsworth and V. Zworykin (U.S.A.).

Unfortunately all but two of those mentioned, and many others also, elected to work on systems embodying mechanical scanning, using the

Nipkow type of disc, the Weiller mirror drum, or various derivatives. John Logie Baird was the first to achieve pictures embodying a degree of light and shade and having movement when, in 1926, he gave a demonstration to members of the Royal Institution. His apparatus consisted of a Nipkow-type disc used in conjunction with a gas-filled potassium photo-cell and thermionic valve amplifiers; the light source at the receiver was a neon lamp. The pictures were scanned in thirty lines per frame, with a frame repetition frequency of five per second. The image area of the received picture was two by one and a half inches.

Other inventors were not long after Baird in producing television pictures and the race was on; a needless race it so happened, because of the limitations of mechanical systems.

The two men who did not conform were Philo Farnsworth and Vladimir Zworykin. Each was working independently on devices which were designed to provide an all-electronic scanning of the image.

Zworykin, who had been a pupil of Rosing's and had assisted him in his early television experiments, came to the U.S.A. after the Russian revolution and joined the staff of the Westinghouse Electric and Manu-facturing Company at East Pittsburg. In spite of discouragement he persisted in carrying out television research and in 1923 filed a patent application for his 'Iconoscope', which was an all-electronic camera pick-up tube embodying the important principle of energy storage between successive scans. It was fundamentally the same in principle as Campbell Swinton's concept of 1911, although it seems that Zworykin had not at that time any knowledge of this prior suggestion.

Farnsworth's camera tube, which he called an image dissector, was also an all-electronic device, but did not use the storage principle. Both men had many years' work ahead of them, battling against indifference, the much-publicized progress of the various mechanical systems and the difficulties inherent in the manufacture of their respective camera tubes.

Meanwhile Baird in England was going from strength to strength, demonstrating in quick succession, the televising of subjects in complete darkness (using infra-red rays), colour television and even stereoscopic television. But impressive as these achievements were, particularly to the lay reader of a daily newspaper, they possessed novelty value only; the limitations in the studio were so rigid as to prohibit any sensible degree of entertainment. The prodigality of Baird's inventions was a function of his need for continual publicity as a means of attracting financial backing. This, it must be emphasized, is not a criticism of Baird the inventor, but rather of an economic system which drove him again and again to seek the headlines before the previous achievements could be assessed and consolidated.

The Marconi Company could not fail to be deeply interested in such a startling development as television and made a point of investigating the various systems which were being put forward, and in particular that developed by Baird. Shortly after the Royal Institution demonstration of 1926, Baird approached the Company with a view to making some sort of arrangement. This approach came to nothing because his apparatus had no patent protection; it was in essence the Nipkow device of 1884.

As to television in general, it was decided within the Company that research and development effort directed towards the field of entertainment should, subject to later review, avoid the video aspect of television. Instead, research should continue on transmitters, receivers and antennas with particular reference to such modulation and transmission problems as were peculiar to the handling of television signals.

But when the B.B.C. rather reluctantly agreed to grant Baird certain transmission facilities for experimental television (these began on 30 September 1929), a reappraisal of the situation took place within the Company. This in no way modified the conviction that a 30-line system could never provide an adequate entertainment service, but it did concede that there were certain commercial possibilities inherent in low definition television. The transmission of news in visual form was one possibility; public address work in which the head and shoulders of a speaker could be reproduced more than life size on a large screen was another.

It was therefore decided to form a television research group; this was constituted and effectively came into operation in August 1930. Its terms of reference were to investigate the commercial possibilities mentioned earlier and to register patents from which useful licence revenue might be derived. As the Company had recently abandoned the manufacture of domestic receivers it did not propose to make domestic television sets, but it was recognized that at some future date a television system providing much higher definition might provide pictures of acceptable entertainment value and so the research team was briefed to investigate the many problems involved in cathode ray tube scanning. Marconi himself in an article in *The Times* for 11 May 1931, referred to this when he said:

Should the intensive work in television now in progress in our laboratories give us, as we hope, at no distant date the results for which we are striving, the public will again be afforded the opportunity of assisting in the creating of a new industry, that of visual broadcasting.

By 1932, N. E. Davis of the Research Department at Chelmsford had produced a v.h.f. transmitter (6·8 m.) suitable for 250 kc/s modulation, covering all the requirements existing at that time for what was regarded as high-definition television. High-gain line amplifiers were also developed. Marconi's lecture to the Royal Institution on 2 December 1932, referred to the possibility of using microwave channels for television purposes.

The first practical results of the work of the Television Section were demonstrated in July 1932, when low definition signals were transmitted from Chelmsford on a wavelength of twenty-five metres and received in Australia. The tests which were carried out with the collaboration of Amalgamated Wireless (Australasia) Ltd., were of two discrete forms, namely:

1. A 'news' picture consisting of a travelling tape bearing a message. This was scanned in ten lines with a repetition rate of twelve and a half frames per second; the receiving display system consisted of modulated neon light projection on to a ground glass screen.
2. A 50-line head-and-shoulders picture of a subject, repeated at a rate of twelve and a half frames per second.

The first-mentioned provided intelligible messages at the receiving end; the second was marred by multiple image effects and imperfect synchronism. The tests were not continued.

A more successful demonstration was given to the York meeting of the British Association between 31 August and 7 September 1932. Again, two different applications were shown:

1. A 'news' picture transmitted from Chelmsford to St Peter's School, York (180 miles). This was sent on a wavelength of 760 m. using a modulation bandwidth of 18 kc/s. The scanning was in fifteen lines per frame at a repetition rate of twenty per second. The picture consisted of message on a tape travelling at a rate which could be increased from 60 to 120 five-letter words per minute; scanning was by means of a light beam and an apertured drum. At the receiver the image was reproduced on a ground-glass screen twenty-five inches by three inches.

2. A transmission from St Peter's School, York, of a head-and-shoulders or full-length picture scanned by a light beam and Nipkow disc. The picture was scanned in fifty lines at a repetition rate of fifteen frames per second. The picture was displayed at the receiver on a ground-glass screen eight inches square.

These transmissions attracted much favourable comment. They were followed in September 1933 with a further demonstration to the British Association, this time at Leicester. On this occasion the display was projected a distance of 20 ft. on to a screen 5 ft. square, being viewed by a large audience. The success of the demonstration gave encouragement to the view that the system was of potential value for public address work. The images were scanned in fifty lines with a frame repetition rate of fifteen per second. Transmission, which was purely local, occupied a band-width of 18 kc/s and was of interest in that the transmission medium was a beam of light, modulated by the signals.

Behind the scenes at Chelmsford improved scanning methods and other features led to the production of a one hundred-line picture, but one still effected by mechanical scanning.

The race to produce a successful high-definition system was now well under way. Although the Baird 30-line transmissions were still being broadcast by the B.B.C. on an experimental basis, it was well known that Baird's Company was actively pursuing the high-definition goal, using improved mechanical scanning devices. Electric and Musical Industries Ltd., had also, by 1931, produced a 150-line, twelve and a half frames per second system, using a lens-drum scanning arrangement, while in the U.S.A. Zworykin had publicly demonstrated his 'Iconoscope' to a meeting of the Institute of Radio Engineers in New York. Such was his progress that by October 1933 Zworykin was able to deliver a paper to the Institution of Electrical Engineers in London describing a 240-line system. This, however, though a remarkable achievement, was not one which was at a production stage. Much had still to be learned about the quantity production of camera pick-up tubes, particularly in the matter of providing a uniform mosaic layer.

Development work at E.M.I. Ltd. was led by the ex-Marconi man, Isaac Shoenberg, who became the presiding genius over a brilliant research team which included Blumlein, Willans, Browne, White and McGee. By 1934 E.M.I. had achieved the design of a Nipkow disc studio flying spot scanner, a 243-line picture at fifty fields per second, using their newly developed interlaced scanning. Before this, however, it had been appreciated that mechanical scanning was approaching its limit in terms of speed and so a parallel research effort had been instituted in 1932 to investigate electronic methods. In this the team were able, by reason of the link between E.M.I. and R.C.A., to have a certain degree of access to Zworykin's work, he being now the leader of the American Company's television research.

In spite of the difficulties of pick-up tube manufacture, Shoenberg became convinced that the all-electronic system was the one of the future, and intensified his effort in that area. The 'Emitron' camera tube resulted; this bore a strong family resemblance to Zworykin's Iconoscope but was the product of quite separate development work.

At this point the interest of Electric and Musical Industries and the Marconi Company began to coincide. Both had long realized that only high-definition television could provide genuine entertainment value and that only an all-electronic system could provide the flexibility in operation which was a prime requirement. But the overall problem was two-headed; one was that the production of video signals on an all-electronic basis demanded considerable expertise in the manufacture of camera pick-up tubes. The other was that the transmission of the extremely wide bandwidth occupied by the video signals called for specialist transmitter knowledge.

Basically, the situation was that E.M.I. possessed a knowledge of camera tube manufacture which Marconi's did not, but conversely, the Marconi Company, by reason of long experience of facsimile transmission and wide-band modulation generally, plus a similar background of antenna design, were in possession of vital knowledge which E.M.I. at that time did not have. Divided, each Company had half of an embryo system at its finger-tips. United, they could be in a position of considerable strength and so it was logical to try to arrange a marriage of convenience.

This was done and in March 1934 the Marconi-E.M.I. Television Company Limited was formed and the complementary special skills co-ordinated. The project was timely, for in that year the trial period which the B.B.C. had allocated to the Baird 30-line system ended and the Government accordingly set up a committee under Lord Selsdon to consider the state of the art in television and to advise the Postmaster-General on the relative merits of various systems and on the conditions under which a permanent public television service might best be provided. In Britain there were four systems worthy of serious consideration, namely those of Baird, A. C. Cossor Ltd., Scophony and Marconi-E.M.I.

Others existed abroad; the Loewe system, the Mihaly-Traub and the Peck.

When in January 1935 the Selsdon Committee published its report, it recommended that high-definition television with a line content of not less than 240 per frame should be adopted, and this automatically eliminated all but two of the contenders, for only Baird and Marconi-E.M.I. could put such a system into the field.

It may be wondered what degree of progress existed in the U.S.A., where the Iconoscope had been born. A delegation from the Selsdon Committee was sent to find out; it reported that while technological progress in America was comparable to that existing in Britain, television stations were only being built on an experimental basis and that no public service was in immediate prospect. A delegation also visited Germany where experimental transmissions were being radiated on two standards, one of 30 lines, $12\frac{1}{2}$ frames per second and the other 180 lines, 25 frames per second.

The Committee, after examining the Baird and the Marconi-E.M.I. apparatus, confirmed that high-definition television was in a sufficiently advanced state to justify the opening of a public service and recommended that the B.B.C. should be responsible for its running. The remaining question had now to be resolved: which of the two systems should be used? To this the Committee's solution had in it the elements of the judgement of Solomon. The rival systems, it was suggested, should be used on alternate weeks until each had been tested thoroughly and evaluated under equal conditions.

The challenge was accepted by both parties and Alexandra Palace in North London chosen as the transmitting site. As it was not possible to design a vision transmitter which would handle both systems, each Company provided its own, but the sound transmitter, built by Marconi's, was common to both. The antenna system, designed by C. S. Franklin of Marconi's, was also shared. The vision wavelength was 6·67 m. and the sound 7·23 m., the radiation bandwidth being 4 mc/s.

Experimental public transmissions by both systems were radiated during the Radio Exhibition at Olympia in August 1936, after which transmissions were discontinued until October, when a series of trial programmes was radiated for two hours daily. The television station formally opened on 2 November 1936.

The apparatus used by the rival Companies was in striking contrast. Marconi-E.M.I. pinned their faith in the small mobile Emitron cameras which could be wheeled easily around the studio floor or used on exterior locations if required. The scanning process was carried out electronically at 405 lines per frame, interlaced to provide two fields per frame, each of $202\frac{1}{2}$ lines. The repetition frequency was fifty fields (25 frames) per second. The Baird Company on the other hand had elected to remain faithful to mechanical scanning of the Nipkow disc type and displayed remarkable mechanical ingenuity in maintaining the speeds necessary to provide their transmission standards which were 240 lines per frame, sequential scanning (i.e. one field per frame) at a repetition rate of twenty-five fields (or frames) per second.

In the Baird studios two distinct types of equipment were employed. One, for studio use where individual subjects were being televised, embodied the special high-speed Nipkow discs and flying-spot scanning. This method being unsuitable for large studio scenes an ingenious intermediate film system was employed in such situations. In this, the scene was filmed and the sound recorded, immediately after which the film was developed and fixed in tanks underneath the camera. The negative was rapidly dried and fed into a scanning unit from which the video signals were derived. The resultant television pictures were delayed by only one minute in all this complex mechanical process.

It has been said that the Marconi-E.M.I. system won on superior picture quality. This is not wholly true for on their day the pictures from the Baird system were comparable with those of its rival. But the Baird apparatus, although a triumph of mechanical ingenuity, was cumbersome, inflexible and expensive in operation. Too late, Baird realized the price he was about to pay for his stubborn adherence to mechanical scanning and hurriedly brought a Farnsworth image dissector into operation, but in February 1937 the Committee recommended that the Marconi-E.M.I. equipment should carry the permanent programme service.

It is natural to have every sympathy with John Logie Baird who had laboured unceasingly for thirteen years to no purpose, at first in poverty and always in ill-health. But the choice was not one in which sentiment could play a part. The Baird mechanical scanning had reached its acme of achievement whereas the Marconi-E.M.I. system clearly had much more flexibility and was capable of considerable future development; events have shown that the choice was a wise one.

It is ironic that Baird, who contributed not a single invention to television as we know it today, should be regarded by the general public as its Father figure, while the names of those who were truly responsible should be known only in electronic engineering circles. But let no one begrudge Baird his niche in the public mind; he was, after all, the first man to produce true television pictures and even though his success led many along the blind alley of mechanical scanning, he was, as P. P. Eckersley once remarked, the aphrodisiac which stimulated others to research, and ultimately to produce a more rewarding system.

Those in the domestic radio receiver industry who saw in the advent of television the promise of a boom comparable with the sound radio bonanza of the 1920s were in for a disappointment. Despite the undoubted interest of the general public, the progress of the sales of home receivers was painfully low. By 1939 the total number of television sets sold amounted only to about 17,000–18,000, virtually all of these in the service area of the London station, which was still the sole source of programmes in the British Isles. The reason for this is not difficult to see. The ultra-rapid acceptance of sound radio had been brought about by the availability of crystal receivers, which were not only modest in price but were also simple enough in construction to be tackled by anyone reasonably adept with his hands; the early valve sets also lent themselves to home construction by the lay public. But these factors were absent at the début of entertainment television. The cost of a receiver was high in relation to the average wage-packet and the circuit complexity was such that only a relative handful of amateurs could successfully attempt home construction.

This painfully slow progress was brought to a complete stand-still by the outbreak of World War II in September 1939, when the London station was closed down on the grounds that its transmissions could provide a ready-made target-homing device for enemy bombers.

The close-down, considered from the parochial standpoint of the British radio industry, was a near-disaster. Up to this time British manufacturers, by reason of practical experience, had a technological lead over the rest of the world, but now these skills had to be diverted to other and, sterner, problems. The situation was, of course, shared by manufacturers all over Europe, but not by those in the U.S.A. who were, under the circumstances, presented with a bonus of six years in which to forge ahead.

32

Research and Development to 1939

For a company to remain in the forefront of progress for more than seventy years is no mean achievement, particularly in electronics, which is more subject to rapid technological changes than most industries. Of the various factors which have contributed to this circumstance, none is more important than the emphasis which is placed on research.

This has always been so since the beginning and so may be regarded as traditional. In the first years all experimental work was done under Guglielmo Marconi's personal direction, most of it being carried out at the Haven, Niton or the establishment at the Needles Hotel, Bournemouth (in fact Marconi continued to use the Haven experimental station until 1926 when it was finally closed).

At the turn of the century, with the transatlantic project the main objective, the relevant experimental work was transferred to Poldhu, Crookhaven and later Clifden, but as there were signs of a demand for stations intermediate in power between the Poldhu giant and the small ships' set, the need was felt for an experimental site near the Chelmsford Works. This was built at Broomfield on the outskirts of Chelmsford. When, in 1905, the Works moved to Dalston, the necessary research and development work in connection with new stations was shared between Broomfield and the Dalston Test Department. In 1908, the Works returned to Hall Street, Chelmsford.

From this time onward Chief Engineer Andrew Gray, foreseeing that more facilities were going to be needed in the near future, periodically put proposals to the Management for an expansion of research activities under the co-leadership of H. J. Round and C. S. Franklin, who had both, as Marconi's personal assistants, shown the necessary qualities as twin spearheads of research. In 1912 his proposal was accepted and a Research Department was constituted under C. S. Franklin. A building in a field opposite the Hall Street Works was placed at the disposal of the new team.

This laboratory functioned fairly well, although Marconi's habit of spiriting Franklin away for special work on the transatlantic stations was not conducive to stability of operation. The laboratory continued to function until the outbreak of war in 1914, when it came under Admiralty direction as an interception station for enemy transmissions. Franklin was allocated to war service on short-wave investigations in Italy and at Portsmouth, and H. J. Round was seconded to Military Intelligence on direction-finding.

In 1917 a Suggestions and Inventions Committee was constituted as an incentive to the staff. In February of the following year Andrew Gray put forward further recommendations for a Research Department and in August 1918 a Research Committee was formed to consider the formation of such a Department against the day when peace should come. A Laboratory Superintendent was appointed to consider the equipping of such an establishment and to look for a good site. When, in 1919, the Admiralty announced its intention of vacating the old laboratory building at Hall Street, it was decided to utilize this as a temporary measure.

In May 1921 the Research Committee was replaced by a Technical Board, which immediately reorganized Company research. By its direction the Research Department was re-formed under the leadership of H. J. Round, while an Independent Research Department was created with C. S. Franklin as Chief. Andrew Gray, who had been walking a diplomatic tightrope for some years with two senior engineers of comparable brilliance on the staff, each with equal claims to assume the title of Chief of Research, must have been relieved at the adoption of this face-saving stratagem. Alas! he had but a brief respite. For a time all was well, but before long his memoranda began to complain of the failure of the two Research Chiefs to keep him informed of what they were doing. 'Eventually,' he laments, 'the reports of the Independent Research Department became reduced to summaries and finally ceased, while the Research Department's report became less and less complete.' It is to be feared that neither Franklin nor Round had any love for paper work and even less regard for any authority other than Marconi himself, whom they viewed with something a shade less than idolatry.

However, the twin departments continued and as an example of the Company's belief in the value of research, the records for 1922 show that the then considerable sum of £40,000 was voted to further this end.

In 1925 Franklin's Independent Research Department consisted of six engineers and twelve technical assistants. The buildings comprised hut accommodation at:

(a)	Burnham Marshes	(b)	Hendon
(c)	Frankley (Birmingham)	(d)	Inchkeith
(e)	South Foreland	(f)	Poldhu (station building and a
(g)	Accommodation at		hut)
	Marconi House, Strand.		

The Research Department, under Round, was staffed by fourteen engineers and fourteen technical assistants. Their buildings consisted of:

(a) The laboratory at Hall Street (Chelmsford) Works
(b) The Broomfield establishment ⎫ both on the outskirts
(c) The Beehive Lane establishment ⎭ of Chelmsford
(d) Accommodation at the New Street (Chelmsford) Works
(e) Accommodation at Marconi House, London.

In addition to its research duties, Franklin's department was responsible for the operation of the B.B.C.'s 2LO broadcasting transmitter, while Round's department had a similar responsibility for the B.B.C.'s long-wave 5XX transmitter, located at the New Street Works.

At this time, other smaller research units were in being. Dr MacLaren and an assistant were working on experimental high-speed recorders, a magnetic drum recorder and the remote (wireless) control of unattended fog guns. In another small department work was being carried out on wireless telephone duplexing, while Marconi and two personal assistants, Mathieu and Kemp, formed another quite separate pocket of research.

Nor was this all. The Works Designs Department at Writtle, near Chelmsford, under the direction of N. (later Sir Noel) Ashbridge, was carrying out work which, although not designated as research, was often so near to it as to be indistinguishable from it. To add to Gray's problems, Guglielmo Marconi was still prone to remove Round or Franklin (or both) for his own purposes at a moment's notice.

Andrew Gray, although he was perhaps too close to the situation to realize it fully, was officiating at the birth of a new era of laboratory practice. Gone were the old happy-go-lucky days of individual inspiration and extempore research, and new disciplines and team work had to take its place. A line of demarcation had to be drawn between research and development; economies in expenditure (particularly in engineers' travelling time to remote sites) had to be effected; the education and training of young engineers must be rationalized and the Works procedures in general needed to be overhauled.

Gray set himself to the task, producing yet another report which set out proposals for reorganization, but although amendments of detail were made, the same general pattern of research was still followed. There was, however, one innovation of note in 1930 when a separate Television Research Group under H. M. Dowsett was formed.

In November 1931, Andrew Gray, now styled Technical General Manager, retired and H. M. Dowsett was appointed in his place, but with the title of Research Manager. These circumstances detonated a mine which had lain under the Research structure for some time. H. J. Round promptly resigned* to set up in practice as a private consultant; two new departments were created, namely Research and Development, the former, as stated, being under the control of H. M. Dowsett and the latter having C. E. Rickard as Executive Head with R. N. Vyvyan in a supervisory capacity. C. S. Franklin, although nominally still Chief of Independent Research, found his Chelmsford staff incorporated into the Development Department.

Understandably, the historical records are blank concerning the politics underlying this explosion and one can only fall back upon the recollections of the few who were on the scene at the time and who are still living.

What can be said with certainty is that the Company was blessed with a galaxy of extremely able engineers, among whom the twin stars Round and Franklin burned with fierce brilliance. Temperamentally as different from each other as chalk from cheese, they were keen rivals and firm friends with a vast respect for each other's abilities. There were, however, three traits which they shared; both had an almost fanatical loyalty to Guglielmo Marconi and no one else; both were essentially 'lone wolf' researchers who were only happy when following their own inspirations and both had a sublime disregard for administrative Authority which to them was synonymous with bureaucracy. In short, they were inspired rebels.

Andrew Gray knew these men better than most, for he also had been with the Company since its early days, when, if a mast was wanted it was selected from the nearest timber yard with no 'nonsense' in the form of requisitions and other paper work. He knew the inhibitions which Company growth must bring upon such men and although frequently goaded by their strong disinclination to report on what they were doing, he had the wisdom to tolerate it, knowing that whatever

* His services were, however, retained as a Technical Consultant and he continued to do much useful work for the Company up to the time of his death in August 1966.

it was it would be ultimately to the Company's benefit. Andrew Gray was a great Chief Engineer and not the least of the facets of his greatness was the shield he interposed between Round and Franklin and the more conservative elements in the Company hierarchy.

But now, with Gray's retirement, the shield was no longer in position. Round, presumably, saw the red light or had it pointed out to him, and got out. Franklin, who carried out nearly all his research at Poldhu and was therefore physically remote from the storm centre, elected to remain, possibly in the erroneous belief that Gray's retirement would not affect him. His reaction when he did find that this was not the case is succinctly described in a letter dated 10 December 1931, written by H. M. Dowsett to a friend and colleague in Bermuda; 'Franklin's staff has been disbanded,' he writes, 'and is now part of the new Development Department. Franklin has made the characteristic reply and has vanished for an indeterminate period. . . .'

Franklin, never wholly at ease in close proximity to Headquarters, became more of a solitary than ever in his fastness at Poldhu, where, to his eternal credit, he continued to provide many valuable patents for the Company. But even this haven was denied him when, in 1934, it was decided to close the Poldhu station and he had perforce to return to Chelmsford. He retired from the Company in 1937 with sixty-five patents registered in his name. One of his last achievements was the design of the sound and vision antenna for the B.B.C.'s first television station at Alexandra Palace.

So in the final analysis, when the dust of the explosion had settled, the road to new concepts of research and development lay clear. It can be argued that the Company emerged from the situation more advantageously than it deserved, but it is difficult to see how the goal could have been gained in any other fashion. Gray had tried palliatives for years and in the end some painful surgery had proved inevitable.

Urgent consideration of the situation now began in earnest, reviewed against the backdrop of Company finances. These were not encouraging. The economy measures taken by the Kellaway administration, although necessary for short-term stability, were now adversely affecting the present and the future. This is reflected in the Company accounts. In 1929, profits were £796,234. By 1935 they had fallen to £259,806, a decline in revenue which was rightly attributed in no small degree to the stringent curtailment of research activities over the years.

The only alternative to still further economies was a decisive step in the opposite direction – expansion. This was a daring thought, the implementation of which would mean nothing less than an act of faith, for it would have to apply to the whole Company structure and not merely its research facilities.

Gradually, however, the idea took hold and as far as research and development were concerned a streamlining process, accompanied by a gradual build-up, occurred over the years 1931–36. But the gap between the initiation of a research project and the emergence of a fully engineered production equipment may well be from five to ten years and so the benefits were not immediately apparent; thus, in 1937, while the total spent on administrative and research salaries was £275,460, the Company profits were only £260,300.

In the meantime the Company had entered into an agreement with the British Thomson-Houston Co. Ltd., Electric and Musical Industries Ltd., The Gramophone Company Ltd., and Philip's Electrical Ltd. to form a pool of scientific data, ideas and inventions. This circumstance gave added impetus to the drive for increased research facilities, for in any such agreement it is incumbent upon every participating Company to pull its weight by making adequate contributions.

The general situation in 1936 was that the Company's research establishments were scattered around the Chelmsford area as relatively isolated units; some of the laboratories were located at the New Street Works where their activities were liable to cause electrical background interference which imposed difficulties upon the testing of low-power equipments. Clearly an integration of establishments was highly desirable; not at the New Street Works for the reasons mentioned, but at a site which was conveniently near the main plant.

After considerable technical discussions, the Managing Director, Mr H. A. White, agreed that a Building Committee should be formed to assess the requirements and to advise on possible sites for entirely new laboratory buildings. This committee was set up in mid-1936 and after examination of many possible locations, advocated the purchase of some 40–50 acres at Great Baddow, a village approximately three miles distant from the main Works.

Negotiations proceeded during 1937, the land purchased and designs for the building agreed. In this was to be housed the Research sections of the Works, Broomfield, the Receiver Group from Writtle, all the Hall Street laboratories and the Marine Receiver section. At the same time the Managing Director authorized provision to be made for at least a doubling of the numerical strength of the existing research personnel.

Building operations continued throughout 1938 and as various laboratory areas became habitable, research sections from the old buildings were transferred, until by March 1939 the new laboratories, equipped with the most modern apparatus, were in full operation.

The augmenting of the numerical strength of the staff proved not so easy. The tradition, established by Marconi himself at the very outset, had been to employ none but the best, and this policy had remained with the passing of the years. But the extra-mural engineers and physicists of 1939 were inclined to look a little askance at these spectacular new laboratories built by a Company whose profits in the past few years had not been impressive, seeing in them not an act of faith but rather one of commercial suicide. Despite this, staff requirements were slowly being met when the onset of World War II changed the whole character of the outlook.

As has been mentioned, the overhaul of the Marconi research effort was only one facet of a general renaissance which included extensions to the New Street Works and the provision of new College premises. In connection with the latter project (of which more will be said in a following chapter), H. M. Dowsett relinquished the post of Research Manager in August 1935 to become Principal of Marconi College. At the same time J. G. Robb was appointed Research and Development Manager.

33

Engineering Training and Inter-Communication

The life blood of any manufacturing organization is its technical staff. This was realized by Guglielmo Marconi at the conception of his Company, and although for a year or so the training of new recruits was carried out by the senior men this rather haphazard state of affairs ended in September 1901, when a residential school for the training of probationer engineers of the Company was opened at Frinton, Essex.

This circumstance made history, for not only was it the first wireless college in the world, it was also the first in which qualified electrical and mechanical engineers on full pay were provided with a training centre where they could be instructed in the latest technological developments.

In 1904 the school was transferred to the Hall Street Works at Chelmsford, and for some time the students were absorbed directly into the general research, development and testing areas.

In October 1911 the school was re-established as a separate department, this time at the Broomfield Research Station. Some instruction was also carried out at Poldhu at this period. The following year saw a considerable expansion of staff occasioned by the opening of the New Street Works and for a time additional training was carried on at other Company research establishments also.

The Great War brought a famine of engineers in the armed forces and every commercial organization was scoured for men. Those engaged on College instruction (and indeed in all other departments) were quickly transferred to the services, decimating the ranks to the point where the College had to cease its activities as a training centre; once again the new recruits had to be drafted direct into the research or development sections.

In 1920 the return of demobilized engineers in need of refresher courses and an increase in the numbers of foreign engineers under instruction at the Works, made it advisable to re-open the College as a separate department.

A property known already as Chelmsford College, situated in Arbour Lane, Chelmsford, was acquired and fitted out with the latest apparatus. Under its Superintendent of Instruction, A. W. Ladner, a scheme of training was instituted which encouraged the Company's graduate probationers to develop their powers of initiative under the guidance of instructor and lecturer engineers specially chosen for their aptitudes in these directions, a policy which continues to this day.

Along with these developments the Company provided facilities for the training of boys and young men within the organization. In 1932 this was given further impetus by providing a scheme whereby the boys were permitted to attend part-time day classes at the Mid-Essex Technical College. Four years later the Marconi Apprenticeship Scheme came into being and has grown steadily ever since.

In 1935, as part of the Company's new expansion policy, the Directors decided to increase the College facilities in every way. The original building was modernized, extended and converted into a residence for about twenty students, while an entirely new college building was erected in the grounds behind it, together with huts for the accommodation of transmitters and complete equipments. The new building contained a main experimental laboratory, two smaller research laboratories, a Standards room, double-screened and provided with a double-screened constant temperature cellar, a lecture theatre, a vacuum laboratory, a common room, a library, photographic rooms and workshop, staff and administrative offices. The new College came into use in October 1936, H. M. Dowsett being the Principal with A. W. Ladner continuing as Superintendent of Instruction.

Post-graduate and resident students soon joined the Company's trainee engineers, together with engineers nominated by customers. Before long, applications for training were being received from all over the world and acceptances had to be strictly limited.

At this time also the New Street Works was reorganized and enlarged, for what, in 1912, had been the most modern and well-equipped factory and office buildings of the day, had by now become inadequate and out of date.

In 1935 the Board, under the urging of H. A. White the Managing Director, had approved a scheme whereby all the engineering, sales and other departments at that time operating from Electra House, London, should be transferred to new buildings (yet to be designed) at Chelmsford.

In the following year designs and estimates were invited for a considerable extension of the New Street Works which would include office accommodation for the Electra House staff also.

As a prelude, work had already been carried out to provide a further extension of the Works main bay, including a new paint spray shop and a second-storey winding shop and plating shop. A separate short-wave research building was also added.

Although a design for the new areas was approved in 1937 it was modified the following year to provide even greater extensions than had originally been contemplated. Building work began with a target of completion by 1940. The outbreak of war in 1939, however, found the new four-storey office block in a sufficiently advanced state to permit the immediate evacuation of some of the staff of Electra House, London, to the new premises, which now carried the title of Marconi House.

The remainder of the Electra House staff were accommodated in other Company establishments at Chelmsford and brought into the new building as, floor by floor, it became habitable.

Thus the new-look Works, built in anticipation of peaceful commercial expansion, began its life not to a fanfare of trumpets but to an *obbligato* of air raid sirens.

But a Works is a useless empty shell, brought only to life by the men and women who tend it. Management/labour relations, always good within the Company, were further strengthened by the various heartening signs of expansion which were evident in the five years prior to the war. A Pensions Scheme was already in being and in 1937 a Welfare Department was inaugurated. A further instance of the high morale which existed in the Company was shown in that year when the Management, instead of making an arbitrary decision as to the hours of work, held a general ballot of all employees, as a result of which a 5-day week of 45 hours was introduced in place of the erstwhile $5\frac{1}{2}$-day week of 47 hours.

It is now universally recognized that one of the best means of bringing home to an employee the importance of his individual effort is to provide him with the news of various Works activities and Company news in general. This was pioneered within Marconi's in 1919, but for various reasons was allowed to lapse until it was reintroduced in 1937 in the form of a House journal entitled the *Marconi News Bulletin*. This was later reconstituted (1950) as *The Marconi Companies and Their People*, which has enjoyed a progressively higher circulation with the passing years and has won several awards in competition with its contemporaries.

Journals of various kinds have for a great many years played an important part in the life of the Company, where the problem of effective inter-communication is particularly acute because its employees are not conveniently under one roof but deployed all over the world.

The first attempt to meet this need was made (as related in Chapter 16) in 1910, with the formation of the Marconi Press Agency Ltd. Its first publication was *The Marconigraph*, a monthly journal which made its bow in April 1911. This magazine's prime function was to disseminate news of particular interest to Marconi wireless operators, but before long its horizons had extended to the point where the original title was no longer apposite and in April 1913 it was retitled *The Wireless World*.

The Year Book of Wireless Telegraphy, first produced in 1913, was another successful publication which continued to appear annually until 1925. Various text-books, written by senior engineers of the Company, were also published, many of them becoming the standard works of reference of the time.

By 1919 the Company's research activities had expanded to a point where they justified the issue of informative papers on advanced technical subjects. It was decided to do this in journal format and the new publication *Radio Review* appeared for the first time in October of that year, but it did not survive infancy and the last issue appeared in March 1920.

As part of the retrenchment policy introduced by Mr Kellaway after the death of Mr Godfrey Isaacs, it was decided to dispose of The Wireless Press (the title of Marconi Press Agency had been changed to this in 1922). The organization was sold to Messrs. Iliffe and Sons in February 1925; the publication of *Wireless World* and text-books was continued (and still does) under Iliffe's, but the Year Book was discontinued.

During those lean years of post-war depression, the Marconi Company's publishing activities were curtailed almost to extinction, and in lieu of its lost journals it now had to rely for such publicity as it could get on outside technical journals and newspapers and on papers read by its engineers at Learned Society gatherings.

The loss of the House journals was even more keenly felt when the Cable and Wireless merger took place. Until that point any success stories concerning the Beam system had been to the credit of Marconi's, whereas after the merger any such publicity would be in favour of Cable and Wireless Ltd. Accordingly, consideration was given to devising ways and means of meeting the situation.

It was finally decided to produce a Company journal having contents of a high technical level which could put forward problems and solutions recently encountered by the research and development engineers; it was to appear monthly and so would have more immediacy than the Institution publications.

In this way *The Marconi Review* came into being; it made its first appearance in October 1928 with H. M. Dowsett as Technical Editor and W. G. Richards as General Editor. In January 1932 Dowsett became sole editor and two years later L. E. Q. Walker was appointed Assistant Editor. In 1939 the latter took over the editorship, a post he holds to date (1968). *The Marconi Review*, which became a quarterly publication in 1937, is held in high esteem in laboratories, universities and kindred establishments throughout the world.

Today the Company publishes five House journals, namely *The Marconi Review, Point-to-Point Telecommunications, Sound and Vision Broadcasting, Aerial* and *The Marconi Companies and Their People*, of which all except *Marconi Review* were inaugurated after World War II. All fulfil different functions, but all have the common aim of disseminating Company information. A steady increase in the circulation figures of all five is the barometer of their success. A Company newspaper, *Marconi News*, on free distribution to employees, has also been inaugurated.

34

The Old-Time Engineers

As this history draws towards the end of what might be termed the Elizabethan era of the Company, it is perhaps fitting to pause and consider one or two of the galaxy of engineers who laboured mightily and to such telling effect in the Company's service.

On 2 January 1933, to the regret of all his associates, the death occurred of George Stephen Kemp, in his seventy-sixth year. In 1896, Kemp, at that time a laboratory assistant to W. H. Preece, Engineer-in-Chief of the Post Office, met Guglielmo Marconi for the first time. The story of this encounter is told by Degna Marconi in her book *My Father, Marconi*:

> My father told me that he set up one of his first demonstrations on the roof of the Post Office in St Martin's-le-Grand where he planned to signal to the Savings Bank Department on Queen Victoria Street. When he looked over the ornate stone balustrade, he saw a red-headed fellow watching him curiously. The man on the pavement caught my father's eye and shouted up, 'What are you doing there?' Marconi called back, 'Come on up and I'll show you.'
>
> The onlooker arrived on the roof with such remarkable promptitude that my father believed he had scrambled up the drain (I sincerely hope not, for the Post Office is a towering eight storeys high). The moment George Kemp reached the rooftop he went to work for Marconi and continued to work for him forever after.

In this manner Kemp, an ex-Naval Petty Officer, became Marconi's first personal assistant. As such he sailed to Newfoundland with him on the epic transatlantic experiment and shared in the triumphs and disappointments which led ultimately to a successful commercial trans-ocean service. All Marconi's subsequent personal assistants displayed great devotion to him, but none more intensely than Kemp, whose activity in implementing the experiments proposed by his leader was tireless. At his death he left a valuable legacy behind him in the form of twenty-one volumes of the day-to-day journal that he kept until his death. It is to the existence of these that the Company is indebted for much of the detail of its early history.

Just over a year prior to Kemp's passing, the veteran Sir Ambrose Fleming resigned his appointment as Scientific Adviser to the Company. Joining Marconi's in that capacity in December 1900 he became the brilliant architect of the original Poldhu station, the inventor of the wavemeter and, in 1904, the patentee of the thermionic diode. Other inventions followed, while his book *The Principles of Electric Wave Telegraphy* became the standard work of reference for many years. His retirement, which occurred on 31 October 1931, did not end his keen interest in electronics which was maintained almost to the end of an incredibly full life. He died in 1945 at the age of ninety-five.

To mention all the outstanding engineers of the Company's first three decades would be to provide a long and tedious list. There are, however, two whose names have constantly recurred throughout these pages, namely Franklin and Round. No history of the Company would be complete without them as they were so frequently the instruments of bringing history into being; so much so, in fact, that the life and technological achievements of either would occupy a book in its own right.

Charles Samuel Franklin was born in 1879, the youngest of a family of thirteen and so weakly that on more than one occasion during childhood his life was despaired of. Somehow he survived and in due course received an engineering and scientific training at the Finsbury Technical College, where he studied under the famous Professor Silvanus Thompson.

Franklin joined the Marconi Company in 1899 and was promptly sent to South Africa as one of the engineers in charge of the wireless apparatus used in the Boer War. On his return he became an installation engineer/wireless operator and was the operator aboard the *Philadelphia* on the occasion when Marconi, who was also aboard, provided irrefutable evidence that wireless waves could cross the Atlantic.

After a two-year spell of installing and demonstrating wireless equipment in Russia, Franklin once more returned home and was soon singled out as one of Marconi's personal assistants. There followed a long and distinguished career in which he eventually became Chief of Independent Research.

Sixty-five patents stand to Franklin's credit; an impressive total indeed, but no less impressive is the longevity of many of the devices he invented. The variable capacitor (patented in 1902), ganged tuning (1907), variable coupling (1907) and many others including the Franklin master oscillator and the coaxial cable, are still in wide usage today.

His most spectacular achievement was of course the short-wave beam system which, after more than forty years, is still the world's mainstay for long-distance radio communication. Considering the speed at which he engineered this it is almost incredible to find that examples of his SWB.1 transmitter of 1924 vintage were still handling daily beam traffic in 1962 and may well be doing so today in some part of the world. This instance is typical of Franklin's immaculate standards of design.

Henry Joseph Round, Franklin's colleague, rival and friend, was born in 1881. His early education was received at Cheltenham and he later studied at the Royal College of Science, London, where he gained first-class honours.

Round joined the Company in 1902 and was seconded to the American Marconi Company's training school for wireless operators at Babylon, Long island (where, as mentioned earlier, his assistant was a youngster by the name of David Sarnoff, later to become an internationally-famous figure and President of the Radio Corporation of America).

Like Franklin, Round was ahead of his time in terms of ideas; for example, in those very early days he devised, in his spare time, dust-core inductances and the elements of wireless direction-finding. In 1907 he published his discovery that light could be generated by applying an electric potential across the semi-conductor silicon carbide, but this fact disappeared into the limbo of forgotten information until it was redis-covered in 1923 to become known as the 'Lossev Effect'. It has since seen practical fruition in the form of semi-conductor devices.

Round returned to England about 1908 and a little later demonstrated to Marconi an arc radio telephone set he had developed during his time in America. He, too, became one of Marconi's personal assistants and was noted for his ability to trace and rectify obscure faults in the apparatus of the period.

His work on the thermionic triode, wireless direction-finding, aircraft wireless and sound broadcasting has been referred to in other chapters. His inventive genius came into full flower in the 1920s when, as Chief of Research, he developed such devices as the 'Straight Eight' receiver, a gramophone recording system, a large-audience public address system, the artificial echo technique for studio productions, new types of micro-phone, gramophone pick-ups, amplifiers, sound recording systems, antenna systems and a great number of other inventions including those of the screened grid valve and the r.f. pentode. In all, Round in his lifetime filed 117 patents.

Franklin and Round. Brilliant engineers both. But to try to find a common denominator to their genius seems well-nigh impossible for the lay observer. Franklin, small, frail, diffident, modest, was happiest when working in seclusion. His was an almost psychic approach to a problem. Colleagues of his Poldhu days have spoken of times when a problem was baffling them all; Franklin, when told of it, would wander off alone across the headland. They would see him suddenly squat down motionless upon the cliff-top and remain there for perhaps an hour or more, oblivious of wind and weather. Then he would return and tell them exactly where the fault lay. He would be right.

Round, on the other hand, was a bluff, sturdy, forthright extrovert, fond of the company of his fellows provided they were not fools. His approach to a technical problem was one of logical deductive reasoning with (preferably) a Dr Watson or so around to act as foils. He had a great capacity for examining a problem from every angle and of turning it inside out, if need be, to arrive at a solution. His subsequent exposition, if he chose to give it, would be so lucid that the recipient would be left with the uncomfortable feeling that he should have thought of it himself. Franklin, no doubt, used much the same diagnostic process, but in a form of inner communion.

There were, however, some common factors. Both men were steadfastly devoted to Guglielmo Marconi throughout their lives. Both were essentially 'lone wolf' inventors who were at their best when given a free hand to originate what they would. Both became Chiefs of Research and in spite of the rivalries inherent in this situation, each had the highest regard for the capabilities of the other. Both were non-conformists to an administrative régime. Round once designed a ship's telephony set, and, without reference to anybody, set up a production batch. When it was eventually discovered, he was on the carpet; the trouble (from the disciplinary point of view) was that these sets were of extremely good design and sold in large quantities, making a considerable amount of money. So, Round, not for the first time, emerged the moral victor. His (and Franklin's) clashes with administration continued, as described earlier; the climax occurred in 1931, after which Round retired to set up in business as a research consultant. Franklin retired in 1937, feeling as he once described it 'That the times were unfriendly so . . . when the time came for the stray cat to get off the stage I was not altogether sorry.'

Thereafter Franklin produced no inventions to the time of his death, which occurred in 1964. Official recognition of his work had come tardily in 1949 when he was created a C.B.E. and awarded the Faraday

Medal. His work on the beam system is commemorated on the obelisk which was erected near the spot where the Poldhu station stood and where he spent his happiest years.

Round, who had been awarded the Military Cross for his direction-finding work in World War I, characteristically refused it on the ground that as it was a medal which was awarded for individual acts of gallantry it was inapplicable. It eventually arrived through the post. Thereafter he received no official British honour whatever, either from the Government or from the scientific institutions, and it was left to the United States to present him with the prized Armstrong Medal, which he received in 1952.

In 1937 Round returned to work for the Company in an advisory capacity and, apart from a break during World War II when, until 1950, he worked for the Admiralty on ASDIC, he continued as a Company Consultant until his death in 1966. Over those last sixteen years he invented new magneto-strictive devices for use in the Marconi International Marine Company's echo sounders; he also introduced the first permanently magnetized nickel transducers, the first belt-recording system for echo sounders and carried out important work on anti-fouling devices for ships. His last patent was taken out in 1962 but he was working out new ideas even on his death bed.

The Company records contain many accounts of the fantastic journeys and experiences of engineers while carrying out installation work in various corners of the earth. One such, concerning Round, occurred in 1912.

The story begins three years previously when the Company signed a contract to build two Poldhu-type stations 500 miles apart on the upper reaches of the Amazon. These stations were vital to the success of a railroad which was being built from Brazil to Bolivia by establishing communication between two Brazilian railheads at Manáus and Porto Velho.

The materials for the stations, including 100 h.p. steam engines to drive the generators, were transported as near as possible to the sites, then manhandled through the jungle and bush along roads cut for the purpose. The task was beset with difficulties but it was done; the stations were completed and communication tests began.

At this point the real trouble started. A clause in the contract demanded that a traffic volume of 5,000 words per day should be maintained, but unfortunately the heavy signal attenuation over the jungle path and the existence of continuous and heavy static made this impossible.

The situation was desperate. The railroad simply had to have the channel of communication and the Marconi Company not only needed the money badly but also additional contracts which hinged on the successful conclusion of the first one.

In February 1912 an expedition led by H. J. Round left England for Brazil with a free hand to do anything which might be necessary. On arrival at destination Round found that communication was only possible for one hour out of the twenty-four; all traffic other than that between 6 a.m. and 7 a.m. was being swamped by static.

Round, remembering the increase in signal strength which had occurred at night during the *Principessa Mafalda* experiments of 1910, first asked, 'What of night signals?' but was told that this, too, was hopeless. Dividing his team into two groups he remained at Manáus while the second group pressed on to Porto Velho. Refusing (as was his wont) to take anything for granted, Round carried out night tests and found that although static was still troublesome, by careful adjustment of the antenna coupling, the signals could be read. In one night, about a month's traffic backlog was cleared.

The immediate crisis was over and the railroad officials understandably became more co-operative. But Round was not satisfied, reasoning that the real trouble was that the wavelength of 2,000 m. was too short for daylight working. (It must be remembered that at this time little was known of the behaviour of the ionosphere, the very existence of which was strongly doubted by many.)

Round decided to lengthen the wavelength of both stations to about 4,000 metres. This would have been a major undertaking even at Poldhu where materials were readily to hand, but in the Amazon jungle the difficulties were increased to the nth degree. However, using such wire as was available, the inductances of the Manáus station were rewound and the station tested.

The first application of power brought near-disaster; all the units of the main capacitor started to break down and it was only by reducing power from 50 kW to 5 kW that they would function at all. However, tests proved that even at this modest power the signal strength as received at Porto Velho was much greater and could now be read from 6 a.m. to 12 noon.

Round then went to Porto Velho and effected the change of wavelength there also, but with similar effects on the capacitor units. He then set to work to clear the trouble in the latter. With the aid of a gang of thirty natives he removed all the units one at a time and cleaned all the tinfoil with boiling oil, a process in which a lot of skin was also cleaned from fingers. To prevent a repetition of the brush discharge and break-down, Round decided to incorporate a surround of zinc. No zinc was, however, available so he commandeered some copper mosquito netting and soldered this around the edges to build them up.

This process took about a month, with the station operational at reduced power the whole time. Every so often, another of the original units would break down, some beyond repair, and it was touch and go whether, in the end, there would be enough 'good' units to make up the capacitance. Eventually, however, the task was completed and the critical moment arrived when the full 50 kW was applied. The capacitor stood up to it and Manáus reported an excellent signal strength.

The final task was to return to Manáus and repeat the capacitor repair in all its tedious detail there. Again success was the reward. The guaran-tees were more than covered and the customer highly appreciative. The final wavelengths used were 2,000 m. by night and 4,000 by day.

The occasion is believed to be the first on which deliberate use was made of wavelengths of considerable difference for day and night working. As a result of the successful improvization with the capacitor units, all those made in the future incorporated zinc protective sheeting.

Stories of remarkable engineering feats are legion. There was, for example, the commercial chain of 30 kW rotary spark stations built in 1910 for the Indian Government, constructed against time and in the face of transport and labour difficulties in readiness for the Imperial Durbar. Or there is the story of C. E. Rickard who transferred from the Marconi Company to the Chilian Navy and took charge of its wireless service. His work in that capacity included a complete wireless survey of the Chilian coastline preparatory to the erection of the 100 kW stations linking North and South. He also directed the erection of the high-power stations at Santiago, Puerto Monte and Punta Arenas. In all, orders for some fifty-seven Marconi stations were received as a result of his efforts.

Again, the adventures of Marconi engineer S. T. Dockray in China in 1919–20 read like fiction, although all were sober fact. The story is too involved to tell in detail here but the outline may perhaps give some idea of the lives which installation engineers led – and in some degree, still lead.

In 1918 a trade agreement was negotiated between the Chinese Government and the Marconi Company whereby some 600 portable wireless telephony stations were supplied. A further contract was signed for the supply and erection of three 25–30 kW Poulsen Arc telegraphy transmitters, one to be sited at Urga, one at Urumchi and the third at Kashgar. In May 1919 the Chinese National Wireless Telegraph Company was formed, being jointly owned by the Chinese Government and the Marconi Company. (The assets of this Company were later transferred to Marconi (China) Ltd.)

At that date China was in a state of uneasy domestic peace with disunity within her borders and a fear of Russian hostility in Mongolia. The chain of three stations was intended to link with the Indian network and to help to unify the control of the northern area.

The radio equipment was packed in England in units not exceeding 150 lb., and cement for the tower foundations in 200 lb. water-tight drums. On arrival at Shanghai the equipment for the Urga station was railed to Kalgan whence it was transported by camel and bullock cart for 800 miles across the Gobi desert. The load, which included three 300 ft. steel towers in sections and 50 h.p. petrol engines, amounted to over 300 tons. The journey took about six weeks.

With the Urga station completed and successfully tested, Dockray returned to Peking only to find that Urga had mysteriously become silent. He thereupon back-tracked to find out what had happened and, nearing the station, he found it. The Chinese and the Mongols in the area had started a local war and Dockray found himself in the middle of it, but managed to reach the Urga wireless station.

After repairing the station, Dockray contacted Peking and told the Authorities what was going on. Suddenly artillery fire broke out and a shell hit the station building, doing a considerable amount of damage and putting it out of action once more. Dockray was uninjured but was captured by the invaders, who turned out to be a small army of White Russian mercenaries fighting for the Mongols. Their leader was General Ungern Sternberg, nicknamed 'The Mad Baron', who charged Dockray with being a British spy and refused to allow him to leave.

Later Dockray, in company with an American and a Dane who were also in the town when it was captured, managed to get away. It was no comfort for them to know that of a party of thirteen who had escaped earlier, only one had survived.

After many hardships and adventures they managed to follow the Kerulan river to reach Manchuli where they were promptly put into quarantine because of bubonic plague, and had to live in a cattle-truck. Eventually they were allowed to leave and in due course reached Peking, where Dockray was awarded the Chinese Order of the Chao Ho for meritorious conduct.

Later that year (1920) the Chinese regained control of Urga and Dockray once again crossed the Gobi and refitted the station. But his task had only begun, for two more stations had yet to be built. After Governmental delays he marshalled the equipment for the Urumchi and Kashgar stations, which had been railed to Fengchen. Here Dockray assembled what was probably the largest caravan in the history of China, consisting of 1,200 camels, 468 ponies and 117 carts, and loaded up. The expedition set out in November 1921.

After a long and arduous trek the caravan arrived at Urumchi only to find that General Yang Tseng-Hsim, the Governor, was not in favour of the wireless scheme and in the following months many obstacles were put in the way of progress. Eventually, however, the station was completed and came on the air in August 1922.

The materials for the final station were stored at Urumchi and Dockray trekked back to Peking for further orders. Again some Governmental delay occurred but at length he was allowed to proceed. Returning to Urumchi, the materials were again loaded and the expedition set out for Kashgar in November 1922.

The route lay across some of the toughest country in China, over rugged mountain ranges and vast rivers. There were seldom any bridges and those which did exist were frail indeed. Over the swift running Yenchi river the caravan – again camels, ponies and carts – had to be carried on improvised rafts which were badly buffeted by ice floes. The hardships were such that twenty of the animals succumbed.

Once the mountains were crossed the going was easier and oases in the form of settlements were reached about once a week; at these, food supplies could be replenished and repairs to the carts carried out. Kashgar was reached on Christmas Eve 1922. Here the officials were most helpful and the constructional work proceeded at speed. Dockray records that the local population believed that the foreigners intended to bury the hearts of several small boys in the tower foundations to ensure that the structures did not collapse; a diplomatic invitation to the inhabitants to witness the foundation work dispelled this rumour.

The station was completed in May 1923. After a short rest Dockray, accompanied by two Chinese servants, decided to return to Peking via India, this roundabout route being in practice the quickest.

On pony-back they crossed the Mintaka pass at an altitude of 15,000 ft. and in August reached Kashmir, thence to Rawalpindi and Calcutta; from Calcutta by ship to Shanghai (surviving a typhoon *en route*). On arrival at Shanghai a spell in hospital was ordered because of scurvy, developed during the long months of hardship. Dockray finally reached Peking just two years after setting off for Urga, but with the satisfaction of knowing that the three stations were on the air.

His expedition was followed some time later by that of another Marconi engineer, C. C. Caspard, whose task was to take Chinese maintenance staff to each of the stations and train them in their working. This party had equally hair-raising adventures; on one occasion some of Caspard's pack animals, loaded with precious fuel, were lost when a flimsy bridge over a gorge collapsed. Caspard knew that fuel was badly needed at the station. He remembered that many miles back he had noticed a quantity of black substance oozing from the rocks, and returning, tested it, finding that, as he had surmised, it was shale oil in some quantity.

A crude refinery was improvised and the resultant liquid – paraffin of sorts – was poured into spare cans. Returning to the gorge, Caspard and his men built another bridge and eventually reached the station. Mercifully the engines kept going on his emergency fuel until fresh supplies of the genuine article could be brought in.

These accounts are only the bare bones but will serve to underscore the capabilities, both physical and mental, which are demanded of the installation engineer. They are by no means isolated instances as the records show. There was, for instance, the expedition led by engineer P. Boucicault in Saudi Arabia in 1931–32. Boucicault first carried out an installation in Mecca by remote supervision – not being of the Muslim faith he had to remain outside the city while Muslims in his team who had previously been trained at Chelmsford, carried out the actual construction work. But this was the easy part; the record of his subsequent treks through the desert on other installation projects is a story of the grim endurance of hunger, thirst and physical disabilities brought on by the intense heat and a meagre diet of rice and goat (or camel if one died). But reluctantly it must, for the moment, remain in the archives.

35

The Passing of Guglielmo Marconi

By the turn of the twentieth century it had become clear that beyond-the-horizon transmission and reception of wireless signals were being made possible by some unknown factor. The transatlantic experiments of 1901 turned the attention of various researchers, notably Heaviside, Kennelly and Marconi, towards the problem of providing a theory to account for the phenomenon. The ionosphere explanation offered by the two former and endorsed by the latter proved, in the event, to be an accurate assessment, but it was not until the 1920s by the efforts of Edward Appleton, Barnett, Breit, Tuve, T. L. Eckersley and others, that the physical existence of the reflecting layers was proven beyond dispute.

The work of T. L. Eckersley and K. W. Tremellen of the Marconi Company in investigating phenomena encountered in wireless direction-finding, has been mentioned earlier. In 1925 Round, Eckersley, Tremellen and Lunnon jointly read an I.E.E. paper on the measurement of field strengths at antipodal and other great distances.* This was an early phase of an extensive theoretical and practical investigation of the properties of the ionosphere that continues within the Company to this day.

The Company's Propagation Section was officially constituted in 1925 under T. L. Eckersley's brilliant leadership. His staff was small, consisting only of Tremellen, F. M. Wright and four wireless operators on loan from Marconi House; G. Millington and R. F. Knight joined the Section in 1931.

The general adoption of the beam system made it vital to find out everything possible regarding the vagaries of the ionosphere as they affected the high frequency spectrum, and the Propagation Section's research effort was dominated by this need for many years. Listening watches were maintained on short-wave stations as one by one they opened up in various parts of the world, and slowly and painstakingly the mass of data so obtained was built up and collated to provide detailed information on the propagational behaviour of various wave-lengths

* Journal of the I.E.E., Vol. 63.

at all hours of the day and night. By 1926 a special form of loop direction-finder had been evolved for data-gathering purposes and the first 'round-the-world' echo signals and scattered signals had been noted. The first attempts at deriving absolute values of the field strengths of short-wave signals (as distinct from aural estimations) were also made in 1925–26.

The first practical fruits of this research were seen in 1927 when K. W. Tremellen constructed the first 'Shadow Charts'. These charts, drawn on transparent paper, could be slid over a Mercator map of the world to show an approximate picture of ionization densities (in terms of a grey scale) at various times of the day or night, over any given route. Such charts, in greatly improved form, are used today in all prediction work. In June 1927, T. L. Eckersley read a notable paper *Short Wave Wireless Telegraphy* to the I.E.E.

The work during 1928 included assistance given to the National Physical Laboratory in the accurate checking of the wavelengths of various world short-wave transmissions. Improved apparatus for signal strength measurement was also devised. In 1929 an important advance in technique was established by using the Somerton–New York facsimile transmitter to obtain information on the heights of the ionospheric layers by measuring the time delays of echoes observed on the facsimile pictures. (The Proc. I.R.E. for January 1930 contains a paper by Eckersley, *Multiple Signals in Short Wave Transmission*, dealing with this work.) A study of 'whistlers' was also made in 1929.

About this time Eckersley and his team were able to predict that the 11-year solar cycle would have an influence on short-wave signals and this was confirmed later.

By 1932 the work of the Section had become of considerable commercial value to the Company by reason of its ability to predict with accuracy the best frequency to use for transmission over a given radio path. This service enabled a radio link service for an overseas country to be planned and tendered for with confidence. Other aspects of propagation research are dealt with in an I.E.E. paper, *Studies in Radio Transmission*, published in March 1932 (T. L. Eckersley and G. Millington).

The 'Shadow Charts', greatly improved by 1932, were compiled from practical reception data on the world's short-wave stations. During 1932, however, Millington foreshadowed future techniques by calculating the values of the ionization contours from theoretical considerations alone. His work was published at the Bucharest C.C.I.R. conference of that year, and although he had subsequently to modify his approach to include other factors which at the time were unpredictable on theoretical grounds alone, the method is now one which provides a high degree of accuracy. Millington also in that year (1932) produced a set of field strength distance contours for wavelengths of fifteen to fifty metres for 1 kW radiated power. These were semi-empirical. They were used in conjunction with the Shadow Charts for many years.

1932 marked the beginning of a prolonged and intensive period of research into critical frequencies, heights, polarization effects and reflection coefficients connected with the ionosphere.

At this period T. L. Eckersley was working ceaselessly on the planning of experiments in connection with polarization effects in a graded medium, magneto-ionic effects, reflection coefficients, reciprocity, phase integrals, refraction theory, upper atmospheric ionization and recombination and other matters; some of his work was of immediate practical benefit and a great proportion of it proved to be of considerable value in the years to come; for example the present systems of ionospheric and tropospheric scatter transmission have their origins in Eckersley's work.

In 1934 the Ongar 40 kW transmitter was experimentally keyed to provide pulses for sounding the ionosphere and much valuable information upon echoes and scattering was recorded photographically. About this time Eckersley suggested the use of spaced frame receivers as a means of providing a polarization-free direction-finding system, and this approach was considerably developed over the years.

The nature and scope of the work continued to increase and multiply, replacing the 'hit-or-miss' experimentation of the early 1900s with a scientific approach to systems installations based on the knowledge acquired by the Section. The prolific number of scientific papers produced by members of the team up to 1939 bear witness to the scope of their interests.

During the 1930s the Propagation Section had also to carry out investigation into the behaviour of v.h.f. and u.h.f. waves. Interest in these was no mere academic exercise, for Guglielmo Marconi, who had, since the successful introduction of the beam system, considerably reduced his own personal research efforts, suddenly revived his interest in very short waves. He chose 50 cms. (600 MHz as his spectrum of investigation; one which had been neglected for over thirty years as it was believed to have no commercial value.

Valves capable of operating at this frequency having been developed, the experimental transmitter and receiver were designed by G. A.

Mathieu and constructed by G. A. Isted. The first demonstrations were given to Italian Government officials in October 1931 from Santa Margherita to Sestri Levanti near Genoa, a distance of eleven miles over sea. In the following month the range was increased to twenty-two miles (Santa Margherita to Levanti). A balanced valve transmitter with three tuned circuits feeding into a dipole antenna with a parabolic reflector were employed, horizontally polarized waves being radiated.

In April 1932 duplex telephony was demonstrated over the circuit, as a result of which the Vatican authorities ordered a telephone channel to be installed from Vatican City to the Pope's palace at Castel Gandolfo, near Rome, a distance of fifteen miles with wooded country along the route. This circuit was put into operation in November 1932, the official inauguration taking place in January 1933. This was the first commercial link ever to operate on a wavelength below one metre.

Shortly after its installation a peculiar effect was noticed at the Vatican City end of the link. At roughly the same time every day the receiver produced a succession of unusual noises which lasted for some seconds. These noises were found to be caused by one of the gardeners who, at the same time every day, pushed a small cart along one of the paths; in doing so he was unwittingly walking broadside through the microwave beam. This phenomenon drew Marconi's attention once more to the possibilities of using radio echoes to detect objects at a distance – that is, what today is termed radar. Because of heavy research commitments in other directions he was, however, unable to carry out any radar experiments until 1935.

Meanwhile the experiments continued. A new transmitter was set up at Santa Margherita. This comprised four of the standard units in a five-unit reflector and radiating on a wavelength of 57 cm. It constituted the most powerful microwave transmitter then in existence. A standard receiver with a single reflector was installed astern of the main deck of Marconi's yacht *Elettra*. The vessel then steamed out to sea for range tests. These showed that signals were receivable at 28 nautical miles, although there was a gradual loss of strength from 11 miles onwards, with deep fading setting in at 22 nautical miles. As the optical range was 14·6 nautical miles it was clear that the microwaves were being deflected earthwards like their longer counterparts, a discovery which was of immediate interest to the far away Propagation Section at Chelmsford.

Next, the transmitter was re-installed at Rocca di Papa, south of Rome, the site being fifteen miles inland and at an elevation of 750 m. above sea level. On 6 August 1933 the *Elettra*, with Italian Government officials on board, left Civitavecchia for further propagation tests. At 58 n.m. (6 n.m. beyond the optical range) good radio telephony was obtained but quality fell off beyond that point; deep fading appeared and at 80 n.m. signals were intermittent. At 87 n.m. signal strength increased again, remaining good up to 100 n.m., after which deterioration set in quickly. Signals disappeared completely at 110 miles' range.

A further test under similar conditions took place on August 10, the maximum range established being 125 miles. Arriving at Golfo Aranci, Sardinia, the receiver was dismantled and re-installed on a signal station tower at Cape Figari, 340 m. above sea level. On the following day signals were received, although with deep fading. At night the signal strengths were not so good as in the day. The distance involved was 168 miles, more than double the optical range of 72 miles.

A full account of these experiments was given by Marconi in a paper read at the Royal Institution of Great Britain on 2 December 1932. In this he referred to the employment of microwaves as 'a new economical means of reliable radio communication, free from electrical disturbances, eminently suitable for use between islands, between islands and the mainland or between other places separated by moderate distances'. He pointed out that the new system was unaffected by fog, and offered a high degree of secrecy by reason of its sharp directive quality.

Marconi then went on, 'In regard to the limited propagation of these microwaves the last word has not been said' and concluded by suggesting practical applications all of which have since become common practice.

In the summer of 1934 Marconi returned to the Mediterranean to demonstrate yet another application of microwaves, this time in the field of direction-finding. For the purposes of the demonstration a microwave radio beacon was installed on a hill behind Sestri Levanti, some 300 ft. above sea level and receiving equipment was fitted in *Elettra*.

For the initial trials the yacht steamed ten miles out to sea then turned about, heading towards Sestri Levanti where, in the bay, two buoys were anchored ninety yards apart to represent a harbour mouth. On board *Elettra* the chart room windows were covered so that navigation was blind. The yacht passed midway between the buoys, the 'blind' helmsman being guided by the 60 cm. microwave radio beam. The manœuvre was carried out several times with complete success on every occasion.

In the event this series of centimetric wavelength experiments proved to be Guglielmo Marconi's last major contribution. In September 1934, after delivering a speech on the applications of microwave and the new development of radio-therapy at an international congress on electro-radio biology in Venice, he suffered a severe heart attack (he had had a severe heart condition diagnosed in 1927). Other attacks occurred in December and the following March.

Marconi was an impossible patient. As soon as he had recovered from an attack he refused to rest. In April 1935 he and his great friend Solari went to Torre Chiaruccia where the Italian Navy had a small experimental station which had been placed at Marconi's disposal. Taking with them a 50 cm. beam transmitter and receiver, they directed the beam across a road and arranged for their car to be driven through the beam. Whenever this was done the reflected energy produced a noticeable hiss in the receiver. This phenomenon was of course nothing new in itself; Heinrich Hertz had demonstrated it in his original work on electro-magnetic waves, but with the abandoning of centimetric waves for communication purposes it had been lost sight of until Marconi's resurrection of their use in the 1931 experiments, when the Vatican City installation had served to rediscover it.

At Vatican City the effect had been a mere side-issue; now Marconi determined to investigate it in the belief that it could be turned to good account. He carried out further successful experiments, this time with an aircraft as the target, but a further heart attack made it impossible for him to continue. The newspapers got wind of his investigations and it was widely believed that the invention of a death ray was imminent.

The latest heart attack kept Marconi confined to Italy for virtually the whole of 1936, although he became well enough to travel within the country or aboard *Elettra*. The spring of 1937 found him resuming his 'echo' experiments but three minor attacks and a severe one in May came as a sharp warning.

It was one which Marconi refused to heed. In June he insisted on accompanying Solari on a tour of inspection of a new wireless station at Santa Palomba, near Rome, and in the following weeks continued his experiments.

On July 17 he had a private audience with the Pope, a meeting for which Marconi had asked. What the two discussed will probably never be known; possibly his stated intention of sailing for England to take up permanent residence there; possibly not.

Two days later, Marconi went to the railway station to see his wife off to Viareggio where she was to spend a holiday and where it had been arranged that he would join her on the 21st. He returned through the hot streets of Rome to his office where he wrote some letters and later drove to Solari's office where the two discussed microwave experiments.

At five o'clock that afternoon, shortly after he arrived home, Marconi suffered yet another heart attack, and at 3.45 a.m. on July 20, he died.

On the evening of the following day, thousands of mourners followed the coffin at the State funeral, while the Italian radio services observed a five-minute radio silence. In Britain, operators and engineers throughout the Post Offices of the nation maintained a two minutes' silence from 6 p.m., the hour of the funeral. The B.B.C. stations likewise fell silent and throughout the Empire the beam stations handled no traffic. The radio silence which Marconi had interrupted when he switched on his first transmitter, came down again in sorrow at his passing.

At Chelmsford a more numbing grief found some expression in the crowded Memorial Service held at the Cathedral and the Requiem Mass sung in the Church of the Immaculate Conception. The overwhelming sense of loss was epitomized in *The Marconi Review* which found mere words so pitifully inadequate that it carried no verbal obituary; a portrait study of Marconi, framed in a mourning wreath of oak leaves, symbolized infinitely more than could ever be said.

.   .   .

Guglielmo Marconi. An enigma of a man. One who became increasingly aloof with the passing of the years, to the point where, at Marconi House, London, he would refuse to share the lift with an employee he did not know personally. Yet this was the man who insisted that Kemp and Paget, his assistants in Newfoundland in 1901, should share in the radio tribute broadcast by the B.B.C. on the thirtieth anniversary of the occasion. The same man who issued a standing order that George Kemp should be able to see him whenever he wished. The same man who inspired his personal assistants to give him a loyalty which it is no exaggeration to describe as dedicated.

There can be no doubt that Marconi sincerely believed that the true role of wireless was as a saver of lives; those who knew him personally have witnessed to his genuine joy when some maritime disaster was averted by its aid. He also believed that closer communication between nations must promote peace; in this connection the realization of the part which wireless had played in the destructive horror of the Great War may have brought inner doubts which led to an increasing withdrawal. Such self-examination was at any rate present when shortly before his death he was elected Lord Rector of St Andrew's University,

Scotland. Asked by the Principal what was to be the title of his inaugural address, Marconi replied that he had chosen 'The Path of the Inventor'. He went on to stress his original intention, namely, to make safe the high seas by giving ships the means of communication. Then, perhaps talking to himself more than to his questioner, he added, 'Have I done the world good, or have I added a menace?'

It could be that this formed at least part of his desire to have audience of the Pope when within a few days of his death; but this is speculation.

In the long view his passing in 1937 spared him a mental crucifixion which must inevitably have come when Italy came to be at war with Britain. Marconi was a patriotic Italian; a member of the Senate who had been since 1923 a member of the Fascist party. On the other hand he had a great affection for Britain, which had given him his opportunity and upon which country his fortunes largely rested. It would seem from the records that, shortly before his death, he had made up his mind to take up permanent residence in England. He was at least spared the agonizing choice which he would have been compelled to make had he lived a few years longer.

Undoubtedly, Marconi was an admirer of Benito Mussolini, whom he saw as the architect of a twentieth century Italian Renaissance. Before condemning him out of hand for this, it must be remembered that Mussolini in his earlier years of power had done much for the Italian people; marshes had been drained to provide fertile agricultural land; the State Railway ran to time and the standard of living had been raised considerably. These and many other benefits had lifted Italy from the slough into which it had fallen and one so conscious of nationality as Marconi could not fail to be heartened thereby. He personally had nothing to gain from Fascism, but the party had a great deal to gain from his association with it, for Marconi was a figure of renown throughout the world; a symbol of the great things of which the Italian nation was capable. There is no evidence that he made the slightest contribution to Fascism and throughout the years of the party's ascendant he was completely immersed in scientific-experimental work.

Let C. S. Franklin, who had a long engineering association with Guglielmo Marconi, sum up his life. Said Franklin: 'Marconi may not have been a great scientist but he was a great man, and to deny that is to deny the facts. Without his steadfast faith, drive and courage, success would not have been possible.'

Two years after his death, the onset of World War II marked the end of an era. The Marconi Company which had started in 1897 as a tiny

organization devoted solely to communication by spark wireless telegraphy, had by 1939 grown to a point where it was internationally
famous, with associated and subsidiary Companies all over the globe.
In the process, its interests had diversified to include sound broadcasting,
television, aeronautical radio communication and navigational aids, and
scientific instruments in addition to a variety of radio communication
systems.

In one major respect the aim had remained unchanged. This was in
research and engineering where Marconi's policy of employing the best
brains available and of ploughing back a generous proportion of the
profits into research and development, was still rigidly adhered to. As
but one consequence of this the Propagation Department was now a
foremost world authority on its subject, and its accumulated knowledge
was proving of inestimable value in planning efficient communications
systems.

In one important respect the outlook on research and development
had changed however. The day of the lone researcher was now, in
1939, all but over and was gradually giving way to the team concept,
to which end the magnificently-equipped new laboratories at Great
Baddow had been specifically designed.

Except for the brief excursion into the domestic sound broadcast
receiver market, the Company still adhered to its original role as a
manufacturer of capital goods and to its traditional 'model-shop'
methods of assembly by skilled craftsmen. The conveyor-belt form of
assembly, which had become standard practice in domestic receiver
factories, had not been adopted – and still are not used to this day – not
because of prejudice, but simply because production runs of such items
as broadcasting transmitters are too small to justify the use of mass
assembly methods, while the services which these equipments will
eventually carry are far too vital to entrust assembly to unskilled
personnel.

Financially the outlook in the late 1930s was promising. Over its
history the Company had weathered some severe storms but now there
seemed every hope that the economic blizzard of the previous years was
being succeeded by favourable trade winds. The Company's policy of
reorganization and expansion was geared to this philosophy; in the
event, however, although the resurgence proved extremely opportune,
it was destined to play a grimmer part than had been anticipated.

PART THREE

36

The Evolution of Radar

If a choice had to be made of the one technical development which most influenced the course of World War II, then radar would be a very strong contender.

Because light waves and radio waves are both electromagnetic in character, differing only in frequency, it was to be expected that radio waves, particularly those of the higher frequencies, would be reflected by objects in their path. Heinrich Hertz, the first man to generate radio waves, set up experiments which proved this expectation to be fact. However, early work on wireless telegraphy diverted attention from the centrimetric waves as all practical experiments seemed to indicate that long ranges (the main aim of the time) could only be achieved by using long wavelengths (low frequencies). As a consequence, virtually no experimental work was done on the 'useless' centrimetric waves for many years and so their reflecting properties were ignored or dismissed as having no practical utility.

There were one or two exceptions however. Tesla, in 1900, suggested that the waves might be used for the detection of moving objects, while Hülsmeyer, a German engineer, actually patented a primitive form of radar in 1904; no interest was shown in it and the subject lapsed for many years.

In 1916 Marconi and his assistant C. S. Franklin, working in Italy, turned their attention to short waves (about two metres) and found in the course of their experiments that these were being reflected by obstacles in the path of the signals. When, in 1922, Marconi was presented with the Medal of Honor of the American Institute of Engineers, he said in the course of his speech:

> In some of my tests I have noticed the effects of reflection of these [short electromagnetic] waves by metallic objects miles away. It seems to me that it should be possible to design apparatus by means of which a ship could radiate or project a divergent beam of these rays in any desired direction,

which rays, in coming across a metallic object such as another steamer or ship, would be reflected back to a receiver screened from the local transmitter on the sending ship, and thereby reveal the presence and bearing of ships, even though these ships be unprovided with any kind of radio.

Marconi, as far as is known, did not pursue the speculation, probably because at that time (1922) he was heavily involved in experimental work which led to the development of the short-wave beam, and Marconi was not one to be sidetracked from a main line of investigation. The matter was not entirely lost sight of however, as is shown by an article written some years later by C. S. Franklin, Marconi's assistant in the short-wave beam work. In *Marconi Review* (supplement to Vol. XIV, No. 103) Franklin commented:

> Shadows and reflections from objects when using such (ultra short) waves had been observed for some years. I was interested in forming a wireless picture using centimetre or millimetre waves in a manner analogous to the optical picture obtained by a camera. It can be done . . . but owing to changing conditions I was never able to get the work organized.

Franklin's tentative experiments were done about 1930. It will be noted that he proposed the use of centimetric and millimetric waves, as used today. It is also interesting to see that he refers to a *picture* (as distinct from a shadow) 'analogous to that obtained by a camera'; could it be that Franklin had in mind the illumination of a target with multiple beams of various frequencies or by sweeping a beam through a band of frequencies?

Meanwhile, progress had been made in a different direction. In 1924 Edward Appleton and M. A. F. Barnett began a series of experiments to determine the height of the F layer in the ionosphere, using techniques which were later employed in continuous wave radar. In the following year G. Breit and M. A. Tuve (U.S.A.) developed a pulsed system for ionospheric sounding – again an approach which was subsequently widely used in radar work.

It was inevitable that the knowledge of these techniques (which was general throughout the scientific world) should bring about investigations of their potential in other directions, notably in the detection of ships and aircraft. Such work, being largely for military purposes, was carried out secretly in various countries during the 1930s.

In Britain the first proposal for the use of pulsed transmission as a means of providing echoes from a target was made in January 1931 by W. A. S. Butement and P. E. Pollard of the Signals Experimental

Establishment at Woolwich. Their apparatus, which operated on 50 cm. and used a rotating beam, was successful in recording echoes over distances of about a hundred yards; but neither the War Office nor the Admiralty were interested and the work ended for lack of support.

In 1935 a committee for the Scientific Survey of Air Defence briefed Robert Watson-Watt, then superintendent of the Radio Research Laboratory at Slough, to investigate the possibility of devising a 'death-ray'. Watson-Watt's reply was emphatically negative regarding lethal radio waves but he suggested instead that electromagnetic waves might be used for the early detection of aircraft and backed his argument by producing a paper entitled 'Detection and Location of Aircraft by Radio Methods'. A practical test followed, in which a Heyford bomber, flying through the short-wave radiations of the B.B.C.'s Empire station at Daventry, was detected on a cathode ray oscilloscope display. This was on 26 February 1935.

As a result, serious experimental work was begun by a handful of scientists at a site near Orfordness, a lonely spot on the Suffolk coast. The results obtained were so encouraging that within a few months a move was made to larger quarters in Bawdsey Manor a few miles away.

By December of that year sufficient progress had been made to warrant a Government decision to build five radar stations to cover the approach to London via the Thames estuary. The success of these promoted the ordering of twenty more stations in May 1937. (For all these, the Marconi Company provided the transmitter 'curtain' antenna arrays; subsequently, further transmitter arrays were erected by the Company for the West Coast and other chains of C. H. (Chain, Home) radar stations.)

By the outbreak of war, Britain was ringed with a chain of C.H. stations to provide early warning of the approach of aircraft. These were supplemented by associated C.H.L. (Chain, Home, Low) stations designed specifically to deal with low-flying aircraft and also shipping, which the C.H. stations could not 'see'. At the same time other types of radar were being developed, notably the G.L. equipment for gun-laying and two types of airborne radar, 'A.S.V.' and 'A.I.'. A.S.V. (Air to Surface Vessels) was first demonstrated in September 1938 while A.I. (Airborne Interception) was flying in experimental form by August 1939.

All this work was done secretly and Germany had no inkling of the state of the art. But the Germans also had radar, derived from their own original research. In September 1939 their 'Freya' type of ground station, which gave early warning of aircraft, was in operation. 'Seetakt', for the detection of shipping, followed soon after. By mid-1940 'Wurzburg', a 50 cm. radar for the control of anti-aircraft guns was proving more effective than its Allied counterpart.

Germany at the outbreak of war had little to fear from hostile aircraft and therefore did not need – at the onset, at least – an elaborate defensive radar chain of the type which was to prove vital to Britain's survival.

In the U.S.A. also, radar was under development. Pulsed radars were demonstrated in 1936, the first practical application, in the form of searchlight control, coming a year later. By 1940 early warning sets were going into large-scale production.

France possessed her own radar just prior to the war. This again was a secret development by French scientists, not a copy of British designs.

It will be seen from this that, contrary to popular belief, Britain had no monopoly of radar at the start of the war. What she did have, which no other country possessed at the time, was a highly organized control system associated with the radar chain, whereby fighter aircraft could be deployed at short notice to areas where they were most needed, without having to maintain flying patrols. No one, in designing the radar chain, could have foreseen the catastrophic fall of France, but when this did happen the radiolocation facilities fitted the desperate need of the time as a hand fits a glove. Without it the Battle of Britain would have been lost.

No mention has been made so far of naval and mercantile marine radar requirements. Very few naval vessels carried radar at the outbreak of war and the first installations were hastily-contrived adaptations of ground and airborne radars. The mercantile fleet possessed no radar at all. In a short space of time, however, equipment specifically designed for service at sea was introduced, born of a series of crash programmes of development and manufacture.

Although the word 'radar' has been used throughout this chapter the term did not come into British use until the war was well advanced. Until that time the technique had been known in this country by the camouflage initials 'R.D.F.' (radio direction-finding). The word 'radar' was of American origin and is an acronym (RAdio Detection and Ranging). It was officially adopted by Britain in order to rationalize the terminology.

37

World War II (Part 1)

The Munich agreement of September 1938, optimistically hailed by Prime Minister Neville Chamberlain as representing 'Peace in our time' was regarded in other quarters as the purchase of a breathing space in which to put the country's defences in some sort of order. For some while prior to the agreement, moves had been taking place to this end and Munich served to accelerate these rather than retard them.

The Marconi Company, in common with many other industrial organizations, had been warned of the possibility of war with Germany. This meant that some extensive crystal gazing had to be indulged in. It was very clear that, if war should come, a considerable further expansion to the existing establishments would be necessary; it was equally clear that a 'wait-and-see' policy would be useless, for a drastic increase in production cannot be achieved overnight. But should the crisis blow over, a ruinous capital outlay and gross over-capacity would result.

It was decided to go ahead with a stepped-up programme of expansion. A large factory was acquired at Vauxhall for sheet metal and frame construction work while the new office building and Works extension at New Street, Chelmsford, were being put into commission with all speed. A Control Centre was built in the Works. The buildings had been camouflaged just after Munich and the fire brigade increased to double strength, as part of the air raid precautionary measures taken. Immediately war broke out (3 September 1939) the Works went on to a seven-day working week and a 24-hour day basis. In the following year premises at Parsons Green, Fulham, Hackbridge and others along the Albert Embankment were taken over.

In 1936 the Marconi Company and E. K. Cole Ltd., had co-operated in a joint venture to manufacture test equipment, and a new jointly-owned Company, known as Marconi-Ekco Instruments Ltd., had been formed to operate as a sales outlet for equipment to be produced at Chelmsford and Southend. The Company had prospered, enlarging its horizons to include a diversity of laboratory research instruments for use in telecommunication and industrial applications; electro-medical apparatus – units for surgery, therapy and diagnosis – were also being manufactured to meet a growing demand.

During the early months of the war large Ministry contracts were placed for all types of test-gear and the limited production areas which had hitherto served were wholly inadequate. The Company accordingly removed to temporary accommodation at St Albans and High Wycombe.

Because of the complications of dual control in war-time the shares belonging to E. K. Cole Ltd., were acquired by the Marconi Company in 1941, thus making the instrument Company, now renamed Marconi Instruments Ltd., a wholly-owned Marconi subsidiary. (A new instrument factory was built at St Albans after the war and the High Wycombe plant and personnel were moved to the new premises by June 1947.)

As some indication of the rate of growth which was taking place, the Company's total floor space in 1937 amounted to 33,007 sq. ft.; this in 1939 had increased somewhat to 399,005 sq. ft. but by 1943 the total area amounted to 739,388 sq. ft. or, by including Marconi Instruments Ltd., 807,388 sq. ft.

The numbers of personnel employed rose from 2,600 in 1937 to 7,408 in 1943. A further 1,072 were employed at Marconi Instruments by that year.

In 1937 the value of the Company's output (at Works cost) was £830,000; in 1939 it was £985,000 while in 1943 it had risen to £3,950,000 with every indication of further rapid increase.

By 1938 the first orders were coming in for the build-up of the three fighting Services, mostly for communications equipment and navigational aids, fields in which the Company was pre-eminent. These were followed later by demands for the most diverse types of equipment but before going on to mention some of these a survey of the overall situation might not come amiss.

In the First World War the Company's part had been very clearly defined. It had supplied a great number of complete communications equipments and systems (using the term 'communications' in its broad sense of including direction-finding apparatus). It had done so in vast quantity because there was no other British firm of anywhere near the size and experience which could mount a commensurate effort. Its activities could thus be clearly defined, as in most cases the Company was the sole participant from the design stage right through to installation and in many cases even the operation.

The 1939–45 War was different for several reasons, not the least of which was the great diversity of uses to which electronics could now be put, and the large number of electronics factories which were then in being. Some were direct competitors, manufacturing transmitters and other capital goods, but many more were involved in the domestic receiver and allied markets; these, although possessing no background of capital goods engineering to professional or Service specifications, were nevertheless well equipped to mass-produce small units. The Governmental Ministries, in order to use the country's electronics resources to the full, and at the same time to preserve the maximum amount of security, evolved a policy of piecemeal manufacture, whereby the several units of a given equipment were individually assembled under several roofs and transported to yet another area – perhaps a military establishment – where building into a complete equipment would be effected. In this manner electronics units could be turned out without any of the manufacturers necessarily having any knowledge of the ultimate nature of the complete equipment. Because of this, no record of destination or usage exists of many hundreds of thousands of such units which were made at the Marconi Works as part of the war effort.

Again, by Government order, a pooling of patents and engineering and production expertise was put into operation, a process which most certainly did not operate to the Company's advantage as the information was, on balance, a unidirectional flow – outwards. The adverse effect of this was not, however, fully felt until the post-war years.

Unlike, for example, a manufacturer of domestic receivers, the outbreak of war brought no great change to the Company in the nature of its customers. It had a relatively small number of these, comprising for the most part Governments, Ministries, Posts and Telegraphs and Broadcasting Authorities, airline companies and so on. In war as in peace, the Company's British clients remained substantially the same, but with a vast increase in demand.

Such a violent step-up in production, while no simple matter even in an organization accustomed to mass production methods, taxes to the limits the resource of a Company which is committed to 'model shop' practice and whose production staff almost entirely consists of engineers, technicians and craftsmen. The situation was rendered even more serious because of the large numbers of physicists, engineers and technicians which were acquired by the Ministries and Armed Forces. By 1943 about 500 highly skilled men had been drafted into the Services, mostly on special duties.

Shortly after the outbreak of war, the Baddow Laboratories as a Marconi entity 'vanished' overnight. In April 1940 the Air Ministry took over part of the research establishment, absorbing T. L. Eckersley and his propagation team into its organization, and in September of that year an Instrument Group under R. J. Kemp was also transferred in order that it might design and construct apparatus to implement the Propagation Group's researches. In May 1941 the remainder of the Baddow Laboratories came under the control of the Admiralty for co-operation with the Admiralty Signal Establishment. In addition, many research and development engineers were removed for special duties in one of the three Services. Thereafter the postal address of the Baddow Laboratories gave rise to considerable perplexity, being simultaneously an Admiralty Signal Establishment extension, an Air Ministry Research Station and an R.A.F. operational station.

These measures, while necessary to the war effort, were a serious blow to the Company as a private manufacturer. Quite apart from the loss of research staff and loss of independent control over the laboratories, the patents taken out by the seconded staff became the property of the Ministry concerned, and as one minor result the Company's real contribution to the war effort in this connection is masked.

Typical of the 'panic' assignments of those early days was an order from the Air Ministry to install SWB8 high-frequency transmitters and associated communications equipment in eleven commandeered motor coaches, as a matter of extreme urgency. By dint of round-the-clock working by the small engineering force detailed to carry out the job (some of the men worked continuously for forty-eight hours at a stretch) the entire project was completed in eleven days from order. Two of these fleets of self-contained mobile transmitting and receiving stations, nick-named respectively 'The Blue Train' and the 'Southern Belle', were shipped to France for emergency communications purposes.

The emergency came within weeks when the German armies, bypassing the Maginot Line fortifications, poured through Belgium and into France. In the chaos which followed the two 'trains' became for many days the only means of communication between the British forces and London. Round-the-clock uninterrupted two-way traffic was maintained, while one 'train' made its way to Marseilles where the equipment was destroyed and the other fell back with the British Army to the Dunkirk area. At the last moment some of the equipment was crow-barred out of the coaches and dumped into the holds of any ships available, after which the fleet of vehicles was driven over the edge of a cliff. One solitary, battered SWB8 transmitter and a receiver eventually returned to Chelmsford to be hastily refurbished and sent out for further service.

One further 'train', 'The Golden Arrow', was later built at the Chelmsford Works and served with distinction in Europe after the D-Day landings; in addition a great number of wartime vehicles were converted to house SWB8 or SWB11 transmitters and receiving equipment. In 1943 alone, some 380 vehicles were so equipped, a conversion rate of one every nineteen hours.

In 1937 preliminary design had begun on an 'all-wave' airborne transmitter-receiver, the AD67/AD77. Just before the war the Royal Air Force became interested in these equipments but requested design modifications to give a larger number of spot frequencies and to provide a new combined communication and direction-finding receiver of improved performance. Negotiations were not concluded until after the outbreak of war; nevertheless by June 1940 production had begun. This was the famous T1154/R1155 or Marconi 'Geep' of which more than 80,000 were manufactured during the war years, although not all by Marconi's, for the designs were subsequently spread to four or five radio firms. These equipments were installed in all the aircraft of Bomber Command, in numerous fighter-bombers, flying boats, reconnaissance aircraft, ground stations, vehicles, R.A.F. air-sea rescue launches and a diversity of other locations as the standard communication and d.f. equipment.

To the Marconi Company also fell the task of engineering the installations in the Wellingtons, Whitleys, Blenheims and Hampdens of Bomber Command, as well as re-equipping the squadrons in the field. For the latter, five units of Marconi engineers were formed and over 2,000 aircraft re-equipped in the early stages of the war, for not until 1942 did the Service Maintenance Units become sufficiently well organized to carry out large-scale installation work. In this way the T1154/R1155 came into service with Bomber and Coastal Commands two years earlier than would have otherwise been the case. In addition, as during the First World War, a training school for R.A.F. officers and other ranks was set up and post-design services on equipments were provided through the medium of Marconi engineers attached to the respective headquarters of Bomber and Coastal Commands.

The table given below summarizes the Company's sales percentage of its main categories of products over three periods, namely 1937, 1939 and 1943:

AREA OF RESEARCH OR MANUFACTURE	1937	1939	1943
	%	%	%
Civil Aircraft Equipment	3·11	1·50	0·1
Military Aircraft Equipment	7·52	16·00	24·2
Broadcasting Equipment	23·57	18·00	2·7
Aerodrome Station Equipment	9·50	4·50	5·1
Govt. Specification	7·50	15·00	10·6
Harbours & Coastal Equipment	1·50	0·70	—
Marconi Marine Company	13·70	7·00	2·3
Other Maritime Companies	2·00	1·20	0·3
Military Equipment	1·82	9·00	8·4
Marconi Instruments Ltd.	0·95	0·30	—
Naval Equipment	3·72	11·00	30·5
Police Equipment	0·98	1·00	—
Marconi Stille Recording Machines	0·50	0·30	—
Stabilovolts	0·10	0·20	2·6
Traffic Services (Assoc. Cos.)	7·70	2·00	1·3
Traffic Services (Other Cos.)	4·15	2·30	0·3
Television Broadcasting Equip.	0·77	—	—
Thermionic Valves	10·00	10·00	7·1
Miscellaneous	0·91	—	4·5
	100%	100%	100%

These figures are instructive as recording the fluctuations in business in peace (albeit when re-armament was going on) and in war; they also illustrate the point made earlier, that the war did not alter the category of equipments being manufactured to any significant extent. It must be said, however, that it is not realistic to read too much into one year's figures as a single large order can to some extent modify a given percentage to give an abnormal value. Such is the case in the sound broadcasting column for 1937, when a big Turkish broadcasting contract over-weighted that year's figure.

Taking the more important of these statistics in order, we see that very little business was done in civil aviation. Business in connection with military aviation on the other hand, was responsible for nearly one-quarter of the total output for 1943. This is largely accounted for by the supply of airborne communications, direction-finding and kindred equipment (the T1154/R1155 contracts have already been mentioned) but one notable addition was the supply of aircraft harness which screened the electronic equipment carried on an aircraft from ignition and other forms of interference. In 1943, 14,320 sets of aircraft screening harness were manufactured.

The broadcasting situation perhaps needs a little more clarification. Even with due allowance for the big Turkish contract there was obviously a great deal of activity in th's area of manufacture in 1937 and in fact it continued through the early years of the war. This was largely because it was recognized quite early on that sound broadcasting could be both a weapon and a source of weakness in the event of war; a weapon as a disseminating agent for propaganda; one which recognized no frontiers; but a source of weakness in that enemy bombers could use the radiated energy to guide them to their targets.

The first requirement then was to reach as many of the peoples of the world with news from Britain. This meant new high-frequency broadcasting stations of high power and a programme organization working on a round-the-clock basis because of the time differences existing in various parts of the world. Thus transmitters and studio equipment were in considerable demand, of which the Company was called upon to supply more than half of the entire need; this in addition to a step-up in the supply of high-power medium-frequency transmitters to augment the B.B.C.'s home service and sound broadcasting equipment of all types for countries overseas.

One very real fear was that the enemy, realizing the great strategic value of the B.B.C. stations to the Allied cause, would mount concentrated bombing attacks to destroy them, and particularly the long-range high-frequency stations.

The great hub of the overseas broadcasting network was the Marconi-equipped station at Daventry which housed a large complex of these transmitters, the destruction of which would be a major achievement for Germany. It was decided therefore to build a 'shadow Daventry' with the utmost despatch, the chosen location being near the small Dorsetshire town of Rampisham. The contract for carrying out the work was placed with the Marconi Company and was completed in six months of high pressure work. The construction of this station was followed by another at Skelton, Yorkshire.

The problem of the enemy's use of British transmissions to guide them to target was tackled by arranging that stations in widely separated parts of the British Isles should share a common wavelength, whereby enemy bombers would be unable to use their direction-finders to home on to a given station. The project in turn raised problems, not the least of which was that an exact phase relationship between the various transmitters must be maintained. This work was also successfully carried out by the Company.

Jamming devices and stations were freely used by both sides during the war as a means of disrupting as far as possible the important radio communications and radar stations. This in turn gave birth to devices which would enable stations to work through the jamming signals. The Company played a significant part in the development of both jamming and anti-jamming devices, one or two of which will be mentioned later.

As the table shows, the demand for broadcasting equipment which in 1939 amounted to 18 per cent of the Company's total manufacture, had, by 1943, dropped to 2·7 per cent, the main requirements having been met.

The figure of 9·5 per cent for aerodrome station equipment in 1937 reflects the pre-war strengthening of the R.A.F. and, to some extent, the air forces of the Commonwealth. The equipments supplied were mostly general-purpose or special-purpose communications transmitting and receiving sets.

These types of equipment also largely account for the percentage supplied to the Army, although here it will be noted that the peak demand came in 1939 (9 per cent) and was still being reasonably maintained in 1943 (8·4 per cent) when army expansion was occurring on various fronts. In addition to the conventional radio equipments for fixed station and mobile work there were large numbers of special assignments such as the 'Cloak and Dagger' portable equipments used by British Intelligence agents behind enemy lines and the radios for Major General Wingate's Chindits in the Burma campaign. By 1943 production was peaking in anticipation of the D-Day landings of the following year.

To detail all the activities of the Company in those days would be to compile a lengthy and tedious list; equipments for desert patrols, tanks, gunnery control, searchlight direction and submarine detection are but a handful. As some indication of the war effort in 1943 it may be mentioned that in that year 10,700 transmitters and 15,000 receivers passed through the Company's Works; these figures do not include direction-finding equipments of which 1,135 were manufactured. Some 34,000 miscellaneous items, ranging from monitors, undulators, echometers, voice frequency bridges and Auto Alarms to switches, morse keys and microphones, also formed part of the 1943 output.

Vacuum tubes and kindred devices were also in large-scale production; these were not so much the standard types of small tube as the

16. The radio room of the liner *Oriana* (1965)

17. Space communications station

18. Radar and television displays at Southern Air Traffic Control Centre

19. An assembly of microcircuits (*c.* 1965) considerably enlarged. The four silicon slices which contain the microcircuits are seen in the centre circle. The actual diameter of the can in which the chips are enclosed (A–A in picture) is 0·37 inch—roughly the cross-section diameter of a small cigarette

20. Flight panel of the Company's Piaggio 166 aircraft, used as a flying exhibition/test-bed

21. Colour television camera in action (1965)

22. Tropospheric
scatter antennas, 1965

23. Part of Marconi
House, Chelmsford,
with thin-line tropo-
scatter antenna on the
roof

'difficult' special-purpose or experimental types, of which the Stabilovolt was an example. The Stabilovolt was originally a German device for providing stabilized power supplies; small-scale manufacture had begun under licence at Baddow in 1936–7 to satisfy a limited demand, but the re-armament programme called for vastly increased numbers for use in aircraft and in a great variety of other equipments. In 1943, 55,500 Stabilovolts were produced, one every eight minutes.

Quartz crystal oscillators were also in heavy demand and it is of interest to note that when in 1926 the Company pioneered the production of these devices, the output was one per week. In 1943, 92,400 were manufactured. This in addition to the 55,500 Stabilovolts and 10,000 vacuum tubes produced during that year.

38

World War II (Part 2)

But in spite of the size of these commitments, by far the greatest volume of the Company's output was produced for the Allied navies. Referring again to the Table given in the previous chapter, it will be seen that in 1943 no less than 30·5 per cent of the total sales were to naval organizations, chiefly, of course, to the Admiralty. At this time 65 per cent of the total Works production capacity was devoted to these ends, as also was a similar percentage of the Company's available design and development resources.

Unlike the war on land, at sea there was no quiescent prelude to the main struggle; the war was fought with ferocity from the first day. In the first four months some 755,392 tons of Allied shipping were destroyed, representing the loss of 222 vessels. These losses would have been greater but for the network of direction-finding stations which the Admiralty had set up to watch the whole Atlantic area and which proved invaluable in locating the enemy and directing British warships to the scene of an attack. Again, with the help of these stations, attacks were frequently avoided by the re-routing of shipping while in other cases the escort vessels were alerted to take counter-offensive action. The major part of this direction-finding equipment was provided by the Marconi Company.

At the same time, massive orders for sea-going communications and d.f. equipment were being fulfilled, both to naval and mercantile marine requirements. Some idea of the scale of supply can be gathered from the fact that a single battleship might carry up to fifty transmitters of various types and an even greater number of receivers. One of the most noteworthy of the receivers manufactured was the Marconi CR100 which became standard in the Royal Navy and was also widely used in the other Services.

The merchant shipping equipment designed and manufactured by the parent Company was installed and serviced by the Marconi Marine Company, one of whose immediate tasks when war was imminent was to extend the already considerable numerical strength of its servicing depots all over the world. In addition it had the equally onerous task of recruiting and training the maximum number of sea-going radio officers. At the outbreak of war, Marconi Marine had about 2,000 radio officers on its strength; by September 1940, despite casualties, over 6,000 were in its service, maintaining communications and assisting navigation in Company-equipped ships from the smallest drifters to the erstwhile passenger liners, now converted to armed merchant cruisers or troopships.

The new and highly secret R.D.F. (later 'radar') was badly needed by both the Navy and merchant shipping, with priority for the former. It was needed to cope with two pressing dangers, attack from the air and attack by submarine, and this called for two types of equipment. At the outbreak of war the Navy's capital ships and cruisers were being fitted with radar equipments to give long-range warning of aircraft, but these were too bulky for use on smaller craft and in any event did not provide adequate facilities for the detection of surface vessels (and in particular, surfaced submarines), although various classes of naval vessels carried the ASDIC anti-submarine device. The general situation therefore was that the large warships were being equipped with early warning radar against air attack and ASDIC for submarine and surface vessel detection: the smaller warships had ASDIC only while the merchant service vessels as individual units had nothing at all.

As a stop-gap expedient, modified Air Ministry-designed ASV (Air-to-Surface-Vessels) equipment operating in the metric band was pressed into service to provide aircraft warning for the smaller ships, while a crash programme for a small radar set suitable for the detection of surface vessels was instituted; this equipment was designed for installation aboard corvettes, frigates and destroyers as a means of keeping watch over a convoy or as an adjunct to ASDIC for the detection of surfaced submarines. The first of these new radars was delivered in 1941. (At the same time orders for an improved form of aircraft warning radar were placed with various companies, including Marconi's. This was the type 281 radar, which when produced, was the most powerful to go into seafaring service.)

Although the introduction of the two categories of radar was valuable in flattening the rising curve of shipping losses for a time, the respite was brief. The modified ASV was unwieldly in that the antenna system was fixed and the ship therefore had to turn in order to get a bearing, while the German scientists soon provided an effective answer to the surface vessel detection radar when it was being used in its anti-submarine role.

As the equipment, like the ASV, operated in the metric band, it was a comparatively simple exercise to design a sensitive receiver that would detect the pulse it transmitted. These, fitted in the U-boats, could pick up the radar transmissions from a considerable range and thus give the submarine commander ample time to submerge, or if he so wished, to 'home' on the signals for an attack; thus the very equipment which had been designed to protect a ship could become the instrument of its destruction.

But in the game of scientific chess, new developments were in hand to remove this hazard. It had long been realized that the use of centimetric wavelengths for radar work would be highly advantageous, but a major problem existed in that conventional thermionic tubes (valves) were incapable of generating significant powers at these wavelengths. In the years immediately preceding the war experimental work had been done on two reasonably promising approaches to the overcoming of the obstacles; one was the klystron and the other the magnetron, but up to the outbreak of hostilities only low output powers had been achieved with either device.

The turning point came in November 1939 when, at Birmingham University, Dr J. T. Randall and Dr H. A. H. Boot constructed the first resonant cavity magnetron, a device which generated considerably more power at a centimetric wavelength than had hitherto been possible. The work was pressed forward with all speed and by September 1940 a wide range of designs had been investigated and laboratory models produced which gave significant power outputs at wavelengths ranging from 2 to 10 cms.

The resonant cavity magnetron, however, had two serious drawbacks; firstly the transition from laboratory model to large-quantity production was difficult because of the high degree of precision and the specialist techniques which were called for in its manufacture, and, secondly, the early magnetrons were extremely unstable and had a disconcerting habit of switching without warning to an entirely different wavelength, a defect which made them virtually useless for the applications in mind.

Nevertheless, development and ultimately production was hastened; one of the few organizations to whom this delicate task was entrusted being the Marconi Laboratories, which undertook production as from August 1940. The difficulties were immense and by the end of the year only twenty per week were being turned out; but in that short time much had been learnt which was to prove of considerable value. In May 1942, production was removed from the Vacuum Laboratories at

Great Baddow to a new building in Waterhouse Lane, Chelmsford, where 9,000 sq. ft. of floor space was available. Before long several hundred cavity magnetrons were being manufactured per month. At peak production in 1945, nearly 2,500 per month were leaving the factory.

To return to the early days; in August 1941 a most important advance was made when Sayers of the British Thomson-Houston Company found that by connecting together alternate segments of the anode (and thereby increasing the wavelength separation between the π-mode and the other modes) the magnetron was rendered much more stable.

The way was now open for the quantity manufacture of centimetric radars of relatively high power, an event which had been eagerly awaited by all three Services but notably by the Air Force and the Navy. By April 1942 batches of amplifier units for the Naval centimetric radar Type 271 were being shipped out of the Chelmsford Works and by the following month over 400 had been produced.

The Type 271 radar, which came into large-scale usage late in 1942 and the early months of 1943, and the centimetric ASV equipment used by R.A.F. Coastal Command, brought as their first-fruits a dramatic increase in the number of U-boats destroyed or damaged, and thereafter a steady drop in the percentage of Allied merchant vessels sunk. The Germans seemed unable to devise effective direct counter-measures against the centimetric equipment, but as soon as it was realized that the Allies had a new device in operation, the strategy of submarine attack was amended pending the arrival of the new German Schnorkel equipment which enabled the U-boats so fitted to remain under water for considerably longer periods than had hitherto been possible. Neither move enabled the Germans to make up the lost ground, however, although convoys in especially dangerous waters, such as the routes to Murmansk and other Russian ports, continued to suffer heavily.

The use of the cavity magnetron was not of course confined to naval and airborne radar; on the contrary it was extensively employed by all three Services in a variety of equipments. Without doubt its development was one of the most important electronic contributions to the war effort.

In the early days of hostilities it was found that German aircraft (and particularly night intruders) were navigating by means of a modified Lorenz beam system, code-named by the enemy as Knickebein ('Crooked Leg') but known to the British authorities as 'Headache'. Jamming measures were at once introduced, at first with modified medical diathermy equipment produced by Marconi's and other companies and then with more powerful transmitters, again suitably modified. A hasty call was made upon the Marconi organization to provide adapted SWB8 and beacon equipments and to install them in various parts of the country; the Company also modified the Alexandra Palace television transmitter to operate as a jamming agent.

These measures proving successful, the Germans in retaliation produced and used a more complex navigational system (X-Gerat), code-named 'Ruffian' by the British, and, in turn, more elaborate jamming equipment was devised to combat this. Then a third system, Wotan (British code-name 'Benito') was provided for the Luftwaffe. Wotan functioned in the manner of the then highly secret British bombing aid 'Oboe' (at the time only in development) but used continuous wave transmission; the new navigation system was more accurate and more difficult to jam than its predecessors and for a short period the Luftwaffe had the advantage. Then an ingenious countermeasure was formulated whereby the signals from the aircraft to the German ground stations were interpolated by similar signals from British ground stations so that the enemy control stations received positional information from the aircraft which was false but at the same time feasible. The answering signals from ground to air, which contained a measurement of range calculated from the falsified information received, were correspondingly inaccurate; as a consequence of this the German navigator often dropped his bomb load on the countryside or even whilst over sea. The ruse succeeded for a considerable time, during which period the airborne navigators blamed their lack of success in bombing the assigned target on to inept ground control, while the ground control personnel blamed the stupidity of the navigators.

'Beam-bending' techniques were also employed whereby British ground transmitters were locked on to the enemy frequency, made to nullify the enemy navigational signals and to provide new ones which led the aircraft in an entirely different direction. In this project also, Marconi's provided much of the equipment.

As a further instance of the electronics game of chess which was being so grimly played, some little while before the navigational aid code-named Gee was first used operationally (March 1942), stations were set up in various parts of the country and began to radiate beamed guidance signals of the J-beam Lorenz type. These had little other function than to lead the enemy to believe that the R.A.F. was introducing a new navigational aid based on this system, and thereby to divert attention to the production of counter-measures against such a system. The stratagem succeeded, and when Gee went into operation its real nature was such a surprise that five months of massed bombing attacks against Germany were to elapse before counter-measures in the form of jamming were encountered.

At the start of the war British radar development was largely concentrated upon its defence potentialities. Germany at that time had no need of an equivalent organization to the British defensive R.D.F. (radar) network, but radar as a weapon of offence had been developed, as was discovered after the fall of France when the large-calibre guns sited along the French coast in the Straits of Dover area began to achieve considerable accuracy in the shelling of convoys, not only in daylight but also during the hours of darkness and even in fog.

In November 1940 two senior engineers of the Marconi Company, N. E. Davis and O. E. Keall, were seconded to the Admiralty to investigate the possibility of counter-measures. The operating frequencies of the German radars were discovered and jamming equipment was set up, first in a hut at the South Foreland but then extending along the coast until at length 127 posts were in being, maintaining a listening watch and standing by to jam enemy transmissions when the order was given, with changes in German wavelengths closely followed by the appropriate countermoves.

One of the great number of special assignments which the Company carried out at short notice was the mass production of an equipment to nullify the radio control of flying bombs (not the V1) which were being launched against shipping by German aircraft at the end of 1943. The problem was especially difficult because the launching plane could effect control on any of twenty frequencies by pre-selection, while, to complicate the matter further, German land stations transmitted similar signals so that which one was effecting control was always in doubt.

By good fortune a specimen flying bomb (christened 'Chase me Charlies') was recovered intact and a little later the control equipment was salvaged from a wrecked German aircraft. Advantage was taken of a design defect to devise jamming equipment and this was hurriedly put into production on a large scale. It proved to be extremely successful in removing master control from the launching aircraft and thereafter the menace of 'Chase me Charlies' was minimized.

In mid-1941 the destruction of the German battleship *Bismarck* illustrated the value of co-ordination by the Navy and the Air Force. From that time onward the two Services were unified in the matter of radio communications by the use of Marconi-designed equipment.

One stratagem which was frequently used by the German Navy on sighting a merchantman steaming out of convoy was to send out a fake distress call giving an entirely different position in order to send any nearby naval vessels scurrying to the 'rescue' and thereby ensuring that they were well out of the way when the attack was mounted. These tactics proved so successful that ways and means had to be found to check them. The problem was solved by the Marconi production of a unit which, when attached to the Company's transmitters, gave the signals an easily distinguished characteristic which was difficult to imitate. This device, known as the Swat Unit, was manufactured in large quantities for use in merchant shipping and proved to be of considerable value in saving lives and ships.

An even more significant contribution to the war effort was the supersonic buoy. This stemmed from an Admiralty requirement in January 1942. The specifications were stringent. The buoy had to radiate supersonic signals which were capable of providing bearings to specially-equipped ships up to a range of 4–5 miles, but which could not be picked up by standard submarine hydrophone. It had to be capable of radiating over a range of different pulsing rates and was to have a running life of three months, radiating for a predetermined period every one or two hours, day and night, but only for fourteen days out of the twenty-eight. The clockwork timing mechanisms had to maintain an accuracy of within ± 15 minutes in three months; the buoy had to be so constructed that it would not drag its moorings or tilt from the perpendicular and must incorporate a detonating charge which would automatically destroy it if it were swept up or broke loose from its moorings.

Such were the stipulations, presented without any indication of the ultimate purpose of the buoys. By October 1942, barely nine months after the initial approach, supersonic buoys meeting the specifications were in production and sea trials were taking place. They were first used in the invasion of Sicily for the guidance of transport and beach-landing craft and later in a similar capacity at the Anzio landings. A Mark II version was developed which could be laid via a submarine's torpedo tubes.

Many other uses were found for these buoys but its biggest role was in the D-Day invasion when, immediately prior to June 6, 1944, large quantities of Marconi Mark IV buoys laid by fast motor launches operating off the French coastline served to mark enemy minefields, sunken wrecks and other hazards. This device thoroughly demonstrated its reliability; throughout the whole of the landing operations not a single failure of a buoy took place.

Another essential feature of the D-Day operations was the jamming of the German radars. This requirement was catered for by two projects which were known respectively by the code names 'Bagful' and 'Carpet'. 'Bagful', which was designed, developed and manufactured by Marconi's from research data supplied by the Telecommunications Research Establishment, was an airborne equipment to intercept and record the frequency and approximate positions of enemy radar stations. This equipment went into large-scale operation a considerable while before D-Day so that by the time the invasion took place an extensive dossier had been built up. Then, on June 6, 'Carpet', a multiplicity of jamming stations, went into action, paralysing the German radar networks while the invasion fleet effected the landings.

In preparation for this, the greatest military operation of all time, the Marconi Marine Company had been instructed to provide facilities for servicing the vast amount of radio communications, echo sounding and radar equipments which were employed on tank-landing craft, and a diversity of other vessels. By D-Day, some twenty-three depots were established along the coast from Ipswich to Littlehampton.

Once the Normandy bridgeheads had been gained, the portable radio communication sets carried by the assault troops and the small wireless vehicles used in the initial phases of the landings were supplemented by large and complex mobile stations installed in prime mover vehicles and caravan trailers. Typical of these was the Marconi-equipped Control Centre of the Second Tactical Air Force.

One of the last special assignments given to the Company was in January 1945 when a Marconi engineer and a hastily recruited party of workmen boarded the *Franconia* at Liverpool and proceeded to strip the smoking-room as a prelude to rendering the area fireproof. That done, two SWB88 transmitters, communications receivers and a host of ancillary equipments were installed. The task, which ordinarily might have taken four months, was completed in ten days.

The installation, although it was not known at the time, was for the use of Prime Minister Winston Churchill and his staff on the occasion of his historic meeting with Franklin D. Roosevelt and Joseph Stalin at Yalta. For the fifteen days of the Big Three conference, round-the-clock communication was maintained with Whitehall. At the end of the conference Churchill made it his business to thank the staff personally, a tribute which was followed later by another from the Controller of the Navy who wrote a personal letter of appreciation to Admiral Grant, the Chairman of the Company.

A few months later, on 8 May 1945, the war with Germany ended, to be followed on August 14 by the capitulation of the Japanese.

Like many another manufacturing organization, the Marconi Company had not come through unscathed. On 27 September 1940, additional factory premises at Vauxhall, acquired only the previous Autumn, were damaged by a bomb and on October 10 they received a direct hit. Fortunately casualties were small, amounting to one killed and two injured, but the building was wrecked. Part of the work was thereupon transferred to other premises which had been taken at Parsons Green while the sheet metal production was temporarily removed to another recently acquired Works at Hackbridge.

Early in the morning of 9 May 1941 a single German aircraft carried out a raid on the Chelmsford Works, scoring direct hits with three of the stick of four bombs dropped. The first detonated in the middle of the main machine shop; the second hit the transmitter erection shop, wrecking it and an adjacent electricity sub-station and setting fire to the paint shop. The Company fire brigade quickly got the fire under control however, while a labour force hastily improvised a new sub-station from spare equipment stored in another part of the Works.

This, as it transpired, was done to no purpose. For on the following day a ticking noise was noticed coming from under the debris of the transmitter erection shop. It came from a delayed action bomb which had to be blown up *in situ* and in so doing the temporary sub-station was completely destroyed.

In this raid seventeen employees were killed and forty injured. Production was badly affected for a short time but temporary quarters were soon found, including a large carpenter's shop which was lent by Crompton Parkinson Ltd., of Chelmsford, pending the erection of new buildings at New Street. After a comparatively brief interval production climbed back to 80 per cent of normal output.

There was a curious sequel to this attack. On 12 June 1945, officers of C Squadron, 8501 Wing, R.A.F., examining a fire-gutted photographic building on Quedlingburg Airfield in Germany, found a scale model of the Marconi and the Hoffmann Works (which occupy neighbouring sites at New Street, Chelmsford) evidently prepared from aerial photographs. The model was recovered and presented to the Marconi Company by the R.A.F. officers. It now stands in the main entrance hall at Marconi House, Chelmsford, near the Roll of Honour.

The growth of the importance of electronics over the forty years or so since the turn of the century is astonishing. In the Boer War wireless equipment had played an insignificant role; useful on occasion, but its use being in no degree critical to the outcome. World War I had seen its status raised from that of a mere 'adjunct to visual and telegraphic signalling' to an indispensable means of communication and co-ordination. The Second World War had seen the beginnings of an entirely new concept in which battles waged between opposing electronic impulses could bring victory or defeat, even though the final issues still had to be settled in terms of human lives. Perhaps the most spectacular instance of this was the Battle of Britain in which radar played so decisive a part, but throughout the armed Services electronic devices for communication and control purposes became indispensable units of the war machine.

39

The English Electric Takeover

In 1943 an extensive survey had been made of the Company's manufacturing position in an attempt to plan a peacetime future, and this was reviewed from time to time as the end to hostilities drew nearer. As some small indication of the administrative complexity which existed during the war years it may be mentioned in passing that the parent Company alone had control over thirty-six factories and other establishments in the area around London, including such diverse premises as garages, the stands of Chelmsford City football club, Methodist Church rooms, a banana warehouse and rooms in two public houses. Many of these were stores acquired on the wartime dispersed-sites plan and were relinquished as a planned run-down of stored materials took effect, towards the end of the war.

On a larger scale there were eight associated and subsidiary Companies in the British Isles, with a further twenty-seven in overseas countries although the future of many of these and particularly those in German-orientated areas, was in considerable doubt.

At the same time a realistic assessment was made of the serious competition for world markets which would build up as soon as the war was over. The potential opposition was considered to fall into one of four categories:

a. Manufacturers of generally similar experience, resources and international background, supported by full-scale research and patents organization.
b. Important companies in the electrical engineering field which had been drawn into the manufacture of electronic equipment during the war and which were believed to be considering a post-war continuance of this type of manufacture.
c. Manufacturers whose pre-war experience had been limited to domestic broadcast receivers, but had been drawn into the capital electronics field by the demands of war. Some of these would probably elect to continue in capital electronics after the war.

d. Government and other National Establishments at home and abroad
which had vastly increased in size and which might be expected to
carry much of their own research for the future.

In all some twenty major 'private-enterprise' organizations were
considered to offer really serious competition, with a host of others
which, although individually would only constitute a nuisance value,
might well in the aggregate account for a significant share of the markets.
Tentative plans were laid in an attempt to place the Company in as
advantageous a position as possible and these were hardened as the end
of the war drew near.

But with the coming of peace, certain factors could not be planned
away. One such was the dire shortage of engineers, particularly the
specialists in research design and development, large numbers of whom
had been drawn off into Service Establishments and were being released
at far too slow a rate for the Company's well-being. This was a desperate
situation because little or no effort had been available for the design of
commercial equipment over the war years, while at the same time the
pre-war designs had steadily grown more and more obsolescent and
even in some cases obsolete. Equipments designed after 1939 had been
for military use only and although many of these promised to have a
commercial future, considerable modification would first be necessary.

Again, the exigencies of war had demanded that production on the
big Government contracts should continue at full pressure until the very
last; the cancellation of most of these at the war's end left the Works
with comparatively little to do. The machines, many of which had
been running virtually around the clock for nearly six years, urgently
needed replacement, and of replacements there were almost none,
because of the famine in materials which was rife throughout the
country. Even such essential materials as window-glass, wood and
building materials were the subject of rigid controls and were surrounded
by an almost impenetrable hedge of restrictions and applications for
permits.

The 1943 forecasts regarding post-war competition proved in the
event to be shrewd and accurate. At home, various companies which,
before the war, had possessed only an electrical or domestic radio background had, over the five years, acquired sufficient experience in the
manufacture of capital electronics goods to essay a peacetime excursion
into the market. Abroad, the formidable electronics industry of the
United States was threatening to sweep all before it, for although its

war effort had been on a massive scale it had never been subjected to the total life-or-death involvement of the character experienced by the British industry with its bomb-damage, its improvisations and its shortages. As a consequence, immediately upon the cessation of hostilities American competitors were able to come forward in strength with more modern equipment for communications, broadcasting and many other purposes.

In short, the overall commercial prospects for the Marconi Company were depressing in the extreme.

On the credit side was the vast store of accumulated knowledge backed by quality engineering of the highest order. And more than this – a something which, like respect for a flag, is too intangible to be expressed in words. Perhaps one could best call it pride – pride of being part of the Marconi organization; of being a Marconi engineer. Sentimental as it may look in print, it is there. It is seen in the extraordinary number of men who have seen over forty years' service with the Company; it is there in the sight of three generations of a family employed in the Works and in the outcry of a retired veteran whose copy of the House Magazine has been lost in the post!

This spirit, always strong in the Company, had been enhanced by the single-minded purpose of the war years, coupled with the personality of the Chairman of those days, Admiral H. W. Grant. In a very short time after his assumption of office the Admiral had captured the loyalty of the Works floor by his seeming determination to know every man personally. During the Chelmsford bombing he was there, ably backed by Mrs Grant who devoted her energies to the Welfare side of the organization. News of the bombing of a Marconi factory in London would send him at top speed to the scene. Stories of the Admiral are legion and there is not one which does not underline his complete identification with his 'Ship's Company' as he called them.

Such factors as these cannot be entered into a Company balance sheet, but they may in some degree help to explain the spirit with which the Marconi organization faced the future in the years immediately following the war.

But events seemingly unconnected with the Marconi fortunes were already conspiring to promote another crisis. In 1945 a Commonwealth Telecommunications Conference was held to consider the future of the cable and radio services linking the countries concerned. This, after deliberation, recommended that the existing services in the U.K., the Dominions and Southern Rhodesia should be acquired by their respective governments, with a unifying Commonwealth Telecommunications Board to replace the advisory Commonwealth Communications Council. This proposal was adopted and as one consequence Cable and Wireless Ltd. became nationalized under the Cable & Wireless Act of 1946, starting its new career as a Government-owned body as from 1 January 1947.

Cable and Wireless (Holding) Ltd., however, had owned the shares of the Marconi Company since the merger agreement of 1929 and since the Government's interest was solely in the traffic operating aspect there was no option but to dispose of Marconi's. This, when it became known, created wide interest in business circles, not only in this country but also in the U.S.A.

Among the big combines considering an offer was the English Electric Company. In July 1946 at an extraordinary meeting of that Company it was proposed that authorization should be given for an offer of £3,750,000 for the whole share capital of Marconi's Wireless Telegraph Company Ltd., the amount to be paid in instalments spread over three years. This proposed purchase, if successfully negotiated, would include the ownership of the Wireless Telegraph parent Company, a 42 per cent interest in the Marconi International Marine Communication Company Ltd. and the entire interest in Marconi Instruments Ltd.

The English Electric Company Ltd. had originated in 1918 when four firms, each a pioneer in its own sphere of engineering, joined forces – Dick Kerr and Co. of Preston (already allied with the Siemens Dynamo Works of Stafford), the Coventry Ordnance Works Ltd., Willans and Robinson of Rugby and the Phoenix Dynamo Manufacturing Company of Bradford. The new Company had a wide sphere of manufacturing interests in the fields of heavy traction, electric power and hydro-electric engineering and, for a time, it prospered. The years of depression from the mid-1920s to 1930 took their toll however, and by the latter date English Electric was in very low water financially.

The tide turned when in that year Mr G. H. Nelson was appointed to the Board and was elected Managing Director. Almost immediately the vigorous measures which he instituted began to bear fruit and by 1933 when he became Chairman (as well as Managing Director) the Company was showing a satisfactory profit. After a recession the following year, brought about by the national economic situation, the turnover graph began to climb steadily and continued to do so year by year. When war broke out, the Company, now considerably expanded, was in the front line of the British manufacturing effort. Vast shadow factories were built and in addition to English Electric's normal products, large-scale armaments manufacture was carried on, including the production of tanks and bomber and fighter aircraft.

In 1942 the firm of D. Napier and Son Ltd. was added to the English Electric Group of Companies. In the following year the Chairman was knighted for his services in connection with the war effort; 1943 also saw his son, Mr H. G. Nelson, elected to the Board of Directors.

Sir George Nelson was that rare combination, a fully qualified practical engineer and an extremely astute business man. He knew that should the Commonwealth Telecommunication Conference elect to recommend the nationalization of Cable and Wireless Ltd., this proposal would almost certainly be implemented. He knew also that this must bring Marconi's into the market and because it had become increasingly evident that the two fields of electric power and electronics were tending to converge, he considered that the acquisition of the Marconi Company would provide a potentially valuable asset. The strong Marconi position in radio communications and capital electronics in general would, he reasoned, provide an improved balance in the basis of the English Electric organization and strengthen its position in competitive overseas markets.

In the light of this philosophy the preliminary financial arrangements were made, as stated, in July 1946 and in the following month the bid was offered and accepted. In such fashion Marconi's Wireless Telegraph Company Ltd., 42 per cent of the shares of the Marconi International Marine Communication Company Ltd., Marconi Instruments Ltd. and small subsidiaries were purchased by English Electric.

It would be quite untrue to imply that the transfer was looked upon with any degree of favour at Chelmsford. From the commercial standpoint the disengagement from Cable & Wireless Ltd. represented a serious loss of revenue because the Marconi Company had hitherto enjoyed a virtual monopoly in the provision of equipment for the operating Company; henceforth, it was realized, any orders gained would have to be contested on an equal footing with competitors.

Again, what was known of English Electric policy and outlook showed it to be considerably out of phase with those which were favoured at Marconi's. This was in great measure due to the hierarchy structure at Chelmsford which consisted almost wholly of engineers – extremely good engineers, be it added – but possessing insufficient commercial leavening with which to combat the cut-and-thrust tactics of the Company's big competitors. The Works output at that time consisted of equipments which were of superlative craftsmanship and finish, built without regard to price, or as Mr F. S. Mockford, at that time Deputy Commercial Manager, put it in 1947 '... with a price a little too high, a delivery a little too long and a specification not quite in line with the customer's requirements' although it could be added that the specification was often out of line by being better than the customer needed.

In justice it must be admitted that there was something to be said for the dominance of the engineering element, for in the one period of the Company's history when this had not been in evidence (in the Kellaway régime) the Marconi organization had sustained considerable losses. Since then, with the engineering power restored, it had been content to jog along, with a steady but unspectacular annual turnover and without much thought given to commercial expansion or for the changing needs which were emerging in the post-war world.

The English Electric takeover was therefore looked on with dismay by many, who saw in it among other things, the submerging of the name Marconi in that of 'big brother'. At best it was painfully evident that the Marconi way of conducting its affairs was incompatible with the bustling drive which characterized Sir George Nelson.

Events moved swiftly; at an extraordinary general meeting of the Marconi Group on 12 August 1946 the Chairman and Managing Director, Admiral H. W. Grant, tendered his resignation. This circumstance might have passed without comment as the Admiral was in his seventy-sixth year, but the simultaneous resignation of the entire board of directors gave promise of further changes. The previous board of thirteen members was replaced by one of five only, with Sir George H. Nelson as Chairman and his son, Mr H. G. Nelson, as one of the directors.

In review, and remote by two decades from the takeover, it is not difficult to appreciate the two completely divergent points of view which existed; we have, on the one hand, Sir George Nelson, by no means the ruthless tyrant that many of his new employees imagined him to be, yet fully determined to bring the Marconi Company to a state of greater prosperity, and on the other hand the hard core of senior Marconi staff who had served the Company faithfully and well according to their lights and who saw no good reason why existing policies should be overset.

No doubt at the time of the Norman invasion no true Saxon had a good word to say for William and his barons, yet today a claim to Norman ancestry is a matter for pride. Likewise in due course English Electric was to infuse new blood and new cultures into Marconi's but this prospect was far from appreciated in 1946, the date of the 'invasion'.

The year 1947, which should have been a particularly auspicious one, being the Golden Jubilee of the Company's founding, passed in an atmosphere of unrest and suspicion. Meanwhile Sir George Nelson was looking for someone to take charge of English Electric's export marketing. His choice fell upon the Managing Director of English Electric in South Africa, Mr F. N. Sutherland, who accordingly received a cable recalling him to England.

F. N. Sutherland had joined English Electric as an apprentice in 1922 after taking his M.A. degree at Cambridge. He had subsequently served at Preston, Stafford, Bradford and London on Works production, technical engineering and management. In 1925 he had been appointed Engineer-in-Chief of the English Electric organization in Brazil and had been largely instrumental in bringing it from a precarious position to one of prosperity. In 1936 he had been transferred to South Africa for a similar process of resuscitation of the Company's interests there, a task he fulfilled with such success that under his direction the Benoni plant, one of the first English Electric works to be built abroad, was constructed and put into operation.

On Sutherland's arrival in England, Sir George changed his mind. It had become very clear that what was wanted at Marconi's was a leader who owed no allegiance to that Company's past methods of operation, and Sutherland had all the necessary attributes. He had a proven reputation of successful management and was well known for his love of a tough fight. He was a highly qualified engineer and an English Electric man to the core, to whom the Marconi Company was little more than a name.

For a month Sir George gave Sutherland no inkling of his intentions. Then, after a visit to the Chelmsford Works with Mr H. G. Nelson, the latter, on behalf of his father, offered him the general managership on the way back. It was accepted.

Early in January 1948 Sir George came to Chelmsford and addressed the employees, breaking the news of the new appointment and thereby causing more consternation. On 19 January 1948, the new General Manager took up his duties.

This was a crucial day in the Company's history; the tension which existed can be imagined and so can the comments. Qualified engineer the new boss might be, but what did he know about electronics? (In fact he knew more than he was given credit for, having had a keen interest in radio for many years past.) From the managerial chair Sutherland faced a latently hostile factory; a host of strange faces and not a single one which he knew he could trust.

For a while he played it carefully; sizing up his key men and establishing the directions in which he could delegate responsibility. To the surprise of the Works the anticipated redundancy notices did not materialize; neither on the other hand did the new boss attempt to fraternize with the Works floor, being too shrewd to compete with Admiral Grant's *bonhomie*. He made no attempt to win the Works with verbal blandishment; he was, he stated uncompromisingly in a newspaper interview, a disciple of Sir George Nelson in the matter of the relationship between workers and management; his aims (he said) were to increase production and to study the well-being of the employees. (At the time it is doubtful whether anyone at Marconi's set much store by the second aim, but events were to prove the doubters wrong. Over the years there was a continual process of improvement in working conditions and social facilities.)*

But strangely enough, there was no explosion. For in those first critical months, although it became plain to the senior Marconi men that the new General Manager was going to run the Company in exactly the way he wanted it, he was at least a man who talked their kind of language. Gradually a realization dawned that their main aim, the prosperity of the Company, was identical with his, the divergences of outlook lying only in the means to be adopted to bring this about. With a common denominator established, the passing months saw a growing spirit of co-operation.

The Sutherland approach was that of deeds, not words. If the Works Floor did not get the informal addresses to which they had become accustomed there was nevertheless plenty of evidence that the new boss was around. New plant, terribly difficult to come by, began to arrive and was installed to increase production. Reorganization of procedures was gradually introduced, to the betterment of working conditions, although the traditional model-shop methods of assembly by skilled craftsmen were still retained as representing the best constructional approach for equipments which had to operate vital services on land,

---

* In connection with these, tribute must also be paid to Mrs Sutherland, who for twenty years worked indefatigably for the promotion of Marconi recreational activities and the general welfare of the employees.

sea and in the air. Over a comparatively short time a new and stream-lined accountancy system was introduced, a new development and planning department implemented, a technical sales organization formed and a new drawing office brought into operation. Buildings were modified and improved after a strenuous behind-the-scenes battle against the Government restrictions then in force over materials. Soon the new spirit which was being infused into the Company was reflected in an upward surge of output and orders; a situation which was promptly converted into positive feed-back in the form of a general increase in wages and salaries.

But these innovations, important as they were, were side issues compared with the overall problem of efficient production and market-ing. From the first days at Marconi's the General Manager had seen clearly that the Company's Achilles heel lay principally in the internal production organization, which consisted of a multifarious collection of small units, groups of which were engaged on kindred tasks but each independently of the other, with considerable wastage of research, development and engineering efforts. The General Manager decided that the moment was opportune for drastic action.

In October 1948 he put a main plan into effect. This, in essence, was the creation of six new sales divisions out of the welter of small units which existed at that time. The six were as follows:

(a) *Service Equipment Division.* This had actually been formed a little earlier (in July). Its function was to be the supplier of radio and radar equipment of British Services pattern.

(b) *Aeronautical Division.* Airborne radio communication and electronic navigational aids. Aerodrome navigational aid equipment.

(c) *Communications Division.* Work appertaining to commercial com-munications and services as used by Posts and Telegraphs Authorities and others.

(d) *Field Station Division.* Portable, mobile and low-powered stationary equipment. (This Division was absorbed into the Communications Division 15.5.50.)

(e) *Broadcasting Division.* Sound broadcasting and television equipment.

(f) *Central Division.* The Company's products not included in the above-mentioned divisions (thermionic tubes (valves), crystals, antenna masts etc.). The Installation Drawing Office and Mast Design sections were included in this division and provided their services to other divisions as required.

The new divisions were not companies in their own right in that they all drew upon the resources of a common Works floor. Each division, however, had its own engineering and sales forces and full authority to conduct its own business. Only in the ultimate was it responsible to the General Manager with whom the responsibility for overall policy decisions rested. The scheme at one stroke provided greater incentives to individuals and at the same time simplified control by establishing six main arteries of information into the General Manager's office instead of the former multitude of capillaries.

At the same period Mr R. J. Kemp was appointed Chief of Research, with a Deputy Chief newly arrived from English Electric in the person of Dr E. Eastwood, a physicist who had had considerable experience in radar engineering with No. 60 Group R.A.F. during the war.

One further event of particular significance occurred during the re-formative period. In 1947 Mr Sutherland returned to England via Brazil where he had some business affairs to deal with. There he had met Mr R. Telford, a Marconi man who was at that time Managing Director of Marconi Brasiliera. Mr Telford had taken his M.A. degree at Cambridge and had joined Marconi's in 1937. Thereafter he had been appointed to various posts of increasing responsibility, the latest of which had been the assignment in Brazil. On the spot, Sutherland formed a high opinion of Telford's capabilities, and when, three years later, he required a man of the right calibre as his assistant, he offered the post to Telford. The offer was accepted. Today (1967) the two are still working in the closest collaboration, Mr Sutherland as Chairman of the Company and Mr Telford as its Managing Director.

Without doubt the reorganization in 1948 of the Company's sales and administrative effort into discrete divisions was an important factor in its subsequent prosperity. A secondary but most vital circumstance was the complete preservation of the Company's basic identity and engineering outlook. Sir George Nelson, having chosen his man, was content to allow him to run the business in his own way, for the good and sufficient reason that it would be, by and large, the Nelson way. His General Manager in turn established Divisional Managers with very wide degrees of freedom, while within the divisions there were groups or sections, the Chiefs of which also exercised considerable powers of decision within their respective areas of influence.

The wisdom of those decisions taken in 1948 can best be gauged by reference to the present day. Over the years, Company expansion has necessitated an increase in the number of product divisions to thirteen but the basic principles and the 'loose rein' practice remain unaltered, having stood the test of time. Facts and figures serve to underline this; for whereas Company turnover in 1947 amounted to £3·171 million, that of 1966 was over ten times greater, at £33,000,000. Furthermore, 50 per cent of the order book of 1966 was in terms of exports, obtained against all comers in the fiercely competitive world of electronics markets.

40

Prelude to the Post-War Scene

It had been the intention to close this history at 1950 as this seemed to be a suitable time. The old Company had been revitalized by the transfusion of executive management from English Electric and was facing up to its post-war problems with quiet confidence. But no matter where an arbitrary line is drawn, something of significance always occurs a little further on.

This history is no exception. For it so happens that in the years between that of the planned termination and the present day, enough Company history has been made to fill another book. There have been two main reasons for this. One is the almost frightening acceleration in the acquisition of scientific knowledge, coupled with the phenomenal growth in electronics applications which the industry has experienced. The other, which is derivative from the first, is the Company's amoebalike partitioning into new divisions in order to take advantage of the diversity of markets which have opened.

In the year 1900 the Marconi aim was simple; it had only one purpose and that purpose was to promote wireless telegraphic communication. Today, in contrast, there is a multiplicity of targets covering radio communications (a vast and complex field in itself), line communications, sound and vision broadcasting (including, of course, colour), closed circuit television and other electro-optical systems, data transmission, automation, computers, space communications, aeronautical communications and navigational aids, radar (another diverse area), microelectronics and others. Many of these main classifications have sub-divisions which are in themselves watertight specialist compartments. The mastery of these commercial outlets has only been made possible by a commensurate expansion in research, to the point where the Marconi laboratories are the largest of their kind in Europe.

'Let us now praise famous men. . . .' says Ecclesiasticus. But it is easy to overlook a later passage in the exhortation which remarks, 'And some there be which have no memorial. . . .' It may be that the reader who

335

has followed the story so far has gained the impression that the Company's prowess was founded entirely upon the efforts of a mere handful of men; those of giant stature such as Round, Franklin and Gray. This is simply not true, although the Company undoubtedly owes them a considerable debt. And although others have been mentioned from time to time, a much greater number of able and devoted engineers have not. Their true memorial is the Company as it stands today.

These comments will apply with even greater force to the chapters which follow and because personalities will rarely be named it should not be supposed that there are none worthy of mention; on the contrary, there are so many as would make a long and tedious list. In this connection it is perhaps an opportune moment to examine the path which electronics technology has followed.

.   .   .

In the earliest years of wireless communication the apparatus used was of a simple character; it was common practice for one engineer to deal with a given installation from start to finish. He would, for example, personally select the timber for his masts, supervise its fashioning, rig the antenna and attend to every detail thereafter. Early sea-going installations were frequently manned by the engineers who had carried out the task of fitting them. Under such circumstances personalities were completely identified with the projects they undertook.

As the years passed, systems grew in complexity and team work became more and more the rule. In parallel with this, research organizations grew commensurately larger as the importance of this vital arm became more appreciated.

The start of World War II accelerated this trend. The exigencies of the desperate years that followed brought a growth of electronics usage and applications which was so vast that even the great companies in Europe and the U.S.A. became mere cogs in a mammoth machine, each making unit contributions to a system and in the process each becoming members of a team. On a wartime C.H. radar station, for example, the radar receivers were provided by one manufacturer, the transmitters by another, the transmitting antennas by a third, the calculators by a fourth, the interrogator equipment by a fifth, the radio communications equipment by a sixth – and so on. Identities were to a significant extent submerged for the common good.

This was likewise reflected in research, where the highly complex devices which were being demanded called for teams of university-trained physicists and engineers for their realization. Thus by the end of the war the trend of the 1930s had become the norm of large-scale electronics manufacture. Team-work was the order of the day, permeating the organization from research, through the development, production and the commercial framework. And with team-work comes the relative anonymity of the individual.

Whether the modern approach to scientific research may still have something to learn from the old-time inventors is a matter for careful consideration; yet protagonists of the 'mass-attack' approach can, as a defence of the method, point to such developments as the transistor, the maser, the laser, colour television, the integrated circuit and many others. Certainly 'mass-attack' has accelerated the growth of scientific knowledge to a considerable degree. Inevitably, however, it brings with it the cloak of anonymity. One suspects that not only the layman, but many electronics engineers also, would be hard put to place names alongside some of the inventions mentioned above.

The circumstance has been dwelt on at some length, partly to record the development of a minor industrial revolution but more particularly to make the point that brilliance in industrial electronic engineering was not a monopoly of a past generation. It exists today.

As with the world trend, so also within the Marconi organization. In the chapters which follow, both the brevity of the account and the modern team-work approach operate against the singling out of personalities; yet they are very much present, for all that. So, in a sense, the remainder of the narrative is a tribute to those 'which have no memorial'.

41

Developments in Radar 1945–1965

As in so many other areas, the development of aviation during World War II was truly staggering. Aircraft efficiencies had improved out of all knowledge; payloads had increased to the point where the aeroplane could compete economically as a freighter or a carrier of passengers. Additionally, the war had bred an air-minded generation by reason of the great numbers of service personnel which had been flown to and from the various theatres of war. Such circumstances made it certain that once the civil airlines of the world got into their stride, the market for commercial aviation radio equipment and navigational aids would be a big one.

The role of radar in commercial aviation was less definite. The great value of radar in wartime had been that it demanded no co-operation from the occupants of an aircraft. But in peacetime such co-operation was freely available and it seemed to many (but not to all) that aviation's navigational needs could be met by the employment of less expensive means such as direction-finders, v.h.f. radio telephones, radio beacons and other devices which, in one form or another, employed aircrew participation.

The prospect for the sale of military radar was more certain. Now that the value of this type of equipment had become apparent to all the world, many countries which had been debarred from using it or had had to be content with radars which were virtually obsolete, were known to be anxious to purchase.

At first a British-American agreement set an embargo on the sale of all but a few of the types of wartime radar equipments which the British Government had stock-piled. As time went by, however, restrictions gradually eased and the Company, which had made a modest start in selling refurbished radars in 1946, found it expedient to establish a Services Equipment Division to handle the growing business. This was formed on 14 July 1948 under the managership of Colonel E. N. Elford, formerly the Company's Assistant Sales Manager. In close co-operation with the Ministries and with each sale individually approved from the security aspect by the appropriate Authority, the new Division expanded steadily. By the end of 1948 it had £1,500,000 worth of contracts on its books.

Another significant event which occurred in 1948 was the arrival within the Company of Dr Eric Eastwood, transferred from the Nelson Laboratories of English Electric at Stafford to become the Marconi Deputy Chief of Research. He brought with him a vast enthusiasm, an incredible capacity for work and an unshakeable belief in the future of radar born of his experience with 60 Group R.A.F. during the war. He also brought a contract acquired by English Electric which called for the re-engineering of a wartime 50 cm. (type 11) radar. This was destined to play a vital part in the Company's fortunes in the markets of military and civil air traffic control.

By this time the activities of the Services Equipment Division had extended beyond the refurbishing of wartime surplus equipments to the building of new radars to wartime designs – with Ministry approval in all cases. But now a completely new turn of events materialized. Relations between the U.S.S.R. and the West had deteriorated to a degree which made it highly advisable for the British Government to look to the country's air defences. As a first step a number of wartime radar stations were refurbished and brought back into operational use; for this, Marconi's rebuilt all the C.H. transmitting arrays on the East and West Coast chains. While this was going on the Company had been entrusted with the preparation of a study contract containing recommendations for a rebuilt ground radar defence system for the R.A.F., Dr Eastwood being in overall charge of this task.

In 1949 the Air Ministry made known its intention to adopt almost wholly the recommendations made in Dr Eastwood's report; these involved the design of a new radar chain to give greatly improved performance. Thereupon Marconi's were called upon to co-operate closely with the Ministry in the designs of new stations (the permanent sites were to be supplemented by mobile equipments).

The huge contracts which followed put the Services Equipment Division and the manufacturing plant virtually on a wartime footing in view of the urgent nature of the requirements. Even so, and in spite of the additional areas acquired and the heavy recruitment of engineers which took place, still more effort was needed. English Electric acquired a former shadow factory at Accrington and more than 100 sub-contractors were eventually appointed.

The main tasks in this stupendous programme were completed by 1955, within a few months of target date. The six years it had taken formed the crucible from which the Radar Division – its name was changed in 1954 – emerged with an expertise in radar engineering which was second to none.

The story of this Division is even more remarkable when it is remembered that these vast Government contracts represented only a part of its activities, for at the same time orders were pouring in from overseas countries anxious to add radar systems to their defence schemes, while yet another section of the Division was dealing with naval requirements.

In the background the laboratories had been extremely active, not only with the Government work, but with new designs for civil and overseas military requirements, for it had been realized that the sale of re-engineered wartime equipments could not go on indefinitely. This proved to be a wise move, for by 1950 both France and the U.S.A. were beginning to offer equipments of post-war design. By that time also, civil aviation had become reorganized and the steadily increasing volume of traffic at the major airports was calling for improved methods of control. An augury for the future came in that year (1950) when the Ministry of Transport and Civil Aviation purchased Marconi radars types 13 (heightfinder) and 14 (centimetric early warning) equipments for use at London Airport and elsewhere.

It will be remembered that when Dr Eastwood joined the Company he had brought with him a Ministry contract for the engineering of the type 11 equipment, a T.R.E. experimental 50 cm. radar. This had been done as it was the Ministry's intention to use the equipment as a component in their mobile defensive radar organization.

In the course of the development, Dr Eastwood had become enthusiastic about the merits of 50 cm. working for civil radar systems, pointing out that it was amenable to the use of high power, that it could be completely crystal controlled, that its operation was virtually unaffected by cloud, precipitation, etc., and that fully coherent moving target indication could be incorporated. (This facility, known as M.T.I., discriminates between responses from aircraft and those from stationary objects such as hills and buildings near the radar site and permits these permanent echoes to be erased from the radar screens.) The advantages overwhelmed the dissentient voices which pointed out that to go to 50 cm. was completely against the trend of the day, which was towards the use of 10 cm. and 3 cm. radars. It was decided to stake the future on 50 cm. equipments.

The first equipment of this type, the S232, appeared in 1954; its performance exceeded the most optimistic expectations. No greater tribute to its advanced design can be paid than by remarking that, while it was joined later by much more powerful equipments and itself suitably modernized in detail, it was still holding a place in the 1967 catalogue.

An early development model of the S232 was installed at London Airport in 1954 for evaluation purposes, as a result of which a fully engineered version was provided in the following year. This was the precursor of a large number of sales, both to ministerial and civil authorities in this country and all over the world.

A new type of radar display employing the now-familiar 'fixed coil' principle had been developed for the R.A.F. ground stations; this could provide the facilities of multiple head selection, video mapping, trace expansion and inter-trace marking – all desirable features for efficient air traffic control. The fixed coil display was at first exclusive to the R.A.F. but in 1954, the Government granted permission to the Company for its sale to NATO countries and later, in suitably modified form, to civil airport authorities.

This device also became a best seller; it did so because it not only met existing requirements but anticipated many of the needs of the future. For the growth of air traffic and the increase of air speeds were such that the plotting of raw radar signals, using the techniques which had originated in the war, was rapidly becoming inadequate. Air traffic controllers needed more positive information at faster rates and technology was extending to meet the needs. The fixed coil display inaugurated a new era of data handling, the forerunner of the highly automated computerized systems of the present day.

Instances of developments in radar techniques in which the Company had some hand during these years include:

The transmission of radar information from the station site to a remote control centre via microwave link (demonstrated at the Farnborough Air Show, 1956).

High power (500 kW) 50 cm. radar. The success of the S232 equipment had led to the development of another radar of the same (50 kW) power which also operated on 50 cm. In 1958 this equipment, the S264, was joined by the S264A which had ten times the output. A special design feature was that its power output stage was in packaged form and could readily be added to existing S264's should the customer wish for a power increase. This output stage consisted of a high-gain power klystron; it was the first of its kind to be incorporated in a production equipment.

In 1959 the first of these 500 kW equipments came into service in New Zealand. The installation represented a considerable engineering feat as the antenna head and transmitting/receiving equipments were built on a high peak overlooking Wellington, with the radar signals passing via a radio link to a control centre at the capital's airport. The equipment is remotely controlled over the link.

In the same year it was announced that the Company was working in close collaboration with the Royal Swedish Air Board on a big military and civil radar system in Sweden. The heart of the system was a high-speed digital computer designed to solve a large number of interception problems simultaneously and to bring various categories of defence weapons – fighters, guided missiles and other anti-aircraft devices – into operation at precisely the right instant. Closed-circuit television, including large-screen colour, formed an integral part. The scheme has since been considerably extended.

In the following year, 1960, the Company exhibited a development model of a coherent parametric amplifier at the Farnborough Air Show. This aroused considerable interest in technical radar circles because of its greatly improved signal-to-noise ratio in comparison with a conventional triode r.f. amplifier. This development was taken a stage further at the 1961 Air Show when an experimental solid state parametric amplifier and mixer was on view; it employed two silicon diffused-junction (variable capacity) diodes, with an X-band klystron as a pump source.

In 1962 an experimental high brightness radar display was introduced and evaluated at London (Gatwick) Airport. This was a valuable development as the phosphors used in conventional plan position indicator displays make it necessary to operate the equipment in subdued lighting conditions. In the final aircraft approach phase, however, it is highly advantageous to the controller to have a radar display which will be bright enough to operate under conditions of high ambient lighting because the aircraft will then shortly be within visual range through the control tower windows. The bright display was subsequently put into production and has come into extensive operational use.

As is well known, radar range and bearing information is conventionally provided by one type of equipment and height-finding by a separate unit. The height-finder obtains its information by a mechanical rotation of the antenna to the general direction of the target, followed by a sweeping of its beam in elevation by means of another mechanical movement, this time a physical nodding of the antenna.

It would obviously be of considerable advantage if range, bearing and height information could be provided in one equipment. A considerable step towards this ideal would be achieved if the height-finding sweep of the lobes could be carried out without mechanical 'nodding'. As long ago as 1950, C. Cockerell (since of Hovercraft fame) and C. D. Colchester (now Assistant Director of Engineering at Marconi's) carried out research to achieve the height-finding operation electronically. This was to be done by sweeping the transmission through a band of frequencies, thereby tilting the lobes in space. A patent (No. 711273) was taken out in this connection.

Further work on this was deferred for some years but in 1962-3 the principles were successfully applied to a 10 cm. equipment. Swept frequency radar is still (1968) not in quantity production, largely because its complexity makes it uncompetitive in price with mechanically nodding height-finders, but the future may tell another story.

Only after the transistor had undergone rigorous evaluation as to performance and, above all, reliability, was it approved for incorporation in production equipment. By the early 1960s however, transistorized radar display equipments were becoming commonplace in the Company's catalogue. A similarly cautious approach has since taken place with microcircuits and these are now in turn coming into more general usage.

Other technological developments in radar which were introduced in the early 1960s include the various forms of tabular display (upon which information derived from a computer or other processor is displayed upon a screen in alpha-numeric characters) and a new approach to air traffic control, secondary radar.

Although the application was new, the basic principle of secondary radar dates back to the I.F.F. (Identification, Friend or Foe) of World War II, in which Allied aircraft were fitted with a small transmitter/receiver, the receiver of which accepted the transmitted pulses from a ground radar station and caused them to trigger the associated transmitter, which sent a distinctive signal back to the ground station, where it was displayed on a cathode ray tube. By this means the ground station acquired not only the conventional information of range, bearing and elevation, but also a positive assurance that an aircraft from which the special signal was originating must be a 'friendly'. (The converse, incidentally, was not necessarily true; an aircraft failing to exhibit the special signal might have had a failure in its I.F.F. transponder or the pilot may have forgotten to switch it on.) A switch on the airborne equipment could set the transponder into squegging oscillation as a distinctive sign of distress; unfortunately the equipment was rather prone to go into the squegging condition without the intervention of the switch so that many an aircraft was reported as being in distress when it was in fact perfectly airworthy.

But those were teething troubles. Ideally the I.F.F. signal provided two additional items of information: (a) that the aircraft was friendly (or hostile, if signals were absent) and (b) that it was not in difficulties (or alternatively, if squegging was observed, that it was). The interrogation system had another advantage in that the return signals from the aircraft were no longer passive reflections from the structure but active signals from a transmitter. Longer ranges of communication with less power could therefore be effected.

Because of the increasing load of duties placed upon the aircrew in fast-flying, complex jet airliners, the automatic transfer of information from air to ground becomes increasingly desirable as the years pass. The basic principles of the wartime I.F.F. were accordingly used as a platform upon which to build a secondary radar system (that is, one which called for a suitable transponder in the aircraft) which provided a number of channels of communication between air and ground over which a continuous flow of data could automatically be sent.

In 1963 the Marconi Company entered into a formal agreement with Compagnie Française Thomson-Houston to collaborate in the development of a secondary surveillance radar system to cover all civil and military modes of operation and satisfy all international (I.C.A.O.) and Eurocontrol requirements laid down for such equipment. The jointly-developed equipment, known as SECAR, was subsequently marketed, with installations (to date) at Brussels and Shannon.

The application of high-speed computers in radar systems has already been mentioned. The need for suitable machines brought the Company into computer manufacture in 1959, with the T.A.C. (Transistorized Automatic Computer). Concurrently with this development, concentrated research was going on into microcircuit techniques, both semiconductor integrated and thin film, and by 1962–3 this had arrived at a point where quantity manufacture could be realized. The microcircuit research findings dovetailed neatly into computer development by providing extremely fast two-state non-mechanical devices of extremely small physical size and high reliability.

As a result, the production of a second-generation computer, MENTOR, was halted and a leap-frogging operation took place to produce a new machine employing microcircuits. This equipment, named MYRIAD, was the first of its type in the world to go into production. It has subsequently sold extremely well.

In May 1961 Colonel E. N. Elford relinquished his position as Manager of the Radar Division, in order to take up special duties for the Managing Director. His place was taken by his former Deputy, Dr T. W. Straker. Colonel Elford retired in January 1963. In doing so he could look back with every satisfaction on the astonishing growth of the Division since its inception. Elford was the architect of its commercial success from its modest beginnings as a department dealing in refurbished war surplus to a thriving Division which has made the Company's name a predominant one in radar systems engineering; a division which in 1965 exported more radar equipment than all other British firms put together and which had a more comprehensive range on offer than any other in the world. As the architect he would be the first to give credit to those who had provided the building materials in the form of shrewd – indeed, inspired – research and development.

By 1965, the year in which we leave this history, no fewer than forty-five 50 cm. radars had been sold, over 50 per cent of which had been exported, and contracts to the value of many millions completed. Four out of the five civil airways surveillance radar sites in the U.K. were equipped with Marconi 50 cm. radars and the microwave links between them were also of Company manufacture. As the story closes, the Division was forming part of a huge international consortium (HUCO) which was bidding for contracts worth £100,000,000 in connection with the NATO Air Defence Ground Environment ('NADGE') project. This consortium was awarded the contracts in the following year.

It would be unjust to close the chapter without recording that a truly significant part in the story was played by various Ministries of the British Government and their associated research establishments which had on so many occasions entrusted the Division with its orders and had collaborated so closely whenever occasion demanded.

42

Developments in Aviation 1945–1965

The revolution which the war brought about in the public's attitude to air travel has already been mentioned. The situation, although not an unpleasant one for the reconstituted airlines of the immediate post-war period, brought with it problems which had scarcely existed in the 1930s.

Of these, by far the greatest was that of air traffic control. The situation had, however, been foreseen and had led to the formation of the International Civil Aviation Organization (I.C.A.O.) in December 1944. Today I.C.A.O. is responsible for a complex code of regulations and recommended practices which form standard procedure for over seventy countries.

As to the means of effecting such control, these had progressed very considerably since the pre-war days. Some of the most significant advances were:

a. The extensive development of v.h.f. air-ground-air communications, which provided a reliable service over line of sight distances.*
b. Airborne and ground station direction-finding equipment had been considerably improved.
c. Hyperbolic position-fixing systems had been evolved. (These consist, in essence, of a chain of ground stations whose special transmission signals are so inter-related as to provide all suitably equipped aircraft with periodic course-correction data.)

* The lay reader should not take the expression 'line of sight' too literally. In communications work a line of sight path is one along which a straight, unimpeded line can be drawn to join the transmitter and the receiver. The length of this line will differ in differing circumstances. Between two ground stations it would not be much greater than the distance between a given point and the horizon, although the line of sight can be extended if both stations use high antenna masts or can be sited on the tops of hills. Significantly greater line of sight ranges can be obtained if one of the co-operating stations is aboard a high flying aircraft, although there comes a point, where, in spite of the plane's altitude, the line no longer clears the earth's curvature. In the case of a ground station in communication with a synchronous satellite (i.e. one which orbits at a speed which keeps it permanently in position over a given point on the earth's surface) the line of sight path is approximately 22,000 miles.

d. The development of primary and secondary radar, both airborne and ground-based.

e. For long and medium range communications, h.f. and m.f. transmitters and receivers had also been subjected to considerable improvement, although the h.f. band was becoming overcrowded. The m.f. band was on its way out of aviation use for the same reason, and because of the band's susceptibility to static and the length of antenna demanded on the aircraft.

It will be seen from this that there was no lack of devices to aid air traffic control. The main problem (which lay with the administrative authorities) was how best to use the newer devices and the old-established ones, such as marker beacons, to maximum advantage.

In the general post-war aviation situation the Marconi Company's trading position was not unfavourable. With an experience of air radio extending back to 1910, it held important patents on many of the aviation electronic devices in current use and also had at its back the experience gained in its massive production of wartime equipments. Without delay, swords were beaten into ploughshares by designing communications sets and navigational aids which were specifically for use by civil airlines.

But if the potential market was there, so also was the competition. This was mainly from the U.S.A., where the internal airlines had not been wholly disrupted by the war (in contrast to those in Britain) and therefore provided an extensive home demand for aviation electronics. This in its turn gave the U.S.A. manufacturers a stable commercial platform from which to thrust into world markets when international airlines became fully constituted.

In order to meet this challenge the Marconi range of airborne and ground communications equipment and navigational aids was built up with all speed; airport requirements in ground radar were met by the Services Equipment Division (or Radar Division as it became in 1954). A foothold was gained with the British aviation industry and among the well-known aircraft of the period which carried Marconi equipment were the De Havilland Comet, the English Electric Canberra, the Armstrong Whitworth Apollo, the Bristol Freighter, the Handley Page Hermes IV, the Percival Prince, the Short Sealand and the Vickers Viscount.

In 1951–2 a considerable technical advance was made in airborne automatic direction-finders with the development of the AD722. This was a sub-miniature radio compass designed for m.f. operation and produced under heavy security classification for the R.A.F. for use principally in fighter aircraft. With an all-up weight of under 10 kg, it was the smallest and lightest of its type in the world. One of the technical innovations it introduced was the departure from the rotating-loop type of antenna in favour of a Bellini-Tosi system which used a sealed iron-cored crossed loop antenna in conjunction with a goniometer, the shaft of which was directly coupled to a scale pointer. This arrangement permitted the antenna to be recessed into the fuselage, with a complete absence of wind-drag. The AD722 was extensively used by the R.A.F. in its fighters and fighter-bombers and was not released from security classification until 1955, when it attracted much attention at its first public showing (which was at the Paris Air Show). Thereafter it achieved massive sales throughout the world.

The fixed-loop system was a significant landmark in design and was later universally adopted. The early direction-finders had large loops mounted externally on the fuselage and were rotated manually to obtain a bearing. This arrangement was followed by the introduction of a smaller loop which could be fitted either internally or externally; in the latter event it was surrounded by a stream-lined casing. The loop was motor-driven and could either be manually controlled or switched to automatic operation; on 'auto' the loop rotated until its axis lay along the line of maximum signal strength, when it would stop. Ambiguity of bearing was avoided by the use of a sensing antenna.

In the immediate post-war years, considerable research was carried out by many companies with the object of designing an airborne navigational aid which would be independent of all ground stations in its operation. The only instrument in this category at that time was the conventional compass.

In order to appreciate the need for a self-contained device it must be remembered that aircraft are in motion through a medium which is itself in motion, and so there can be no fixed relationship between speed through the air and speed over the ground. As an extreme example early types of aircraft could be flying at an indicated airspeed of perhaps seventy knots while remaining virtually stationary over a landmark, if the head wind was of sufficient force.

Rarely, however, does an aircraft experience a direct head or tail wind; far more often it is flying in a cross-wind of varying intensity. This causes the machine to fly crab-fashion at an angle to the direction in which its nose is pointing. The drift angle, as it is called, must be allowed for in flying a course; but up until the 1950s no cockpit device existed that would give the pilot this information instantaneously and continuously. True, both the ground speed and drift can be calculated from information derived from ground stations but this inevitably refers to conditions which occurred in past time, since when a change in wind velocity might well have imposed an entirely new set of conditions of which the pilot would be unaware. Furthermore, such calculations are only possible where a chain of such ground stations exist and there are still a great many parts of the world where they do not.

It will be seen from this that a self-contained airborne navigational aid which provided instant information on ground speed and drift angle was highly desirable and a considerable amount of research was going on in this connection, in Britain, the U.S.A. and other countries. One possible line of approach was to measure the physical changes which occur when a moving body changes its speed or direction, and, indeed, inertial guidance systems are now in development, but these, although acceptable for short-time flights (such as those of guided weapons) present formidable engineering problems when applied to long-distance, day in, day out, flights as performed by commercial aircraft.

In the late 1940s an intensive investigation into the various possibilities was being carried out at the Telecommunications Research Establishment (T.R.E.) of the Ministry of Supply and it was there that J. E. Clegg (then of T.R.E.) designed the first experimental self-contained airborne navigational aid to give promise. This was not an inertial system; instead, it made use of the well-known 'doppler effect'.

This derives its name from Christian Johann Doppler, the celebrated Austrian physicist who, in 1842, published a paper on the behaviour of light and sound sources when in motion relative to an observer. Doppler found that the frequency of the waves emitted by such sources appeared to the observer to increase when the source was approaching him and to decrease as it receded. (Familiar instances of this are the shrill note of a locomotive's whistle as a train approaches at speed and its dying fall as the train recedes, and the shift towards the red end of the visible spectrum which is noted from a star which is moving rapidly away from our own solar system.)

The important aspect of this effect as far as its practical application is concerned is that the observed amount of increase or decrease in frequency is in direct relationship to the speed of the source relative to the observer. The difficulty lies in measuring the difference in frequency accurately.

349

T.R.E. carried the experimental work to a point where a practical device seemed feasible and then awarded a development contract to Marconi's. At the Great Baddow laboratories the project was continued under the leadership of M. Morgan; experimental models were produced and given flight trials by the R.A.F. With the basic research completed the prototype was taken over by a team led by G. E. Beck at the Writtle establishment where the design was translated into a fully engineered form.

By 1952 a number of doppler equipments were available to the R.A.F. for evaluation and lessons learned from the trials were incorporated into the final version, which went into quantity production in 1954, for use in the R.A.F. and (later) in the air forces of certain Commonwealth governments. The design and development work had been carried out in conditions of secrecy under the code name 'Green Satin'. Not until another two years had elapsed (i.e. in 1956) was security lifted to the point where it was permissible to speak of the existence of this 'black box'.

The AD2000, as it was termed, was a pulsed doppler which provided the requisite information as to ground speed and drift by measuring the frequency difference between beams of radio energy transmitted earthward from the aircraft and the scattered energy which returned from the earth's surface as a consequence. These measurements, together with data from the aircraft's gyro compass, were fed into a small digital computer which processed it to provide an automatic and continuous flow of navigational information which could include immediate position in latitude and longitude, track guidance, distance run and distance to go, and estimated time of arrival.

This was the first doppler navigator in the world to go into production. Three years later (1957) with the security classification lifted to some extent, the Company were able to announce that a doppler navigator for civil airlines, the AD2300 was in production. This equipment differed from the military doppler in various ways, notably in that it employed a continuous wave system instead of the pulsed approach.

The advent of this equipment was received with caution by the airlines and with undisguised suspicion by their aircrews. To the former it was just another black box which would have to justify its existence beyond question before inclusion, and to the latter it represented yet another addition to the welter of instrumentation in the modern airliner. Understandable sentiments, both.

However, certain airlines agreed to give the doppler equipment a trial under routine flight conditions, but usually with a Marconi engineer flying with it at first to brief the aircrew on its operation. Once familiarization had been achieved, the conversion of the crew members was usually rapid, the general attitude being summed up by the captain who stated in his report, 'Having now flown with doppler I would be much happier with it aboard than without it.'

In due course sampling orders were placed by the major airline operators and later, after stringent evaluations, whole fleets were equipped with Marconi dopplers. As is usual with inventions, other organizations which had been researching along similar lines were quickly off their marks and into production and today the presence of doppler navigators on intercontinental airliners is the rule rather than the exception. The evolution of this device has been given at some length as an excellent instance of how a government Ministry can, and frequently does, benefit industry, not only by placing initial development contracts but also by creating commercial 'fall-out' in due season.

Concurrent with the doppler development, active research was going on to anticipate the needs of the future in new designs of automatic direction-finder and communications equipment. It was evident that aircraft were going to fly faster and faster and that air traffic would become denser and denser as the years went by. With a large number of instruments to watch over and a decreasing amount of time in which to make decisions the pilot and navigator urgently needed relief from the burden of finnicky tuning adjustments to their radio equipment.

A new automatic direction-finder, the AD712, introduced in 1957, made aviation history by being the first airborne equipment in the world to abandon manual tuning as the means of station selection. Instead, any desired frequency between 100–415 kHz and 490–1799·5 kHz was available in steps of 0·5 kHz, merely by turning a calibrated switch. This was made possible by the development of a completely new type of crystal control which locked to within ± 50 Hz of the chosen frequency – a degree of accuracy which had never before been attained in this category of equipment.

Another feature of the AD712 was the use of a Bellini-Tosi cross-loop fixed antenna mounted in a resin-filled fibre glass casing, designed for external mounting on the fuselage but imposing negligible drag. This was not, however, an idea adapted from the sub-miniature AD722 mentioned earlier; it was rather the reverse, for the design of 'big brother' had begun before that of the sub-miniature. The latter, however, was a Ministry order of high priority and the philosophy of the fixed-loop/goniometer combination was transferred in a scaled-down form from the AD712, the development of which took second place.

It is perhaps of interest to mention briefly here a battle lost. Aeronautical Radio Incorporated (ARINC) had become a powerful organization which laid down standards and parameters to which American manufacturers of aviation equipment conformed by agreement. In a David-and-Goliath attempt to fight off American influence, the new automatic direction-finder was not designed to ARINC standards. It was an abortive gesture, for in the circumstances it stood virtually no chance of being used in American aircraft. Thus although the AD712 sold extremely well in the home market and in areas of the world where the American influence was not dominant, it is a fair assumption that its advanced design would have made a significant impact on the American market had it conformed to U.S. standards. The lesson was learned. The next range of equipments was manufactured to conform to ARINC standards.

Nowhere is reliability so important as in aviation equipment. It was because of this that the Company (and, indeed, the majority of its competitors) continued to manufacture valved transmitters and receivers for some years after the invention of the transistor. Yet at the same time it was almost painfully clear that the solid-state device was something which aviation electronics designers had long wished for. Its small size and weight, its relatively small power supply requirements (no heater windings and low h.t. supplies) and its modest cooling demands were all of considerable value in airborne equipment. The unknown factor was reliability and, indeed, caution was soon seen to be justified, for the early transistors proved to be too sensitive to temperature changes and vulnerable to power supply surges.

By 1956, however, very considerable improvement in transistor performances had been effected and the solid state device was already becoming widely used in other areas of electronics manufacture. One thing remained in doubt, its reliability under the environmental conditions of an aircraft in regular service; it was believed to be satisfactory but to believe is not the same as to be sure.

Two parallel plans were put into effect; one emphasized the doubt, the other the belief. The former was an advanced development programme in which transistorized amplifiers of all types and operating frequencies were subjected to far more strenuous conditions than any aircraft would provide. The latter was the implementation of designs for a whole new range of airborne equipments to be built around transistors.

As the designs evolved, the components associated with them were rigorously tested. From these tests, clear patterns of secondary causes of failure emerged over and above the well-understood primary causes. One by one these were analysed and eradicated. Mechanisms, too, were subjected to conditions which were considerably more severe than would ever be encountered in service. Severe standards were set in quality control procedures, performance testing and monitored 'soak' testing.

Four years were taken over these programmes, and when all was done the resulting equipments, designated the 'Sixty Series', were introduced at the Farnborough Air Show, 1960. They set new standards in reduced size, weight and power consumption and (as was subsequently proved) in reliability and ease of maintenance. These equipments became very widely used in British and overseas aircraft and the unprecedented amount of research and development which went into them was in due course amply justified by the contribution of many millions of pounds which they made to Company turnover.

Progress in aviation in the post-war years has been truly spectacular. Before the war the general public opinion was that civil flying was only for rich fools. The war changed that outlook almost completely; today we find the working man and his family flying to and from foreign countries as a normal part of the annual holidays. Businessmen and engineers are also inveterate users of the airlines because of the economic saving in doing so.

Such demands have not only brought about a staggering growth in the manufacture of civil aircraft but also in the number and complexity of the electronic devices, both ground-based and airborne, which control the air traffic and aid its navigation. The time has long passed when the electronics equipment was an after-thought, to be stuffed away in odd places in the aircraft; today it is vital, almost to the point where the airliner is designed around its electronics systems. A similar situation also exists in the design of military aircraft, the operation of which depends so heavily on 'black boxes'.

In the furtherance of safety in the air – and the aircraft is statistically the safest form of mechanized transport – the Marconi Company has played its part.

43

Sound Broadcasting 1945–1965

Even before World War II the world's broadcasting authorities had become concerned at the prospect of an acute shortage of available frequencies and the constant increase in co-station interference. For a while it had seemed that international agreement and the development of the crystal-controlled oscillator would serve to keep order; unfortunately, the benefits of crystal control were largely offset by the general increase in transmitter powers which had been a marked feature of the war years.

With the l.f., m.f. and h.f. broadcasting bands over-full the B.B.C. had to look to the higher frequencies, and in particular to the 87·5 MHz–100 MHz band which was allocated to broadcasting but was virtually empty. Towards the end of World War II the matter was being given active consideration.

If new stations were to be built to operate in this frequency band, another important question had to be settled, namely the type of modulation to be used. For many years amplitude modulation (in which the audio signals are impressed upon the amplitude of the radio frequency carrier) had been unchallenged. Now it had a rival in frequency modulation. In f.m. the carrier amplitude remains constant and the audio signals are applied to vary the frequency. This approach had gained considerable favour in the U.S.A. and by 1944 it was well established in that country with more than 500,000 f.m. receivers in use.

Frequency modulation was not in itself new; a form of f.m. had been used as long ago as 1902 in connection with the Poulsen arc. It was then forgotten until the early 1920s when the Westinghouse Company in the U.S.A. worked on it briefly. For some years before this Major Edwin Armstrong of the U.S.A. had been doing a considerable amount of work on static interference – at the time an apparently unrelated subject. Another investigator in this field was H. J. Round of the Marconi Company who had patented various anti-static circuits. The two met and exchanged notes during the 1914–18 War; a firm friendship developed.

Armstrong carried out much experimental work in devising anti-static circuits but without significant success. Eventually he came to the realization that the effect of a static discharge was to modulate a carrier in amplitude and there seemed little prospect of developing a circuit which could discriminate at all times between the natural and the man-made amplitude modulation. This channelled his thoughts towards other forms of modulation and in particular the neglected f.m.

It is not within the province of this history to relate the story of Armstrong's long struggle to perfect his new system and of the diffi-culties he encountered in convincing the American manufacturers and broadcasting authorities of the worth of his invention. That he did so at last is a tribute to a great inventor, to whom we are also in debt for the supersonic heterodyne (superhet) receiver. (There are, incidentally, some of Armstrong's letters to Round and an early f.m. receiver which he presented to his British friend, in the Science Museum, London.)

So, to return to the B.B.C. In addition to the project of building v.h.f. sound stations there was also a choice of modulation systems to make. Just before the end of the Second World War H. L. Kirke, then Chief of the B.B.C. Research Department (and one of the Writtle broadcasting pioneers) mounted an investigation into the possibilities of inaugurating a national f.m. system. The Marconi Company, looking to the future and with the export market much in mind, had f.m. transmitting equipment in an advanced state of development.

As a result of H. L. Kirke's experimental work at Alexandra Palace, Oxford and Moorside Edge (near Huddersfield), the Government, in a White Paper, recommended that the B.B.C. should press ahead with the work on f.m. transmission while continuing the l.f. and m.f. services for an indefinite period.

Early in 1947 the Corporation placed a contract with Marconi's for a 25 kW f.m. broadcasting transmitter and in March of the following year work began on a new B.B.C. transmitting station on Wrotham Hill in Kent. This was completed by August 1950.

In order to assess f.m. against a.m., two sets of transmitting equipment were installed, both of Marconi manufacture. One was amplitude modulated, operating on a frequency of 93·80 MHz (3·2 m.) and having an unmodulated power output of 18 kW. The frequency modulated equipment had an output of 25 kW and radiated at a mean carrier frequency of 91·4 MHz (3·28 m.) with a maximum frequency deviation of ± 75 kHz. It incorporated the patented Marconi F.M.Q. modulation system developed by W. S. Mortley at the Baddow Research

Laboratories. In this a quartz crystal oscillator is connected through a quarter-wave network to a balanced modulator, the susceptance of which varies with the modulating signal; this in turn varies the frequency of the crystal oscillator. Both transmitters were controlled and monitored from a single control console.

The high-gain antenna system, which was designed by the B.B.C., was common to both types of transmission. The antenna consisted of a cylinder 110 ft. long and $6\frac{1}{2}$ ft. in diameter; it incorporated eight tiers, each consisting of four folded slot radiators spaced at 90° intervals on the circumference. This arrangement provided omni-directional radiation, horizontally polarized.

This antenna was manufactured by Marconi's who also developed and manufactured the feeder system. It was mounted on a 360 ft. lattice steel mast designed and built by British Insulated Callenders Construction Company Ltd.

The antenna and transmission line were designed to provide either the simultaneous radiation of one 18 kW a.m. and one 25 kW f.m. transmission or three 25 kW f.m. transmissions in the 87·5 MHz to 95 MHz band, the latter thus permitting the simultaneous radiation of the Home, Light and Third programmes* if the experimental period showed that f.m. was the superior system.

Rarely can an experiment of this size have been mounted; certainly not in Britain. For here was a station costing somewhere in the region of £250,000, transmitting six days a week to an official audience of only fifty or sixty technical observers. Yet it was necessary, for a long-term period of high-power testing was essential before committing the whole country to an f.m. service.

From these comparison trials f.m. emerged the winner. The coverage of the Greater London area was admirable and the service area of the Wrotham station extended as far as Oxford. The quality of reproduction was excellent.

Early in 1954 the B.B.C. placed orders with Marconi's for twenty-six v.h.f. f.m. transmitters and these were followed a little later by others which brought the total to thirty-eight. Two, each of 10 kW power, were to be used in parallel at Wrotham, while the remainder, of 4 kW each, were for use in parallel pairs, six to a station; two to radiate the Home service, two the Light and two the Third. As new television stations were being built at the same time the masts at these were designed to carry both television and sound f.m. antennas.

* The B.B.C.'s Third Programme service had begun (on m.f.) in October 1946.

From that time to the present day the Company has supplied very considerable numbers of f.m. transmitters of various powers to the B.B.C. and to many overseas countries, particularly those in Scandinavia.

At the outset the B.B.C. had hoped that the inherent freedom from interference and capacity for high-quality reproduction which f.m. offers would 'sell' the service to the point where medium-frequency receivers would eventually become obsolete. So far there is little sign of this and it seems that the medium-frequency service will be with us into the indefinite future. Two factors are involved in the circumstance; one is that the average purchaser of a domestic receiver demands 'that it shall get foreign stations', even though he may subsequently make little or no use of this capability; the other is that, in general, receiver manufacturers have too often sacrificed quality of reproduction by building down to a price.

It was fortunate therefore that the B.B.C., in the immediate post-war years, set about improving its medium-frequency service in parallel with its plans for f.m. This improvement was desirable since there were many pockets of indifferent reception of the medium-wave stations in various parts of the country and it had been realized from the beginning that the service would have to continue for many years.

The most promising road to improvement was considered to lie in the provision of a large number of low-powered stations operating on shared wavelengths, each station being strategically placed to cover a 'black spot' with the same programme as the main station. The biggest obstacle to this project lay in the scarcity of skilled engineers to man them; indeed, in view of the large number of booster stations envisaged, it would be impossible to muster such a strength of staff.

The main hope for getting the project off the ground lay in the provision of unmanned stations, for during the war years a fair degree of success had been achieved with unattended low-power telecommunications transmitters. In an attempt to meet the need the Marconi Company, shortly after the war, began the design of a small m.f. broadcasting transmitter which would be capable of operating for long periods without attention.

The complete equipment consisted of three discrete transmitters, each of 660 W output, operating in parallel via a combining unit. Remote control was effected from a distant 'parent' station by the imposition of coded 'tones' or pulses on the lines over which the programme was fed, or by the use of time clocks.

The three transmitters operated on a common frequency and into a common antenna system. Each incorporated an automatic monitor which gave a continuous check on the audio and radio frequency stages; should one transmitter develop a fault it would automatically switch itself off, the remaining two continuing the service at 4/9 original power; if two of the three failed, the third would continue at 1/9 original power.

This equipment, the B.D.210C, proved extremely successful and large numbers of these and subsequent types of booster (or gap filler) stations have been used by the B.B.C. and overseas broadcasting authorities.

In view of this success it was natural that attention should turn to the possibility of running high-power stations unattended. Here, however, a much more complex situation existed, for whereas the small transmitters used air-cooled valves, the high-power transmitters of the period employed water-cooled valves in their main stages. Water-cooling (pioneered, incidentally, by Marconi's) is basically efficient but demands a complex of heat exchangers, pumps, filters, water insulating columns and water-flow interlock devices and these are not conducive to easy remote control.

This main barrier was removed shortly after the war when, in close collaboration with Marconi's, the English Electric Valve Co. began the manufacture of high-power air-cooled valves. Immediately, the B.B.C. and the Marconi Company began a joint project in unattended high-power transmitter design to such effect that in January 1952 a 200 kW m.f. installation was put into unattended operation at the B.B.C.'s Daventry station, carrying the Third Programme service. This installation, which is remotely controlled from another building on the station, has proved eminently satisfactory over the years and marked the beginning of an important new phase in the simplification of transmitter operation.

(It is perhaps fitting that the installation should have been at Daventry, where the B.B.C., a quarter of a century earlier, took delivery of their first high-power low-frequency broadcasting transmitter from the Marconi Company. This transmitter, which remained in service until 1948, had replaced the historic 5XX which had originally radiated the B.B.C. l.f. broadcasting service from the Chelmsford Works.)

The pioneering of unattended transmitter design for low-, medium- and high-power broadcasting proved to be an intelligent appraisal of market requirements. The shortage of highly-skilled engineers was by no means peculiar to Britain; in particular, new nations were emerging which urgently needed their own national radio networks but which had neither the time nor the resources to train broadcasting engineers in quantity. To all such the simplicity of operation which Marconi's offered in a new range of air-cooled transmitters proved invaluable. In addition to the requirements of the newcomers to broadcasting, a heavy demand was also experienced from old and highly-valued customers – Finland, Denmark, Norway, Argentina, Egypt, South Africa, India, Pakistan, Cyprus and many others.

More recent techniques for the higher-power transmitters have veered away somewhat from air-cooled to vapour-cooled valves. This is mentioned as illustrating how research work can sometimes lie dormant for many years, awaiting an appropriate time to grow to fruition. For vapour-cooling is no new idea; it was first put forward in 1933 by P. E. Privett, a Marconi engineer, and was subsequently patented (No. 432891) in August 1935. It was not, however, commercially exploited until well into the 1950s when the demand arose for even higher powers than could conveniently be provided by air-cooled valves; this brought about a re-investigation of the possibilities of vapour-cooling. The method employed bears only a superficial resemblance to that of water-cooling and is far more efficient; for a given flow of water, vapour-cooling will dissipate some twenty-seven times as much thermal energy as does a water-cooling system.

Another important innovation in high-power broadcasting was the development of the Tyler high-efficiency Class C circuit for power amplifiers. This has been used to excellent purpose in the Company's high-power m.f. transmitters and is also employed under licence by other manufacturing organizations.

In recent years there has also been a trend towards the use of solid state devices, both for high-voltage, high-power rectification and in various stages of the transmitter proper. The present high reliability of high-power solid state rectifiers owes much to development work begun in the Company in the early 1950s and continued thereafter. The use of solid state devices has now reached the point where, in a current Marconi 10 kW sound broadcasting equipment there is only one thermionic valve, the final amplifier. The increases in simplicity of operation and reliability, together with the reductions in physical size of broadcasting transmitters, have, over the two decades under discussion, been remarkable.

Transmitter development work within an organization such as Marconi's is clearly the combined efforts of a highly-skilled team, each member of which makes valuable contributions to the design. In such circumstances it is invidious to single out one name at the expense of the others; yet this account would be incomplete without reference to B. N. MacLarty, the Company's Engineer-in-Chief between 1954 and 1963.

B. N. MacLarty joined Marconi's in 1921, just in time to be in at the birth of electronic aids for civil aviation. As a youthful engineer he fitted the first airborne radio equipment (the types AD1 and AD2) into civil aircraft. He was also intimately concerned with the start of British broadcasting, being one of the team which built the pioneer sound broadcasting station 2-MT at Writtle, near Chelmsford. This, it may be remembered, was the first station in this country to provide a regular series of programmes.

In 1926 he transferred to the B.B.C. Research Department, continuing to work on transmitters. In his twenty-one years with the British Broadcasting Corporation he was responsible for the design and construction of all their main stations, including the 100 kW h.f. transmitters at Daventry. In 1935-6 he directed the design and installation of the B.B.C.'s first television station (Alexandra Palace).

He rejoined Marconi's in 1947 as deputy engineer-in-chief and succeeded G. M. Wright as Engineer-in-Chief on the death of the latter in 1954. During B. N. MacLarty's period of office many notable broadcasting transmitter designs were evolved and these are now in wide service in this country and throughout the world.

44

Developments in Television 1945–1965

It will be recalled that the B.B.C. television high definition service began in 1936, using Marconi transmitters and antenna and an E.M.I. modulator and studio equipment. The complete system had been provided by a company registered in 1934 as the Marconi–E.M.I. Television Co. Ltd., a fusion of the television interests of both manufacturers.

Upon the outbreak of war, the London (Alexandra Palace) station, which was the only one in the British Isles, closed down for the duration. The final pictures were those of a Mickey Mouse cartoon, the closing words of which, appropriately enough, were 'I t'ank I go 'ome' – a catch-phrase of the time deriving from the famous Hollywood actress Greta Garbo. There was no closing-down speech. Just 'I t'ank I go 'ome'. Then silence for the next seven years. The blank screens were symbolic of the trading aspirations of Marconi–E.M.I. Ltd.

But when the end of the war approached, collaboration between the television engineering elements of Marconi and E.M.I. began again. One outcome of this was a proposal that the pioneering standards of 405 lines positive modulation should be abandoned for a higher line standard. In the U.S.A. a public service operating on 525 lines and using negative modulation had been operating since 1941 and it was argued by Marconi–E.M.I. that as only a relative handful of television receivers existed in the London area (all at least seven years old), the re-start of the service would be an excellent opportunity to raise the line standard, 525 lines, negative modulation, being favoured.

To give substance to this opinion, television equipment using negative modulation was built. It was assembled at the E.M.I. plant at Hayes, Middlesex, after the war at the time when a committee under Lord Hankey was investigating the future of television on behalf of the Government. Lord Hankey's committee was invited to inspect the operation of the equipment, which provided an improved picture with no white flashes from static interference. Strangely, the committee never made the journey to Hayes and when its report was published its main recommendation was that the B.B.C. should recommence the service on the original standards. Thus was a golden opportunity missed. On 7 June 1946 the television service was resumed from Alexandra Palace, using the pre-war equipment.

It was at this time that the Marconi Company was experiencing a considerable internal crisis. Behind-the-scenes negotiations concerning the English Electric take-over had been going on for some considerable while past and within the Marconi senior management the issue was not seriously in doubt. The Company would come into the English Electric Group, and soon.

This situation necessitated some new thinking in many directions, one of which was the future role of Marconi's in television. The crux of the matter was this: the Company itself was debarred by prior agreement from offering thermionic valves or kindred devices for sale. If, however, it became a part of English Electric there would be nothing to prevent that Company from entering the valve market, which would naturally include the manufacture and sale of television camera tubes.

One important consequence of this would be to upset the pre-war Marconi relationship with E.M.I. The formation of Marconi–E.M.I. Television Ltd. was in no sense an amalgamation between the two companies as a whole; only their television interests were involved. These interests were complementary; Marconi's possessed the transmitter expertise, E.M.I. the Emitron camera and particularly the skills of camera tube manufacture; neither company was in active competition with the other and so a *mariage de convenance* was strictly logical at the time of its inception.

As a takeover was almost certain to take place the fundamental question was whether the Company should extend its activities to include television studio equipment in general and camera channels in particular, thus putting it in direct competition with E.M.I. Although (in the event of an English Electric takeover) Sir George Nelson would without doubt have the final say in the matter, he would be guided in his decision by the views of the Marconi management.

The decision involved too great an element of crystal ball–gazing to be an easy one to make. For one thing, there was at that time little or no indication that television would ever attain the popularity of sound radio. The three pre-war years had seen only about 2,000 licences issued – a painfully slow rate of growth. If this trend was maintained in the post-war period the inevitable outpouring of money into camera research would yield no significant return.

Another factor on the 'against' side was that although the Marconi valve laboratories were highly experienced in general thermionic work, the skills did not extend to camera tube manufacture. Even if camera tubes were 'bought in', the manufacture of cameras was an unknown area.

Last, but not least, the decision to gamble would inevitably mean the dissolution of the Marconi–E.M.I. television partnership which had served well enough in the building of the London station and would no doubt continue to do so. Dissolution would mean the automatic creation of a formidable competitor which already possessed the thoroughly proven Emitron and Super-Emitron camera designs.

As a probing exercise, Marconi engineers, sent to the U.S.A. to report on the current state of the art, returned with some moderately encouraging news. Television sales were showing signs of a boom, while, on the technical side, the orthicon camera tube which had been developed there before the war had undergone considerable subsequent improvement and had emerged as the image orthicon. This device, which embodies principles different from those of the iconoscope or Emitron type of tube, possessed certain advantages. Its cylindrical shape made a simplified camera design and housing possible. Electrically it eliminated the spurious shading effects associated with the early iconoscopes and it was more sensitive and could therefore be used at lower lighting levels. Unfortunately, however, these advantages could only occasionally be realized in selected laboratory tubes; quantity production was another matter. The first image orthicons were like the little girl in the rhyme; when they were good they were very very good and when they were bad (which, more often than not, they were) they were horrid.

As a stop gap expedient the Marconi Company utilized its cross-licensing agreements with the Radio Corporation of America and purchased existing camera designs and those of associated equipments from that source. These were re-engineered Marconi-fashion to become the Mark I camera channel. This used American three-inch image orthicon tubes.

In view of the hazards it is surprising to find that a decision was made to go into production with television studio equipment. This act of faith – for it seemed to be little else at that time – was followed by the English Electric takeover in August 1946. One of the consequences of this was the reconstitution of the Marconi valve laboratory as the English Electric Valve Company Limited. By 1947 work was in hand for the development of an image orthicon camera tube.

With the London television station in service again the B.B.C. invited tenders for the installation of a second transmitting station to be located at Sutton Coldfield near Birmingham. This brought the first crunch, for E.M.I. Ltd. had retaliated by actively moving into the Marconi home ground – the transmitter market – and tendered for the contracts as a competitor. In the event E.M.I. were awarded the responsibility for the high-power vision transmitter and Marconi's provided the high-power sound transmitter, the medium-power vision and sound equipments, the antenna and the feeder systems. The alliance was at an end; the Marconi–E.M.I. Television Company was officially dissolved in 1948. The Sutton Coldfield station came on the air on 17 December 1949.

The immediate prospect in the camera field was not encouraging. The B.B.C. had evaluated the Marconi Mark 1 camera and were not impressed with its studio performance. The Super Emitrons under the controlled lighting conditions of a studio were undoubtedly superior. The prospects for sales of the Mark 1 were, however, somewhat more hopeful for outside broadcasting work, for when dealing with a scene under natural lighting (and in particular under overcast conditions) the sensitivity of the image orthicon showed up to advantage. In this field the B.B.C. was at least interested.

The newly formed (1948) Broadcasting Division was not unduly despondent. Overseas, the market was showing some promise. In September 1949 the Division had staged the world's first public demonstration of 625-line large screen television at the International Television Exhibition in Milan. This had impressed the Italian broadcasting authorities and it was hoped that orders would be placed. (In due course they were, and on a large scale, both for transmitters and studio equipment.) Only six Mark 1 cameras had been made; these were guinea-pigs from which an improved strain could be bred. Much had been learned from them in a short time and already a Mark 1B, a considerable improvement, was on its way. Heartening too was the promise in the image orthicon approach and the thought that the camera's dependence on American tubes might soon be at an end with the development of English Electric Valve Co.'s model.

This feeling of optimism received a fillip in 1950 when the Mark 1B was accepted by the B.B.C. who began to make increasing use of these cameras in their numerous outside broadcast exercises. On 27 August 1950 television spanned the English Channel for the first time with an outside broadcast from Calais and on September 30 the first live air-to-ground television broadcast from an aircraft in flight took place. Marconi image orthicon cameras were used on both occasions.

By this time the B.B.C. were pushing ahead rapidly with their plans for television coverage of the British Isles. The service came to the North of England on 12 October 1951 when the Holme Moss station began transmissions. This station, at that time the most powerful in the world, was all-Marconi. The Corporation's plans were well advanced for further stations at Kirk o'Shotts (Scotland) and Wenvoe (near Cardiff) with others to follow at Pontop Pike (Yorkshire), Divis (Northern Ireland), Les Platons (Channel Islands) and Meldrum (near Aberdeen). Still more were in the planning stage.

On the studio front, a Mark II camera had been developed which, it was hoped, would break into that market. Its specification included a 4-lens turret, an electronic viewfinder and, for the first time, an English Electric Valve Co. three-inch image orthicon.

An early order for these cameras came from the United Nations organization for use at the U.N. Headquarters building. Three Mark II's were permanently installed. This camera was also chosen to provide large screen pictures at the Telekinema at the Festival of Britain. The great breakthrough into the studio market came in 1951 with overseas contracts for the supply and installation of complete television services (transmitters, antennas, cameras and associated studio equipment) in Canada, Spain and Bolivia. At home, the B.B.C. ordered six Mark II camera channels and associated equipment for their new Lime Grove studios. The Broadcasting Division were over the hump in camera manufacture and from this time onward orders multiplied considerably. By 1953, well over £1,000,000 worth of camera channels had been sold.

A heavy demand for transmitters was also being experienced. The Kirk o'Shotts station which came into service on 14 March 1952, used Marconi sound transmitters, medium-power vision transmitter and antenna system. Wenvoe (Cardiff), the fifth B.B.C. station, was similarly equipped when it came on the air on 15 August 1952. A month earlier an all-Marconi station (transmitters and studio equipment) was ordered for Venezuela. Other equipments were being exported to Canada, the U.S.A., Italy, Yugoslavia, Siam, Australia and Japan.

On 21 August 1953, the B.B.C.'s Studio E at Lime Grove came into service, using the six Mark II cameras mentioned earlier. This was a significant occasion, for it was the first on which the B.B.C. had relied solely on image orthicon cameras in a studio. The provision of the Mark

II's was a temporary measure, pending delivery of a new type of camera which embodied a radical development in image orthicon camera tubes. Behind this lies an interesting facet of technical history.

The story goes back to 1947 and a visit to the U.S.A. by G.E. Partington, a senior engineer of the Company. At the Radio Corporation of America's Lancaster plant he saw an experimental image orthicon which had originally been developed for the United States Navy; the tube incorporated a light-sensitive mosaic of $4\frac{1}{2}$-inch cross-section instead of the standard 3-inch. This tube had considerable disadvantages; it was physically unwieldy, demanding a long camera housing and long lenses, while its sensitivity was considerably lower than that of a 3-inch tube. Its only merit was its low-noise performance.

At that time R.C.A. had just developed the Vidicon photo-conductive camera tube, a device which was much simpler in construction than an image orthicon. High hopes were entertained for this new tube and as a consequence work on the $4\frac{1}{2}$-inch image orthicon had been all but abandoned.

One man at R.C.A., O. Schade, had been carrying out work on image processes, using sample $4\frac{1}{2}$-inch tubes, of which a few had been made. These had given Schade a firm belief in the latent possibilities of the $4\frac{1}{2}$-inch tube and during a visit by another Marconi engineer, L. C. Jesty, the R.C.A. man demonstrated the device to his visitor, who was considerably impressed.

Later that year Partington again visited R.C.A. and also saw the $4\frac{1}{2}$-inch tube demonstrated by Schade. It was microphonic; it had a poor target; but Partington stated in his subsequent report that it was the finest picture he had ever seen – at least, in areas where the target was good. It resolved 800 lines/picture height all over; it had a signal-to-noise ratio of better than 40 dB, while redistribution effects and electronic 'ghosts' were virtually absent.

Partington became a $4\frac{1}{2}$-inch enthusiast on the spot and on his return he and Jesty urged their chief, L. H. Bedford, to authorize the development of $4\frac{1}{2}$-inch camera tubes. But the domestic upheaval of complete Company reorganization, and in particular the creation of the English Electric Valve Co., delayed matters and it was not until 1951 that Bedford got agreement for E.E.V. to develop $4\frac{1}{2}$-inch image orthicons and eventually manufacture them. Concurrently, Marconi's were to design a new camera around it.

Manufacture of the $4\frac{1}{2}$-inch target proved a particular nightmare; rejects in the early stages were almost one hundred per cent. Other problems arose because it had been ambitiously decided to lengthen the image section considerably in order to provide extra magnification, thus permitting the use of lenses of the same size as employed with the 3-inch.

There were many occasions when those involved in the project wished that Schade of R.C.A. had kept the prototype tube to himself and all the time (recalled Partington) there was the chilling thought that the excellent picture quality he and Jesty had witnessed might have owed as much to the genius of O. Schade as to the construction of the tube itself.

The camera design also posed major problems, most of them deriving from the dimensions of the long, thick tube it had to accommodate. In these matters the advice of the B.B.C. had been sought at an early stage and the camera design proceeded in close collaboration with the Corporation's engineers.

Gradually the problems, both with tube and camera, began to sort themselves out and after three years' intensive work the day arrived when a realistic demonstration could be given. As a result of this the B.B.C. ordered the cameras for use at Studio E, Lime Grove, but as the opening date for the studio was in advance of manufacturing schedules, Mark II's were installed as a stop-gap. The new cameras, designated Mark III's, became available at the end of 1954.

Unfortunately, teething troubles predominated. The early tubes of the production run did not repeat the performance of the prototype in terms of sensitivity, resolution and signal-to-noise ratio and (as if this were not enough) they were also prone to microphony. The first batch delivered to Lime Grove had this defect and the B.B.C. were not amused. 'Thereafter,' wrote Partington wryly, 'the great industry of dropping dustbin lids began.' The $4\frac{1}{2}$-inch tubes were withdrawn and the Mark III cameras were converted to use the standard 3-inch (fortunately the Mark III had been designed to use either type).

It was a desperate time at English Electric Valve Co., but by May 1955 the concentrated research effort had succeeded to the point where the B.B.C. removed the ban. By June 22 the $4\frac{1}{2}$-inch image orthicons were on the air.

Microphony was still something of a problem in production batches for a while, but this was eventually dealt with. In the studios the production teams gradually got the feel of the new equipment and as they did so the picture quality improved to the point where the 3-inch could no longer compete. Early in 1956 nearly all existing Mark III cameras were housing $4\frac{1}{2}$-inch tubes, which were now consistently meeting the desired specifications.

Those engineers who had contracted ulcers in the hectic research and development phases had their reward in 1957, when the B.B.C. decided to standardize on the $4\frac{1}{2}$-inch camera tube, both for studio and outside broadcast work. A further honour came in 1961 – this time from the U.S.A. – for English Electric Valve Co. and the Marconi Company jointly shared with the Radio Corporation of America, the coveted 'Emmy' award of a gold statuette for outstanding contributions to electronic technology in respect of the $4\frac{1}{2}$-inch image orthicon and the Mark III camera. Today, the $4\frac{1}{2}$-inch tube is recognized as a world standard for black-and-white pictures.

In the early 1950s considerable discussion arose in this country as to whether a colour television service should be started. It was strongly felt in some quarters that Britain, which had pioneered black-and-white, should not lag too far behind the U.S.A. where a colour service was already in being. A Television Advisory Committee had been set up to provide recommendations for the future of television and, as one facet of it, the question of a colour service. One of the findings of this Committee was that any system which was eventually adopted should be fully compatible – that is, that the colour transmissions should also be capable of being received as black-and-white pictures on a conventional receiver.

Following on this report the Marconi Company staged a complex demonstration of compatible colour television at English Electric House in the Strand, London. The demonstration, which opened on 11 May 1954, was the first of its kind in Britain. It did not set out to influence opinion as to which system to employ; on the contrary, three different approaches were shown side-by-side. Visitors were able to compare the respective picture qualities afforded by a full bandwidth, three-channel (red + green + blue) system, an N.T.S.C.* type of transmission (in which the colour information is contained in a sub-carrier within the main carrier envelope) and a system in which the colour information is contained in a separate carrier external to that which carried the luminance (black-and-white picture) information.

In addition, two types of colour camera were shown (one a three-tube equipment and the other a two-tube experimental camera) and a considerable variety of ancillary colour equipment.

* National Television System Committee, the American authority which laid down the standards used in the U.S.A. where compatible colour television was introduced as a public service in 1953.

The exhibition created very considerable interest among the hundreds of invited guests, which included the technical and lay press. It underlined the concentration of research effort which even at that early stage, the Company had put into the subject. In the event another thirteen years were to elapse before a national colour service came into existence, but in the interim a considerable business in colour television equipment was built up in overseas markets, particularly with the U.S.A.

On 6 June 1954, Eurovision, the network of microwave radio links and coaxial cables which permits programme exchanges between participant countries, was inaugurated. This featured the Fête des Narcisses at Montreux and also a camera tour of Vatican City. Marconi equipment played an important role in these exercises.

Another first was on September 26 when a B.B.C. programme was transmitted 'live' from a ship at sea. This was radiated from the British Railways car ferry *Lord Warden*, which carried Marconi transmitting equipment for the occasion. The experiment was entirely successful.

By 1953 British television, which had got off to a slow re-start in 1946 was steadily gaining viewers, largely because a large area of the British Isles was now covered by B.B.C. stations. The number of licence holders had topped the 2,000,000 mark. The B.B.C. decided that the time had come to replace the veteran (1936) installation at Alexandra Palace with a much more powerful station, to be sited at the Crystal Palace. Marconi's were awarded the contracts for the provision and installation of the entire transmitting equipment.

The Crystal Palace station provided an excellent example of the rapid technological progress which was being made. It was to have an effective (vision) radiated power of 200 kW – twice as much as any other B.B.C. station – which would make it the world's most powerful Band 1 transmitter. This was effected by the parallel operation of two Marconi 15 kW vision transmitters, feeding into a high-gain antenna system. Encouraged by the success of parallel-operated sound transmitters at Daventry two years earlier, Marconi engineers had tackled the much more difficult problem of phasing two vision equipments and a method of doing so had been perfected. The Crystal Palace installation was the first to use this approach.

The transmitters were newly-designed, built around a new type of tetrode manufactured by English Electric Valve Co. These equipments, while providing an effective radiated power which was twice that of Holme Moss, only occupied one-quarter of the floor space of those at the northern station.

Programme service (using a temporary antenna) began from the Crystal Palace station on 28 March 1956 and Alexandra Palace ('Ally Pally' to all its friends) closed down. Part of the original vision transmitter was eventually moved to Chelmsford where it was added to the Company's collection of historical exhibits. On 18 December 1957 Crystal Palace officially came into full-power service using its main antenna system.

The B.B.C. had begun colour test transmissions from a studio at Alexandra Palace in October 1956. On November 5 of that year the first series of experimental colour transmissions to include 'live' pictures were radiated from the Crystal Palace station. The cameras used were supplied to the B.B.C. by the Marconi Company.

The most important single event in the history of British television in the 1950s was the formation of the Independent Television Authority. This followed on the report of the Broadcasting Committee (1949) which in May 1952 recommended the introduction of an alternative service to that provided by the B.B.C. In the following year the first report of the Postmaster-General's Television Advisory Committee recommended that the new service should operate on Band III frequencies. In November 1953 a Government memorandum made specific proposals for independent television and the Royal Assent was given on 30 July 1954. A few days later the Independent Television Authority was set up by the Postmaster-General under the chairmanship of Sir Kenneth Clark. Shortly after, Sir Robert Fraser was appointed the Authority's Director-General.

The framework of independent television seemed to many at the time to be cumbersome, but the subsequent years have shown it to work well. The Independent Television Authority owns the transmitting stations and has jurisdiction over the programme and advertising content. It derives its revenue from the programme contractors it appoints and the programme contractors in turn derive their revenue from advertisers. Unlike the approach employed in the U.S.A. and other countries, the Independent Television Authority does not permit the direct sponsorship of programmes and limits the amount of advertising time, which may only be inserted in 'natural breaks' in the programme – usually at intervals of fifteen or thirty minutes.

The technical story of the inauguration of the new service is one with which the Marconi Company was closely connected; the magnitude of the effort needed to put independent television on the air at short notice can only be outlined here.

In September 1954 it was announced that the I.T.A. had placed a contract with Marconi's for three vision and three sound transmitters to operate in Band III. At the same time, very large orders for camera channels and other studio equipment began to pour in from programme contractors appointed by the Authority.

At Chelmsford, this promoted something of a crisis, for although some preparations had been made as soon as it became likely that a commercial service would materialize, heavy contracts already existing with the B.B.C. and overseas customers were loading the Works almost to capacity.

Accordingly, established procedures and working hours went by the board. Research and Development departments, confronted with problems peculiar to the hitherto little-used Band III (the phasing of parallel-operated transmitters at those frequencies, for instance), worked around the clock to solve them. The Propagation Department set about the task of recommending suitable transmitting sites and the preparation of theoretical field-strength contour maps, while the Works floor and associated areas tackled the seemingly impossible production targets. Unable to recruit specialist installation engineers in sufficient numbers, recently retired veterans were invited to return to active service, while those already on the strength voluntarily abandoned all thoughts of annual holidays.

On 22 September 1955 the first I.T.A. station, situated at Croydon, came on the air to serve the London area; the installation comprised one prototype vision transmitter and its associated sound transmitter and antenna system (the permanent equipment, including standbys, was installed a little later). The station, Marconi-built, was completed in seven months from the clearance of this site. It is perhaps of interest to record that the engineer in charge of the work was that same Christopher Caspard whose exploits in China in the mid-20s are mentioned in Chapter 34. He was one of the old brigade who came out of retirement at the Company's invitation.

In June of that year the Company established a Television Centre at St Mary Abbot's Place, London, to provide training facilities for the personnel of various programme contractors. This service was extensively used; later, when the main flood of training requirements had abated, the Centre was used as a temporary studio by the B.B.C. The 'Tonight' programme was one of those which started life at St Mary Abbot's.

It says much for the courage of those responsible for the I.T.A.'s organization that plans for national coverage were well advanced even before Croydon came on the air. It must be remembered that the coverage area of a Band III transmitter was very much an unknown quantity and that the great majority of domestic receivers in use in the country were incapable of tuning to anything but a Band I station. Not a few wagged their heads and gloomily forecast a brief inglorious existence for commercial television. New domestic television receivers with wavechange switching to cover Band III were now available and also converter units which could be used with the older models, but the question was – would the public buy? And having bought, would they respond to the advertising? For if they did not, the advertisers would soon return to their old-established media and without their support independent television could not survive.

The Croydon (London) station was therefore very much the guinea-pig. But long before the health of this animal could be established other stations were coming on the air. These included:

Litchfield (Midlands) Opened 17 February 1956. Marconi antenna and feeder system.

Winter Hill (Northern, Lancashire) Opened 3 May 1956. An all-Marconi station.

Emley Moor (Northern, Yorkshire) Opened 3 November 1956. An all-Marconi station.

Black Hill (Central Scotland) Opened 31 August 1957. An all-Marconi station.

St Hilary (South Wales and the West) Opened 14 January 1958. Marconi antenna and feeder system.

Chillerton Down (Southern) Opened 30 August 1958. An all-Marconi station.

Burnhope (North-Eastern) Opened 15 January 1959. An all-Marconi station.

Thus (with the inclusion of the Croydon station), six out of the first eight I.T.A. stations were wholly supplied by Marconi's, as well as the antenna systems for the remaining two. Add to this the new B.B.C. stations which were being built at that period and the heavy overseas orders which included three stations for the National television service ⟨in Australia (Brisbane, Adelaide and Perth), and some idea can be gained of the strenuous life lived in the Broadcasting Division at that time.

Orders for other B.B.C. and I.T.A. stations, too numerous to detail here, followed, while in the studio field the Mark III camera was in due course superseded by improved models. The Division has continued its tradition of making history, as for example on 11 July 1962, when the first transatlantic transmissions via the Telstar satellite employed Marconi cameras, as did the colour transmissions five days later.

CLOSED CIRCUIT TELEVISION

Television is so closely associated with broadcasting that one tends to forget that the early workers in the field thought of it in terms of visual line telegraphy. It was not until 1911 that the distribution of the video signals via a radio carrier was suggested by A. Sinding-Larsen (a prophetic utterance as the generation of radio waves by thermionic valves was unknown and television pictures having light, shade and movement had never been produced). Then, by the time television had arrived, sound broadcasting had become so widespread that the obvious thing to do was to provide vision entertainment via radio also. The original concept of transmission over wire conductors fell into oblivion.

It was revived in the U.S.A. in the late 1940s and in the early 1950s the Marconi Broadcasting Division also began to explore the possibilities of using the television camera for industrial, professional and commercial purposes. Experimental demonstrations were given to various potentially interested parties, including large gatherings of medical students and nurses; the 'remote eye' of the camera enabled these to watch surgical operations being performed, giving them close-up views which would not have been possible if they had been in the operating theatre itself.

Closed circuit television made the world's headlines in June 1951 when observers aboard the Admiralty vessel *Reclaim* saw, on television screens, the nameplate of the submarine *Affray*, lying in forty-seven fathoms in the English Channel. The submarine had vanished without trace two months previously and the identification was the climax to a systematic examination of wrecks over a wide area, using a television camera lowered to the sea-bed and connected by cable to the monitor screens in *Reclaim*. The camera was of Marconi manufacture and had hurriedly been adapted by the Admiralty to operate under water. Not only was *Affray* positively identified but the television camera also disclosed the fault in the schnorkel equipment which had sent the vessel to the bottom.

As a result of this success the Company entered into an agreement with Siebe, Gorman and Co. Ltd., the specialists in underwater apparatus, to pool their respective skills and design equipment specifically for underwater work. This bore fruit in 1954 when the Marconi-Siebe, Gorman camera provided positive identification of pieces of the Comet aircraft which had mysteriously disintegrated in mid-air near the island of Elba in January of that year. By examination of the recovered wreckage, aviation experts were able to determine the cause of the tragedy and to safeguard against it for the future.

Although underwater television equipment has only a limited market, its use in these two tragic circumstances underlined the value of closed circuit t.v. in instances where first-hand human observation is dangerous, inconvenient or impossible. In the early days of its development as a tool, standard cameras were used, but before long relatively small, simple and robust camera channels were being designed; these bore a similar relationship to the broadcast camera as the photographic box camera does to the expensive professional model in that they could be handled by the lay operator after only a brief period of instruction.

As a deliberate policy the Company concentrated its main effort into the production of high-quality equipment for use in heavy industry, particularly in steel works and electrical power-generating stations, but, in general, for any environment in which rigorous ambient conditions exist. Other types of camera are manufactured for use in educational establishments. Gradually the volume of business built up to a point where it became expedient to hive it off from the Broadcasting Division and this was done in 1959 when it became the Closed Circuit Television Division.

Colour equipment is not extensively used for closed circuit work, partly because it is expensive, but mainly because the additional complication is, in a great number of cases, unnecessary – for example if the remote observation of dials and gauges is being carried out, the information is complete in its black-and-white form. Colour is, however, of value in certain instances such as hospital work or in aircraft flight simulator equipment.

Since Closed Circuit Division became a separate entity the volume and range of its business has continued to expand steadily. Although it is, strictly speaking, outside the dateline boundary to refer to 1968, it might perhaps avoid confusion to mention that in that year its title was changed to Electro-Optical Systems Division as better expressing the enlarging scope of its activities.

45

Developments in Communications
1945–1965

Although sound broadcasting and television are forms of communication, it has long been the convention to reserve this term for transmissions of a non-entertainment character, such as commercial or military intelligence or weather reports. These may be in the form of telephony or telegraphy and may be sent broadcast, or transmitted by radio link from point to point or over line conductors. Aviation communication is of course a branch of this work, but because of its specialist nature has been dealt with in a separate chapter.

The Marconi Company has first and last been a communications organization. It began as such in 1897 and despite its diversification of interests as new applications of electronics were realized, the provision of communications systems to Posts and Telegraphs and military authorities has always been a major activity.

In common with all its other enterprises the private-venture development of communications equipment came to a virtual standstill during World War II and it was not until peace came in prospect that much consideration could be given to the design of equipments to compete in the post-war world.

At this point it is perhaps of interest to record that the S.W.B. ('short wave band') series of high-frequency transmitters were still strongly in evidence after the war. The first SWB's (affectionately known as 'Swabs') had been designed by C. S. Franklin in the mid-1920s and it is known that at least one or two of the originals were still in daily service in the 1960s. However, subsequent generations had been developed from the SWB1 and by 1954 these had extended to the SWB 11X.

One of the earliest advances of the immediate post-war period was mechanical and not electronic. This was the adoption of the Page cabinet method of construction. This was devised by F. R. Page, a senior engineer of the Company, to supersede the heterogeneous transmitter cabinet sizes which had hitherto been used. In essence it is a module form of assembly whereby a transmitter of any size can be built up from standard parts and units to form cabinets and enclosures of generally similar appearance. The Page method of assembly not only gave Marconi transmitters a characteristic appearance; by rationalizing the manufacturing process to produce standard units, significant cost reductions were made. The method is still in wide use today.

In 1948 an important advance in h.f. transmitter design took place. Up to that time the SWB series of equipments were essentially h.f. amplifiers to which a modulator could be added for telephonic broadcasting purposes, or telegraph equipment for P and T type communications work. With the adoption of more sophisticated systems, such as single sideband or independent sideband operation, a new design approach was necessary. As a consequence the main stream of h.f. transmitter design forked into two specialist channels, one to serve broadcasting needs and the other telecommunications.

For telecommunications work the two basic requirements are for power amplifiers with a high order of linearity and for equipment which will provide the facility of a rapid change of frequency. These two factors perhaps call for brief explanation to those not in electronics.

A linear amplifier is one in which there is a linear relationship between instantaneous anode current and grid voltage. In lay terms it may be described as an amplifier in which distortion is reduced to a minimum. Two of the early improvements in linearity performance were provided by E. Green's quarter-wave network (*circa* 1945) which was first incorporated in the TF732 communications transmitter and the r.f. feed back system (later used in the H551 communications transmitter) which was based on a patent by V. O. Stokes.

Improvements in valve design also made important contributions to the linearity aspect. The evolution of thermionic valves (particularly high-power triodes and tetrodes) which were suitable for high frequency operation and which had higher gains, better linearity and improved cooling facilities have, over the years, made for very considerable advances in transmitter design.

In order to appreciate the importance of rapid frequency changing it is first of all necessary to recall that h.f. communications depends upon the existence of ionized layers surrounding the earth. There are two main layers, the Kennelly-Heaviside layer at 50–90 miles up and the Appleton layer at about 170 miles. The h.f. radio waves on reaching these layers are reflected and diffracted earthward again, and may reach the earth's surface in an area which is perhaps 1,000 miles or more from the station. Here the wave is re-reflected back to the ionosphere only to be returned to earth once more; this process may be repeated several times and in such a manner the signals travel onward in a series of hops between ionosphere and ground.

If there had been no ionosphere, round-the-world radio communication would have been virtually impossible until the advent of satellite working. The ionosphere is not, however, an ideal reflective mirror from the point of view of the communications engineer. It owes its existence to the action of the ultra-violet content in the sun's rays which ionizes gases in the upper atmosphere, thereby releasing electrons, and it is these free electrons which effect most of the bending back of the radio waves to earth. It follows therefore that the height and density of the layers are dependent upon the position of the sun in relation to the earth. They alter in height and density at sunrise and sunset; there are also seasonal changes, while solar flares, if severe, can play havoc with h.f. communications for hours or even days.

With all these circumstances, and others, the h.f. communications engineer has to contend. Having no control over the ionosphere he has to study its vagaries and work with it. Fortunately, some of the variations are predictable – for example the diurnal changes can be off-set by changing the frequency of the transmitter and receivers to one which is more suitable under the changed conditions.

In earlier days the changing of the transmitter frequency was carried out manually; this was a long and laborious process which called for the services of a highly-skilled engineer; there was, moreover, the added disadvantage that the transmitter became unserviceable twice a day for a considerable period while re-tuning was being carried out.

One of the first steps to speed the process was the abandoning of plug-in inductors (coils) in favour of a complete set of these devices mounted on a turntable, by which means the desired inductor could rapidly be brought into operation. This method, however, was soon superseded by one which employed variable inductors ganged (coupled) to variable capacitors filled with sulphahexafluoride (developed specially for Marconi's by Napiers of Acton, an associate company within the English Electric Group). By motorizing such an assembly, a press-button change of frequency to any one of a number of pre-selected 'spot' frequencies was made possible. By such means all stages in the transmitter could be retuned simultaneously in a matter of seconds, with no skill demanded from the operating personnel. These methods were incorporated in the H.S. series of communications transmitters and enabled the whole band from 4 MHz to 27·5 MHz to be covered.

Transmitters of this type were installed in the extension of Rugby Radio, the G.P.O.'s main long-range transmitting station, which was opened in July 1955. Twenty-eight of these units, each of 30 kW peak envelope power, and much of the associated equipment, were supplied and installed. All are remotely controlled by press-button from a central control position.

A further important step towards simplifying the frequency-changing process came in 1959. This abolished all forms of operational tuning in the transmitter's h.f. amplifying stages by using a special form of distributed amplifier developed by two senior Marconi engineers, V. O. Stokes and B. M. Sosin. This type of amplifier was not in itself new, having been used previously in oscilloscopes, but had never before been successfully employed for transmitter work at high power.

Its salient feature is that it is not frequency-conscious and will accept an input of any frequency within the h.f. band and amplify it – in fact, more than one input can be amplified simultaneously. This is in complete contrast to the conventional radio amplifier, which will only amplify the one input for which it is adjusted and every stage of which has to be re-tuned in order to operate at another frequency. The great merit of the wideband amplifier is that a change of frequency can be effected merely by turning a switch on an associated drive unit.

The first equipment of this type to go into production (the HS113) had an output power of 1 kW. Its introduction created great interest and it rapidly became a best seller.

The distributed amplifier technique was taken a stage further when the successful introduction of solid state (semiconductor) devices into transmitter technology permitted the use of a circuit patented by V. O. Stokes in 1947. This enabled a valved power output stage embodying a new form of motor-driven tuning to be added to a distributed amplifier, thus providing the means of building transmitters with a peak envelope power of up to 30 kW but which were tuned (and this automatically) only in the final stage.

The 'Stokes' automatic tuning circuit gave two considerable advantages. It enabled rapid tuning of the final stage to be carried out and at the same time ensured that the transmitter output stage at all times presented a correct matching impedance to the antenna system regardless of changes in antenna conditions occasioned by the weather.

This new approach, christened the Marconi Self Tuning (MST)

system, constituted a tremendous advance upon previous techniques. By utilizing new types of semiconductor power rectifiers, the power supply components could be made much smaller and this made it possible to build them into the transmitter units. The saving of space thus afforded, together with the compactness of the distributed amplifiers, enabled the overall size to be reduced to the point where the cost of buildings and installation could in some instances be halved.

Again, the extreme simplicity of operation, which included a 15-second frequency change, made one-man control of a station a practical possibility, thereby reducing operating costs. At the time of the introduction of MST in 1963–4 there was nothing like it on the market and the advantages it offered created world sales. Since that time well over £10,000,000 worth of this type of equipment has been sold.

In Britain and a number of other countries the pole-and-wire system of telephonic and telegraphic system of communication is a familiar, if unattractive sight. It is an economic proposition in countries such as ours where there is a high density of population, an equable climate (whatever we may say to the contrary), where there are relatively short distances to be covered, and where the terrain is easy to negotiate.

In many areas of the world these factors are absent. There are, for instance, many parts of the African continent where it would be all but impossible to use a pole-and-wire system to span the mountains, jungle or desert which lie between centres of population. Pole-and-wire is vulnerable to storms, floods and wild animals (giraffes and elephants are notorious for the destruction of overhead wires) while in very remote areas the local inhabitants prize copper wire very highly.

Very High Frequency (v.h.f.) radio, which had been considerably developed during the war, held promise of commercial application in such areas and, in the immediate post-war period, extensive research and further development were being carried out. A series of equipments was planned, aiming at such targets as simplicity of operation, compactness, ability to withstand extremes of temperature, reliability and privacy of communication.

Technically, the v.h.f. band was in many ways suited to the project. Although the range of such a station in ground-to-ground operation is limited to a little more than 'line-of-sight' – that is, a straight line could be drawn between transmitter and receiver – the twenty-five to forty-five miles so covered is a useful distance and can be extended to several hundred miles, if need be, by the use of small unattended repeater stations at intervals along the route. The physically small size of the antennas makes it possible to concentrate the radiated power into a fairly narrow beam, which in practice is subdivided into a considerable number of separate channels over which separate telephonic or telegraphic messages can be carried simultaneously. The system is therefore somewhat akin to pole-and-wire except that the 'poles' in the form of repeater stations are perhaps thirty miles apart and the 'wires' or channels are invisible.

A considerable business in such systems was effected in the 1950s and this continued thereafter. At that time, many former colonies and protectorates, particularly in Africa, were gaining independence and needed efficient communications systems urgently. Nigeria, for example, needed a nation-wide system linking all the main centres of population and entrusted the Company with the task of providing most of it. When completed, the country possessed what was then the world's largest v.h.f. communications network.

Many other systems of this character were installed in various 'new' countries in the African continent and in other areas of the world from the 1950s onward. As the number of simultaneous channels which can be employed increases with frequency,* it was natural that the higher frequency bands – the ultra-high and super-high frequencies – should also be developed. The employment of these (and particularly s.h.f.) was not merely a question of adjusting the frequency of the existing transmitters, but rather of new design throughout. This is largely because conventional thermionic valves do not readily operate at frequencies above about 3,000 MHz and as a consequence other types of devices had to be employed. One such is the travelling wave tube which was originally developed in Britain by R. Kompfner (Physics Department, Birmingham University) in 1942. This device provides the cardinal requirements of amplification and a wide bandwidth and (in considerably improved form) is still in common use today (1967).

Unfortunately for the radio communications engineer there is no single frequency band which he can use for all purposes. Very powerful stations operating at very low and low frequencies (v.l.f. and l.f.) can cover considerable distances but are limited in the amount of information they can carry. Medium-frequency stations are limited in reliable range to a few hundred miles and do not permit the simultaneous transmission of a number of messages. High frequency (h.f.) stations give round-the-world coverage but because this is achieved by a series of reflections of the

*Whereas a capacity of forty-eight telephone channels is typical of a v.h.f. link, an s.h.f. link can provide about six hundred.

signals between earth and the ionosphere there is a zone of silence which prevails from a short distance beyond the station to the area where the sky-wave first returns to earth after ionospheric reflection (the 'skip-distance' effect). High frequency transmission has the further disadvantage that it can provide only a few separate channels of intelligence per carrier.

Very High Frequency (v.h.f.) communication between ground stations, as we have seen, needs repeater stations at about thirty-mile intervals if long-distance working is to be effected, but can carry a fair number of simultaneous messages. This situation continues with the ultra- and super-high frequencies; the range performance becomes more optical in character (obstructions along the path throw sharp radio shadows) but, by way of compensation, the channel-capacity is greater.

By using the appropriate frequencies the radio communications engineer is able to meet most range requirements. There is, however, a gap in the above summary; this exists between the thirty-mile (approximate) range of the v.h.f. station and the return to earth of the first ionospheric reflection of the h.f. station, which can be about one thousand miles distant. The gap can be filled in many cases by using v.h.f. point-to-point repeaters as described, providing that the intervening terrain is suitable. This, however, is not always the case and the method becomes impossible if the required destination is an island some hundreds of miles from the mainland with no conveniently spaced chain of islands upon which to place repeaters (nature is seldom so obliging!).

It is not surprising therefore to find that much research effort was being applied in the post-war period to devise means of filling this gap. Such research had its roots in the studies of the behaviour of the ionosphere, pioneered by such workers as Sir Edward Appleton and T. L. Eckersley from about 1919 onwards.

At Marconi's the study of the behaviour of radio waves had figured prominently in the Company's activities since the earliest days. In 1919 a specialist department to study wave propagation was set up under T. L. Eckersley's leadership. By the start of World War II the Propagation Group had removed to the new laboratory areas at Great Baddow; it was then taken over by the Government and incorporated into an Ionospheric Bureau which functioned at Baddow throughout the war.

In 1939, Eckersley read his classic paper 'Analysis of the Effect of Scattering in Radio Transmission' before the Institution of Electrical Engineers. The phenomenon of scatter transmission had first been observed in 1927 when the Marconi research team noted it as a curious side effect of the first beam transmissions and Eckersley had devoted considerable attention to it from that time onward.

One of the members of the wartime Ionospheric Bureau team was D. K. Bailey, a gifted American research worker. In daily contact with Eckersley, Bailey became intensely interested in the former's scatter theories and on his return to the U.S.A. continued his investigations in collaboration with R. Bateman and R. C. Kirby, working at the National Bureau of Standards and in close collaboration with the Lincoln Laboratory of the Massachusetts Institute of Technology. A practical communications system evolved from this work; the technique involved the radiation of a v.h.f. radio beam (in the 30–60 MHz range) at a certain critical angle to the horizontal plane; the waves are scattered in the lower ionosphere and a tiny proportion of this energy returns to earth at a distance of some hundreds of miles from the source.

In Britain, a little later, the Post Office carried out experimental work on these lines between a station in the Shetlands and one in Jersey. The Department of Scientific and Industrial Research co-operated in these experiments using a receiving station at Slough, while Marconi's built a receiving station at the Great Baddow laboratories. This work began in 1952 and built up in intensity as the promise in the ionospheric forward scatter system was more and more substantiated.

In 1956 the Admiralty, using a modified Marconi high-power television transmitter, began experimental transmissions from Gibraltar, beaming the signals into the ionosphere across the Bay of Biscay, with the scattered radiation coming to earth in the area of the British Isles. The Ministry of Supply, the D.S.I.R., the G.P.O. and the Marconi Company set up stations in order to evaluate the received signals. As a result of these tests Marconi's were later assigned the task of designing and building a v.h.f. ionospheric scatter link between the Isle of Wight and Malta, a distance of about 3,000 miles. This (to date) still remains a record distance between scatter stations which are in everyday service. The contract was carried out on behalf of the Air Ministry.

The first permanent ionospheric scatter station to be built in Britain, however, was at a United States Air Force station at Kingston Blount in Oxfordshire. This formed the European terminal of a link between the U.S.A. and England, with a repeater station in Iceland.

Almost coincident with the development of the ionospheric scatter system came another, in which the scattering is effected in the troposphere, about five miles above the earth's surface. The scattering, in this instance, is not caused by ionization but by random irregularities, associated with variations in the refractive index of the earth's atmosphere, at this height. For early tropospheric scatter operation the frequency band 200–3,000 MHz was used but this has in recent years been extended upwards in frequency to 5,000 MHz and beyond.

As would be expected from the relatively low height at which the scattering takes place, the range of tropospheric scatter transmission is considerably less than that obtained with the ionospheric system. With the skyward beam aimed as low as possible the effective range is between 200–400 miles. Because of the much higher frequencies employed, the number of simultaneous channels which can be carried is considerably greater than with the ionospheric scatter approach – from 24 to 120 channels.

As with ionospheric scatter, the principle of operation of tropospheric scatter is based on fundamental research work carried out in Britain. Despite a certain delay in British development because an allocation of operating frequencies was not immediately forthcoming (during which period American development went ahead) various British companies were quickly off the mark when this situation was rectified. The Marconi Company carried out extensive research work during the mid-1950s period and thereafter, operating an experimental link between Galleywood, near Chelmsford, and Start Point in Devonshire. As a result of this groundwork another profitable market was opened up.

It cannot be claimed that either of the forward scatter systems is elegant. Brute force plays a significant part in their operation for in both cases a great deal of transmitter energy is wasted; only a tiny part is scattered earthward, the remainder being lost in outer space. Nevertheless, together, they serve to bridge the range gap referred to earlier and are thus valuable assets to the radio communications engineer.

For more than forty years the high frequencies have been the main carriers of the world's long-distance radio traffic, both in telegraphy and telephony.

In spite of the system's disadvantages (its dependence upon the vagaries of the ionosphere and the limited number of simultaneous messages that can be transmitted on one carrier wave) there has, until recent years, been no other which could rival it.

This was not for want of trying. For instance, considerable work has been done over a period of years on the use of meteor trails as passive reflectors of v.h.f. transmission (the lower end of the band is used). This is a workable system provided that simultaneous optical paths exist between the transmitting station and the meteor trail and the trail and the receiving station, but because of the brief time of this occurrence the signals have to be recorded in readiness and then transmitted at high speed when the correct aspect is present. It follows from this that the system can only be used for telegraphic purposes.

Other approaches made in the early post-war period included the use of the moon as a passive reflector, the signals being directed from an earth station to the lunar surface and reflected from there to reach earth again. This method also had serious limitations; the moon's surface is not an efficient reflector and in any event could only be used when optical paths existed between it and both stations simultaneously.

Thus, h.f. communication was never seriously challenged until the advent of the artificial satellite. At the time of writing (1968) h.f. is still the main bearer of the world's long-distance radio messages for two reasons, one of which is that a complete global system of satellite communication between countries calls for a vast amount of international co-operation and organization and this takes time; another is that such a service cannot so far compete economically with the long-established h.f. circuits. Again this is probably a matter of time, although it is held in some authoritative quarters that h.f. communication will never be completely ousted.

Whether this is so or not, there can be no doubt that satellite working is easily the greatest single advance in communications over the past forty years. It is also unique in that, for the very first time in the history of radio, the power to exploit the system has passed out of the hands of electronics engineers into the hands of those whose business is with space vehicles. It is a disturbing fact (and one which we may in due course regret) that, to date, neither Britain nor her continental neighbours have the means of putting a large telecommunications satellite into orbit and can therefore only participate in the new form of communication on something of a grace-and-favour basis.

Satellite communication came into being as a technological fall-out from the East-West arms race. The development of rockets capable of delivering large war-heads over thousands of miles also made it possible to position vehicles to orbit the earth as artificial satellites, and from this it was a logical step to the equipping of these vehicles with electronic instrumentation.

The principle of satellite communication is simple. Provided that an optical path simultaneously exists between the space vehicle and two communication stations on the ground, the 'line-of-sight' frequencies (v.h.f. and those above) are freed from their over-the-ground limitations of 25-40 miles. One ground station sends its signals towards the satellite where they are picked up, amplified, and fed into a small transmitter which re-radiates them to the second ground station. With a similar return circuit in operation, two-way communication between the ground is effected.

Putting the principle into practice is not nearly so simple. Aboard the satellite the complex transmitting-receiving equipment must be powerful enough to do the work, yet extremely light in weight, reliable, and consuming the minimum amount of power. It was the need for such equipment that accelerated the development of microcircuits. In the present state of the art the power supplies are special forms of batteries, the energy of which is supplemented by that developed by solar cells – devices which produce electric current from the sun's radiation – mounted on the satellite's external surface. This arrangement can only provide a relatively low power but it is doubtless only a matter of time before more efficient means – possibly nuclear – can be produced economically.

This power limitation at the satellite creates problems at the ground stations, where special amplifying techniques, such as the maser or the parametric amplifier, have to be used in conjunction with large-diameter dish antennas in order to make the most of the weak signals.

On 10 July 1962 the Telstar satellite became the instrument of a successful television broadcast from the U.S.A. to Europe and this was followed by an experimental colour television broadcast in the following September. (It is perhaps of interest to note that on both occasions Marconi television cameras were used at the American end of the circuit.) Telstar orbited at a comparatively low height and so an optical path to the two ground stations was only formed at intervals. The present technique is to put the satellite in orbit at a much greater height (about 23,000 miles) at which distance it encircles the earth at a speed which keeps it almost stationary over a given point on the earth's surface. By this means the selected ground stations always have an optical path to it and thus a 24-hour service can be maintained. Such systems are termed 'synchronous'.

So far, the Marconi Company has concentrated on the development of ground stations for satellite working and has done well in this area. In 1965, Cable and Wireless Ltd. placed an order with the Company for the design and construction of such a station for use in connection with the American National Aeronautical and Space Administration (NASA) man-on-the-moon project. This APOLLO station was built on Ascension Island. Since then (but out of the time-scope of this history) many other orders have been equally successfully completed; the volume of business has been such as to necessitate the formation of a Division specializing in space communications work and the Company is easily the largest British manufacturer.

46

Developments in Marine Communications 1945–1965

Because little has been said in this account regarding marine radio communications it might be thought that the seafaring aspect, which was Guglielmo Marconi's main interest when he founded his Company, has become insignificant over the years.

Nothing would be further from the truth. The explanation is simple; in 1900 a separate Company was set up to handle the mercantile marine business, which was steadily growing, and the subsequent activities of the Marconi International Marine Communication Co. Ltd.* would easily fill another book.

The two Companies are, however, closely knit in that the parent organization has been the manufactory for most of the maritime equipment marketed and serviced by the Marconi Marine Company, so perhaps a brief account of the latter may serve to bring the partnership into perspective.

In one respect Marconi Marine still adheres to a commercial policy adopted nearly seventy years ago, in that, to British shipowners at least, a rental maintenance system is offered.

With this, the equipment is installed on a hire basis and qualified radio officers are provided to operate and maintain the equipment while at sea. Any work which may be necessary on it while the ship is in port is done by shore-based Marconi technicians; Marconi Marine has over 250 depots and agencies established in ports all over the world, from which these technicians operate. A further service is provided whereby the analysis of ships' traffic accounts can be undertaken by Marconi Marine staff; this relieves the shipowner of all responsibility in connection with payments to British and foreign telegraph administrations. Even in instances where the equipment is sold outright, the majority of purchasers prefer to use Marconi radio officers and pay separately for inspection and maintenance as necessary.

* Now Marconi International Marine Co. Ltd.

At the inception of the Marconi Marine Company in 1900, its head-quarters office was at 18 Finch Lane, London E.C., the home of the parent Company. It moved to Watergate House, London, W.C., upon the removal of the Marconi organization to that address in 1907, and again moved in 1910, this time to Marconi House in the Strand. Its registered office remained here until 1960, when it came to Marconi House, New Street, Chelmsford, where certain units of the Marine Company had been working since just before World War II. Two years later, upon the completion of a new building, Elettra House, Westway (also in Chelmsford), Marconi Marine transferred there (Elettra House was officially opened in 1963). From here its staff of around 3,000 radio officers and technicians is controlled.

In the formative years at the turn of the century the sea-going equipment provided was exclusively concerned with wireless communication, but over the years the service has enlarged to include such devices as automatic distress call alarms, special lifeboat equipment, direction-finders (manual and automatic), echometers for various purposes, marine radar, sound systems for intercommunication and public address work, and closed circuit television for use as a 'remote eye' and for entertainment purposes aboard ship. Today, the Marconi Marine Company offers by far the most comprehensive range of marine electronic equipment and services of any in the world.

This necessarily brief outline may serve as a background to the Marconi Company's activities as the principal manufacturing arm.

The first major extension to the use of wireless as a communications system was the development of direction-finding equipment. The first direction-finding device to be used at sea was an experimental Marconi equipment, installed aboard the (first) *Mauretania* in 1912. This used crystal detection and had a range of about eighteen miles. H. J. Round's introduction of thermionic valve (tube) amplifiers into d.f. equipment provided a considerable increase in sensitivity and in the early stages of World War I a chain of such stations was built around the coasts of the United Kingdom. Ship-borne radio direction-finders and land-based radio beacons using thermionic valve amplifiers quickly followed.

The years between the two wars were notable for the further improvements made to thermionic valves (tubes) and for the extension of their usage, both in communications work and in other applications. In particular the era saw the gradual decline of the use of spark transmission and the ascendance of valved transmitter techniques.

In 1931 another important electronic device came aboard ship for the first time in the form of the supersonic echometer, introduced by Marconi's.

In 1948 the major overhaul of the Company structure described in an earlier chapter placed the manufacture of marine electronic equipment within the province of the then newly-formed Central Division as part of its responsibilities (these, broadly speaking, included all branches of Company activity except broadcasting, radar, aeronautical and communications work). In addition to the manufacture of mercantile ships' equipment for Marconi Marine, the Central Division supplied naval equipment direct to the customer.

For a while after the war the equipments offered were wartime designs modified if necessary to align with peacetime conditions; this gave a breathing space which was used to design a new range of equipments.

The war at sea had thoroughly demonstrated the value of radar for shipping and a considerable demand for such equipment was foreseen. Development of mercantile and naval radar was therefore given high priority, as a result of which sea-trials of a new design, Radiolocator 1, were taking place in the early post-war period. This equipment went into full-scale production in 1947-8, and, considering the traditional caution which shipping interests very properly show in adopting any new device upon which lives will depend, it was most favourably received. Encouraged by this, design work was intensified and over the years the various marks of Radiolocator equipment have come into wide use.

In 1950, orders were received by Marconi Marine for the re-equipment of all lighthouses around the British coastline. This meant that every marine approach and marker radio beacon in the British Isles bore the Marconi label.

Radio beacons are in many respects equivalent to lighthouses. Instead of radiating a beam of light, radio energy is transmitted; this is modulated by a repetitive call-sign (peculiar to the beacon as a means of identification) followed by a long dash of continuous transmission to enable vessels which are fitted with direction-finding equipment to obtain a bearing from it. Radio beacons are thus a valuable supplement to conventional lighthouses, particularly in foggy weather. Such equipments are designed for automatic working; they require no attention other than normal periodic servicing and adjustment of the time periods to meet local conditions. A 20-watt medium frequency beacon of the 1950s had a range of fifty to seventy miles.

The 1951 International Conference for the Reorganization of Maritime Radio gave further impetus to this category of business, in that it brought a new regulation into force which made it compulsory that all installations should be in duplicate. Considerable orders arose, many from overseas. A typical instance was that of the Portuguese Lighthouse Department which in 1955 placed an order for eight equipments for supply and installation in duplicate at four of their lighthouses. The single Marconi installations which had served these up to that time were removed and re-installed at other lighthouses along the Portuguese coast.

In 1954 the Queen and the Duke of Edinburgh carried out a Commonwealth tour, for which occasion the Shaw Savill liner *Gothic* was fitted out as a floating headquarters. The *Gothic* was already equipped with Marconi radio but the normal installation was heavily supplemented to meet the onerous requirements of State and naval traffic, the heavy demands of the Press and B.B.C. correspondents and the commentators who were covering the tour. Orders for new electronic equipment were placed in 1952 and Marconi Marine and the parent Company co-operated with the Admiralty over the supply and installation. High-power radio telephone and high-speed radio telegraph equipments were fitted to provide long-distance coverage. One of these was an SWB 11X 7 kW transmitter – the first occasion on which a transmitter of this power had ever been installed on a merchant vessel.

The steady expansion and progress of the Company's maritime interests were such that the management decided that the time was opportune to segregate these Central Division activities into a discrete Maritime Division. This took effect in April 1954.

One of the notable trends of the mid-1950s was the growth in the use of the very high frequencies (v.h.f.) for maritime purposes. The Company, in its research and development, anticipated this movement by some few years and by the time it was under way was in production with a new range of maritime v.h.f. equipments.

In January 1957 the Hague International Conference made important recommendations regarding the use of v.h.f. at sea and for ship-to-shore communication. Technical and operational standards were laid down with the objective of providing easy ship-to-shore contact for vessels entering or leaving any port. The Marconi equipment fully met the specifications and sold well. Typical of these was the 10-watt transmitter-receiver NTS402 which provided a rapid selection of up to fifteen pre-selected crystal-controlled channels in the 154 to 165 MHz band, with a combined simplex-duplex facility. This equipment was marketed by

Marconi Marine as the 'Nautilus'. Much of the practical development of this and other v.h.f. equipments was carried out aboard the Marine Company's 72 ft. motor yacht *Elettra II* which is fitted out as a floating laboratory.

The British Post Office was quick to utilize the benefits of The Hague Conference and on 5 September 1958 a new public correspondence service, using v.h.f. radio telephony, was inaugurated. To mark the occasion Viscount Simon, Chairman of the Port of London Authority, embarked in *Elettra II* and, from a position off the Kent coast, spoke by radio telephone to Mr Ernest Marples, then Postmaster-General, who accepted the call at the G.P.O. stand at the Radio Exhibition.

The G.P.O.'s North Foreland station, which provided the shore link, had been equipped with v.h.f. frequency-modulated transmitters and receivers manufactured by Marconi's. It is also perhaps of interest to recall that the wireless licence issued to *Elettra II* for that year (1958) was the first ever issued to a ship authorizing the use of v.h.f. for public correspondence with a Post Office or equivalent shore station.

Earlier in the year – in January – a 'Nautilus' installation aboard the liner *Mauretania** had inaugurated the Southampton Harbour Board's new port operation and information service, while a little later a similar installation aboard the Shaw Savill liner *Southern Cross* had carried out long-range tests with a new v.h.f. shore station operated by the Melbourne Harbour Trust. (These were not, of course, public correspondence stations.) Since 1958 the British Post Office has greatly extended its service to cover the major ports of the British Isles.

Overseas, the sales of v.h.f. radio telephone equipment continued to rise. The port of Karachi was comprehensively equipped in 1957–8 and at the close of 1959 the Authorities of the chief port of East Pakistan, Chittagong, placed a large order for the establishment of a radio telephone network to improve communications within the port area and the Khamapuli river.

In March 1960, Marconi Marine received an order for the supply and installation of a full range of marine communication and navigational aid equipment to the new P & O luxury liner *Canberra*. It is perhaps of interest to compare this installation with that carried by Atlantic passenger ships at the turn of the century. Whereas the latter comprised only a battery-operated spark transmitter and a coherer receiver (which was less sensitive than a crystal set) the *Canberra*'s main equipment included the following:

* The second *Mauretania*.

A single sideband transmitter and two associated receivers in addition to a 'Globespan' transmitter and two 'Atalanta' receivers to deal with normal radio telegraph and telephone traffic in the medium, intermediate and high frequency bands. Special radio telephone terminal equipment to enable passengers to make private calls from first-class cabins and from ship-board telephone kiosks.

Emergency equipment comprised a 'Reliance' m.f. transmitter, an 'Alert' guard receiver and an 'Autokey' automatic keying device. Two of the liners Class A lifeboats were fitted with 'Salvare' transmitter/receivers.

Radio aids to navigation included automatic direction-finding equipment and a Seagraph III recording echometer with a separate visual indicator. A complete television system was also provided to enable passengers and crew to see television programmes at various ports of call, or when out of range of these, to watch teleciné programmes derived from the ship's film library.

A similar order was also in process of installation at this time (1960) for the liner *Oriana*.

The principle of the distributed amplifier, which offers a wideband coverage of the high frequency band without re-tuning has already been mentioned in the chapter 'Developments in Communications'. This was also introduced for maritime purposes in 1959–60, although the development of the sea-borne equipment was done independently by the Maritime Division.

The first ship in the world to be equipped with amplifiers of this type was the G.P.O. cable-laying vessel *Monarch* which already carried a complement of Marconi equipment. Two parallel-connected NT213 wideband amplifiers were provided, giving an output of 2·8 kW peak envelope power. The drive was provided from the primary stages of either of two NT201 single sideband h.f. transmitters; alternatively these transmitters, each rated at 1 kW output could be used as independent units. A v.h.f. transmitter/receiver also formed part of the order, enabling the ship to communicate on the international inter-ship/port control and public correspondence frequencies.

A further large order for maritime transmitters and direction-finding equipments came in December of that year 1960. This time it was for installations aboard two weather ships, *Weather Adviser* and *Weather Monitor*. A little later a third ship, *Weather Recorder*, was also similarly fitted out.

By 1961 the NT203 wideband amplifier was selling in large quantities both at home and overseas, the Royal Navy being a particularly heavy buyer. In November the Admiralty placed a further large order (nearly £1,000,000) for large numbers of another new type of equipment, the 500W m.f./h.f. independent sideband transmitter NT204. This incorporated a further technical advance, termed (rather loosely, perhaps) a frequency synthesizer; this device reduced frequency-changing on the transmitter to a mere turning of switch controls.

The output of this unit, at a level of 10W, formed the input of the main amplifier. This embodied distributed amplifier techniques in its final r.f. amplifier stage so that the latter required no tuning at all. The penultimate stage was tuned, but in the simplest manner.

Only those who have spent hours in the laborious manual re-tuning of a conventional transmitter can fully appreciate the significance of the transition to the new techniques. At the time of its introduction the NT204 was the only one of its kind in the world to provide continuous coverage of the entire maritime band in one small compact equipment.

47

Expansion and Reorganization in the 'Sixties'

By the early 1960s it had become very evident that the formation of specialist, largely autonomous, divisions which had been put into effect in 1948, had paid off handsomely. The Company turnover in 1964 was almost exactly ten times as great as that of 1947, while the divisions themselves had grown from modest dimensions to almost the stature of large companies in their own right.

This expansion brought its own problems. Manufacture had long since overflowed from the parent plant at New Street, Chelmsford, and was being carried on in numerous establishments, mostly (but not all) within a few miles' radius of the parent plant.

Even by 1950 it had become apparent that an additional factory of some size was needed and plans were laid to build this at Basildon New Town where a suitable site was available alongside the London to Southend arterial road. This factory, built on a ten-acre site and having an area of approximately 158,000 sq. ft. (it has subsequently been considerably enlarged) was completed in May 1954, although staff began to move in earlier than this, as soon as a given area was finished. Basically intended for the manufacture of the physically lighter types of equipment, it is the home of the Aeronautical and Closed Circuit Television Divisions,* although a diversity of other equipments is made there.

By 1961 the need had again arisen for a further manufacturing area and this time an existing factory was acquired at Wembley, Middlesex. This formerly belonged to E.M.I. Electronics Ltd., and was taken over as a staffed and equipped working entity. It provided an additional area of approximately 85,000 sq. ft. and at the time of its acquisition employed between 400–500 people.

In the Baddow Laboratories in the late 1950s the Semiconductor

* Now Electro-Optical Systems Division.

Physics Group was conducting exhaustive investigations into the possibilities of fabricating whole circuits within tiny slices of semiconductor, typically germanium or silicon. At the same time, development teams at the Television Laboratories at the Waterhouse Lane establishment were exploring another approach to the manufacture of microcircuits, namely by the 'thin film' technique; both approaches had originated in the U.S.A. as part of that Government's massive guided missile and space satellite programmes, and in the U.S.A. sufficient success had been achieved to show that here were embryonic technologies which in due course must exert a powerful influence on electronics design in many areas.

The two techniques, semiconductor and thin film, are well documented and need no detailed description here except, perhaps, to point out that the generic description of microcircuits is in a sense misleading, implying as it does that the important feature is the small physical size. While it is true that this is a striking characteristic and is of considerable value in certain categories of equipment (it certainly is in the design of electronic equipment for satellites), nevertheless there are many other departments of electronics manufacture in which small size is of no particular importance. But microcircuits can provide a characteristic which is of prime interest to all branches of electronics, namely an intrinsic reliability factor much higher than can be attained in conventional components.

This reliability does not derive from any 'magic' property of the semiconductor or thin film but from the low mass of the completed microcircuits and the fact that far fewer interconnections are involved (interconnections are a major cause of failure in conventional circuits). A further advantage, which is of particular value in computer work and certain other areas, is that because the interconnections are so minute in length, the response times of computers using microcircuit techniques are faster than can be achieved with conventional components, where the interconnections are of necessity of much greater physical length. To see why this should be so it must be remembered that electricity is not an instantaneous flow in a conductor but travels at a speed which approximates to 0·7 ft. per nanosecond. Thus to a machine which operates in microseconds (10^{-6} sec.) or nanoseconds (10^{-9} sec.) any saving in terms of lengths of interconnections represents a faster operating speed.

A little earlier it was said that microcircuit techniques *can* provide greater reliability, but whether they do or not depends largely upon the skills employed in manufacture. A badly-made microcircuit can be every bit as troublesome as badly-made conventional components. The process demands basic materials of an extremely high and uniform degree of purity and rigid control at every stage of manufacture. At the onset these techniques were largely foreign to conventional electronics manufacture, savouring more of microscopy and photography than of the familiar pliers and soldering-iron approach. For this reason some years were spent at the Baddow Laboratories exploring, not only the physics of semiconductors, but also the new fabrication techniques and the evolution of methods of large-scale manufacture.

This last was vital, for to date no method of economic manufacture on a small scale has been evolved in the semiconductor approach. But at length the main problems were solved and it was decided that the time was opportune to create a Microelectronics Division to tap the new (and to many at that time) highly problematical market.

This was done in December 1964. Plans had also been laid to establish a separate factory where the microcircuits could be manufactured under ideal conditions. In June 1965 the factory, situated at Witham, Essex, came into production; at the same time plans were in being for a much larger factory on an adjacent site.*

A considerable expansion of the broadcasting and closed circuit television development groups was also effected during 1964 with the occupation of a new £750,000 establishment at Waterhouse Lane, Chelmsford, when the floor space devoted to television development work was increased to 37,000 sq. ft.

In March 1965 the Specialized Components Division moved from their original manufacturing quarters at Guy's Farm, Writtle, to a new factory at Billericay, Essex, where over 8,000 sq. ft. of floor space was available. This Division, which had been formed in July 1962, has as its primary function the design and manufacture of specialized components which are unobtainable (to the specifications demanded) from outside sources of supply. In addition to providing for the Company's needs in this respect, some of the range of components made are available to outside purchasers. In the period 1962–5 these activities expanded to the point where nearly three hundred components were on general offer.

Yet another increase in the Marconi range of interests came in June 1965 when the business of Stratton and Company Limited, manufacturers of professional radio communications receivers and accessories since 1923, was acquired. As this Company had marketed its products under the well-known name of Eddystone, its title was changed to Eddystone Radio Limited.

* This is now in operation.

Table I shows the principal factories and establishments, together with their locations, as in 1965. From this it will be seen that the Marconi manufacturing effort is indeed a dispersed one. In fact this is by no means the whole of the picture for there are a number of smaller establishments which are not tabulated.

Table 1

COMPANY	LOCATION	DESCRIPTION
The Marconi Co.	New St., Chelmsford	Head Office & Factory
,, ,, ,,	Gt Baddow, Nr Chelmsford	Research Laboratories
,, ,, ,,	Waterhouse Lane, Chelmsford	Factory
,, ,, ,,	Widford, Essex	Factory
,, ,, ,,	Witham, Essex	Factory
,, ,, ,,	Billericay, Essex	Factory
,, ,, ,,	Basildon, Essex	Factory
,, ,, ,,	Felling, Gateshead	Factory
,, ,, ,,	Wembley, Middlesex	Factory
,, ,, ,,	Hackbridge, Surrey	Factory
,, ,, ,,	Rivenhall, Essex	Establishment
,, ,, ,,	Writtle, Essex	Establishment

MANUFACTURING SUBSIDIARY COMPANIES		
Marconi Instruments Ltd.	St Albans, Herts	Head Office & Factory
W. H. Sanders (Electronics) Ltd	Stevenage, Herts	Head Office & Factory
Eddystone Radio Ltd	Birmingham	Head Office & Factory
Marconi Italiana S.P.A.	Genoa, Italy	Head Office & Factory

The phenomenal increase of electronics applications over the two decades following World War II made for a particularly exciting phase of the Company's history. Each new development, whether originating within or outside the organization, had to be considered (usually in its embryo form), and a decision made as to whether it should have a place in the Company's development and manufacturing programmes. Selections, however stringent the scrutiny, do not always behave according to plan; some, which seem to have every prospect of vigorous growth, languish; others, after an inauspicious start, flourish beyond expectation. In between these minority extremes come those which develop along predicted lines. The ratio of successes to failures is a measure of managerial acumen.

Such new projects begin as relatively unimportant sideshoots in a Division which is most logically equipped to nurture them. Over the years the good ones grow to become a valuable branch of the Division's manufacturing activities. The best evolve to the point where they show the capabilities of becoming a main trunk.

By 1965 the original four manufacturing Divisions of the Sutherland reorganization of 1948 – Communications, Broadcasting, Aeronautical and Radar – had expanded so very considerably that their structures were in danger of becoming unwieldy, while in certain instances the 'side-shoots' referred to above merited consideration for more intensive cultivation. The Managing Director, F. N. Sutherland, in consultation with the senior management, decided that the time was opportune for a second reorganization.

The first steps took the form of a re-shuffle of senior executives. This was precipitated by the appointment of Dr E. Eastwood, the Director of Engineering and Research, to the posts of Director of Research of English Electric and Chief Scientist of Marconi's. Thereupon the directorate was divided, H. J. H. Wassell becoming Director of Engineering and G. D. Speake the Director of Research. Two further senior appointments were made at this time; D. G. Smee (formerly Assistant General Manager) became Commercial Director and A. W. H. Cole (formerly Manager of the Communications Division) became Director of Product Planning.

These appointments were the preface to a massive divisional redeployment from which emerged thirteen manufacturing divisions. Each division was classified into one or other of three major groups, namely, Telecommunications, Electronics and Components. Table 2 at the end of this chapter gives a summary of the functions of each division as set down in 1965.

The final phase of this major structural organization came in November of that year when F. N. Sutherland was appointed Chairman both of The Marconi Company and of Marconi Instruments, with R. Telford succeeding him as Managing Director of Marconi's.

Examination of Table 2 will show that the 'new deal' involved no departure from traditional policy. No entry into the consumer goods market was contemplated; manufacture, as in the past, was to be confined to the area of top-quality capital goods for sale in world markets. The fundamental change lay in the creation of specialist divisions to exploit to the full the potentials of such relatively new developments as space communications, computers, microcircuits and automation. This not only made for a more flexible Company structure; by releasing the younger developments from the constraint of being merely sections of very large divisions and promoting them to full divisional status with a fair degree of autonomy, incentives were materially increased and morale further strengthened.

Although events beyond 1965 have no part of this history it is perhaps pertinent to remark that at the time of writing, when three years have elapsed since the re-formation, the wisdom of the change has been completely justified. Annual sales, which, in 1965, were amounting to some £30,000,000, have since increased (1967 figures) to £70,000,000.

Table 2

RE-FORMATION OF COMPANY DIVISIONS, 1965

(1) TELECOMMUNICATIONS GROUP
consisting of:

(a) *Broadcasting Division.* Formed 11.8.1948. Virtually unchanged by the reorganization. Continued to be responsible for the Company's activities in sound and television broadcasting.

(b) *Radio Communications Division.* Formed 15.8.1965. A new Division resulting from the fission of the old Communications Division. Responsible for radio communications other than radar, aviation and mercantile marine. Took over the naval radio communications business previously handled by Maritime Division.

(c) *Line Communications Division.* Formed 15.8.1965. A new Division, responsible for telegraph and digital equipment used in line transmission work. This was formerly part of Communication Division's activities.

(d) *Space Communications Division.* Formed 13.9.1965. A new Division taking over work previously done by Radar Division, Communications Division and the Research Laboratories.

(e) *Mercantile Marine Division.* Formed 13.9.1965. A new Division with activities based on those of the old Maritime Division, but without responsibility for the supply of naval equipment (see Radio Communications Division).

(2) ELECTRONICS GROUP
consisting of:

(a) *Radar Division.* Formed 15.7.1948 as Services Equipment Division (renamed Radar Division, April 1954). Virtually unchanged by reorganization except for removal of some aspects of space communication work. Continued to be responsible for Company's activities in ground radar, both civil and military.

(b) *Aeronautical Division.* Formed 11.10.1948. Virtually unchanged by reorganization. Continued to be responsible for airborne radio communications and for electronic navigational aids both for airborne and airport usage.

(c) *Computer Division.* Formed 25.1.1965. Responsible for the provision of electronic digital computers in the fields of radar defence, civil air traffic control and communications systems.

(d) *Closed Circuit Television Division.* Formed 23.11.1959. Continued to be responsible for industrial, educational and commercial television equipment in applications other than broadcasting usage. (*Note:* Re-named Electro Optical Systems Division 1.1.1968.)

(e) *Mechanical Products Division.* Acquired (as Scanners Ltd.) 16.1.1951. Became 'Marconi Works, Felling', 1958. Title changed to Mechanical Products Division 3.9.1962. Responsible for mechanical engineering (e.g. radar heads, turning gear, microwave dish antennas, etc.) as required by other divisions. Products also available as direct sales to external customers.

(f) *Automation Division.* Officially constituted 21.10.1965. Responsible for the industrial application of Myriad computer systems (in conjunction with English Electric), automated systems for area traffic control and also for the development of cathode ray type displays for all branches of computer graphics.

(3) COMPONENTS GROUP
consisting of:

(a) *Specialized Components Division.* Formed 2.7.1962. Virtually unchanged by reorganization. Continued to manufacture special components both for Company divisions and for outside sale.

(b) *Microelectronics Division.* Formed 1.12.1964 from the microelectronics section of Semiconductor Physics Group at the Baddow Research Laboratories. Responsible for the development, manufacture and sale of microelectronic devices and for providing a comprehensive design and advisory service, both for Company divisions and for external users. (*Note:* became Marconi-Elliott Microelectronics Ltd., 4.7.1968.)

(c) *Hackbridge Establishment.* Formed 1935. Virtually unchanged by reorganization. Continued to be responsible for the design and manufacture of crystals and specialized crystal-derived products.

48

A Last Look Round

Although a successful company is continually adding to its history, practical considerations force a chronicler to set a date beyond which his record does not go. In this instance the time chosen is 1965, although the reader will have detected a little cheating here and there when an over-stepping of the dateline seemed to be justified.

In many ways 1965 is a propitious year upon which to finish; the varying fortunes of the Company have been followed from its formation in 1897 to the point where it was on the threshold of yet another era of development. Now is the time to cry 'Enough!' except to mention a few unconnected matters which have perversely refused to fit logically into the preceding chapters.

In October 1961, Lord Nelson of Stafford (Sir George had received a baronetcy in 1955 and had been raised to the peerage as the first Baron Nelson of Stafford in 1960), retired from the chairmanships of Marconi's Wireless Telegraph Co. and Marconi Instruments Ltd. after fifteen years in these offices. His son, the Hon. George Nelson, became Chairman of Marconi's, with Sir Gordon Radley as Deputy. Sir Gordon, who had retired from the post of Director-General of the G.P.O. in May 1960, also became the new Chairman of Marconi Instruments.

A matter of months later – on 16 July 1962 – Lord Nelson died at the age of seventy-four. The influence of this remarkable man upon the fortunes of the Marconi organizations is difficult to over-estimate. Certainly his business flair brought the Company back on the rails towards prosperity. But over and beyond this he was a humanitarian whose concern for the welfare of his employees found many practical expressions.

The Hon. H. G. Nelson, who succeeded to the title of Lord Nelson of Stafford, officiated as the Marconi Chairman until October 1962 when, on his appointment as Chairman and Chief Executive of English Electric, his place was taken by Sir Gordon Radley. At the same time

Mr F. N. Sutherland* became Deputy Chairman of The Marconi Company as well as its Managing Director.

Throughout this book constant reference has been made to 'the Marconi Company'; perhaps this is as convenient a point as any to recall that, properly speaking, this title (but with a capital 'T') only dates from 1963. A brief recapitulation of the various titles which the Company has borne over the years might be of interest.

In the beginning in 1897 the draft prospectus bore the name 'Marconi's Patent Telegraphs Ltd.' The original document carries a written amendment, apparently in Marconi's handwriting, changing the title to 'The Wireless Telegraph and Signal Company' and this became the official designation, registered on 20 July 1897.

In the annual report of 1899 it was recommended that the title should be changed to 'Marconi's Wireless Telegraph Company Limited'. Guglielmo Marconi seems to have been singularly averse to having his name used; he made it very clear at the time that the proposed change was not of his seeking. Nevertheless the recommendation was adopted at the Annual General Meeting held on 23 February 1900 and the new title was registered on March 14 of that year.

At that time the Company's aim was to seek the commercial exploitation of 'patents granted to Mr Marconi in respect of an improved method of transmission of electrical impulses and signals and the apparatus therefor.'

The discovery of the thermionic triode and, more particularly, the great extension of its applications which occurred from the 1920s onward, brought such a diversification of the Company's activities that the title was no longer apt. Nevertheless it was retained until 21 August 1963 when it was changed to 'The Marconi Company Limited'. This no doubt brought relief both to the customers and to the Press, who had, up to that time, derived a considerable variety of designations from the old title but seldom the correct one.

Seventy years is a long time to have been in business, especially in electronics, which is notorious for rapid changes. Toward the close of this history it is tempting to probe into the whys and wherefores of such longevity. Such a project is, however, quite beyond the powers of a mere historian; the most he dare do is to suggest one or two of the more obvious factors and to leave the ultimate assessment to the economists and other experts.

First, let us consider briefly the genius of Guglielmo Marconi. This did

* Now Sir Neil Sutherland, C.B.E.

not wholly lie (as so many believe) in his contributions to wireless but in many relatively unknown directions.

One of these was his knack of selecting the right man for the job, coupled with his insistence that nothing but the best engineering effort was good enough. One example of this must suffice, namely his employment of Professor J. A. Fleming for the design of the first high-power transmitter at Poldhu. Fleming was the foremost available authority on high-power, high-frequency electrical engineering and his services could not be acquired for a song; yet Marconi engaged him without hesitation at a time when the Company's finances were severely strained and almost everyone who should know said that his transatlantic project was impossible. This precept of 'the best, regardless' is one which has remained with the Company, even though Marconi has been dead these thirty years.

Again, the young Marconi, with a wisdom beyond his years, instituted (also in 1901) a scheme for the training of probationer engineers and furthered it by every means in his power. Thus he built for future decades at a period when the present was precarious; when sales were few and the Company was losing money heavily. Since that time the world's oldest wireless college has been consistently enlarged and improved; in 1955 an entirely new lecture, tutorial, laboratory and administrative building came into service, with the former college building converted into a students' residence. Additionally, the Company possesses one of the most advanced training and educational schemes in the country. Its long-term value can be seen, not only in the number of senior posts held within the Company by ex-apprentices, but also in the number of chief engineers and other senior executives in broadcasting and Posts and Telegraphs organizations all over the world who spent their early years at the Chelmsford Works.

Guglielmo Marconi's zeal for expenditure on research did not endear him to his accountants and to the more commercially-minded among his directors. He, however, held the view that a generous plough-back of income into research and development was essential to long-term success, and when sufficient income was not available (as in the early years was invariably the case) he had no hesitation in drawing on capital to do so. However, his faith in his Company's future proved to be justified and he would have been proud of the present laboratories at Great Baddow, Waterhouse Lane and elsewhere had he lived to see them.

These, then, are a few of the corner stones upon which the Company structure has rested for seventy years; precepts which have been followed from the first. Top quality in engineering, craftsmanship and materials; a thorough training of youth for the future and a generous feedback of profits into research and development. None of these are ingredients for short-term success; all are vital if a company is to stay for an indefinite distance.

Index

frequency control, automatic methods of, 201–2
frequency modulation, 354–6
Furnival, Captain J. M., 167, 170, 240, 242

Gee, British air navigational aid, 318–9
'Geep' transmitter/receiver, 309
General Electric Co. (U.S.A.), 180–1
General Post Office, see British Post Office
German commercial 'war', 129–35
Gesellschaft für Drahtlose Telegraphie, 33
Glace Bay (Canada) station, 73, 77–81, 102, 111, 123–4, 127, 153
Gramophone Company, The (H.M.V.), 199–200
Grant, Admiral H.W., 326, 329
Gray, Andrew, 87, 90, 111, 123, 127–8, 267–8, 270
Green, E., 376

Hague, The, International Conference, 1957, 390
Hall, H. Cuthbert, 89, 110, 125
Hambling Committee, 1922–3, 239–40
Hankey Committee, 1945, 361–2
Haven Hotel, the (experimental station), 40, 42–3, 62, 92, 267
Heaviside, O., and Kennelly, A. E., 82, 216
Hendon–Birmingham h.f. link, 217
Hertz, Heinrich, 18, 19, 20
His Master's Voice, see The Gramophone Co.
Homeric radio telephone service, 248
Hounslow aerodrome, 236
House of Commons demonstration, 1898, 37
House of Commons Select Committee, 1907, 115
HS113 distributed amplifier equipment, 378–9
HUCO consortium, 1965, 345
Hughes, Professor D. E., 22–3

I.C.A.O. (International Civil Aviation Organization), 346
Ice Patrol, 1913, 141–2
Iconoscope, 259, 262
I.F.F. (Identification Friend or Foe), 343–4

ignition coils, for automobiles, 125
ignition system for aircraft (screened), 238
image dissector, 259
image orthicon television camera tubes, 363, 365–8
Imperial Airways, formation of, 239–40
Imperial chain of wireless stations, 143, 206–7
Imperial Conference, 1921, 207
Imperial and International Communications Ltd., 231
Imperial Press Union Conference, 1920, 186
Imperial Wireless Scheme, 116, 136–7, 143–8, 204–15
Independent Television Authority, 370–2
International Conference on Safety of Life at Sea, 1914, 140–1
International Convention on Wireless Communication at Sea, 1906, 125, 132
International Conference for the Reorganization of Maritime Radio, 1951, 390
International Radio Telegraphic Conference, 1912, 138
International Television Exhibition, Milan, 1949, 364
International Wireless Telegraphy Conference, 1903, 96
International Wireless Telegraphy Conference, 1906, 115–6
Inverforth, Lord, 231
ionosphere, 82, 216, 291, 302, 376–9, 382–3
and high frequency communication, 376–9; and Ionospheric Bureau, 381–382; and ionospheric scatter, 382–3; research into, 216, 291, 302, 382
Isaacs, Godfrey, 130, 131, 134–5, 137–8, 143–8, 198, 208–9, 226–7
career of, 226–7
Isted, G. A., 292
Italian Navy detector, 68
Italian Navy, and Marconi apparatus, 35, 37, 76

Jackson, Admiral Sir Henry, 29, 164
Jameson Davis, 28, 35, 89
jamming, 45, 52, 53, 312, 317–9, 321
Jesty, L. C., 366

wireless telegraphy stations—*cont.*
Broomfield, Essex, 97; Leafield, 206, 207; Lizard, Cornwall, 63, 83; Niton, Isle of Wight, 62; Ongar, Essex, 204; 205, 291; Poldhu, 63–73, 77, 78–83, 95, 98, 101, 102, 218–23, 269, 271
Falkland Islands, 161
France: Wimereux, 44–5
Germany: Nauen, 158, 159
Hawaiian Islands, 86
Ireland: Ballycastle (Rathlin Island), 38; Clifden, 113, 116, 117–20, 123, 124, 136, 205, 226; Crookhaven, 65–66; Letterfrack, 153
Italy: Coltano, 96, 137, 164
Norway: Stavanger, 155
Portugal, 135
Russia, 103
Scotland: Frazerburgh, 101
South Africa, 208–9; Durban, 50, 126; Kimberley, 50, 51; Slangkop, 126

Spain, 131–2
United States of America, 155; Belmar (New York), 157; Cape Cod (South Wellfleet), 64–5, 66, 82, 124; New Brunswick, 154, 155; Tuckerton, 154–5
Wales: Caernarvon, 154–5, 204, 207; Towyn, 154, 206
Wotan, German aircraft navigational aid, 318
Writtle broadcasting station, 2MT, 188–190, 192, 195
Wynn, R. T. B., 195

X-Gerat, German aircraft navigational system, 318

Yalta conference, 1945, 321

Zworykin, V., 259, 263